WORLD TAX SERIES

 **THE LAW SCHOOL OF**

INTERNATIONAL PROGRAM IN TAXATION

STANLEY S. SURREY,
Professor of Law and Director, International Program in Taxation

WILLIAM S. BARNES,
Assistant Dean and Director, World Tax Series

WALTER W. BRUDNO,
Research Associate in Law and Editor, World Tax Series,
for the United Kingdom and Commonwealth Countries

HENRY J. GUMPEL,
Research Associate in Law and Editor, World Tax Series,
for Certain European and Latin American Countries

CONSULTING EDITORS,
for Other Countries Included in World Tax Series

CORRESPONDENTS,
for All Countries Included in World Tax Series

NORMAN SHETHAR,
Editorial Associate

in consultation with

THE UNITED NATIONS SECRETARIAT

HARVARD UNIVERSITY

WORLD TAX SERIES

William Sprague Barnes, Director

TAXATION IN BRAZIL

HARVARD LAW SCHOOL

INTERNATIONAL PROGRAM IN TAXATION

LITTLE, BROWN AND COMPANY

BOSTON · TORONTO 1957

The law stated in this volume is as of January 1, 1957, with the exception of the Income Tax Regulations promulgated by Decree No. 40,702 on December 31, 1956.

PRINTED IN THE UNITED STATES OF AMERICA

The Riverside Press

CAMBRIDGE, MASSACHUSETTS

Published simultaneously in Canada by Little, Brown & Company (Canada) Limited

TAXATION IN BRAZIL

*This volume of the World Tax Series is primarily the
work of the following staff member and correspondent:*

Henry J. Gumpel

and

Rubens Gomes de Sousa

ACKNOWLEDGMENTS

In each volume of the World Tax Series, a member of the editorial staff has worked in close collaboration with correspondents abroad. In this volume, Henry J. Gumpel, LL.B., M.S., Jur. D., Latin American and European Editor of the World Tax Series, has collaborated with Rubens Gomes de Sousa, Professor of Tax Law, Faculty of Economics and Administration, University of São Paulo, Brazil. Mr. Gumpel is primarily responsible for all the chapters dealing with the income tax and the excess profits tax and Professor Gomes de Sousa for the introductory chapters and the chapters dealing with other taxes.

Mr. Gumpel wishes to acknowledge, with thanks, the assistance of John F. Costelloe, Tax Director, Radio Corporation of America, New York; Donald H. Gleason, General Tax Executive, Corn Products Refining Company, New York; and Richard C. Munsche, Head, Tax Department, The Coca-Cola Export Corporation, New York, who are members of the Advisory Board; and of Walter de Campos Birnfeld, Attorney, Rio de Janeiro; and Mr. Manoel R. Cruz Filho, a staff member in the Rio de Janeiro office of Price Waterhouse & Co.

Professor Gomes de Sousa wishes to acknowledge, with thanks, the assistance of Alcides Jorge Costa, Professor of Tax Law, School of Business Administration, Catholic University of São Paulo; and of Fabio Monteiro de Barros, Assistant Professor of Tax Law, Faculty of Economics and Administration, University of São Paulo.

Finally, we acknowledge the generous gift of the Ford Foundation to the International Program in Taxation, which established the framework within which this series has been undertaken. We are especially grateful for the contributions of the corporations which have made possible the preparation and publication of the World Tax Series.

PREFACE

The World Tax Series consists of reports on national tax systems of countries throughout the world. There is generally one country report in each volume. Each report contains a description of the tax system as a whole and a detailed analysis of the most important taxes, especially the income tax. As far as possible, the contents of the reports are arranged according to a uniform pattern which is explained in the Introduction.

The United Nations, and the League of Nations before it, had long recognized the need for providing systematic information on national tax systems and had initiated a series of publications, dealing especially with the taxation of foreign income and foreign taxpayers. In August, 1951, the Economic and Social Council of the United Nations passed the following resolution, which was recommended to it by the Fiscal Commission, where the United States Delegate had originally proposed it:

> *The Economic and Social Council*
>
> *Having in mind* that the promotion of trade and investment between countries is of great importance in the economic development of Member countries;
>
> *Having in mind* that the establishment of a modern tax structure constitutes an important factor in attracting foreign trade and investment and in promoting national development;
>
> *Having in mind* that the availability of comprehensive and authentic information on the tax systems of Member countries serves these aims; and
>
> *Having in mind* that the United Nations is best suited to obtain the basic information on national tax systems from Member governments;
>
> *Requests* the Secretary-General to consider:
>
> (a) The publication of a world tax service, providing a continuous service of information on national tax laws and administration;
>
> (b) Keeping this service on a current basis by the publication of loose-leaf or booklet supplements;
>
> (c) Inviting governments in each of the countries to be covered by the world tax service to co-operate in supplying the legislative documentation and other materials;
>
> (d) The possible co-operation of universities in this undertaking.

The Harvard Law School offered to cooperate in this undertaking. United Nations officials, working in close collaboration with members of the Law School faculty, prepared an outline and plan of organization for the contemplated series of reports on national tax systems. Further discussions led, in 1952, to the establishment at the Law School of an International Program in Taxation, which has been carried forward as part of the Harvard Law School program in International Legal Studies. Training and research activities were initiated under the Program with the aid of a grant from the Ford Foundation. The World Tax Series project was undertaken as a part of the Program in 1954, when the minimum financial support necessary to commence this work was obtained from the contributions of corporations.

A uniform method of preparation is generally followed for all of the reports of the World Tax Series. Preliminary drafts are prepared by the Program staff with the assistance of correspondents abroad and consultants both here and abroad. Materials in the Harvard Law Library, supplemented by materials provided by a number of tax authorities abroad, form the foundation for the description and analysis of each tax system. The collection of laws, regulations and basic texts at Harvard is available to all interested persons who wish to consult these sources.

The analytical research on original sources and commentaries is usually done by an individual member of the Program staff and then checked by the correspondent. In some cases, the correspondent has provided the basic information which the staff uses in the preparation of the report. A number of correspondents have come to Cambridge to work with the staff in completing the drafts for their respective countries. In each instance the final draft of a report is reviewed before publication by members of the staff with the advice of officials of the United Nations.

An advisory board, composed of persons familiar with international tax problems, has assisted the staff by making important recommendations on the scope and arrangement of the Series. Particular reports have been checked by members of the Advisory Board and other tax experts here and abroad. The final arrangement of the material has been worked out with the advice of consultants from the United Nations Secretariat and from tax publishing houses.

The World Tax Series is designed to present a comprehensive perspective of the various tax systems. It is not expected that reports will furnish final answers to all the questions that can arise under a particular tax system. The over-all description of the tax structure and the detailed analysis of the principal taxes in each report of the World Tax Series provide basic tools for comparative tax research. This research has hitherto been difficult because of the lack of any convenient source where information could be obtained on a comparative basis. The Series also provides tax practitioners in the United States and elsewhere with technical information which will enable them to discuss tax questions with their advisers abroad. It may be useful to governments engaged in tax reforms or in international tax negotiations. The information on the techniques used in other countries may be helpful to teachers of taxation as well as to those carrying on technical assistance in the fiscal field.

Only through the use of the reports will their shortcomings become

evident. Readers are urged to suggest specific improvements to be incorporated in the future reports and in the periodic supplements by
means of which it is planned to keep the information in the basic
volumes up-to-date. The ultimate purpose is to achieve a design for a
truly comparative approach which may be useful not only in the field of
taxation but in other fields of law as well.

INTRODUCTION

The Arrangement of the Report

The World Tax Series seeks to achieve two basic goals: (1) to describe each tax system in its own legal and administrative terms, and (2) to present each system so it can be compared, point by point, with others. Therefore each report in the Series presents, in Part I, a description of the tax system of a country and, in Part II, a detailed analysis, under uniform topic headings, of its income tax. If, in any country, taxes other than the income tax require detailed treatment, they are covered in Part III.

Part I

The four chapters of Part I describe the background and the entire tax structure in its own setting.

Chapter 1 gives the background information needed for an understanding of the tax structure as a whole. Chapter 2 summarizes taxes on net income. It serves as more than an introduction to their detailed analysis in Part II in that it presents an over-all perspective of them in terms of their own legislative and administrative design. Chapter 3 summarizes taxes on capital, and Chapter 4 summarizes taxes that may differ greatly in purpose and approach but that are all taxes on transactions.

Readers should examine Part I to understand the framework of the whole tax system before they look up any specific point of law in Parts II or III. Familiarity with the description of taxes on income in Chapter 2 is particularly important.

Part II

Part II of each report, Chapters 5 through 13, contains a detailed analysis of taxes on net income, and its chapters all have the same titles and the same major subdivisions in each report. As the Table of Contents shows, the analysis follows the over-all sequence of answering these questions: Who pays the income tax? What is the tax imposed on? How is the tax computed? How is the tax administered?

While this sequence is broad enough to embrace all the problems presented by any income tax, it is designed primarily for analysis of detailed provisions, and, in Part II, the legislative and administrative pattern of any particular country's income tax, which is explained in Chapter 2, has intentionally been forsaken.

Individuals, corporations, and other taxpayers. In describing who pays the income tax, each report makes the basic distinction between individuals and corporations. Where the distinction is between physical persons and juridical persons, the latter are referred to as "entities" in the Series. The first section of Chapter 5 of each report describes the status of individuals as taxpayers, and the second describes the status of corporations.

Somewhere between individuals and corporations are various kinds of organizations and associations, some of which are taxed directly to their members, and some of which are taxed as entities. In the third section of Chapter 5, each of those intermediate organizations is described separately and, as far as possible, in terms of comparison and contrast with the tax status of individuals and of corporations.

The international aspects of income taxation. In order to emphasize international problems related to income taxation, the technical definitions of who is a resident and who is a nonresident are included among the criteria identifying the various classes of taxpayers described in Chapter 5, at the beginning of the analysis of the income tax.

Chapter 11 (International Aspects of Income Taxation) consolidates all discussion of the foreign income of residents and the domestic income of nonresidents. The remaining chapters of the analysis are concerned only with the domestic income of residents. There are references throughout to the sections of Chapter 11 where equivalent problems are discussed in relation to nonresidents or to foreign income.

The fourth section of Chapter 11, relating to tax treaties, covers only the major effects of those treaties on the basic, internal tax law. The United Nations volumes on International Tax Agreements provide full texts of them in English.

Schedular and global income tax systems. The disparity between income tax systems known as "schedular" and those known as "global" or "unitary" is, actually, largely a matter of emphasis. Every "global" system, by one adjustment or another, makes some distinction in the treatment of, and ultimate tax rates on, income from capital, income from labor, and income from capital and labor combined (investment income, income from personal services, and business income). The characterization of a system as "schedular" or "global" is retained in the descriptive material on income taxes in Part I, but it does not affect the arrangement of Part II.

Income tax return forms. An important part of each report in the Series is a reproduction of the country's most recent available individual and corporate income tax return forms, with translations where necessary. The forms are not always facsimiles, but they show each item in the position corresponding to its place on the page of the original return.

The Numbering System

Each topic covered in this, and in other, books in the Series is numbered. These numbers furnish a complete system of cross reference. By giving the same numbers to the same topics in each book, considerable uniformity has been provided throughout the Series. In Part I, only the chapters are identical, but in Part II both the chapters and the major headings are virtually the same in every report. In Part III, a separate chapter covers each of the principal taxes requiring analysis.

Each chapter is indicated by its number followed by a diagonal stroke. Thus, 5/ always refers to Chapter 5. The major headings within each chapter are numbered consecutively following the stroke. For example, in every report Chapter 7 is "Business Income" and the second major heading is "Deductions." Thus, its paragraph number is 7/2. Further subheadings are numbered consecutively following the period (e.g., "Compensation for Services" under "Deductions" is usually 7/2.3), but rules of taxation vary so widely from country to country that these subheadings cannot be uniform. In general, where the same subject matter appears in different countries, the titles and numbers of the subheadings are the same in each report, but the editorial staff of the Series considered it unwise to impose a perhaps artificial and misleading uniformity merely for its own sake.

Cross references and references in the index are made to heading numbers rather than pages. Thus, 9/10.5 is a reference to Chapter 9, tenth major heading, fifth subheading. The Summary of Contents gives each paragraph number, its title, and the number of the page on which it begins. A quick examination of the detailed Table of Contents at the beginning of each chapter will familiarize the reader with the workings of the system.

Bibliography and Sources

In each report of the Series the Bibliography includes a narrative description of the sources of tax law in the country, an explanation of how they are reported, and a list of abbreviations.

It also lists the sources of law as described above, books, articles, and all other works either used as source material for the text or recommended for further reference.

Citations

In the report there are many citations to relevant sections of laws and regulations, but few direct quotations or translations. The substance and effects of tax provisions are explained instead of merely paraphrased. Wherever possible, examples further clarify the explanations, but there are no explicit comparisons with laws of the United States or of any other country.

References

At the end of the text, the section of the book called References gives a table of statutes and regulations mentioned in the report and the numbers of the sections in which they appear. In common law countries, a table of cases is also provided. This section is designed to help readers find the application or interpretation of any particular section of a statute or judicial decision.

The Index

All subjects and terms in the Index, both in English and in the language of the taxing country, are in one alphabetical list. Each foreign word or term in the list is cross-referenced to its English equivalent. In addition to consulting the Index, readers are advised to use the detailed table of contents at the beginning of each chapter.

The Terminology of the Report

A difficulty in preparing the World Tax Series has been the variety of words used, both from country to country and within particular countries, to describe concepts which are functionally identical. Wherever such variety exists, one word that best describes the function has been applied consistently throughout the Series. For example, "the Government" has been adopted as a shorthand term for "the taxing authorities." Of course, where the context demands the identification of a particular office or administrative division, it is named, and all such offices are described in Chapter 1 and, in more detail, in Chapter 13.

Words Used in Determining Taxable Income

One of the best examples of the verbal confusion in this field is the variety of words used to describe the way total amounts received and accrued during a taxable period are narrowed to establish taxable income. Some of them are abatements, allowances, credits, deductions, exclusions, and exemptions. Within every system different items are covered by each of these terms with little consistency.

In the preparation of these reports a standardized vocabulary is being developed. It is by no means complete yet, but the following terms and definitions represent a beginning.

Gross receipts. "Gross receipts" is the total amount, both in cash and accruals and in goods, services, or other benefits, received by a taxpayer during the taxable period. In addition to items that are within the definition of income, "gross receipts" is used to include any items received which are not so considered.

Exclusion. "Exclusion" is that amount received by a taxpayer that is not considered within the concept of income for tax purposes and which, therefore, is usually not entered on an income tax return. Examples of "exclusions" might be gifts, life insurance proceeds, or returns of capital.

Not all tax systems refer to these items as exclusions. Some may call them exemptions, adjustments to income, or deductions.

Gross income. "Gross income" is the total of all the items included in the concept of income that a taxpayer receives during a taxable period. It is usually synonymous with the term "gross profits," which is used in some systems in connection with the income of a business.

Exemption. "Exemption" as used in the analysis of the income tax has two applications. (1) to classes of taxpayers, and (2) to items of income:

1. An "exemption" granted to a taxpayer is the elimination, by law, of that individual or entity from the operation of the tax. Foreign diplomatic personnel and charitable institutions are frequent examples of persons exempt from tax.
2. The word "exemption" applied to income means the elimination of a certain item from the scope of tax, even though that item is recognized as income. An example of an exemption from income might be interest from certain government securities.

As applied to taxes on capital or transactions, the term "exemption" has a similar dual application. It may refer to a person or to a type of capital or of transaction declared by law to be beyond the scope of the tax.

Deduction. "Deduction" is an expense or other amount that the law declares a taxpayer may subtract from his gross income in arriving at net income. "Deductions" may include both expenses incurred by the taxpayer in acquiring his gross income, usually called "cost deductions," and other disbursements not directly related to earning income. Examples of the former may be wages, rent, and advertising expenses, and of the latter, medical expenses, charitable contributions, and interest due on the taxpayer's personal debts.

Net income. "Net income" is the amount remaining after narrowing the tax base by subtracting exemptions and deductions from gross income.

Allowance. "Allowance" is any part of net income on which the tax rate is zero. As opposed to deductions, "allowances" do not correspond to actual expenses but are concrete amounts or percentages established by the tax law. The most common "allowances" are those for cost of living granted to the taxpayer for himself and for his dependents (often called personal exemptions), and the minimum amounts which entities must earn before they become subject to tax.

Thus "allowances" may enter into the tax calculations of both individuals and entities. They differ from exemptions in that they apply to definite amounts or percentages of income, while exemptions apply to types of income or classes of taxpayers.

Presumptive income. "Presumptive income" is that amount presumed to have been derived from some activity of or from some property owned by the taxpayer, without reference to how much income, if any, he actually received. An example might be the rental value presumed to be received by the owner of a house, even though he occupies it himself. "Presumptive income" should not be confused with the various methods, either available to the taxpayer or imposed by the Government, of estimating the income that the taxpayer actually did receive.

Taxable income. "Taxable income" is the result obtained after subtracting allowances from net income and after making the adjustments to net income required by law. It is the amount to which the income tax rates are actually applied and on which tax liability is computed.

Credit. "Credit" is any amount that a taxpayer is permitted to subtract from the total tax on taxable income computed according to the process described above. "Credits" are usually granted by a government for taxes already paid. Examples of possible credits are those for taxes withheld on wages or salaries during the taxable period; or those for tax on income earned abroad, when the country of origin has taxed that income. Another frequent example of a credit is the fixed amount certain governments allow taxpayers to subtract from their total tax liability for dependents. A "credit" for taxes paid must not be confused with a mere deduction for them.

Other Terms

Real Property and movables. The term "real property" ordinarily designates land and interests therein, accretions, buildings, and fixtures. Whether or not a particular interest is considered an interest in land depends on local law and is stated in each report. Where the term "immovables" has a specialized meaning different from "real property," that difference is explained.

All other kinds of property are "movable." "Personal" and "personalty" seem inadequate because of the confusion that may result from speaking of the personal property of an entity. "Movable property" includes intangibles as well as tangible property, though the distinction between those two is made whenever necessary throughout the Series.

International tax concepts. Nationality, citizenship, domicile, residence, permanent establishment, and "doing business" all describe relationships between taxpayers and a taxing country and produce differing tax liabilities. Since, from one country to another, the same words often describe different relationships and bring forth different results, devising an integrated, standard terminology for the World Tax Series would be more artificial than helpful.

In general, persons with close ties to the taxing country are taxed by that country on their income from all sources. Persons without such close ties are taxed only on that part of their income derived from the taxing country. The particular tie that usually decides the extent of an individual's tax liability is his presence in the country for a specified length of time during the tax year, and the word usually applied to a person in the country for the required length of time is "resident." However, nationality or some other criterion besides physical presence may determine the extent of an individual's tax liability in a particular country.

The term "resident" as applied to corporations and other entities generally includes those organized in the taxing country and is often extended to include entities organized elsewhere but managed in the taxing country or having other ties with it. In each report, the criteria determining who is a "resident" are given in Chapter 5, and the legal consequences of that determination are analyzed in Chapter 11.

BIBLIOGRAPHY AND SOURCES, WITH LIST OF ABBREVIATIONS

Primary Sources

The various income tax laws of Brazil are from time to time consolidated and republished in the form of a comprehensive and organized enactment called Regulations. These Regulations are sanctioned by, and promulgated under, a presidential decree and, from the date of their publication, subject to further amendments, constitute the statutory law.

The text of this report is based on the Regulations which were promulgated by Decree No. 36,773 of January 13, 1955. This decree consolidated and republished the previous Regulations (approved by Decree No. 24,239 of December 22, 1947) and the amendments thereto, up to and including those enacted by Law No. 2,354 of November 29, 1954. The Income Tax Regulations were again republished by Decree No. 40,702 of December 31, 1956, to supersede Decree No. 36,773, but they were not available in time to be included herein. Reports indicate that only minor changes in numbering have been introduced. The particular articles and their subdivisions which are cited in this study are listed consecutively in the Table of Statutes. The "Sole paragraphs" are cited and listed as "Sole §."

Administrative decisions on income tax matters are made by the *Primeiro Conselho de Contribuintes* which, literally translated, means the First Council of Taxpayers. It is referred to in the text as "Tax Court" and in case citations as "CC." There are three separate administrative tax courts in Brazil, but only this one has jurisdiction over income tax matters.

Rulings on the application of the Regulations are made by the *Divisão do Impôsto de Renda,* which is the Income Tax Division of the Ministry of Finance and is referred to in the text as "Income Tax Division." In citations to its rulings, it is abbreviated as "DIR."

The *Revista Fiscal e de Legislação de Fazenda* (abbreviated in the text as *Rev.*) is an unofficial bi-monthly publication edited by Tito Rezende in which statutes, articles, decisions, and rulings in the field of taxation are currently reproduced. The publication is divided into sections, one for each major tax. The Income Tax Section includes the decisions of the Tax Court and the rulings of the Income Tax Division of the Ministry of Finance, numbered consecutively for each year. Examples of citations in the text to them are:

CC, *Rev.* 1950, No. 117 (for decisions of the Tax Court)
DIR, *Rev.* 1951, No. 1,018 (for rulings of the Income Tax Division)

Citations to the Constitution (abbreviated in footnotes as "Const.") refer to the Brazilian Constitution of 1946, which replaced the Constitutional Charter promulgated under the regime of President Getulio Vargas in 1937.

References to the *Código Civil,* or Civil Code, which codifies the private law in Brazil, and the *Código Comercial,* or Commercial Code, which codifies the commercial law, are given in full. The *Lei das Sociedades Anônimas,* or Corporation Law, is cited as Corp. Law.

Abbreviations Used in This Book

CC — Tax Court (*Primeiro Conselho de Contribuintes*). See above under PRIMARY SOURCES.

Corp. Law — Corporation Law (*Lei das Sociedades Anônimas*). See above under PRIMARY SOURCES.

DIR — Income Tax Division (*Divisão do Impôsto de Renda*). See above under PRIMARY SOURCES.

Reg. Art. — Articles of the Income Tax Regulations (*Regulamento*). See above under PRIMARY SOURCES.

Rev. — Tito Rezende and J. O. Castro Viana, Junior, *Revista Fiscal e de Legislação de Fazenda.* See above under PRIMARY SOURCES.

Rezende — Tito Rezende and J. O. Castro Viana, Junior, *Impôsto de Renda — Anotações.* See below under INCOME TAX.

Rezende, *Anotações* (1st ed.) — Tito Rezende and J. O. Castro Viana, Junior, *Impôsto de Renda — Anotações* (1st ed.). See below under INCOME TAX.

Rezende-Viana *Consolidação* — Tito Rezende and J. O. Castro Viana, Junior, *Consolidação das Leis do Impôsto de Renda.* See below under INCOME TAX.

Sousa — Rubens Gomes de Sousa, *Impôsto de Renda.* See below under INCOME TAX. Citations in this text to paragraphs appear as: Sousa, §31.

Sousa, *Compêndio* (1st ed.) — Rubens Gomes de Sousa, *Compêndio de Legislação Tributária* (1st ed.). See below under GENERAL AND HISTORICAL WORKS ON TAXATION.

Sousa, *Compêndio* (2d ed.) — Rubens Gomes de Sousa, *Compêndio de Legislação Tributária* (2d ed.). See below under GENERAL AND HISTORICAL WORKS ON TAXATION.

General Bibliography

General and Historical Works on Taxation

Araujo, Petronio Baptista de, *O Impôsto sôbre a Transmissão da Propriedade,* Fundação Getúlio Vargas, Rio de Janeiro, 1954. A theoretical discussion of the tax laws affecting transfers of property.

Baleeiro, Aliomar, *Limitações Constitucionais ao Poder de Tributar,* Edição

Revista Forense, Rio de Janeiro, 1951. An excellent book on the constitutional aspects of taxation.

————, *O Impôsto sôbre a Renda*, Livraria Editora Bahiana, Bahia, 1938. Still useful for its theoretical approach and for its history of income taxation in Brazil, though out of date.

————, *Uma Introdução a Ciência das Finanças* (2 vols.), Edição Revista Forense, Rio de Janeiro, 1955. An excellent discussion of each of the major taxes.

Elementos de Direito Tributário, Edições Financeiras S.A., Rio de Janeiro, 1954. The condensation of a seminar conducted by various professors.

Gomes de Sousa, Rubens, *Anteproyeto de Código Tributário Nacional*, Imprensa Nacional, Rio de Janeiro, 1951.

————, *Compêndio de Legislação Tributária* (1st ed.), Edições Financeiras S.A., Rio de Janeiro, 1952. A textbook for students which provides the only description of Brazilian tax law as a whole.

————, *Compêndio de Legislação Tributária* (2d ed.), Edições Financeiras S.A., Rio de Janeiro, 1954. The income tax chapters in this book have been superseded by the same author's *Impôsto de Renda*. See "Sousa" under ABBREVIATIONS USED IN THIS BOOK.

————, *Estudos de Direito Tributário*, Edição Saraiva, São Paulo, 1950. Collection of opinions and essays on taxation.

International Tax Agreements (6 vols.), United Nations, Department of Economic Affairs, New York, 1948–56. A collection of all international tax agreements in force, published in English, French, and Spanish editions.

Loureiro, Raul R., *Questões Fiscais*, Edição Saraiva, São Paulo, 1953. Collected studies and opinions on taxation.

Sá Filho, Francisco, *Estudos de Direito Fiscal*, Imprensa Nacional, Rio de Janeiro, 1942. A collection of legal studies and opinions on taxation.

Silva, Gerson Augusto da, *Sistema Tributário Brasileiro*, reprinted from Report of the Economic and Financial Committee of the Ministry of Finance, Rio de Janeiro, 1948. Outdated in some areas, this report on the tax system contains much useful information, presented with sound judgment.

Trabalhos da Comissão Especial do Código Tributário Nacional, Ministry of Finance, Rio de Janeiro, 1954. A published committee report which provides a critical survey of Brazilian tax law.

Ulhôa Canto, Gilberto de, *Temas de Direito Tributário*, Edições Financeiras S.A., Rio de Janeiro, 1955. Collected opinions and essays on taxation.

Veiga, Filho, *Manual de Ciência das Finanças* (4th ed.), Monteiro Lobato & Cia., São Paulo, 1923. Chapter XV contains a general history of taxation in Brazil.

Viveiros de Castro, Augusto Olympio, *Tratado de Impôstos* (2d ed.), Imprensa Nacional, Rio de Janeiro, 1910. Chapter II contains a historical survey of taxation in Brazil up to that time.

Economic Background of Tax System

Baleeiro, Aliomar, "Estados Discriminação de Rendas e Reforma Constitucional" ("The States, the Apportionment of Tax Revenue, and Constitutional Reform"), 143 *Revista Forense* 7 (1952), reprinted in 30 *Revista de Direito Administrativo* 11 (1952).

Banco Nacional de Desenvolvimento Econômico do Brasil and United Nations

Economic Commission for Latin America Joint Working Group, *Analysis and Projections of Economic Development, Part II, Economic Development of Brazil*, United Nations Document E/CN. 12/364, 1955, and its addition 4, 1955.

Camacho, J.A., *Brazil*, Royal Institute of International Affairs, London and New York, 1954.

Hugon, Paul, *O Impôsto* (2d ed.), Edições Financeiras S.A., Rio de Janeiro, 1951. A study of the economic effects of taxation in Brazil.

Joint Brazil-U.S. Economic Development Commission, *The Development of Brazil*, Institute of Inter-American Affairs and Foreign Operations Administration, Washington, 1954.

Kafka, Alexandre, *Brazil*, in Beckhart, Benjamin Haggot (ed.), *Banking Systems*, Columbia University Press, New York, 1954.

Kafka, Alexandre, "The Brazilian Exchange Auction System," 38 *The Review of Economics and Statistics* 308 (1956).

Monteiro de Barros Filho, Theotonio, *Estrutura Financeira do Brasil*, in Laufenburger, Henry (ed.), *Finanças Comparadas*, Edições Financeiras S.A., Rio de Janeiro, 1953. A brief but able synopsis of the economics of taxation in Brazil.

Prado Junior, Caio, *História Econômica do Brasil* (3d ed.), Editora Brasiliense Ltda., São Paulo, 1953. A study of economic and fiscal institutions in Brazil. Excellent, but reflects the author's political beliefs.

Spiegel, Henry William, *The Brazilian Economy; Chronic Inflation and Sporadic Industrialization*, Blakiston, Philadelphia, 1949.

Vianna, Victor, *Histórico da Formação Econômica do Brasil*, Imprensa Nacional, Rio de Janeiro, 1922. A study of economic factors in the development of political and administrative institutions in Brazil.

Wythe, George; Wight, Royce A.; and Midkiff, Harold M., *Brazil: An Expanding Economy*, Twentieth Century Fund, New York, 1949.

Income Tax

Bevilaqua, Clovis, *Direito das Obrigações* (4th ed.), F. Alves, Rio de Janeiro, 1936.

Boucher, Hercules, *Conceitos e Categorias de Direito Tributário* (2d ed.), Livraria Freitas Bastos, Rio de Janeiro and São Paulo, 1955. A description of the Income Tax Regulations in dictionary form.

————, *Estudos de Impôsto de Renda e Contabilidade*, Livraria Freitas Bastos, Rio de Janeiro and São Paulo, 1950. A study of tax accounting.

————, *Estudos de Impôsto de Renda e Lucros Imobiliários*, Livraria Freitas Bastos, Rio de Janeiro and São Paulo, 1953. A study of the tax on gains from the sale of real property.

Carvalho de Mendonça, J. X., *Tratado de Direito Comercial* (8 vols., 4th ed.), Livraria Freitas Bastos, Rio de Janeiro, 1947.

Cesarino, Junior, A. F., *Sociedades Anônimas Estrangeiras*, São Paulo, 1934.

Gama, Cerqueira, João da, *Tratado da Propriedade Industrial* (3 vols.), Edição Revista Forense, Rio de Janeiro, 1946.

Gomes de Sousa, Rubens, *Imposto de Renda*, Edições Financeiras S.A., Rio de Janeiro, 1955. Supersedes income tax chapters of Gomes de Sousa, *Compêndio de Legislação Tributária* (2d ed.) (see above under GENERAL AND HISTORICAL WORKS ON TAXATION) and incorporates the Income Tax

Regulations of January 13, 1955. Chapters and paragraph numbers correspond with those in *Compêndio* (2d ed.).

Nogueira, Ruy Barbosa, "Atividade Jurídica e Atividade Funcional," 27 *Revista de Direito Administrativo* 412 (1952).

Reinach, "O Impôsto de Renda No Sistema Tributário do Brasil," 4 *Serviço Social*, No. 33, São Paulo, 1944.

Rezende, Tito, and Castro Viana, Junior, J. O., *Consolidação das Leis do Impôsto de Renda* (2 vols.), Revista Fiscal e de Legislação de Fazenda, Rio de Janeiro, 1955. A shorter version of *Impôsto de Renda — Anotações* by the same authors.

————, *Impôsto de Renda — Anotações* (2 vols., 2d ed.), Revista Fiscal e de Legislação de Fazenda, Rio de Janeiro, 1953. (1st ed., 1948.) The standard work on the income tax.

————, *Novo Regulamento do Impôsto de Renda*, Revista Fiscal e de Legislação de Fazenda, Rio de Janeiro, 1955. A one-volume condensation of *Impôsto de Renda — Anotações* by the same authors.

Excess Profits Tax

There is no literature on the excess profits tax act of 1956 yet, but the following works on the excess profits tax of 1944 may be useful in interpreting the new law.

Ascarelli, Tullio; Gomes de Sousa, Rubens; and Pereira de Almeida Filho, João Baptista, *Lucros Extraordinários e Impôsto de Renda*, Livraria Martins Editora, São Paulo, 1944.

Rezende, Tito, *O Impôsto sôbre Lucros Extraordinários*, Revista Fiscal e de Legislação de Fazenda, Rio de Janeiro, 1946.

Sales and Export Taxes

Campos, Francisco, opinion in 37 *Revista de Direito Administrativo* 480 (1954).

Gil, Otto Eduardo Vizeu, *Impôsto sôbre Vendas e Consignações*, Edições Financeiras S.A., Rio de Janeiro, 1954. A commentary on the sales tax in the Federal District, containing much information of general application.

Gomes de Sousa, Rubens, opinion in 25 *Revista de Direito Administrativo* 404 (1951).

————, opinion in 32 *Revista de Direito Administrativo* 453 (1953).

————, opinion in 229 *Revista dos Tribunais* 37 (1954).

————, Ulhôa Canto, Gilberto de; and others, *O Impôsto sôbre Vendas e Consignações no Sistema Tributário Brasileiro*, Edições Financeiras S.A., Rio de Janeiro, 1955. Introductory chapters on the sales tax in general and in Brazil, and chapters by local experts on the tax in each of the states and the Federal District.

Maximiliano, Carlos, opinion in 4 *Revista de Direito Administrativo* 375 (1946).

Morais, Antão de, opinion in 31 *Revista de Direito Administrativo* 474 (1953).

Rezende, Tito, *Impôsto sôbre Vendas e Consignações*, Revista Fiscal e de Legislação de Fazenda, Rio de Janeiro, 1955. A study of the sales tax of the Federal District, containing much information of general application.

Romeiro, Jorge Alberto, opinion in 144 *Revista Forense* 84 (1952).

Federal Excise (Consumption) Tax and "Impôsto Unico"

Gomes de Sousa, Rubens, opinion in 41 *Revista de Direito Administrativo* 486 (1955).

Rezende, Tito, and Péricles, Jaime, *Consolidação das Leis do Impôsto de Consumo* (2d ed.), Revista Fiscal e de Legislação de Fazenda, Rio de Janeiro, 1952. A one-volume condensation of the *Manual do Impôsto de Consumo* by the same authors.

————, *Manual do Impôsto de Consumo* (9 vols.), Revista Fiscal e de Legislação de Fazenda, Rio de Janeiro, 1951–56. Comprehensive study and commentary on the federal excise tax.

Ulhôa Canto, Gilberto de, opinion in 25 *Revista de Direito Administrativo* 410 (1951).

————, opinion in 29 *Revista de Direito Administrativo* 279 (1952).

Stamp Taxes

Péricles, Jaime, and Rezende, Tito, *Consolidação das Leis do Impôsto de Sêlo*, Revista Fiscal e de Legislação de Fazenda, Rio de Janeiro, 1953. A one-volume summary of the *Manual do Sêlo* by the same authors.

————, *Manual do Sêlo* (3 vols., 6th ed.), Revista Fiscal e de Legislação de Fazenda, Rio de Janeiro, 1949–50. Comprehensive commentary on the federal stamp tax.

Municipal Business Tax

Miranda Guimarães, Ylves José de, *O Impôsto de Indústria e Profissões, Teoria e Prática*, Edição Saraiva, São Paulo, 1954. A discussion of the theory of the municipal business tax, and a commentary on its operation in the City of São Paulo.

Monteiro de Barros Filho, Theotonio, opinion in 200 *Revista dos Tribunais* 64 (1952).

Valladão, Haroldo, opinion in 28 *Revista de Direito Administrativo* 414 (1952).

Periodicals

Taxes in Brazil

There are no periodicals in Brazil devoted entirely to taxation, but the following carry frequent articles on the subject.

Diário da Justiça, Rio de Janeiro. The only official reports of all federal court decisions. Not indexed.

Diário Oficial, Rio de Janeiro. The official gazette.

Revista de Direito Administrativo, Getúlio Vargas Foundation, Rio de Janeiro. A legal publication which devotes much space to taxation.

Revista de Finanças Públicas, Economic and Fiscal Committee of the Ministry of Finance, Rio de Janeiro. Emphasizes the economic aspects of taxation.

Revista dos Tribunais, São Paulo. A legal review with sections for opinions and decisions of the Supreme Court, the Federal Court of Appeals, the Supreme Judicial Court of São Paulo, the Judicial Court of the Federal District, other state supreme courts, and the district courts.

Revista Forense, Rio de Janeiro.   A legal review, not devoted exclusively to taxation, which publishes articles, selected court decisions (mostly of the Federal Supreme Court and the Federal Court of Appeals), and legislation of general interest.

Rezende, Tito, and Castro Viana, Junior, J. O., *Revista Fiscal e de Legislação de Fazenda,* Rio de Janeiro. The standard reference work for the tax practitioner.   See above under PRIMARY SOURCES.

General Economic References

Annual Report on Exchange Control Restrictions, International Monetary Fund, Washington.

Brazilian Bulletin, Brazilian Government Trade Bureau, New York.

Conjunctura Econômica: Economics and Business in Brazil (International edition), Rio de Janeiro.   An English-language monthly that provides many useful economic statistics.

Foreign Information Service, First National City Bank of New York, New York.

Monthly Bulletin, British Chamber of Commerce in Brazil, Rio de Janeiro.

CONTENTS

At the beginning of each chapter there is
a detailed Table of Contents of that chapter.

Preface   vii

Introduction   xi

Bibliography and Sources, with List of Abbreviations   xix

PART I. DESCRIPTION OF THE TAX SYSTEM

Chapter 1

Background of the Tax System

1/1. Historical and Political Background   5
1/2. Economic and Fiscal Background   9
1/3. Constitutional Provisions on Taxation   21
1/4. Legal Background   24
1/5. Tax Administration   30
1/6. Synopsis of the Tax Structure   41

Chapter 2

Summary of Taxes on Income

2/1. History of the Income Tax   46
2/2. Introduction   47
2/3. Taxation of Resident Individuals   48
2/4. Taxation of Resident Business Enterprises   53
2/5. Taxation of Nonresidents   57
2/6. The Excess Profits Tax   59

Chapter 3

Summary of Taxes on Capital

3/1. Description of Taxes on Capital 61
3/2. Taxes on Real Property 61
3/3. Inheritance and Gift Taxes 70

Chapter 4

ⅹ Taxes on Transactions

4/1. Description of Taxes on Transactions 78
4/2. Sales Tax 80
4/3. Export Tax 81
4/4. Customs Duties 81
4/5. The Federal Excise (Consumption) Tax 82
4/6. The "Impôsto Unico" 82
4/7. Stamp Taxes 83
4/8. The Municipal Business Tax 83
4/9. The Real Property Transfer Tax 84
4/10. The Tax on Exchange Remittances 84

PART II. ANALYSIS OF THE INCOME TAX

Chapter 5

Classes of Taxpayers

5/1. Resident Individuals 90
5/2. Resident Corporations 91
5/3. Other Resident Taxpayers 93
5/4. Nonresidents 96
5/5. Tax-Exempt Individuals 101
5/6. Tax-Exempt Entities 102

Chapter 6

Principles of Income Determination

6/1. Concept of Taxable Income 106
6/2. Books and Records 112

6/3. Accounting Periods   115
6/4. Accounting Methods — Cash Basis and Accrual Basis   118
6/5. Valuation of Assets   120
6/6. Reserves   122
6/7. Head Office and Branch Office Accounting   124
6/8. Attribution Rules   125
6/9. Alternative Methods of Determining the Tax Base   126

Chapter 7

Business Income

7/1. Gross Profit   131
7/2. Deductions   132
7/3. Depreciation   140
7/4. Business Losses   144
7/5. Nondeductible Expenses   149
7/6. Additions to Income   152
7/7. Exclusions from Income   155
7/8. Special Taxation of Reserves   156

Chapter 8

Income from Personal Services

8/1. Compensation for Services as an Employee   161
8/2. Income from Professional Services and Other
         Independent Work   166
8/3. Income-Spreading Provisions   168

Chapter 9

Income from Capital

9/1. Interest Income   172
9/2. Income from Dividends and other Distributions   176
9/3. Annuities, Pensions, and Life Insurance   183
9/4. Income from Rent   183
9/5. Income from Royalties   186
9/6. Presumptive Income   187
9/7. Taxation at Source of Income from Capital   187
9/8. Capital Gains   188
9/9. Liquidation and Reorganization   192

Chapter 10

Income from Special Activities and from Miscellaneous Sources

10/1.   Natural Resource Extraction   200
10/2.   Agriculture   202
10/3.   Other Activities Subject to Special Treatment   203
10/4.   Income from Miscellaneous Sources   204

Chapter 11

International Aspects of Income Taxation

11/1.   Scope of Discussion and Definition of Terms   208
11/2.   Income of Residents from Foreign Sources   208
11/3.   Income of Nonresidents from Sources in Brazil   211
11/4.   Tax Treaties   221

Chapter 12

Computation of the Tax

12/1.   Individuals   223
12/2.   Entities   237

Chapter 13

Tax Administration and Procedure

13/1.   Returns and Payment of the Tax   250
13/2.   Review of Returns and Assessment ex officio   255
13/3.   Information at the Source   257
13/4.   Protests and Review Procedure   258
13/5.   Claims for Refund   261
13/6.   Time Limits on Assessment and Collection   262
13/7.   Penalties   263

PART III. ANALYSIS OF OTHER TAXES

Chapter 14

The Excess Profits Tax

14/1.   In General   270
14/2.   The Taxpayer   271

14/3. Income Subject to Excess Profits Tax   271
14/4. The Excess Profits Credit   272
14/5. Computation of the Excess Profits Tax   278
14/6. Special Types of Taxpayers   280
14/7. Returns and Payment of the Tax   281
14/8. Administration of the Tax   281

⊹ Chapter 15

Sales and Export Taxes

15/1. Background of the Sales Tax   284
15/2. Taxpayer and Taxable Event   286
15/3. Tax Base   292
15/4. Tax Rates and Computation of the Tax   293
15/5. Administration of the Tax   295
15/6. The Export Tax   298
15/7. Concurrent Sales Taxes   299

Chapter 16

Excise Taxes

16/1. Introductory   301
16/2. Description of the Federal Excise Tax   301
16/3. The "Impôsto Unico"   309
16/4. State and Municipal Excise Taxes   313

Chapter 17

Stamp Taxes

17/1. Description of Stamp Taxes   314
17/2. The Federal Stamp Tax   315
17/3. State and Municipal Stamp Taxes   319

Chapter 18

Business Taxes

18/1. Background of the Business Tax   321
18/2. Classes of Taxpayers   322
18/3. Base and Rates   325
18/4. Other Taxes on Business and on Miscellaneous Activities 326

Chapter 19

The Real Property Transfer Tax

19/1.	In General	329
19/2.	Classes of Taxpayers	329
19/3.	Taxable Event	330
19/4.	Base of the Tax	331
19/5.	Rates and Computation of the Tax	334
19/6.	Administration of the Tax	334

References   337

Index   345

PART I
DESCRIPTION OF THE TAX SYSTEM

 The first four chapters of this report describe the tax system and its background. The various taxes are presented in summary form following the pattern of Brazilian law. The more important taxes are analyzed in Parts II and III.

CHAPTER 1

BACKGROUND OF THE

TAX SYSTEM

1/1. Historical and Political Background
    1/1.1 Colonial Period
    1/1.2 Kingdom and Empire
    1/1.3 The Republic from 1889 to 1945
    1/1.4 Federal Structure
    1/1.5 Governmental Structure
        a. Executive
        b. Legislative
        c. Judicial

1/2. Economic and Fiscal Background
    1/2.1 Resources and Population
    1/2.2 The Brazilian Economy
    1/2.3 Public Finance
        a. Social Security Funds
        b. Compulsory Loan
        c. Public Expenditures
    1/2.4 Banking and Currency
    1/2.5 International Trade
    1/2.6 Import Duties
        a. Exemptions and Reductions
    1/2.7 Exchange Control
        a. Exchange Rates
        b. Control of Imports and Exports
        c. Foreign Investment in Brazil

1/3. **Constitutional Provisions on Taxation**

1/3.1 Basic Tax Provisions
1/3.2 Exclusive Tax Jurisdiction
1/3.3 Concurrent Tax Jurisdiction
1/3.4 General Classification of Taxes
1/3.5 Tax Immunity Based on the Constitution

1/4. **Legal Background**

1/4.1 In General
1/4.2 Forms of Business Organization
  a. Individual Proprietorship
  b. "Sociedade em nome coletivo" or "Sociedade com firma"
  c. "Sociedade de capital e indústria"
  d. "Sociedade em conta de participação"
  e. "Sociedade em comandita" and "Sociedade em comandita por ações"
  f. Limited Liability Company ("Sociedade por quotas de responsibilidad limitada")
  g. "Sociedade anônima"
1/4.3 National Fiscal Code
1/4.4 Sources of Tax Law — In General
1/4.5 Statutory Sources of Tax Law
  a. Statutes
  b. Decrees
  c. Decree-laws
  d. International Agreements
1/4.6 Other Sources of Tax Law
  a. Case Law ("Jurisprudência")
  b. Circulars, Instructions to the Service, and other Administrative Orders
  c. Usage and Custom

1/5. **Tax Administration**

1/5.1 Organization of the Federal Tax Authorities
1/5.2 Organization of State and Municipal Tax Authorities
1/5.3 Powers of Investigation
  a. Searches and Seizures
  b. Inspection of Books and Records
1/5.4 Administrative Proceedings
1/5.5 Judicial Remedies
1/5.6 Role of Lawyers and Accountants in Tax Practice

1/5.7   Enforcement
1/5.8   Fines and Penalities
1/5.9   Collection of Delinquent Taxes
1/5.10   Periods of Limitation

1/6.   **Synopsis of the Tax Structure**
1/6.1   Allocation of Tax Revenues
1/6.2   Federal Revenue
         a. Import Duties
         b. Excise Tax
         c. "Impôsto unico"
         d. Income and Excess Profits Taxes
         e. Exchange Remittance Tax
         f. Stamp Tax
         g. Comparative Importance of Federal
            Sources of Revenue
1/6.3   State Revenue
         a. Rural Land Tax
         b. Real Property Transfer Tax
         c. Inheritance Tax
         d. Sales Tax
         e. Export Tax
         f. Stamp Tax
         g. Comparative Importance of State Sources
            of Revenue
         h. The Sales Tax on Interstate Sales
1/6.4   Municipal Exclusive Taxes
         a. Urban Real Property Tax
         b. License Taxes
         c. Business Tax
         d. Amusement Tax
         e. Stamp Tax
         f. Constitutional Problems in Municipal
            Taxes
         g. Importance of Allocations of Revenue
            to Municipalities

1/1.   Historical and Political Background

1/1.1   Colonial Period

Portuguese explorers landed in Brazil in 1500. At first Portuguese economic activity there was limited to the extraction of natural products such as redwood, gold, and semiprecious stones. No local industries were established until the middle of the sixteenth century. Even then they were restricted, and the importation of raw materials and of manufactured products was prohibited except from or through Portugal.

Local taxation rates were as high as 20% for the production taxes, called *quintos* (fifths), but the chief sources of colonial revenue were direct exploitation by the Crown and the farming of land concessions.

1/1.2   Kingdom and Empire

In 1808, when Napoleon's armies invaded Portugal, the Portuguese court took refuge in Brazil, which was then raised to the status of a kingdom united with Portugal. The ban on imports was lifted and customs duties were instituted at a basic rate of 24%, reduced to 16% on imports from Portugal and to 15% on imports from England.

After Napoleon's downfall, King John VI of Portugal returned home, leaving his son Dom Pedro in Brazil as Prince Regent. In 1822, Dom Pedro declared Brazil independent of Portugal and was crowned as Emperor Pedro I. By the Imperial Constitution of 1824, the new country was divided into provinces roughly corresponding to the present states. These provinces were granted limited political autonomy but no taxing powers. The Constitution was amended in 1835 to grant to the provinces the right to levy all taxes not specifically reserved to the Crown, but most taxes then in use were on the reserved list.

Unfavorable economic conditions, aggravated by the war of 1864–1870 with Paraguay and by discontent precipitated by the abolition of slavery in 1888 without indemnity to landowners, led to the proclamation of the Republic in the following year.

1/1.3   The Republic from 1889 to 1945

The republican Constitution of 1891 reserved to the federal government all taxes considered to be national in character and reserved to the states those taxes on property and business that were considered to be local. No limitations were imposed on the power to levy taxes other than those specifically designated, so that, as to the remaining taxes, there was no restriction on the overlapping of state and federal jurisdiction.

In 1930, immediately after his assumption of power, President Getulio Vargas suspended the Constitution of 1891. The new Constitution, voted in 1934, reserved the income tax, which had been instituted in 1922, to the federal government and the sales tax to the states. For the first time, municipal governments received an exclusive power to levy taxes. Taxes on real property as well as license and amusement taxes were reserved to them, and they were granted a 50% share of the state business tax (18/1.2). A new provision in the Constitution, designed to prevent different units of government from levying the same tax, made a federal tax prevail over a conflicting state tax, once the identity of the taxes was declared by a resolution of the federal Senate.

The Constitution of 1934 was replaced in 1937 by a Charter proclaimed by Vargas as Chief of State. The Charter retained the essential tax features of the previous Constitution, including the clause to prevent overlapping taxation. However, the executive arm of the federal government used its privilege of legislating by decree during congressional recess to absorb all effective power, since no congressional elections were called until Vargas' resignation in 1945. The Constitution now in force was adopted in September 1946 (1/3.1).

The historical development of some of the major taxes is discussed in connection with their analysis in later chapters of this study.

1/1.4   Federal Structure

The Republic of Brazil is composed of 20 states, four federal territories, and a federal district; it has no possessions, colonies, or mandates. Each state is in turn divided into a varying number of municipalities (townships), of which there are at present some 3,000 in the entire country.

Federation in Brazil arose not as the merger of independent states relinquishing certain of their powers to the central government, but rather as the assumption of autonomous powers by political entities which were originally components of an essentially centralized country.

The states are free to vote their own constitutions, provided they adopt the republican form of government, observe the principle of separation of powers, and respect the individual liberties guaranteed by the federal Constitution. All powers not specifically reserved to the Union by the federal Constitution may be exercised by the states; and even in certain matters so reserved the states may issue complementary legislation.

The municipalities are assured, in the Constitution, of autonomy in matters relating to their own specific interests. Otherwise, the state constitutions govern their administrative capacities.

The four federal territories, which are sparsely settled areas on the northern and southwestern borders of Brazil, are administered by governors appointed by the President. They have no legislative powers, and legislation applicable to them is voted by the federal Congress in the same way that it votes legislation of a national character. However, their taxing power is similar to that of the states.

The Federal District, comprising the city of Rio de Janeiro and its immediate vicinity, is the nation's capital. It is administered by a mayor appointed by the President, but its legislative power is exercised by an elective council. The tax jurisdiction of the council is similar both to that of a state and that of a municipality.

1/1.5 Governmental Structure

a. EXECUTIVE. The President is elected for five years and may not be re-elected for the immediately following term. He is assisted by a cabinet of 10 ministers who, although appointed by the President and responsible to him, may be summoned before Congress for discussion of the affairs and policies of their respective departments.

b. LEGISLATIVE. The federal Congress is composed of a House of Representatives and a Senate. Representatives are elected in each state, on the basis of population, for a four-year term. Three senators are elected from each state for an eight-year term.

Bills in matters of finance and taxation must originate in the House of Representatives. The President may veto any bill in whole or in part, but a vetoed bill which is confirmed by a majority of two thirds in a joint session of Congress automatically becomes law.

State governors and legislative assemblies are elected along the same lines. Municipal legislative powers are exercised by elective councils. All elections are by the direct and secret vote of literate citizens of both sexes over 18 years of age.

c. JUDICIAL. There is both a state and a federal judiciary. State judiciaries usually comprise one-judge district courts and a state court of appeals, composed of a varying number of justices, which has final jurisdiction in matters of federal, state, and municipal law, except for those matters in which the federal Supreme Court has final jurisdiction, as explained below.

The federal judiciary maintains in each state from one to four one-judge federal district courts with jurisdiction in all cases to which the federal government or a federal agency is a party. Appeal in such cases is to the federal court of appeals, composed of nine justices and sitting at Rio de Janeiro. Proposals to increase the number of such courts to three or four to act as federal circuit courts of appeals are presently under consideration.

The federal Supreme Court sits at Rio de Janeiro and is composed of eleven justices. It retains appellate jurisdiction in all cases finally decided by the state or the federal courts of appeals in which the decision is challenged as being in violation of the federal Constitution or a federal statute, or as being in conflict with a decision of another state court of appeals, the federal court of appeals, or the Supreme Court itself in its interpretation of a federal statute.

1/2.   Economic and Fiscal Background

1/2.1   Resources and Population

Brazil has an area of 8½ million square kilometers (3¼ million square miles), which is larger than the continental United States excluding Alaska. A wide variety of geographical and climatic conditions allows almost every type of cultivation. The country possesses valuable mineral resources, including iron ore, manganese, gold, silver, and lead, but it lacks fuel. Oil has been found in only small quantities, and the coal is of low grade.

The south and west of Brazil are developing rapidly, in contrast to vast regions in the north. The population was estimated to be 58 million in 1955. It is concentrated in the south and, in general, along the Atlantic coastline.

1/2.2   The Brazilian Economy

The Brazilian economy has grown rapidly in recent years. Between 1947 and 1953, estimated national income in real terms (i.e., at constant prices) increased by 50% (Table 1). In current prices, however, estimated national income more than doubled during that period. The inflationary development is illustrated by a comparison between industrial production on the one hand and wages and prices on the other; whereas the physical volume of industrial production increased by 75% between 1946 and 1955,[1] money wages in the same period increased not less than 266%. Correspondingly, the cost of living index for the Federal District rose by 195% and the wholesale price index by 222%. Almost one third of the country's national income is produced in the state of São Paulo, which constitutes only 2.9% of the area and 17.6% of the population of the country.

Table I: *Indexes of national and per capita income, 1947–1953.*[a]

Year	National Income[b]	Per Capita Income[b]
1947	94	96
1948	100	100
1949	107	104
1950	121	116
1951	128	119
1952	135	123
1953	141	125

[a] Source: Statistics of National Income and Expenditure, United Nations Statistical Papers, Series H, No. 8, September, 1955, p. 20.

[b] Index numbers are computed in terms of 1939 prices; 1948 = 100.

[1] *Conjunctura Econômica*, Index of the Physical Volume of Industrial Production, Series 29, p. 37. The figure used for 1955 is a preliminary one.

Brazil has a predominantly rural economy in which agriculture engaged more than half of the total working population and produced more than one third of the total national income in 1953. The principal agricultural crop is coffee, which is also Brazil's leading export (Table 4). It is followed in importance, in money terms, by rice, corn, and cotton, of which the last is also an important export.

Industrial production ranks second, after agriculture, as a source of national income. Although it now produces less than one fifth of the total, it is becoming more important, and the country, led by the state of São Paulo, is engaged in rapid industrial development. Between 1940 and 1954, industrial production expanded at an average annual rate of 7.3%.

Trade and services each accounted for about 12% of national income in 1953.

1/2.3 Public Finance

The federal government is granted the power to monopolize or regulate certain branches of industry and commerce in the interest of the national economy, which it has used to establish ceiling prices on commodities. In addition, certain activities, such as international and interstate transportation and communication, are reserved specifically to the federal government to exercise directly or by concession.

The public sector [2] is becoming more important in the Brazilian economy. From 1947 to 1952, the expenditures of the public sector rose from 17.8% of net national product at market prices to 22.3%.

During the same period, total government receipts increased, but at a slower rate than expenditures. In 1952 they were Cr$ 70,382.2 million, constituting 20.6% of national product. 23.2% of these receipts came from direct taxes, 65.5% from indirect taxes, and 11.4% from nontax receipts (Tables 2, 3; Chart 1).

The major sources of tax revenue collected by each level of government are summarized in 1/6.2–1/6.4.

a. SOCIAL SECURITY FUNDS. More than 30 independent funds and agencies administer social security schemes in Brazil, each operating through its own budget. These institutions collect contributions from both employers and employees, and the federal government is usually required to contribute sums equal to the contributions made by the employees.

The total employee contributions range from 5% to 7% of their wages; the employers' contributions take the form of charges on their payrolls at the same rates as those imposed on the employees.

---

[2] This term, as used here, includes all government units at the federal, state, and municipal levels, and all federal government agencies except those in which there is mixed ownership, such as the Volta Redonda Steel Mill.

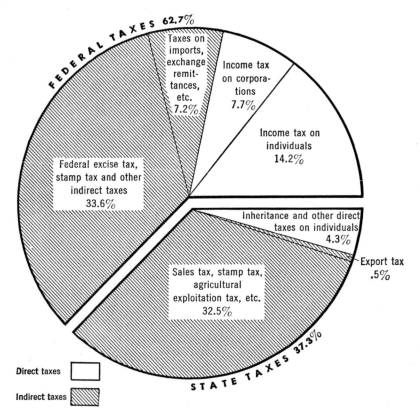

Chart 1: *Percentage distribution of tax receipts of public sector, 1952.*[a]

[a] Source: U.N. Document E/CN. 12/364/Add. 4 (1955), p. 15.

Social security funds compose a greater proportion of total institutional savings (40%) than do the funds of any other group of institutions.

b. COMPULSORY LOAN. Law No. 1,474 of November 26, 1951, introduced a compulsory refundable loan to be collected during the years 1952 through 1956. Law No. 2,973 of November 26, 1956,[3] has extended the validity of this charge for 10 years beginning with the taxable year 1957. This loan is made up of three elements: (1) 15%–25% of the income tax of any individual who pays an income tax of more than Cr$ 20,000; (2) 15% of the income tax of all taxable entities; and (3) 4% of the amounts credited by taxable entities to their reserves.

c. PUBLIC EXPENDITURES. During 1952, current expenditures on goods and services accounted for the bulk of government expenditures (51.6%), followed by capital outlays (26.2%), and transfer payments (21.8%)

[3] *Diário Oficial* of November 26, 1956.

Table 2: *Receipts of the Public Sector, 1947–1952.*[a]

(Millions of Cruzeiros and Percentages of Total Receipts)

	1947[b] Cr$	%	1948[b] Cr$	%	1949[b] Cr$	%	1950[b] Cr$	%	1951[c] Cr$	%	1952[c] Cr$	%
Direct taxes												
Taxes on income of individuals [d]	4,811.6	16.7	5,026.6	14.8	6,139.4	15.1	7,403.7	15.9	9,738.4	15.7	11,563.1	16.4
Taxes on corporations	1,639.3	5.7	2,220.6	6.5	2,312.2	5.7	2,622.7	5.6	3,467.0	5.6	4,788.3	6.8
Sub-total—direct taxes	6,450.9	22.4	7,247.2	21.3	8,451.6	20.8	10,026.4	21.6	13,205.4	21.2	16,351.4	23.2
Indirect taxes												
Taxes on imports, exports and exchange remittances	2,472.7	8.6	3,103.7	9.1	3,355.9	8.3	3,472.9	7.5	5,616.0	9.0	4,842.1	6.9
Consumption, sales and excise	16,324.5	56.7	19,049.7	56.1	23,305.9	57.5	27,387.1	58.9	36,189.3	58.2	41,177.0	58.5
Sub-total—indirect taxes	18,797.2	65.3	22,153.4	65.3	26,661.8	65.8	30,860.0	66.4	41,805.3	67.3	46,019.1	65.4
Sub-total—tax receipts	25,248.1	87.7	29,400.6	86.6	35,113.4	86.7	40,886.4	88.0	55,010.7	88.5	62,370.5	88.6
Nontax receipts [e]	3,532.2	12.3	4,536.8	13.4	5,408.1	13.3	5,589.3	12.0	7,135.7	11.5	8,017.7	11.4
TOTAL RECEIPTS	28,780.3	100.0	33,937.4	100.0	40,521.5	100.0	46,475.7	100.0	62,146.4	100.0	70,388.2	100.0

[a] Source: U.N. Document E/CN. 12/364/Add. 4 (1955), p. 15. For further breakdown of these figures, see Table 3, p. 13.
[b] Accounts for these years are closed.
[c] Those portions of the figures for 1951 and 1952 that are attributable to the receipts of municipalities are based on budget estimates.
[d] Including inheritance and property taxes.
[e] Including sales of physical assets, which are quantitatively insignificant.

Table 3: *Analysis of tax receipts, 1947–1952.*[a]
(Millions of Cruzeiros)

	1947[b]	1948[b]	1949[b]	1950[b]	1951[c]	1952[c]
DIRECT TAXES						
Taxes on individuals						
Federal government						
Budget (income tax)	2,239.9	2,025.0	2,473.3	2,965.3	4,624.7	5,208.9
Extrabudgetary (poll tax)	57.0	65.8	73.8	83.0	88.5	103.2
Social security (employee contributions)	1,377.6	1,541.0	1,968.4	2,322.0	2,792.6	3,517.2
State governments (gift, inheritance, real property taxes)	654.5	804.1	914.5	1,019.3	1,271.3	1,469.8
Municipal governments (real property taxes)	482.6	590.7	709.4	1,014.1	961.3	1,264.0
Subtotal (direct taxes on individuals)	4,811.6	5,026.6	6,139.4	7,403.7	9,738.4	11,563.1
DIRECT TAXES ON CORPORATIONS						
Federal government (income tax)	1,639.3	2,220.6	2,312.2	2,622.7	3,467.0	4,788.3
SUBTOTAL — DIRECT TAXES	6,450.9	7,247.2	8,451.6	10,026.4	13,205.4	16,351.4
INDIRECT TAXES						
Federal government						
Budget						
Import duties	2,149.3	1,935.8	2,015.3	1,989.2	3,360.7	3,169.4
Tax on exchange remittances	—	698.3	952.9	1,052.4	1,788.4	1,268.7
Federal excise, *impôsto unico*, etc.	6,430.4	6,894.8	7,682.4	8,852.0	11,829.1	13,236.0
Subtotal — federal government budgetary indirect taxes	8,579.7	9,528.9	10,650.6	11,893.6	16,978.2	17,674.1
Extrabudgetary						
Tax on imports and exports	53.7	61.7	60.0	61.7	65.4	70.0
Taxes on payrolls, freight, passenger fares	583.4	547.8	612.9	646.9	736.8	800.6
Tax on fuels (for Highway Department)	756.4	1,142.5	1,207.0	1,441.4	1,800.0	2,167.1
Social security (employer contributions)	1,236.2	1,379.0	1,743.6	2,115.8	2,567.0	3,260.1
Social welfare agencies (employer contributions)	526.8	602.4	711.3	823.3	966.8	1,105.0
Price and production control agencies	154.7	152.3	243.9	244.0	252.7	256.0
Other agencies	103.5	110.4	119.0	136.6	159.9	148.4
Subtotal — federal government extrabudgetary indirect taxes	3,414.7	3,996.1	4,697.7	5,469.7	6,548.6	7,807.2
State governments						
Export tax	269.3	407.9	327.7	369.6	401.5	334.0
Sales, stamp, agricultural and industrial exploitation taxes, etc.	5,683.8	6,989.1	9,444.4	11,270.3	15,986.4	17,941.8
Subtotal — state government indirect taxes	5,953.1	7,397.0	9,772.1	11,639.9	16,387.9	18,275.8
Municipal governments						
Business tax, stamp taxes, amusement taxes, etc.	849.3	1,231.4	1,541.4	1,856.8	1,890.6	2,262.0
SUBTOTAL — INDIRECT TAXES	18,797.2	22,153.4	26,661.8	30,860.0	41,805.3	46,019.1
TOTAL TAX RECEIPTS	25,248.1	29,400.6	35,113.4	40,886.4	55,010.7	62,370.5

[a] Source: Unpublished appendix to U.N. Document E/CN. 12/364 (1955).
[b] Accounts for these years are closed.
[c] Receipts of the municipal governments for 1951 and 1952 are based on budget estimates.

(Chart 2). From 1947 to 1952 government capital formation rose 239%, while in the economy as a whole capital formation increased 148%.

In the federal budget of 1952, the largest outlays were for the following ministries, in order of their importance: Finance (including the service of the public debt), Communications and Public Works, Defense, and Education. Outlays for these four departments comprise more than 60% of the federal budget. All social security and social welfare agencies and most publicly owned enterprises are outside the federal budget.

1/2.4 Banking and Currency

Brazil has no central bank. Central banking functions are shared by the Treasury, the Bank of Brazil, the Rediscount Department and the Bank Loan Fund (both legally distinct from the Bank of Brazil but operating under the general supervision of its president), the Exchange Department of the Bank of Brazil and the Superintendency of Money and Credit.

The Bank of Brazil, which is Brazil's largest commercial bank, is the

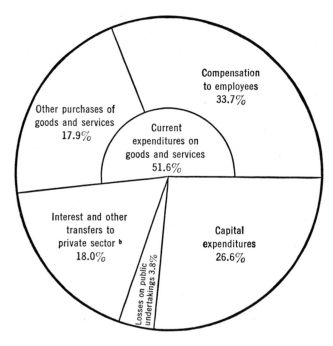

Chart 2ᵃ: *Percentage distribution of expenditures of public sector, 1952.ᵇ*

ᵃ Source: U.N. Document E/CN. 12/364/Add. 4 (1955), p. 13. The percentages shown include expenditures made by the federal government, the states, and the municipalities. For the municipalities, only budget estimates are available.

ᵇ Includes largely social security benefits, family allowances, and subsidies to private educational and health institutions.

official bank of the federal government, which owns a majority of its stock. The bank is managed by a president and a board composed of the directors of its seven departments. The government chooses the president and all the directors.

Monetary policy is formulated by the Council of the Superintendency of Money and Credit, which is presided over by the Minister of Finance. The Superintendency of Money and Credit exercises credit control and the general supervision of banks. It has the power to regulate the note issue, to fix the rediscount rate and the interest rate on loans to banks, and has the general supervision of exchange operations.

The unit of currency is the cruzeiro (Cr$). The Treasury issues the currency on application from the Bank Loan Fund and the Rediscount Department, subject to approval from the Superintendency. Issues made under general legislation must be backed by 25% gold or foreign exchange reserves. Actually, however, the Treasury borrows from the Credit Department of the Bank of Brazil, and the Department borrows from the Rediscount Department, which obtains the currency from the Treasury.

The Bank Loan Fund and the Rediscount Department are the lenders of last resort, under the general supervision of the Superintendency. The Rediscount Department does not have the sole privilege of rediscounting in Brazil since this is shared by the other banks.

The Bank Loan Fund (*Caixa de Mobilização Bancária*) was created in 1932 as a depression measure to enable banks to mobilize their frozen assets. The Bank Loan Fund is authorized to make loans to banks under very liberal conditions and not subject to limit. The rates of interest may vary between 6% and 10%.

At the end of 1954 there were 398 domestic banks in Brazil with 3,628 branches and 37 branches of foreign banks. In addition there are a number of cooperative and other credit establishments carrying on a limited banking business. Their distribution, with reference to population, is very uneven, varying from one office per 100,000 persons in the north, to one office per 10,000 in some of the cities of the south. Most branches are organized as corporations.

The federal government has established a National Economic Development Bank and two regional development banks. Many states also own official banks that act as their fiscal agents.

Commercial banks require the authorization of the Minister of Finance to initiate operations and are under the continued supervision of the Inspectorate of Banks in the Superintendency of Money and Credit. Banks are required to submit periodic reports, and, in case of mismanagement, the Superintendency has the power to intervene in the administration of a bank and even to liquidate it. Banks are required by law to keep cash reserves equal to 15% and 10% of their sight and time deposits, respectively.

Commercial banks are engaged mainly in granting short-term credit through discounts and loans. The credit instrument that is most widely used is the "duplicata" which serves the purposes of a bill of exchange (15/1.2). Bills of exchange and promissory notes are also used. Banks have shown a preference for discounts as compared to loans. The former vary in their maturity; they commonly reach but rarely exceed 120 days and renewals are rare. Current account loans are either for six months or a year.

The assets and liabilities of Brazilian commercial banks more than doubled between 1951 and 1954. More than 90% of the assets of the commercial banks are made up of loans and discounts to different sectors of the economy. For both years, the highest figure is registered for trade, followed in importance by industry and by loans and discounts to the three levels of government. Loans to agriculture made up a small percentage of the total, due to the fact that agriculture is financed principally through loans made directly by processors and traders. Traditionally, banks have not invested in real estate, except in buildings for their own use. Mortgage loans also make up a very slight percentage of the total, as do Treasury bills, which only accounted for 2 million cruzeiros in 1954 among total assets which, excluding contra accounts, reached 425 billion cruzeiros.

There has been an increasing competition among the banks to attract deposits for which they pay a high rate of interest, even in the case of current accounts. There are, however, established maximum rates which are 3% per annum on current account deposits, except for so-called popular deposits, which carry 5% per annum, and 6% per annum on fixed term deposits for one year.

There is no deposit insurance in Brazil, and this is understood to have accounted at times for the leniency observed by the monetary authorities toward banks in difficulties.

In recent years, there has been a trend toward increasing indebtedness to the monetary authorities, which at present amounts to more than 10% of their outstanding loans. A great part of this indebtedness is made up of emergency loans to smaller institutions. However, rediscounting for purposes other than emergency has increased notably, thus enabling the monetary authorities to use rediscounting as a tool of credit control.

1/2.5 International Trade

Brazil's imports and exports reached Cr$ 55 and 43 billion respectively in 1954. Coffee constituted almost two thirds of all Brazilian exports, the next largest items of which were cotton and cocoa (Tables 4, 5). Quantitatively, Brazilian exports have been losing ground as a percentage of world trade, though at least until 1953 this decrease was amply compensated by a rise in the average prices of her export commodities.

Table 4: *Exports 1954.*[a]

(Billions of Cruzeiros and Percentages of Total Value)

Commodity	Value		% of total value	
Total food				
Coffee	25		58.1	
Cocoa	5		11.6	
Other food	1	31	2.4	72.1
Total raw materials				
Cotton	7		16.3	
Other raw materials	3	10	7.0	23.3
Total other exports		2		4.6
TOTAL EXPORTS		43		100.0

[a] Source: United Nations Yearbook of International Trade Statistics, 1954, pp. 77, 78.

Table 5: *Imports 1954.*[a]

(Billions of Cruzeiros and Percentages of Total Value)

Commodity	Value		% of total value	
Total food				
Unmilled wheat	3		5.5	
Other food	4	7	7.2	12.7
Total manufactured goods				
Iron and steel products	4		7.3	
Other manufactured goods	7	11	12.7	20.0
Total machinery and transport equipment				
Road motor vehicles	5		9.1	
Other machinery and transport equipment	13	18	23.6	32.7
Petroleum products		8		14.5
Other imports		11		20.1
TOTAL IMPORTS		55		100.0

[a] Source: United Nations Yearbook of International Trade Statistics, 1954, pp. 76, 77.

Brazil's imports cover a wide range of products, with machinery and transport equipment accounting for almost one third of total imports, in money terms, in 1954. Next in order of importance come petroleum products, iron and steel, and unmilled wheat. In quantitative terms,

Brazil's imports increased until the first quarter of 1955, after which they decreased. This reduction, coupled with the tightening of the foreign exchange system, lessened the pressure on the balance of payments, which closed with a surplus at the end of 1955.

1/2.6 Import Duties

The following presentation of import duties is limited to a brief summary, in view of the fact that the Brazilian tariff [4] is presently scheduled to be replaced by an entirely new act.

All imported articles are subject to duty unless specifically exempt. Duties are, in almost all cases, specific, i.e., expressed in fixed amounts of money per unit of weight, length, or size. These duties are imposed under the current tariff, which is divided into five sections consisting of 35 chapters, which in turn are subdivided into 1,894 paragraphs. Each paragraph covers a category of dutiable goods. Ad valorem duties are the exception and apply to certain articles of small size or weight but of high price, such as precious metals or stones. In addition, ad valorem duties are imposed in respect of nonclassified products, i.e., of products not specifically included in any one of the 1,894 paragraphs of the tariff and not capable of classification by comparison with any other products specifically included in them. Duties on such articles are either 40% (general) or 33% (minimum).

The tariff automatically indicates the duties to be paid, which are either (1) minimum duties, applicable to goods from countries applying the same type of duties to Brazilian goods, or (2) conventional duties, applicable to goods specifically provided for in trade agreements, or (3) general duties, applicable to all other cases.

The specific duties imposed by the 1940 tariff have been revised and increased by about 40% in each case under the General Agreement on Tariffs and Trade (GATT), of which Brazil is a member. That revision was approved by the Brazilian Congress under Law No. 313 of July 30, 1948, and made effective by Presidential Decree No. 25,474 of September 10, 1948. In spite of this revision, regulation of foreign trade is largely dependent upon nonfiscal measures such as the requirement of import licenses, instituted temporarily by Law No. 842 of October 4, 1949,[5] and upon exchange control (1/2.7).

a. EXEMPTIONS AND REDUCTIONS. Exemptions from, or reductions of, import duties are regulated by a special statute [6] which is particularly

---

[4] Approved by Decree-law No. 2,878 of December 18, 1940. The draft of a new act is about to be completed by a special committee of the Ministry of Finance and will be submitted to Congress in the near future.

[5] This law has been supplemented by regulations issued under Decree No. 27,541 of December 3, 1949, and its effective period has been successively extended.

[6] Decree-law No. 300 of February 24, 1938.

concerned with the following categories of goods: machinery for mining and refining oil and coal, machinery for the manufacture of cement and of plate glass, agricultural machinery in general, and fertilizers. Other exemptions or reductions are frequently granted by other statutes, either permanently or temporarily, for specified articles, but all exemptions or reductions are dependent upon the fact that the imported article has no equivalent produced domestically in a quantity sufficient to supply the market. This is ascertained in each case by a special committee of the Ministry of Finance, which periodically issues a list of equivalent domestic products. A product included in such lists is automatically ineligible for exemption from, or reduction of, import duties, and is, moreover, transferred to the least favorable category of exchange.

1/2.7   Exchange Control

a. EXCHANGE RATES. Exchange control restrictions were introduced in Brazil in 1931 and have been frequently modified since then. The present system, which dates substantially from 1953, provides for a free market for invisible and most capital transactions (the average free market rate in September 1956 was Cr$ 66.67 per US$ 1.00); an official exchange rate of Cr$ 18.36 buying and Cr$ 18.32 selling per US$ 1.00 (with a 10% tax discussed in 4/10. on practically all payments made through the official market); and a series of exchange rates for the bulk of import payments and export proceeds, which operates through the control mechanism described below.

b. CONTROL OF IMPORTS AND EXPORTS. Practically all imports and exports require official authorization.

Imports by the government and of some essential products are paid for through the official market, with varying fixed premiums added, depending on the nature of the product imported. Such imports are subject to qualitative control.

Most imports, however, are controlled through a method of allocating currencies, which are sold at auction to the importers. These imports are classified into five categories in order of their importance.[7] For each category, a varying amount of foreign exchange is allocated each month for auction to prospective importers of merchandise in that category. A minimum addition to the official exchange rate is fixed for each category, and the actual rate, above that minimum, is determined

[7] Category I: Commodities needed to promote employment and agricultural income, and necessities such as pharmaceutical products. Category II: Essential raw materials. Category III: Other raw materials and highly essential spare parts and equipment. Category IV: Fresh fruits, less essential spare parts and equipment, office machinery, and certain consumer goods. Category V: All other products.

through the auction procedure. The holder of an exchange certificate secured at an auction must, within 30 days, file an application for an import license, which is granted to him automatically. This system is operated by the Foreign Trade Department of the Bank of Brazil (*Carteira do Comercio Exterior*, known as CACEX), which periodically revises the categories and the respective surtaxes, acting by authority granted under Decree No. 34,893 of January 5, 1954.

Exports are also subject to license, which, in the case of coffee, is issued by the Brazilian Coffee Institute, and exporters are required to surrender the proceeds of their exports through an authorized bank. The effective rates for export proceeds are obtained by adding to the official rate a bonus which varies with the commodity exported.[8]

The excess of import premiums over export bonuses is sizable and in 1954 contributed one third of the total federal revenue.

The Bank of Brazil, through its Exchange Department and Foreign Trade Department, is in charge of the control of the system, under the direction of the Council of the Superintendency of Money and Credit. This council directly allocates the maximum foreign exchange to be used by government departments and public entities on the basis of a semi-annual budget submitted by them. The Exchange Department authorizes incoming and outgoing payments of most transactions, organizes the auctions in the different cities, and issues the exchange certificates. The Foreign Trade Department issues the import and export licenses; classifies the imports in order of essentiality with the approval of the Superintendency; exercises control over prices, measures, weights, classification and types declared in export and import operations; and determines the percentage of total exchange auctioned to be allocated to each category of imports. The Department also hears the recommendations and suggestions regarding import and export licensing presented by the Advisory Commission on Foreign Trade.

c. FOREIGN INVESTMENT IN BRAZIL. Foreign investment and remittances of earnings are in principle effected at the free market rate. However, if the investment is registered with the Council of the Superintendency of Money and Credit and is classified by it as being of "special" interest to the national economy, remittances of earnings may be made, up to a maximum of 10% annually, at a rate equal to "the cost of exchange,"

[8] As of January 1, 1956, exports were classified in the following categories. Category I (no commodities). Category II (coffee and bananas) Bonus: Cr$ 18.70 for proceeds in convertible currencies and "multilateral currencies," and Cr$ 17.19 for proceeds in other currencies. Category III (raw cotton, cocoa beans, sawed pine wood, leaf tobacco, piassava, castor seeds, soybeans, raw hides and skins) Bonus: Cr$ 24.70 for proceeds in convertible currencies and "multilateral currencies," and Cr$ 22.95 for proceeds in other currencies. Category IV (all other exports) Bonus: Cr$ 31.70 for proceeds in convertible currencies and "multilateral currencies," and Cr$ 29.67 for proceeds in other currencies.

i.e., the official rate plus the weighted average of the bonus paid to exporters at the time of remittance. In the case of loans, credit, and other financing classified as being of "special" interest to the national economy, principal repayments and interest totalling no more than 8% per year may be authorized at the "cost of exchange" by the Council of the Superintendency of Money and Credit, provided the original capital was transferred through the official market or used abroad for a specific, authorized purpose.

In addition, the purchase of equipment in foreign currency for the production of commodities classified in the essential categories (I, II, and III) may be authorized by the Foreign Trade Department. Annual installment payments on such equipment may not exceed 20% of the total amount financed. Exchange for such equipment may be granted by the Exchange Department at the official rate, provided the importer prepays a surcharge. The Exchange Department may also permit payment to be made, in whole or in part, through the free market. Capital goods used in the production of commodities other than those classified in the three essential categories may be imported in accordance with the above provision only with the authorization of the Superintendency of Money and Credit.

1/3. Constitutional Provisions on Taxation

1/3.1 Basic Tax Provisions

The Constitution provides in Art. 141, § 34, that no tax shall be imposed unless authorized by law, and that none shall be collected in any fiscal year unless authorized by the budget. Therefore, the act of Congress approving the budget and the estimate of revenues for the next fiscal year (which, in Brazil, is the calendar year) refers specifically to each individual tax. Since the Constitution sets a deadline (November 30) for voting the budget, the intent of the rule is to prevent new taxes, instituted by law after that date, from being collected before a new budget has been approved. Thus, a tax created by law after November 30, 1956, i.e., after the approval of the 1957 budget, can only be collected after January 1, 1958. This rule of "annuality" has been extended, in some court decisions, to apply to an increase in the rates of existing taxes, on the theory that the budget act refers to taxes as regulated by law as of the date the act was passed, but there are conflicting decisions on this point. Retroactive legislation is prohibited.

Under the Constitution, all federal taxes must be uniform throughout the country. Similarly, taxation of interstate or intermunicipal transactions is prohibited, except for fees or tolls used for building and maintaining roads.

Although the Constitution restricts the power to impose taxes to those jurisdictions possessing the power to legislate, the assessment and collection of taxes may be delegated to administrative or to quasi-private agencies. An example is the collection of social security contributions, instituted by the federal government but collected by agencies of the Ministry of Labor, by associations of manufacturers, by chambers of commerce, and by labor unions (1/2.3a).

One of the individual liberties guaranteed by the Constitution assures "all Brazilians and resident foreigners" of equal treatment under the law. This clause has been invoked in support of higher taxation of nonresidents, e.g., in the matter of inheritance taxes (3/3.7).

1/3.2   Exclusive Tax Jurisdiction

The Constitution attributes certain taxes, by name, to the Union, others to the states, and others to the municipalities; such taxes may be called "exclusive" in the sense that only the government to which the Constitution assigns them by name may impose them. Federal exclusive taxes are listed in Art. 15 of the Constitution and described in 1/6.2; state exclusive taxes are listed in Art. 19 and described in 1/6.3; and municipal exclusive taxes are listed in Art. 29 and described in 1/6.4.

1/3.3   Concurrent Tax Jurisdiction

According to Art. 21 of the Constitution, taxes other than the exclusive taxes of each government may be instituted by either the federal government or the states. These may be called "concurrent" taxes. The Constitution seeks to prevent overlapping of such taxes by a provision making a federal concurrent tax supersede an identical state concurrent tax, even though the latter was instituted first. Since this rule depends upon judicial action being taken by an interested taxpayer, identical federal and state taxes may, and sometimes do, remain simultaneously in effect where no taxpayer initiates legal action. However, since Art. 21 of the Constitution provides that the revenue from concurrent taxes must be shared with other levels of government, such taxes are rarely imposed by the states and are of little importance (1/6.1). For an example of a concurrent tax, see 15/7.2. Problems of overlapping taxation do not arise in the income tax field because the income tax is a federal exclusive tax.

1/3.4   General Classification of Taxes

The general concept of a levy (*tributo*) includes three different types: (1) taxes proper (*impôstos*) in the sense of public revenue for general government expenses; (2) fees [9] imposed in return for specific public

[9] As defined by Decree-law No. 2,416 of July 17, 1940.

services rendered or available to the individual taxpayer; and (3) special assessments (or improvement taxes), defined as exactions imposed to defray the cost of public works which increase the value of private property. Constitutional limitations in matters of taxation, unless they specifically indicate otherwise, apply to taxes *in the general sense* (*tributos*), i.e., to all three types of exactions; namely, taxes proper, fees, and special assessments. Both fees and special assessments may be simultaneously instituted and collected on all three levels of government and thus may be called "common" taxes to distinguish them from exclusive and concurrent taxes which may only be imposed at one level.

The general definition of a fee is frequently interpreted in such a way as to widen the taxing powers of the particular government by enabling it to institute taxes which it might not otherwise be empowered to levy (1/6.4f). This is made possible in practice because: (1) the Constitution grants the power to impose fees in a generic manner, without specific reference to designated services; (2) Decree-law No. 2,416 does not define fees in terms of charges on particular taxpayers in return for specific services; (3) judicial review is not always demanded by taxpayers in this matter, and, in those cases which have come before the courts, there is a tendency to uphold a broad definition of the fee concept.[10]

Special assessments have never come into general use and are of no great practical importance in the tax system of Brazil. Under Art. 30, Sole §, of the Constitution, two specific limitations apply to special assessments: (1) the total amount collected may not exceed the cost of the public work, (2) each individual taxpayer may not be assessed for more than the benefit accruing to his property as a result of the public work. Under Law No. 854 of October 10, 1949, such benefit is determined by comparison between appraisals conducted before the inception and after the completion of the public work by the administrative authorities, subject to judicial review.

1/3.5 Tax Immunity Based on the Constitution

General immunity is provided by Art. 31 of the Constitution to the Union, the states, and the municipalities, from mutual taxation of public property, revenue, or services. This immunity refers only to taxes proper, and does not extend to fees or to special assessments. It has, however, been extended by federal statute,[11] the constitutionality of which has been contested and upheld, to autonomous federal, state, or municipal agencies and public corporations possessing administrative and financial autonomy. Sales by units of government are not exempt from the federal excise tax under this provision, however, since that tax

[10] For example, see 15/6.3 (export taxes disguised as fees).
[11] Decree-law No. 6,016 of November 22, 1943.

is imposed on the consumption of goods and therefore is considered to be a tax on the transaction as such (16/2.1).

Apart from governmental agencies, Art. 31 grants immunity from taxation to churches of every denomination, to registered political parties, and to educational and charitable institutions. The matter of tax immunity has given rise to much litigation concerning the power of the federal government to grant exemption from state and municipal taxes. The trend of decisions in the state courts is to deny such power, but the Supreme Court has recognized it in specific cases when the exemption is granted to an entity exercising delegated federal powers.

1/4. Legal Background

1/4.1 In General

Legislation on matters of civil, commercial, and criminal law is federal and uniform throughout the country. Principles and provisions of civil and commercial law apply in taxation unless the tax laws provide otherwise.

1/4.2 Forms of Business Organization

The forms of business organization existing in Brazil are essentially those which are found in every civil law system. Brazil is different from the common law countries in that there are several types of business organization with independent legal personality (corporation, limited liability company, and certain variations of the corporate form). Furthermore, there are hybrid forms of organization which in some respects resemble corporations, in others, partnerships. The type of business entity most commonly used is the limited liability company (1/4.2f).

a. INDIVIDUAL PROPRIETORSHIP. An individual engaged in business who is a resident of Brazil must register his business as an individual firm with the Commercial Registry (*Junta Comercial*), stating its purpose and allocating to the firm a certain amount of capital. He thereby becomes subject to the rights and responsibilities of commercial and industrial firms under the laws regulating the activities of such firms in Brazil.

b. "SOCIEDADE EM NOME COLETIVO" or "SOCIEDADE COM FIRMA." This is a form of general partnership in which all of the partners contribute to the capital of the firm and are liable for the debts of the firm. Not all the partners need to be merchants (*comerciantes*). The rules pertaining to this form of association are found in Arts. 315–316 of the Commercial Code.

c. "SOCIEDADE DE CAPITAL E INDÚSTRIA." This is a form of general partnership in which one or more partners contribute only their services.
The partner rendering only services to the firm is not personally liable
for its debts unless he contributes money or property or becomes
manager of the firm. The applicable rules are Arts. 317–324 of the
Commercial Code.

d. "SOCIEDADE EM CONTA DE PARTICIPAÇÃO." This is essentially a joint
venture in which one active partner unites with one or several others
who contribute money or services in one or more business transactions.
Only the active partner (the *sócio ostentivo*, or *gerente*) acts in the
name of the firm towards third parties. The venture is organized by
mere agreement of the participants and without the formalities otherwise required in the formation of commercial organizations; it does
not have a firm name and is not registered. The applicable rules are
Arts. 325–328 of the Commercial Code.

e. "SOCIEDADE EM COMANDITA" AND "SOCIEDADE EM COMANDITA POR
AÇÕES." The *sociedade em comandita* is a limited partnership. It is
formed by two or more individuals, at least one of whom is subject to
unlimited liability for the debts of the firm, whereas the limited partners
(*sócios comanditários*) are liable only to the extent of their capital
contribution, as stated in the partnership agreement. The total amount
of the subscriptions of the limited partners must be recorded with the
Commercial Registry. The limited or silent partners may not take part
in the management of the firm, but they have a right to be informed
about its business and financial operations. The applicable rules are
Arts. 311–314 of the Commercial Code.

The participation of the limited or silent partners may be represented
by shares of stock, in which case the company is called a *sociedade em
comandita por ações*. This form combines features of a corporation
with those of a partnership, and it is subject to the provisions of the
Brazilian Corporation Law,[12] except as specifically modified.[13] The partners whose liability is unlimited [14] are the managers (*gerentes*) or directors [15] (*directores*) of the company; they are nominated for an unlimited
time in the bylaws of the company, and their names may appear in the
firm name; they may be removed from office only by a resolution of shareholders representing at least two thirds of the capital of the company.

[12] Decree-law No. 2,627 of September 26, 1940.
[13] Corp. Law Arts. 163–166.
[14] Their liability is, however, subsidiary to that of the company. Corp. Law Art.
165.
[15] In the sense in which this term is used in Brazilian corporation law, i.e., corresponding to the administrative officers of a U. S. corporation; see below under
sociedade anônima.

f. LIMITED LIABILITY COMPANY ("SOCIEDADE POR QUOTAS DE RESPONSIBILIDAD LIMITADA"). The limited liability company (a form of organization which is common in civil law countries) combines features of a partnership with those of a corporation. It is similar to a partnership in that it may have as few as two associates (who may be either individuals or legal entities [16]) and particularly in that the various formalities and publicity requirements to be observed by a corporation do not apply to it. On the other hand, the limited liability company is similar to a corporation in that it is a legal entity. The quotas (shares) of an associate are transferable only with the consent of the other associates.[17]

The number of limited liability companies in Brazil by far exceeds that of corporations proper. This form of organization is well suited to smaller or medium-sized enterprises whose participants wish to limit their liability to third parties and is not normally used by business enterprises of substantial size. It is unsuitable where the capital of the enterprise is raised through a public subscription and transferable stock certificates (especially bearer shares) or debentures are issued. On the other hand, it is an advantageous form of business for a small group of investors who intend to maintain control of an enterprise. A limited liability company is under no legal obligation to publish its annual balance sheet, statement of profit and loss, minutes of the meetings of its members, or notice of such meetings; it is not required to register its shares or participations with the local stock exchange or to have a fiscal committee. The principal participants in a limited liability company are protected by the provision that the other associates cannot assign their quotas to third parties without the principals' consent.[18] Limited liability companies, like other entities, may at any time be transformed into corporations.

g. "SOCIEDADE ANÔNIMA." This is the Brazilian counterpart of a United States corporation and of the joint stock company in other English-speak-

[16] A foreign corporation or nonresident individual may be an associate in a limited liability company organized in Brazil. In this case, however, it is customary to have at least two additional associates who are residents of Brazil, because the manager of the company must be a resident of Brazil and the holder of an interest in the company; if he were the only other associate, his death would result in the dissolution of the company.

[17] The formation of limited liability companies in Brazil was authorized by Law No. 3,708 of January 10, 1919. The contract of organization of this type of company is regulated by the Commercial Code of Brazil. In matters not provided for in the contract of organization, the provisions of the Corporation Law (Decree-law No. 2,627 of September 26, 1940) are applicable (Law No. 3,708, Art. 18).

[18] It should, however, be noted that the share of an individual associate becomes, upon his death, part of his estate. This is important if the principal participant is a foreign corporation or nonresident individual in cases where shares are placed in the hands of a nominal participant who is a resident of Brazil. An assignment of the shares held by the resident nominal participant cannot be executed after his death.

ing countries, and the legal rules governing its formation and opera-
ions are similar.[19] For the purposes of the present study, the term
"corporation" refers to this type of entity, and the following special
characteristics may be noted.

A Brazilian corporation must have at least seven stockholders. The
directors of the corporation are its administrative officers, and they must
be residents of Brazil. It is customary to have five directors, of whom
three constitute a quorum. There is also a fiscal committee (*conselho
fiscal*) which is composed of three or more members and an equal
number of alternates, who examine the accounts of the corporation [20] and
submit to the annual general meeting of the stockholders of the company
a report on its affairs and operations.

The publicity requirements which corporations must meet under
Brazilian law are fairly extensive. The following information must be
published in the official gazette: the annual balance sheet and statement of profit and loss, the annual report of the directors, the review
by the fiscal committee of the commercial and financial operations of
the company, the minutes of all stockholders' meetings, notices of such
meetings, and all amendments of the bylaws. All corporations domiciled in Brazil must list their shares and debentures with the stock
exchange closest to their head office and file certified copies of their
financial statements, the names of the directors, and any changes that
may have been made in accordance with the bylaws within 30 days
after such listing.[21] If the corporation intends to have its shares traded
in on an exchange, it must meet certain qualification requirements.

1/4.3   National Fiscal Code

The draft of a national fiscal code, which incorporates the fundamental
substantive and procedural rules common to all taxes and other government levies, was prepared at the request of the federal government in
1953.[22] The draft was subsequently revised by a commission appointed
by the government, and it has since been under discussion by Congress,
the Administration, and the legal profession.

1/4.4   Sources of Tax Law — In General

The sources of the law of taxation (*direito tributário*) are the statutes,
international agreements, case law, administrative regulations (*circulares,
portarias*, etc., see below at 1/4.6b), and usage and custom.

[19] The basic law regulating *sociedades anônimas* is Decree-law No. 2,627 of
September 26, 1940 (*Lei das Sociedades por Ações*).
[20] At any time, but at least quarterly.
[21] Administrative Order of the Ministry of Finance No. 39, February 15, 1950
(*Diário Oficial*, February 17, 1950).
[22] Gomes de Sousa, *Anteproyecto de Código Tributário Nacional*, Imprensa
Nacional, Rio de Janeiro, 1951.

1/4.5 Statutory Sources of Tax Law

a. STATUTES. Art. 141, §2, of the federal Constitution expresses the principle that nobody is obliged to do, or to refrain from doing, anything unless the law so prescribes; and §34 of the same constitutional article states, in specific application of the principle just mentioned, that no tax or other exaction for public purposes (*tributo*) shall be imposed or increased unless authorized by law. Therefore, a statute is the only source of tax law. Moreover, the law of taxation presents the peculiarity that the legality of the collection of a tax requires not only one statute, but two, namely the statute imposing the tax and the budgetary law.[23]

b. DECREES. A decree, although a law in the generic sense, is an order of the executive branch of the government as distinguished from statutes which emanate from the Legislature. As a rule, the statutes limit themselves to the fundamental questions of the particular area they are concerned with, leaving the regulation of the detail to the Executive; it is usual for the statutes to include a provision authorizing the Executive to implement them, or at times expressly ordering it to do so. This implementation of a statute, i.e., the determination of the detail relative to its execution and application, is effected by the Executive through decrees which bear the name of regulatory decrees or simply regulations.[24] Two important principles must be observed in this matter: (1) Regulations must strictly adhere to the provisions of the statute which they purport to implement and cannot create new law; to the extent that they violate this restriction, they are unconstitutional as constituting an invasion of the legislative power;[25] (2) A statute whose application depends on detailed implementation does not become effective unless and until the respective regulations are issued.[26]

c. DECREE-LAWS. A decree-law is a mixture of a decree and a law (in the sense of a statute, or act of the Legislature). It is an act emanating

[23] Art. 141, §34, of the federal Constitution prescribes that except for customs duties and taxes levied in times of war, no tax or other public exaction can be collected without previous budgetary authorization. In contrast to revenue laws proper, which introduce or increase specific taxes and which are permanent until repealed or amended, the budget law deals with the collection of taxes and it is valid for one year only.

[24] As an example, the presently valid Income Tax Regulations (which constitute the body of the income tax law) were promulgated by the Executive under Decree No. 36, 773 of January 13, 1955.

[25] Supreme Court, 130 *Revista Forense* 105 (1950); São Paulo State Court of Appeals, 182 *Revista dos Tribunais* 681 (1949). An example of the introduction, by the Executive, of a new rule of substantive law without statutory basis (Art. 97, §5, of the Income Tax Regulations) is cited at 9/4.2.

[26] Supreme Court, 124 *Revista Forense* 67.

from the Executive, but dealing with matters which are within the
domain of the Legislature. Actually, decree-laws are without constitutional foundation, not only because the Constitution defines the powers
of the Legislature (Arts. 65 and 66) and of the Executive (Art. 87), but
also because it forbids both branches of government to delegate their
functions (Art. 86, §2). However, the decree-laws which were promulgated during the period when the Constitutional Charter of 1937 was
in force (and when the functions of the Legislature were taken over by
the Executive) remain valid to the extent that they are not in conflict
with substantive provisions of the present Constitution.

d. INTERNATIONAL AGREEMENTS. Finally, international treaties and
conventions are primary sources of tax law; they are of importance
mainly in connection with customs duties and matters of double taxation.
According to Art. 66 (I) of the Constitution, an international agreement
entered into by the executive branch of the government becomes effective
only if and when it is ratified by the Legislature.

1/4.6   Other Sources of Tax Law

a. CASE LAW ("JURISPRUDÊNCIA"). This designation applies to the decisions of the judiciary, but it is also (although improperly) applied to
those of administrative authorities. Under the Brazilian system, which
in this point is different from that of the common law countries, decisions by the courts are not a primary source of law, because they need
not be followed in all other similar cases. A decision rendered in one
case has binding effect only for that particular controversy; it is, in
other similar cases which arise, only of persuasive authority and may
with this limitation be cited to support a complaint or a defense. Decisions
of the administrative authorities are occasionally invested by the statutes
with normative power, which means that they must be followed, in
identical cases, by the lower authorities.

b. CIRCULARS, INSTRUCTIONS TO THE SERVICE, AND OTHER ADMINISTRATIVE
ORDERS. Administrative orders, or directives, are variously called "circulares," "portarias," and "ordens de serviço." While the terminology used
is not definitely fixed, it may be stated that circulares are administrative
orders issued to the public at large, while portarias and ordens de serviço
are internal directives issued to subordinate officials. These instructions are sometimes not officially published, but they must, in every case,
be based either on a statute or a circular. The administrative pronouncements listed here must not be confused with rulings in individual cases
(decisões); while the latter constitute important precedents, their formal
authority is limited to the decided case. On the other hand, circulares,

portarias, and *ordens de serviço* are general rulings intended to clarify the meaning and scope of tax laws. They may be invoked by a citizen who claims that he has relied on them or that a government official has failed to apply them in his case.

The administrative pronouncements discussed here must, like regulations (1/4.5b), be confined to carrying out the laws or decrees to which they refer. However, like regulations, they sometimes tend to extend or restrict the scope of statutory law.

c. USAGE AND CUSTOM. Usage and custom represent the rules of conduct according to which the application of a law, or the exercise of an authority, proceeds regularly and continuously. Different from other areas of law, the law of taxation does not recognize the introduction of a new rule of law or the abrogation of an existing one by usage or custom. The interpretation of a law through continued custom, however, is possible in the field of taxation and comparable in its effect to that of official rulings, although more limited in its application because of the lack of a written rule. The individual can always allege in his favor that which the government has repeatedly considered as the sense or meaning of any law, if it should revise this understanding to his detriment; the taxpayer can also demonstrate his good faith and prevent the imposition of penalties by pleading that he relied on a consistent practice followed by the government.

1/5.   Tax Administration

1/5.1   Organization of the Federal Tax Authorities

Chart 3, reproduced on page 31 indicates in greatly simplified form the organization of the Federal Ministry of Finance and those of its subordinate agencies which are concerned with taxation. The chart is supplemented by explanatory notes, which are arranged according to the letters assigned to the various departments in the chart. The solid lines in the chart indicate that a direct hierarchical order exists among the various agencies, and the broken lines indicate advisory or independent relationships not within the direct hierarchical order.

Notes to Chart 3

A. *Minister of Finance.* The Minister of Finance is a political official and is dependent upon his advisers for carrying out the technical functions of his department. The advisers (usually about five) are invariably drawn from among high-ranking officials of the Ministry, and they are personally appointed by the Minister. The choice of the advisers largely determines the policy of the department. The Minister is charged with making the final administrative decision on appeals from the tax courts (F) in certain

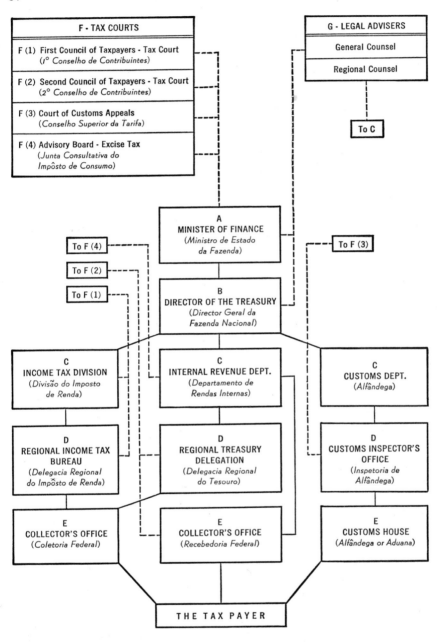

Chart 3. *Organization of the federal tax authorities*

cases (13/4.3). This function is, in practice, always delegated to one of the advisers, who, in turn, relies on the opinion of the General Counsel (G).

B. *Director of the Treasury.* The Director of the Treasury is the highest-ranking permanent (nonpolitical) official in charge of tax matters, although his freedom of decision is, in practice, somewhat limited by the Minister's advisers. He also has the final decision on administrative appeals concerning claims for refund, which are outside the jurisdiction of the tax courts (see 13/5.1). Otherwise, the Director of the Treasury does not decide actual tax controversies but issues general directives to the subordinate agencies called *circulares* (1/4.6b).

C. *Income Tax Division, Internal Revenue Department, and Customs Department.* The Income Tax Division, Internal Revenue Department, and the Customs Department are agencies of equal standing directly responsible to the Director of the Treasury. The Income Tax Department is in charge of income and excess profits taxes, and the Internal Revenue Department of all other federal taxes; the Customs Department is responsible for import duties. At the head of each department is a Director who is a permanent official. While the Director does not decide actual tax controversies, he issues general directives in the form of circulars and special rulings at the request of taxpayers (see page 29 and Chapters 5 through 14, *passim*).

All of the above government departments are located in the national office of the Ministry of Finance.

D. *Regional Income Tax Bureau, Regional Treasury Delegation, and Customs Inspector's Office.* There are in each state two independent federal offices of equal standing, the Regional Income Tax Bureau (D) and the Regional Treasury Delegation (D), which are subordinate agencies of the Income Tax Division (C) and the Internal Revenue Department (C), respectively. The jurisdiction of these agencies covers the territory of a state, and their offices are located in the state capital. In addition to these two, there is a Customs Inspector's Office in each of the maritime states. Each of the offices discussed here is in the charge of a Regional Director (called "Inspector" in the case of the Customs Office) who handles assessments, renders administrative decisions in contested cases arising in his territory, and who is further responsible for a vast number of administrative matters. While taxpayers' requests for rulings are directed to the next higher authority (C), the Regional Directors give advisory opinions in connection therewith.

E. *"Coletoria Federal," "Recebedoria Federal," and Customs House.* *Coletorias* are local federal collection offices which are distributed in varying numbers over the states. They are, for administrative purposes, subordinate to the Regional Treasury Delegation (D), but they also handle income tax matters and report in connection therewith to the Regional Income Tax Bureau (D). The function of the officials attached to a *coletoria* is merely to collect taxes and to forward papers to or from higher administrative agencies; they have no power of decision. The revenue agents are in direct contact with the taxpayer. They are, for administrative purposes, stationed at the *coletorias,* but they report to and receive their instructions from the Regional Directors (D).

The cities of Rio de Janeiro and São Paulo present important exceptions to the *coletoria* system. The counterpart of the local *coletorias* in these two cities is the *recebedoria federal,* whose administrators, besides their regular duties as cashiers, have the same powers of assessment and administrative decision as the Regional Directors (D) with respect to taxpayers subject to their jurisdiction.

F. *Tax Courts.* The various administrative tax courts are listed in the chart under F. Regarding the First and Second Councils of Taxpayers and the Court of Customs Appeals (F1, F2, and F3 in the chart), see 13/4.3. In addition to these three courts, there is the *Junta Consultativa do Impôsto de Consumo,* composed of three taxpayers and three officials and presided over by the Director of the Internal Revenue Department (C), which gives advisory opinions on taxpayers' requests for rulings in connection with the federal excise (consumption) tax. The ruling is issued by the Director, who may disregard even the unanimous opinion of the Council.

The former *Junta de Ajuste de Lucros* (Excess Profits Tax Council) was abolished by Law No. 2,862 of September 4, 1956, and its functions assigned to the First Council of Taxpayers (Tax Court).

G. *Legal Advisers.* The table of organization provides for a General Counsel and Regional Counsels for each state. The General Counsel is the legal adviser to the Minister of Finance and Director of the Treasury, and the three Directors listed in the chart at the C level. The Regional Counsels perform similar functions for the three Directors listed in the chart under D. They are subordinate to the General Counsel. None of these legal advisers, however, represents the Treasury in court. This function is assigned to officials of the Federal Ministry of Justice.

1/5.2   Organization of State and Municipal Tax Authorities

The administrative organization in the states and municipalities is considerably simpler than it is on the federal level. There is, in all states, a Secretary of Finance, who is a political appointee like his federal counterpart, and under him a Director of Revenue, who is a permanent official responsible for the assessment of taxes and the administrative decision of tax controversies. In the more important states, this official is assisted by departmental directors (one for each major tax), who handle the routine assessments; the authority to render administrative decisions, however, is always reserved to the Director of Revenue. Most states have a tax court, which is always outside the administrative hierarchy and whose decisions are appealed to the Director of Revenue and, in some cases, to the Secretary of Finance. The organization and functions of the legal personnel closely follow the federal pattern.

In most municipalities there is only a Director of Revenue (permanent official) directly under the mayor who is in charge of all municipal tax matters. Appeals from the rulings and decisions of the Director go to the mayor. Only the most important cities, like Rio de Janeiro (Federal

District) and São Paulo, have a Secretary of the Treasury and a tax court. The administrative organization in these cities is similar to that of the states.

1/5.3 Powers of Investigation

a. SEARCHES AND SEIZURES. Federal, state, and municipal tax officials have the right to enter business premises at all times during usual business hours and to search for material evidence of tax violations; they must have a court warrant to enter into places of residence. All relevant movable property except business books and records found at places of business, or deposited in warehouses, or in transit, may be seized by administrative officials when they constitute, or are suspected to constitute, material evidence of a tax violation.

All evidence must be obtained by fair and lawful means and may be contested by the taxpayer. Correspondence is inviolable, except as part of business records, but in at least one case the Supreme Court held that information obtained through wartime mail censorship was acceptable as supporting evidence of tax fraud.

b. INSPECTION OF BOOKS AND RECORDS. Under Art. 17 of the Commercial Code, books of account and business records are immune from inspection by third parties except under a court order indicating specifically what parts of such books or records should be inspected as material evidence in litigation.

By federal statute, however, tax inspectors have access, in connection with all major federal taxes, to all records and books of account, both fiscal and commercial, and are not confined to any particular portion of the books and records. State and municipal tax authorities have not been granted a similar privilege by federal law, and consequently, their powers of inspection are restricted to such books and records as may be prescribed by state or municipal law.

Refusal on the part of the taxpayer voluntarily to submit his commercial books and records for inspection by state or municipal tax authorities will be construed as presumptive evidence against him. The same rule will apply in all cases where nonexistence of fiscal or commercial books or records is alleged, unless positive proof of their destruction by fire or other circumstances beyond the taxpayer's control is presented. Books and records must be preserved until the period of limitations has run for all transactions recorded therein.

1/5.4 Administrative Proceedings

Tax controversies brought before the administrative authorities are decided successively at two levels. On the first level, the competent authority [27] issues a ruling on a petition or claim submitted by the taxpayer or on a protest (*reclamação*) against an assessment or the findings of a tax inspector. Unless the ruling orders a further examination, it must fully dispose of the case and give the reasons for its decision. If the authority decides in favor of the taxpayer either entirely or in part, it must submit its ruling to the higher authority for review (so-called appeal "ex officio").[28] The collection of the tax is suspended from the time when the taxpayer's protest is filed until the decision thereon is rendered.

The taxpayer may file an appeal (*recurso*) against a ruling adverse to him with the appropriate administrative tribunal. In order to appeal, the taxpayer must deposit the amount of the deficiency asserted by the contested ruling with the collector's office either in cash or in government bonds.[29] Full payment of the contested tax is required in the case of property and other recurrent taxes, and any overpayment which may be determined is applied against the tax for later years.

On the federal level as well as in most states and in some municipalities, the administrative tribunals are courts or boards which are composed of taxpayers and Treasury officials in equal numbers; the presiding judge, who, by tradition, is always a taxpayer, casts the deciding vote in case of a tie. A unanimous decision of the board or court which is entirely favorable to the taxpayer is final. If the decision is not unanimous, the Treasury may appeal it to the Minister of Finance, the state Secretary of the Treasury, or the mayor, as the case may be.[30] A decision of the tribunal in favor of the government (whether unanimous or not) exhausts the taxpayer's administrative remedies and he must resort to the judicial remedies discussed at 1/5.5, except that he may petition the court or board for a reconsideration on the basis of new arguments.

In the states and municipalities which have no administrative tax court or board, appeals are directed to the Secretary of the Treasury or the mayor.

1/5.5 Judicial Remedies

The Federal Code of Civil Procedure [31] provides uniform rules for proceedings in all civil actions not otherwise specifically regulated, and

[27] Usually the head of the department, or, in federal cases, the official in charge of the regional bureau.

[28] Unless the amount in controversy does not exceed a certain amount, which is usually Cr$ 5,000.

[29] If the deficiency exceeds a certain amount, usually Cr$ 5,000, the taxpayer may be allowed to offer a surety.

[30] The officials referred to have no authority to revise the decision of the court or board. They can either affirm it or reinstate the ruling of the lower administrative agency.

[31] Decree-law No. 1,608 of September 18, 1939.

such uniform rules apply, in matters of taxation, to four types of controversy which may be instituted by a taxpayer:

1. A suit for judicial revision of a ruling terminating administrative proceedings; suit must be instituted within 30 days of the receipt of notice of the final administrative ruling; the deposit made by the taxpayer in the course of administrative proceedings will be held until final judicial decision is entered. Surety is not acceptable in judicial proceedings.
2. A suit for judicial revision of a ruling by a lower administrative authority which confirmed an assessment or the findings of a tax inspector and which imposed a tax or a fine or both. The prerequisites are the same as in (1) above.
3. A suit for the refund of a tax or a fine or both; the prerequisites in this case are the same as in (1) above, except that a deposit is not required.
4. A petition for a declaratory judgment on an actual instance of fact, no declaratory judgments being given on hypothetical cases; suit may be instituted at any time prior to the inception of administrative proceedings against the taxpayer, and no deposit is required except on a motion by the Treasury. A declaratory judgment is not enforceable in itself, but may be used either as the basis for a refund claim, or as a defense against enforcement by distraint as explained below.

Under Art. 141, §24 of the Constitution, a court order called a *mandado de segurança,* the equivalent of a writ of mandamus, may be secured against any administrative act or ruling alleged to be unconstitutional or illegal which is injurious to a vested right and cannot otherwise be redressed. Under the provisions of Law No. 1,533 of December 31, 1951, the petition must be filed within 120 days from the date of the act or notice of ruling, no deposit being required. In urgent cases, the court may enjoin the act or ruling without a hearing; otherwise a hearing is held within five days, and the court enters a decision. In matters of taxation, the writ of *mandado de segurança* may be used only after a ruling has been issued by a lower administrative authority. The practical advantages of the *mandado de segurança* are its ability to stay the effects of the administrative act or ruling and its precedence in court calendars. Partly for these reasons, however, this method of procedure has been somewhat abused, and in recent cases the courts have been showing an increasing tendency to restrict its application to cases where unconstitutionality or illegality is apparent beyond a reasonable doubt.

In tax cases, a district court decision adverse to the Treasury is always appealed ex officio to the higher court of jurisdiction, unless the amount in controversy is not in excess of Cr$ 5,000. Even in that case, however, it may be appealed by the Treasury. Conversely, a district court decision adverse to the taxpayer may always be appealed by him, unless the amount involved is not in excess of Cr$ 2,000, in which case the decision is final unless it is appealed on constitutional grounds.

Adjudicated refund claims may not be enforced through a lien on government property or funds. Such claims are met through specially budgeted funds, in the chronological order in which payment orders issued by the courts are filed by the interested parties with the appropriate disbursing agency. Consequently, such claims may sometimes be held in abeyance for a considerable time; they accrue 6% interest from the date of final judgment.

It may be tentatively said that, except in cases of *mandado de segurança,* the average time lapsing from inception to final adjudication of a judicial tax case is, in the larger cities like Rio de Janeiro or São Paulo, from eighteen months to two years.

1/5.6   Role of Lawyers and Accountants in Tax Practice

In all judicial proceedings representation of the taxpayer by a qualified attorney-at-law is mandatory, whereas in administrative proceedings the taxpayer may appear in person or be represented by a properly appointed person not necessarily a qualified lawyer. Consequently, the conduct of administrative litigation is a proper field of action for accountants.

It is the usual practice in Brazil to entrust the preparing of tax returns, certified statements, and all similar material required by tax laws and regulations to accountants. In most small and medium-sized corporations not having a legal department, it is the general rule to rely entirely upon the accountant attached to the staff (usually as the company's treasurer) for guidance and advice in all matters of taxation, and to consult an outside lawyer only in questions involving specific legal points of particular difficulty.

Even in large corporations, tax matters are primarily dealt with by the treasurer's department, which may consult with the legal department. Most important Brazilian corporations, and practically all foreign-owned corporations, engage independent auditors in addition to maintaining qualified accountants on their staffs. Such independent auditors are sometimes used as tax consultants, in addition to, or in lieu of specialized lawyers. In general, it is not improper for a trained person, not formally qualified as a lawyer, to give expert advice in legal matters in the field of taxation as well as in other fields.

There are in Brazil numerous individuals or firms called *despachantes* who, as "dispatchers" of papers through government agencies, undertake to advise on tax matters and even to represent clients in administrative cases. *Despachantes* are not an organized profession, except for customs *despachantes* who intervene in all dealings of importers with customs authorities but whose activities are strictly regulated by federal statute.[32]

[32] Decree-law No. 4,014 of January 13, 1942, as amended by Decree-law No. 9,832 of September 11, 1946.

1/5.7 Enforcement

A federal statute [33] provides for the enforcement of tax claims by distraint. Under this act, if a taxpayer fails within the prescribed time to pay or contest a tax assessment or fine, or fails within 30 days to comply with a final administrative ruling or to file suit as indicated above, the Treasury will secure a court warrant for his personal or real property to be seized in an amount sufficient to cover the claim and defray the court costs. If in the course of prior administrative litigation the taxpayer has made a deposit, seizure is carried out against the property thus deposited; but if a surety has been offered, seizure is carried out against the surety's property. After a final decision adverse to the taxpayer is entered, the property already under seizure is sold at public auction and any proceeds over the adjudicated claim plus court costs are returned to the taxpayer. If the decision is in favor of the taxpayer, the seizure will be lifted and the case closed.

A finally adjudicated tax claim is a first lien on all of an individual taxpayer's personal and real property, joint property, marriage property, and the income from all of them. It is similarly a first lien on the entire assets of a legal entity and on the income therefrom. The same rule applies to successors of the original taxpayer and to sureties offered in connection with administrative tax litigation.[34]

A legal entity taking over all assets and liabilities of another in liquidation succeeds to all claims whether pending or adjudicated. A legal entity taking over assets and/or liabilities of another in a reorganization will be held jointly liable with the latter.

Claims for real property taxes and fines automatically pass to the person acquiring such property,[35] unless (1) a full statement of clearance is secured by the former owner of the property and transcribed into the deed of sale or assignment, or (2) the property is acquired at public auction following its seizure for taxes against the former owner thereof.

Claims for taxes and fines precede all other public or private claims in bankruptcy, liquidation, receivership, or similar proceedings.[36] Although the Consolidated Labor Law [37] assures a similar precedence to employees' claims for wages or termination pay, the courts invariably decide in favor of tax claims on the ground of their public nature.

Finally, no sale or other transfer of property between private parties even by judicial order as in the case of enforcement of judgments, settlement of estates, or liquidation of legal entities declared bankrupt

[33] Decree-law No. 960 of December 17, 1938.
[34] Decree No. 22,866 of June 28, 1933.
[35] Civil Code, Art. 677.
[36] Decree-law No. 960 of November 17, 1938, Art. 60.
[37] Decree-law No. 5,452 of May 1, 1943.

or under receivership, can be effected unless a full statement of clearance is presented in respect of all taxes attaching to the property transferred.

1/5.8   Fines and Penalties

All statutes imposing taxes deal, in varying degrees of elaboration, with the matter of penalties. These are almost exclusively in the form of fines, or sometimes in the form of an increase in the tax rate, which may in turn be combined with a fine. Confiscation as a penalty is prohibited by the Constitution. Since criminal law in Brazil is exclusively federal, no tax violation can be defined as a crime by a state or municipal statute. Federal law does not treat tax violations, except smuggling,[38] as independent crimes.

Criminal offenses punishable by imprisonment can be committed in connection with tax matters, such as wilfully entering false statements of fact into books of account, resisting a lawful order of an administrative or judicial authority, or suppressing or destroying evidence. In all such cases, the penalties provided by criminal law will not exclude the civil penalties provided by fiscal law.[39]

Except for minor violations of regulations, no penalty may be imposed without a hearing by the appropriate authority. Penalties for criminal offenses are imposed only by judicial authority; all other penalties are imposed by administrative authority, but they are always subject to judicial review.

The general rule, both administrative and judicial, is that tax penalties are incurred irrespective of intent; consequently, the master is always liable for his servant, as well as the successor for his predecessor.[40] Intent is always a factor in determining the amount of the fine whenever this is left by the statute to the discretion of the authority with a minimum and a maximum expressed in percentages of the defaulted tax.

It is a criminal offense for a tax official to demand payment of a tax not legally due, unless there is reasonable doubt as to statutory construction. Both the offer and the acceptance of a bribe are punished as crimes. A tax official divulging or utilizing, beyond the interests of the revenue service, information obtained in line of duty and relating to the financial position or the nature and state of the affairs of a taxpayer, is guilty of a crime.[41]

[38] Criminal Code Art. 334. The penalty is imprisonment for from one to four years.
[39] For a detailed list of such criminal offenses, see Sousa, Compêndio (2d ed.) §§35 and 36 (1954).
[40] Supreme Court, 71 Arquivo Judiciário 10, 105 Revista Forense 68.
[41] Penal Code, Art. 325. The penalty is imprisonment for from six months to two years and a fine of not less than Cr$ 12,000.

1/5.9   Collection of Delinquent Taxes

In order to enforce the collection of taxes owed, the law permits the administrative authorities to refuse the delinquent taxpayer the right to buy tax stamps, to dispatch merchandise through the customs, or to take part in any other transaction with a government department. Thus, a delinquent taxpayer is practically prevented from engaging in commerce or industry. It should be noted, however, that the legal disabilities attaching to the status of a delinquent taxpayer are removed if the taxpayer deposits the amount in question (for the purpose of an administrative appeal) or appoints a surety. In these cases, the enforcement measures are discontinued.[42]

Such provisions apply only to taxes due to the federal government. They constitute an effective means of indirectly forcing taxpayers to discharge their obligations as and when due. Interest for taxes and fines in arrears is usually imposed at a fixed rate (10%),[43] but this does not constitute a sufficient incentive for the delinquent taxpayer to settle the matter promptly except for the income tax (13/7.2). Interest is not construed as a penalty and therefore is not a bar to the imposition of any fines which may be applicable.

A percentage (usually 50%) of the amount collected as a fine is allocated to the tax inspector who initiated the investigation leading to the discovery of a tax deficiency or violation. This practice is often questioned, but it remains prevalent at all three levels of government.

1/5.10   Periods of Limitation

With the exception of the Income Tax Regulations (13/6.), tax statutes, whether federal, state, or municipal, prescribe no time limitations on assessment or collection, but only on the power to impose fines and penalties. This period is usually five years.

Under Arts. 177 and 178 §7(II) of the Civil Code, the statute of limitations is two years on all personal obligations up to Cr$ 100 and thirty years on those in excess of Cr$ 100. But recently the Supreme Court has held that since the Civil Code regulates only matters of private law, its provisions are not applicable to matters of public law such as taxation.[44] There are, consequently, no precise time limitations on assessment and collection other than those prescribed in individual tax laws. On the other hand, the government may issue deficiency assessments only if the original assessment was based on an error of fact or law.

[42] Decree-law No. 5 of November 13, 1937, as amended by Decree-laws No. 42 of December 6, 1937, and No. 3,336 of June 10, 1941.

[43] The penalty has recently been increased for deficiencies of income tax (13/7.2).

[44] 129 *Revista Forense* 118 and 426 (1950); 21 *Revista de Direito Administrativo* 73 and 78 (1950); 186 *Revista dos Tribunais* 936 (1950).

It may not do so on the basis of a change in the administrative or judicial construction of a statute.[45]

Conversely, the periods of limitation applying to taxpayers' claims for the revision of administrative assessments or rulings or for the refund of overpaid taxes are clearly defined by a federal statute.[46] Under this law the time limit for a petition is one year if brought in administrative, and five years if brought in judicial proceedings.

1/6. Synopsis of the Tax Structure

1/6.1 Allocation of Tax Revenues

In determining the revenue of each level of government — federal, state, and municipal — the allocations provided for by the Constitution must be taken into consideration.

The major allocations of the revenue collected by the federal government are:

1. 10% of the revenue from the income tax, to the municipalities, except state capitals.
2. 60% of the revenue from the *impôsto unico,* divided according to a formula designed to redistribute the revenue to its source of origin, as explained in 16/3.1.

The major allocations of revenue collected by the states are:

1. 20% of the revenue from nonexclusive taxes, to the federal government.
2. 40% of the revenue from nonexclusive taxes, to the municipal governments.
3. 30% of the excess of tax collected in any municipality (except a state capital) over the revenue that the muncipality collects from its own taxes, to the municipality.

Looking at these allocations of revenue from the point of view of the recipient, the federal government receives 20% of the tax revenues collected by the states from nonexclusive taxes.

The state governments receive a percentage of the *impôsto unico,* which the federal government collects.

The municipal governments receive from revenues collected by the federal government:

1. 10% of the income tax.
2. A percentage of the *impôsto unico.*

---

[45] See Federal Court of Appeals in *Rev.* 1954, No. 4. Similarly, administrative orders modifying the established construction of a statute apply only to cases arising subsequent to the order.

[46] Decree No. 20,910 of January 6, 1932.

They receive from the revenues collected by the states:

1. 40% of all nonexclusive taxes.
2. A municipality in which a state collects more tax revenue than does the municipality itself, receives 30% of the excess.

1/6.2 Federal Revenue

The following are the federal exclusive taxes (1/3.2) levied under the authority of Art. 15 of the Constitution:

a. IMPORT DUTIES. Import duties are imposed on the importation of natural or manufactured products that are to be consumed in the national territory.

b. EXCISE TAX. The excise tax (16/2.) is imposed on the producer or importer of specified goods under Art. 15(II) of the Constitution, which authorizes the imposition of taxes on the consumption of goods.

c. "IMPÔSTO UNICO." The *impôsto unico* (16/3.) is the only excise tax authorized to be levied on liquid and gaseous fuels, lubricants, domestic mineral products, and electricity.

d. INCOME AND EXCESS PROFITS TAXES. The income tax (Chapters 5–13) is levied on the gains derived from capital, from labor, or from a combination of both. The income tax on business enterprises is actually a tax on profits. The excess profits tax (Chapter 14) was reintroduced in 1956.

e. EXCHANGE REMITTANCE TAX. The exchange remittance tax (4/10.) is levied on actual or constructive transactions made for the purpose, or with the effect, of transferring funds from Brazil to foreign countries.

f. STAMP TAX. The stamp tax (17/2.) is levied on legal documents and instruments regulated by federal law.

g. COMPARATIVE IMPORTANCE OF FEDERAL SOURCES OF REVENUE. Under the federal budget for 1957 [47] for a total estimated revenue of 98,257 millions of cruzeiros, the total estimated tax revenue is 84,642 million.

The 1957 budget estimate of the revenue from the major federal taxes is as follows:

	Millions of Cr$
Income tax	35,151
Excise tax	32,247
Stamp tax	11,593
Impôsto unico	1,100
Import duties	2,760
Exchange tax	1,440

[47] Approved by Law No. 2996 of December 10, 1956.

It is apparent from the table that the excise tax alone exceeds all other federal taxes except the income tax in financial significance. In addition, it is possible to consider the sales tax, which in most states contributes about 70% of the entire tax revenue, as essentially a tax of the same nature as the excise tax. Therefore, inasmuch as most staple commodities are subject to both sales tax and excise tax, the burden to the individual taxpayer actually is the aggregate of the two taxes. It is apparent that the Brazilian tax system still relies to a very large extent on taxes on transactions as distinguished from those on capital and income, and that the per capita burden resulting from this form of taxation is very high.

1/6.3   State Revenue

The following state exclusive taxes are levied under the authority of Art. 19 of the Constitution:

a. RURAL LAND TAX. The rural land tax (see 3/2.5) is imposed on the ownership of real property located outside of urban and suburban limits.

b. REAL PROPERTY TRANSFER TAX. The real property transfer tax (Chapter 19) is levied on the transfer of title to real property, or of rights therein inter vivos. It includes the contribution of such property or rights to the capital of legal entities.

c. INHERITANCE TAX. The inheritance tax (3/3.) is imposed on the passing of title to real or movable property by reason of death.

d. SALES TAX. The sales tax (15/1.) is levied on the sale or other transfer of movable property for a consideration.

e. EXPORT TAX. The export tax (15/6.) is imposed by the producer state on the export of natural or manufactured products outside the national territory.

f. STAMP TAX. The stamp tax (17/3.) is imposed on legal documents and instruments regulated by state law.

g. COMPARATIVE IMPORTANCE OF STATE SOURCES OF REVENUE. The states do not use all the taxing powers granted to them by the Constitution.[48] The fact that Art. 21 of the Constitution requires them to allocate 60% of all revenue from nonexclusive taxes to the federal government and the municipalities in whose territory the taxes were collected has discouraged them from levying such taxes. The export tax is of such limited scope and measure that it is of no great importance. Therefore,

[48] For further discussion of the use by the states of the sources of revenue available to them, see Aliomar Baleeiro, *"Estados, Discriminação de Rendas e Reforma Constitucional"* ("The States, the Apportionment of Tax Revenue and Constitutional Reform"), 143 *Revista Forense* 7 (1952), reprinted in 30 *Revista de Direito Administrativo* 11 (1952).

the sales tax, which is the only important state exclusive tax, has become the mainstay of all state tax systems. In all states except Amazonas it is a multipoint tax, imposed each time an article is sold. In Amazonas it is imposed only on the first sale, but the rate of tax there is 8%, as compared to an average of 2½% to 3% in the other states.

h. THE SALES TAX ON INTERSTATE SALES. A federal act,[49] designed to prevent double taxation of interstate sales, states that when goods produced in one state are shipped to a branch or agent of the producer in another state for purposes of sale, the sales tax is due to the producer state at the time of shipment. Any balance in tax arising from a markup in prices when the goods are actually sold is also due to the producer state and not to the state where the sale took place (15/1.3).

1/6.4 Municipal Exclusive Taxes

The following municipal exclusive taxes (1/3.2) are levied under the authority of Art. 29 of the Constitution.

a. URBAN REAL PROPERTY TAX. The urban real property tax (3/2.6, 3/2.7) is a tax on the ownership of vacant or improved real property, located within urban or suburban limits.

b. LICENSE TAXES. License taxes (18/4.4) are taxes on the issuance of permits to exercise activities subject to municipal regulation or control.

c. BUSINESS TAX. The business tax (18/1.) is a tax on engaging in industry, commerce, and professions, irrespective of the financial results.

d. AMUSEMENT TAX. The amusement tax (18/4.1) is a tax on the admission to, or participation in, any exhibition, performance, or other activity staged for purposes of entertainment.

e. STAMP TAX. The stamp tax (17/3.) is a tax on municipal affairs or transactions pertaining to the municipal economy.

f. CONSTITUTIONAL PROBLEMS IN MUNICIPAL TAXES. The business tax has come to be the foundation of the municipal tax system (see 4/8.). Because of its complicated and costly administration, however, its operation under acceptable legal conditions has been beyond the means of most of the smaller townships. This has led to the assessment and collection of the business tax in certain municipalities as a stated percentage of the amount paid by each taxpayer under the sales tax, which converts it into an addition to the sales tax. Since the sales tax is exclusive to the states, and since the municipalities have no power to institute taxes other than their own "exclusive" taxes, a substantial percentage of municipal

[49] Decree-law No. 915 of December 1, 1938.

tax revenue comes from sources the constitutionality of which may be open to question.

A typical example are the taxes (sometimes described as fees) imposed by a large number of municipalities, under varying definitions and methods, which fall directly on agricultural or industrial production. A systematic treatment of such taxes could not be attempted owing to their infinite variation. Their common factor is that they are assessed on the value of production, either gross or net. The sales tax, the excise tax, and even the income tax are sometimes used as the means for indirectly determining the basis of assessment. An extreme instance of taxes imposed by the municipalities under the guise of fees is to be found in taxes, sometimes defined as nonfiscal revenues such as "port charges," based on the value of goods loaded, unloaded, or even in transit, and imposed by certain municipalities situated along the Amazon and the São Francisco Rivers.

g. IMPORTANCE OF ALLOCATIONS OF REVENUE TO MUNICIPALITIES. According to estimates based on the federal budget figures for 1955, the distributions of revenue from the income tax would provide about Cr$ 600,000 to each qualifying municipality for the fiscal year 1955,[50] This amount is of no great significance to the larger and more developed townships, but in the case of minor ones it is equal to or even in excess of their estimated tax revenue for 1955. Such municipalities rely upon the federal allocations as the basic element of local finances. The elements determining the qualifications of a municipality are laid down by the state constitutions, and since the federal Constitution of 1946 some states have reduced such requirements to an absolute minimum. In this way, those states secure for increasingly larger portions of their territory the allocation of federal aid, thereby alleviating their own share of the burden of the financial requirements of their townships.

[50] Source: *Revista de Finanças Publicas* (unofficial publication of the Ministry of Finance), vol. 15, Nos. 170/171, p. 2 (February-March, 1955).

CHAPTER 2

SUMMARY OF TAXES

ON INCOME

2/1. History of the Income Tax

2/2. Introduction

2/3. Taxation of Resident Individuals
  2/3.1 The Schedular Tax
  2/3.2 The Complementary Tax
  2/3.3 The Withholding Tax
      a. Income from Bearer Securities
      b. Wages and Salaries
      c. Gains from the Sale of Real Property

2/4. Taxation of Resident Business Enterprises
  2/4.1 What Is Business Income
  2/4.2 Methods of Taxation and Tax Rates
  2/4.3 Actual Profits
  2/4.4 Reserves
      a. Reserves not Deductible
      b. Special Taxes on Reserves

2/5. Taxation of Nonresidents

2/6. The Excess Profits Tax

2/1. History of the Income Tax

The introduction of a general income tax in Brazil, although proposed at the time of the Empire and again in the Constitutional Assembly of 1891, did not become a reality until 1922. The taxation of income in the 19th century had been limited to some types of receipts such as the emoluments of public officials and corporate dividends. The first Constitution of the Republic (1891) made no reference to the income tax, which thus remained a subject of concurrent legislation by the federal Union and the states. No state, however, made use of its prerogative to introduce a general income tax.

The first federal income tax law of 1922 [1] was limited to a sole article which merely introduced the tax and described its general characteristics. This law, like subsequent and increasingly elaborate income tax laws of Brazil, received its basic orientation from the income tax law of France.

The field of income taxation first became an exclusively federal area under the Constitution of 1937 and it retains this position under the present Constitution of 1946.

The first income tax law of 1922 was followed by a number of regulatory decrees which were combined into one consolidated text in 1932.[2] This enactment was the object of fundamental changes in the following years [3] and a new consolidated law was published in 1947.[4] Additional amendments [5] resulted in another consolidation and republication of the existing body of law by Decree No. 36,773 of January 13, 1955. The "Regulations" published under this decree represent the presently valid income tax statute. They were amended again by Law No. 2,862 of September 4, 1956, and Decree No. 39,995 of September 13, 1956.

2/2. Introduction

The income tax applies to all individuals and entities which are either residents of Brazil or derive income from Brazilian sources. The methods of taxation are, however, different for the various classes of taxpayers.

Resident individuals are subject to a dual income tax, namely, a schedular tax at fixed rates which differ for the various types of income, and a complementary tax at progressive rates which is computed on total income. Certain types of income (agricultural and foreign income) are subject to complementary tax only.

Resident entities are subject to uniform rules of taxation on the ground that all income of these entities (corporations, limited liability companies, commercial partnerships, etc.) is from one source only, namely, from business. Only income from Brazilian sources is subject to this tax. The tax is computed at slightly progressive rates which have been continuously increased during the last few years.

[1] Law No. 4,625 of December 31, 1922, Art. 31.
[2] Decree No. 21,554 of 1932.
[3] Decree-laws No. 4,178 of 1942, and No. 5,844 of 1943; Law No. 154 of 1947.
[4] Decree No. 24,239 of December 22, 1947.
[5] By Laws No. 1,474 of 1951, and No. 2,354 of 1954.

The rules on the taxation of business income of entities also apply to an individual engaged in business with respect to his income from that source. For purposes of the complementary tax on the individual's total income, his income from business is combined with that from nonbusiness sources.

The foregoing describes in very brief outline the system of taxation by assessment, i.e., on the basis of an annual return filed by the taxpayer.

Besides the system of taxation by assessment, there is, in respect of certain types of income, taxation by withholding at the source. Where the withholding system applies, the tax liability of the recipient of the income is fully satisfied through payment of the withholding tax, and the recipient is not required to include this income in his return for purposes of the assessed tax. Withholding of tax at the source is required on all income of resident taxpayers (individuals or entities) from bearer securities and from wages and salaries which are within certain minimum limits.

The system of taxation by withholding of tax at the source applies to all income of nonresidents from sources in Brazil, regardless of the nature of the income and whether the recipient is an individual or an entity (2/5.).

2/3. Taxation of Resident Individuals

All individuals who are physically present in Brazil for an uninterrupted period of at least twelve consecutive months are residents for income tax purposes, regardless of their nationality, intent, or the reasons for their stay. Conversely, all individuals (Brazilians or foreigners) who have not completed twelve full months of residence in Brazil, or who remain absent from the country for more than twelve months, are nonresidents. Resident individuals are subject to assessed income tax on both domestic and foreign income, whereas nonresidents are taxed by withholding at the source on income from Brazilian sources. For taxation of nonresidents who are engaged in business in Brazil through a permanent establishment located there, see 2/5.

In order to arrive at an equitable distribution of the tax burden and to take account of the nature of the income as well as the needs of the taxpayer, the income tax on resident individuals is composed of two taxes, called schedular tax and complementary tax. The proportionate rates of the schedular tax, which give weight to social factors, vary with the type of income but not its amount; this tax, therefore, considers only the nature of the income. The complementary tax, on the other hand, is a progressive tax and depends entirely on the amount of the taxpayer's annual income, regardless of its nature.

2/3.1   The Schedular Tax

For purposes of the schedular tax, the income of an individual is classified into eight categories or schedules which are listed below with the schedular tax rate applying to each.

		Schedular Tax Rate
Schedule A:	Interest from nominative government securities	3%
Schedule B:	Interest from other sources and certain other income from capital	10%
Schedule C:	Compensation for personal services as an employee	1% [6]
Schedule D:	Compensation for independent personal services	2%
Schedule E:	Income from real property	3%
Schedule F:	Income from distributions by entities, business income of individuals, and foreign income	No schedular tax
Schedule G:	Income from agriculture	No schedular tax
Schedule H:	Income from gainful occupations not includible under another schedule	5%

Gross income for purposes of the schedular tax is defined as the gain derived from capital, from labor, or from both combined; in addition, certain receipts which do not meet these qualifications are deemed income by statutory prescription. On the other hand, not all receipts which come under the general definition of income constitute gross income for tax purposes. It follows from the nature of the Brazilian income tax system as a schedular system that receipts, in order to qualify as gross income, must also be capable of being included in one of the schedular classifications whose scope is determined either by common understanding or by specific statutory rule.

Gross income under each schedule is reduced by specific statutory deductions which are different for each type of schedular income. The resulting net schedular income is taxed at the proportionate rates shown above, regardless of its amount. The schedular tax does not provide for family allowances or other expenditures affecting the taxpayer's ability to pay. However, an individual whose net annual income under all applicable schedules does not exceed Cr$ 60,000 is not obliged to pay any schedular tax because he is, by statutory definition, not a taxpayer unless his net income reaches this minimum amount.

It is evident from the table reproduced above that no schedular taxes apply under Schedules F and G. These schedules, therefore, merely

[6] But see 2/3.3b.

serve the purpose of classifying certain income for purposes of the complementary tax. While the absence of a schedular tax under Schedule G is in the nature of a tax benefit for individuals engaged in agriculture,[7] the reason for the exemption of Schedule F income from the schedular tax is different. Schedule F includes two types of income which are entirely unrelated to each other, namely, income from business (whether the taxpayer's own business or one in which he has made an investment) and income from foreign sources. Business income is subject to a tax, similar to the schedular tax imposed on individuals, in the hands of the entity which earns it. It is the policy of the law not to burden this income with another proportionate tax imposed on the individual owner, partner, or shareholder when it becomes available to him either through its mere computation, as in the case of a sole proprietorship or commercial partnership, or through distributions made by a corporation or other legal entity in which the individual owns shares. Rather than provide for a schedular tax rate for the business income of individuals, the law achieves the same result by substituting the tax imposed on the business for the individual's schedular tax. For purposes of the progressive complementary tax, the individual's business and nonbusiness income are combined.

Foreign income of individuals is not subject to schedular tax because it is not derived from activities carried on in Brazil; this income is, however, subject to complementary tax. In this respect the tax situation of an individual is different from that of a corporation or other business entity which is taxable only on income from Brazilian sources. There seems to be no valid theory supporting this difference, and its actual importance is very limited in view of the established interpretation of the law according to which foreign income is taxable only if remitted to Brazil, and the practical impossibility of enforcing the reporting by individuals of such foreign income as is remitted.[8]

The rule that income from all transactions for profit which cannot be classified under another schedule is taxable under Schedule H has given rise to difficulties of interpretation. The statute itself lists five different types of income as qualifying under Schedule H and, in addition, "net profits from the assignment of any right." It is obvious that a

---

[7] Agricultural income of a corporation or other entity constitutes business income and is taxed as such under the rules set forth at 2/4.

[8] The rule that individuals are subject to the complementary tax on "all" income from foreign sources necessarily implies that they are taxed on foreign business profits and dividends, if remitted to Brazil. On the other hand, a resident individual who is engaged in business in Brazil is, with respect to his business profits, subject to the rules applying to corporations and other entities which are *not* taxed on foreign income. It would therefore appear that foreign dividends are taxed only if derived from private investments of the individual, but not if they originate in his business. There are, at this time, no administrative or judicial decisions which would clarify this question.

literal interpretation of this provision would go far in destroying the schedular tax system because there are few transactions, if any, which do not involve an assignment of some right. The interpretation of this provision by the government as well as the courts has, therefore, been most restrictive. In particular, gains from the sale of property are not taxed unless they are realized in a business and thus subject to the rules on the taxation of business income (2/4.) or unless the statute expressly provides for their taxation as it does for gains realized by individuals from the sale of Brazilian real estate (2/3.3c).

2/3.2   The Complementary Tax

As a balancing factor to the schedular tax, whose rates depend on the nature of the income only and not its amount, the complementary tax is levied at progressive rates on the entire amount of an individual's income regardless of its character. Gross income, for purposes of the complementary tax, is the sum total of net income under all applicable schedules; it follows that only income which qualifies under one of the schedules enters into the computation of the complementary tax. Gross income is reduced by deductions called "abatements," which are partly in the nature of family allowances (Cr$ 50,000 for the taxpayer's spouse, Cr$ 25,000 for each child and certain other dependents) and partly in the nature of deductions for certain personal expenditures (interest on personal debts, life insurance premiums, casualty losses, medical expenses, and charitable contributions).

The rates of the complementary tax range from 3% in the lowest bracket (net income between Cr$ 60,000 and Cr$ 90,000) to 50% in the highest (net income exceeding Cr$ 3,000,000). Since the different rates apply only to the portion of income within a given bracket, the effective tax is always less than the rate applicable to the portion of income falling into the highest bracket will indicate.

The first Cr$ 60,000 of taxable income are not subject to complementary tax. An individual whose net annual income for purposes of the schedular tax does not exceed Cr$ 60,000 is subject neither to the schedular tax nor to the complementary tax. The same is true if the net schedular income of an individual (which becomes gross income for purposes of the complementary tax) is greater than Cr$ 60,000 but is reduced to an amount equal to or less than that figure by statutory "abatements." This follows from the rule already referred to that individuals whose net annual income does not exceed Cr$ 60,000 are not taxpayers under the law. Expressed differently, the individual income tax becomes operative only if at least the minimum amount of net income is present for purposes of both its components — the schedular tax and the complementary tax.

The total income tax of an individual (schedular tax and complementary tax) may be subject to certain percentage increases depending on the individual's family situation; and if the total tax equals or exceeds Cr$ 20,000, it is increased by an addition which is in the nature of a compulsory refundable loan (see 12/1.3b).

2/3.3   The Withholding Tax

A brief survey of the withholding provisions applying to residents of Brazil may be conveniently made under three headings, namely, income from bearer securities, wages and salaries, and gains from the sale of real property.

a. INCOME FROM BEARER SECURITIES. The reason for taxing income from bearer securities (dividends from bearer shares, interest from bearer bonds, etc.) at the source is that the owner of the securities is usually unknown or, at least, not easily identified. In order to make the tax effective and to assure its equal application, it is based on the mere fact that payments of a certain type are made, and the characteristics and personal circumstances of the taxpayer are disregarded. The withholding tax applies to individuals and entities alike and it is based on gross income, making no allowance for tax-free amounts, for deductions, or, in the case of individual recipients, for family or personal expenditures. The tax liability of the recipient is fully satisfied by payment of the withholding tax and he is not required to include the income subject to withholding in his return. For reasons of administrative control, the fiscal obligations are imposed on the payor of the income. Payment of the tax must usually be made within 30 days from the date when withholding is required, i.e., at the time when the income is paid, credited, or remitted by the withholding agent to the individual or entity entitled thereto or, upon the taxpayer's request, to a third party.

The rates of the withholding tax are at present as follows: [9]

On interest from government bonds made out to bearer	6%
On interest from other bearer bonds or debentures	21%
On dividends (in cash or in stock), distributions to holders of participating certificates and founders' shares, and certain revaluation gains in connection with reorganizations (if the distributions are made on bearer securities)	28%

b. WAGES AND SALARIES. Withholding of income tax on wages and salaries of employees (as well as the compensation of owners of individual businesses, partners, and corporate officers) was introduced by the Income Tax Regulations of January 1955. Because of their limited scope, the present withholding provisions are an effective substitute for the

---

[9] As modified, in part, by Law No. 2,862 of September 4, 1956. These rates are increased by additions in the nature of a refundable compulsory loan.

assessed income tax only in respect of employees and workers in the lower income brackets.

The employer is required to withhold income tax for every month in which the wages or salary of an employee amounts to more than Cr\$ 5,000.[10] If the monthly compensation of the employee exceeds Cr\$ 10,000, the withholding provisions apply to the portion thereof between Cr\$ 5,000 and Cr\$ 10,000. The tax is determined from a withholding table attached to the Regulations which is revised whenever necessary to give effect to changes in family allowances and tax rates.

If the amount of compensation paid by not more than one employer does not exceed Cr\$ 10,000 in any one calendar month, the tax liability of the employee is fully satisfied by withholding, and he is not required to file a return.

c. GAINS FROM THE SALE OF REAL PROPERTY. Gains from the sale of real property located in Brazil are subject to special rules of taxation and taxed at a preferential rate if realized by an individual.[11] The tax on the gain is collected from the seller. It is therefore not a withholding tax in the proper sense of the term and its designation as such by the Income Tax Regulations merely serves the purpose of making the technical withholding provisions of the statute applicable. The tax is levied at the flat rate of 10%, computed on the gain from the sale. This gain, however, is reduced by varying percentages (between 10% and 30%) depending on the seller's holding period, so that the effective tax will always be less than 10% of the actual gain.

2/4. Taxation of Resident Business Enterprises

2/4.1 What Is Business Income

The rules governing the taxation of business income are laid down in the part of the Income Tax Regulations which deals with "juridical persons," i.e., entities with legal personality of their own such as corporations, limited liability companies, and their variations as they exist under Brazilian law (1/4.2). The application of these rules is extended to sole proprietorships, commercial partnerships, and unincorporated entities engaged in business with the help of the legal fiction that individuals and others who continuously and regularly effect transactions for profit in their own names assume the status of legal entities for income tax purposes. Disregarding the legal construction by which the desired result is achieved, the rule is that all individuals and entities which are engaged

---

[10] The following summary considers the amendments by Law No. 2,862, effective January 1, 1957.

[11] If realized in a business, such gains form part of the business income and are subject to the rules explained at 2/4.

in business are subject to the same rules of taxation irrespective of the form of organization under which the business operates.✓

Corporations, limited liability companies, and other entities organized under the commercial law are merchants with respect to all their activities. Consequently, all income of these entities constitutes business income for tax purposes regardless of how the same kind of activity and the same income would be classified in the case of a nonmerchant. Individuals, on the other hand, are merchants and as such subject to the commercial law and to taxation under the rules applying to business income only with respect to their business activities. Nonbusiness income of an individual is subject to the various schedular taxes and to complementary tax, as explained at 2/3. Independently, the business firm owned by the individual is a taxable entity and as such subject to taxation under the rules applying to business income. A resident individual engaged in business is therefore required to file two annual income tax returns. On the return filed as owner of the business, the individual computes his income and tax exactly as would a corporation. On the return filed in his individual capacity, the individual reports his nonbusiness income for purposes of the schedular and complementary taxes, but he also includes his buisness income, which is subject to complementary tax under Schedule F as explained at 2/2.

The "residence" of a business, for income tax purposes, is at its seat, i.e., where its management is located. A foreign corporation or other entity "resides" in Brazil, for income tax purposes, if it is doing business in Brazil through a permanent branch or agency located in the country. The same is true in the rare situation where a nonresident individual has a permanent business establishment in Brazil.

The tax treatment of the Brazilian branch of a foreign business firm is peculiar in certain respects. As an establishment which is located in Brazil and doing business there, the branch is subject to the assessed tax on its business profits (15% on the first Cr$ 500,000 of taxable income and 20% on the excess over Cr$ 500,000), the same as an entity organized under Brazilian law. Being, on the other hand, an integral part of a nonresident foreign organization, the branch is further considered subject to the withholding tax (at the existing rate of 20%) imposed on all income of nonresidents from sources in Brazil (2/5.); this tax falls due as soon as the branch profits are determined, irrespective of any actual credit or remittance to the home office. While double taxation of branch profits would not seem to be the inevitable result of the dual nature of the branch, the rule discussed here is firmly established in the income tax law of Brazil, and it has the support of the highest courts.[12]

---

[12] A certain mitigation of the double taxation of branch profits is accomplished by the exemption from the withholding tax of profits which are reinvested in Brazil by the branch.

2/4.2 Methods of Taxation and Tax Rates

In the usual situation, the "actual profits" of a business form the basis of taxation. The law further provides for two alternative bases of taxation, namely, "presumed profits" and "estimated profits." Taxation on the basis of "presumed profits" is an elective method of determining the tax base which is available to certain smaller enterprises (with capital not exceeding Cr$ 100,000 and gross annual income not exceeding Cr$ 500,000), but in no event to corporations, limited liability companies, or the Brazilian branch of a foreign entity; under this method, taxable income is represented by an amount equal to 8% of gross income. Taxation on the basis of "estimated profits" is a method by which the government can determine the tax base if the computation of actual profits is prevented through the fault of the taxpayer. Under this method, taxable income is expressed in terms of a percentage of the assets, the capital, or the gross income of the enterprise.

The rate of tax is 15% with an addition of 5% applying to the portion of taxable income exceeding Cr$ 500,000. In view of the deductibility of the preceding year's income tax, the effective rate of the tax is usually less than 15% or 20%. In addition to the tax, a charge in the nature of a compulsory refundable loan amounting to 15% of the tax is collected.[13] These rates apply whether taxable income is determined on an actual, presumed, or estimated basis.

2/4.3 Actual Profits

The term "actual profits" refers to the book income of a business as determined by accepted accounting methods with certain adjustments required by law for income tax purposes. Similar to the exemption from income tax of individuals with annual *net* income of not more than Cr$ 60,000, there is an exemption for corporations and other entities whose *gross* annual income is Cr$ 150,000 or less. However, if gross income exceeds Cr$ 150,000, no part of the income is exempt; in this respect, the rule is different from that for individual taxpayers.

The business profits which form the basis of the income tax on actual profits are determined primarily from the commercial books of the taxpayer. It follows that the application of this method is dependent on the maintenance of proper books and records and that the method becomes inapplicable if the taxpayer fails to keep reliable and intelligible books; in this situation the tax is computed on estimated profits. Apart from a number of formal rules which must be observed notwithstanding their antiquated nature, the taxpayer is free to rely on any system of accounting which gives a detailed and comprehensive picture of his activities during the year and which is followed consistently.

[13] See 12/1.3b.

Since book profits rather than gross income are the starting point for the determination of taxable income, the law does not give a definition of gross income for purposes of the business income tax as it does in the case of the nonbusiness income of individuals, and it does not mention cost of goods sold. The catalogue of allowable deductions given in the law is brief and incomplete. The statute allows the deduction of all expenses incurred in connection with the particular business activity and necessary to produce the gross profits and to maintain the productive source. Besides this very broadly defined deduction for general business expenses, only a few deductions are specifically listed; [14] this enumeration, however, is in the nature of definitions and limitations rather than of an exhaustive description of allowable deductions. A number of important deductions such as that for taxes (including the income tax paid during the business year on the income of the next-preceding year) are not specifically referred to in the statute but are covered by the general expense allowance referred to.

Only business income which is derived from Brazilian sources is subject to tax. The law specifically lists certain transactions which are deemed to result in income from both Brazilian and foreign sources and gives rules for the determination of the domestic portion of the income which is the only part subject to tax.

Income which has already been taxed — such as dividends on bearer shares on which tax is withheld by the distributing entity for the account of the distributee — is excluded from taxable income for purposes of the tax on business profits.

Since all income received by an entity is considered business income and taxed as such, there is no distinction between ordinary income and capital gains. All profits and gains from whatever source form part of the business income and are taxed under the same rules.

2/4.4   Reserves

The discussion of reserves, from the viewpoint of the income tax, covers two different and unrelated subjects. One deals with the question whether reserves constitute allowable deductions for purposes of the income tax on business profits. The other refers to special taxes, in addition to the regular income tax, on certain reserves of corporations and other entities.

Under Brazilian law only entities with independent legal existence are deemed capable of having reserves. A sole proprietorship or partnership,

[14] The Income Tax Regulations list interest, bad debts, depreciation of movable property, depletion, the deduction for obsolete machinery and equipment, charitable contributions, and certain specific deductions available to insurance companies, capitalization banks, and public utilities. Depreciation of buildings and other improvements of real property is not recognized under Brazilian income tax law.

although considered an "entity" for purposes of the business income tax, cannot have reserves in the proper sense because its profits are always at the disposition of the owner or partners as soon as determined. The same rule applies to the unincorporated Brazilian branch of a nonresident foreign corporation or other entity.

a. RESERVES NOT DEDUCTIBLE. Reserves in the technical sense of the term must, under Brazilian terminology, be distinguished from "provisions." "Provisions" are noncash expenses such as depreciation, amortization, depletion, and bad debts, which are deductible for income tax purposes within the limits set by the law. "Reserves" in the technical sense are appropriations of surplus, profits in suspense, and excess "provisions." The rule is that all reserves formed during the year, regardless of their purpose, must be included in taxable income.

b. SPECIAL TAXES ON RESERVES. If the total surplus and reserves of a *corporation* exceed the amount of the paid-in capital stock, the excess is subject to a special tax of 30%, which is essentially a tax on excessive accumulations of surplus.

The 30% tax on reserves applies only to corporations organized under Brazilian law, not to other incorporated or unincorporated entities or, as already pointed out, to the Brazilian branch of a foreign entity. The tax is imposed only once; if surplus and reserves are increased from one year to the next, the tax falls only on the increase not previously taxed.

The tax on excess reserves is imposed on the shareholders, but withheld and paid by the corporation for their account. If the amount of the excess reserves is capitalized or distributed to the shareholders, the 30% tax is in lieu of all individual income taxes which are usually incurred through transactions of this kind.

Furthermore, a special charge of 4%, in the nature of a refundable compulsory loan, is imposed on the surplus and reserves of all business entities except sole proprietorships. The legal reserves of corporations (6/6.2) and the special reserves of insurance companies and certain savings institutions are not subject to this charge. The validity of the charge has been extended by Law No. 2,973 of November 26, 1956, until the taxable year 1966 (base year 1965).

2/5. Taxation of Nonresidents

The general rule is that nonresidents of Brazil are taxed at the source on all their income from Brazilian sources. No distinction is made between nonresident individuals and entities. The present rate of the withholding tax is 20% except on income which, because of its nature, is subject to a higher withholding rate in the hands of a resident (e.g., dividends on bearer shares for which a withholding rate of 28% is in effect); in these cases, the higher withholding rate applies to nonresidents also. Royalty income of nonresidents is taxed at the rate of 25%. With the exception of income from real property,[15] the withholding tax on nonresidents is based on gross income.[16]

The rules just stated are subject to certain qualifications. While it is generally correct that all income of nonresidents is taxed by withholding at the source, it is also true that there is only one concept of taxable income and that nonresidents should not be taxed on receipts which are not considered taxable income to residents.[17] Furthermore, while the withholding tax is generally based on gross income, the courts and the Administration have been careful to limit its application to payments which are in the nature of income as distinguished from gross receipts or a return of capital, and they have refrained from imposing the tax where a payment cannot be conveniently apportioned between income and capital.

The application of the withholding provisions to business income of nonresidents from Brazilian sources depends largely on the form in which the business is transacted. The profits of an entity which is organized under Brazilian law — e.g., the Brazilian subsidiary of a foreign corporation — are subject to the assessed tax on business income; they become, in addition, subject to the withholding tax only if they are credited to a nonresident or actually remitted abroad. The profits of the Brazilian branch of a foreign entity are, as already discussed (2/4.1), subject to the withholding of tax on nonresidents in addition to the assessed tax on business profits for the reason that the profits of the branch are those of the home office by operation of law as soon as they are determined. The rules of taxation of direct business transactions of a foreign firm in Brazil are not uniform and not always clearly defined. Income from direct sales of merchandise or other property to Brazil is considered not subject to withholding tax because the profit is not derived from Brazilian sources. Income from the licensing of patents, processes, and similar intangible rights is subject to withholding at the source at the rate of 25% computed on gross income; regarding this type of property, however, the question whether a particular transaction is in the nature of a sale or a license agreement is far from settled. Income from technical or other services rendered by a nonresi-

[15] Regarding this type of income, a nonresident individual or entity is entitled to the schedular deductions available to a resident individual taxpayer.

[16] Taxable income from the distribution of foreign motion pictures in Brazil is deemed to be equal to 30% of the gross amount made available to the foreign producer or distributor, so that the tax in effect amounts to 6% (20% of 30%) of gross income.

[17] This rule has not been observed regarding royalty income of nonresident authors which has been held to be subject to the withholding tax. Resident authors are exempt from tax on this income under the Constitution of Brazil.

dent to a Brazilian firm is subject to taxation at the source if the services are rendered in Brazil.

2/6. The Excess Profits Tax

The excess profits tax was reintroduced in Brazil by Law No. 2,862 of September 4, 1956; the effective period of the new law is limited to four years.

The excess profits tax is imposed on all individuals and entities which are liable for income tax on business profits, unless the amount of their annual profit (as adjusted for income tax purposes) does not exceed Cr$ 300,000. The income subject to excess profits tax is the amount by which the adjusted business profits exceed 30% of the invested capital, defined as the total of paid-in capital, reserves, and undistributed profits. The taxpayer may increase invested capital through a revaluation of fixed assets acquired prior to 1951 and the capitalization of reserves which were set up prior to 1956. These increases in capital are subject to special taxes of 10% and 12%, respectively, in lieu of the regular income tax which would otherwise be payable, provided that they were made by October 31, 1956.

The rates of the excess profits tax are graduated according to the ratio which "excess" profits bear to "normal" profits, i.e., an amount equal to 30% of the invested capital. There are two alternative methods of computing normal profits, one based on the average profits for the three years from 1947 to 1949, and the other on percentages of gross income during the current base year.

CHAPTER 3

TAXES ON CAPITAL

3/1. Description of Taxes on Capital
    3/1.1 In General

3/2. Taxes on Real Property
    3/2.1 In General
    3/2.2 Persons Subject to Real Property Taxes
    3/2.3 Persons Exempt from Real Property Taxes
        a. Federal, State, and Municipal Governments
        b. Churches of every Denomination
        c. Political Parties
        d. Benevolent and Educational Institutions
        e. Other Exemptions
    3/2.4 Base of the Tax in General
    3/2.5 Base of State Tax on Rural Real Property
        a. Determination of Base
        b. Valuation
    3/2.6 Base of Municipal Tax on Unimproved Urban Real Property
    3/2.7 Base of Municipal Tax on Improved Urban Real Property
        a. Determination of Base
        b. Items Excluded from Tax Base
        c. Valuation
    3/2.8 City Planning through Real Property Taxes
    3/2.9 Rates and Computation of the Tax
        a. State Tax on Rural Real Property
        b. Municipal Tax on Improved Real Property
    3/2.10 Fees Levied on Real Property
        a. Municipal Water and Sewerage Fees

   b. Municipal Street Pavement Fees

   c. State and Municipal Road Fees

3/3. Inheritance and Gift Taxes

   3/3.1 In General
   3/3.2 Jurisdiction
   3/3.3 The Taxpayer
          a. General Rule
          b. Exempt Persons
   3/3.4 Tax Base
   3/3.5 Exempt Transfers
   3/3.6 Valuation of Transferred Property
   3/3.7 Tax Rates
   3/3.8 Administration

3/1. Description of Taxes on Capital

3/1.1 In General

In the Brazilian tax system, direct taxation of capital is relatively unimportant as compared with the taxation of income and of transactions. The only typical taxes on capital which are specifically listed in the Constitution are those which are imposed on the value of real property, and these are allocated to the states and municipalities (3/2.). They yield little revenue and do not, in any case, constitute a major burden on business enterprises or other economic activity.

The foregoing statement does not imply that other forms of capital taxation are not authorized by the Constitution; such taxes, however, would fall into the category of "concurrent" taxes (1/3.3) whose proceeds would have to be shared with other governments, and they are therefore of little interest to the states and municipalities.

In addition to real property taxes, this chapter discusses the state inheritance and gift taxes (3/3.). While the federal Constitution regards these as transfer taxes rather than taxes on capital, the classification used here appears more relevant to their true economic significance.

3/2. Taxes On Real Property

3/2.1 In General

The Constitution recognizes three types of taxes on real property as "exclusive" taxes.

   1. A tax on rural real property, either improved or unimproved, which is allocated to the states.[1]

   [1] Const. Art. 19(I).

2. A tax on urban (including suburban) unimproved land, which is allocated to the municipalities.[2]
3. A tax on urban (including suburban) improved real property, which is also allocated to the municipalities.[3]

It should be observed that the latter two taxes are distinct and separate from each other. Distinguishing between rural and urban property is a matter for the various states to legislate on,[4] which they have done in statutes called *Leis Orgânicas dos Municípios* (Municipal Organization Acts). The distinction is usually based on the relative importance of municipal public works existing in each area. Consequently, a municipality may gradually absorb into its own taxing power areas previously within a state's, which, on occasion, has caused friction. Where there is no conflict regarding the nature of an area as rural or urban, there is no possibility of a state tax and a municipal tax being simultaneously imposed on the same property.

Although all three real property taxes are essentially of the same nature, there are certain differences in the determination of the tax base. The state taxes on rural real property and the municipal taxes on unimproved urban property are computed on capital value, whereas the municipal tax on improved urban real property is computed on rental value.

The term "real property," as defined in Art. 43 of the Civil Code, includes the following:

1. The land with its surface and its natural accretions and appurtenances, including trees and growing crops, the air space above, and the subsoil below.
2. All that which has been permanently affixed to the soil through human agency, such as seeds planted in the land, or buildings and other constructions erected thereon in such a way that they can not be removed without being destroyed, changed, broken, or damaged.
3. All property of an inherently movable nature which the owner keeps on the premises for the purpose of their industrial use, beautification, or convenience.

Item (1) above is included in the base of each of the three taxes on real property. Item (2) is occasionally included in the state tax on unimproved real property and both municipal real property taxes. Item (3) may, constitutionally, be included only in the municipal tax on improved urban real property, but it never is. The bases of each of these taxes are given in detail in sections 3/2.4–3/2.7 below.

3/2.2 Persons Subject to Real Property Taxes

All three types of real property taxes are imposed on the ownership of property and not on the income therefrom or the exploitation thereof

---

[2] Const. Art. 29(I).   [3] *Ibid.*
[4] Supreme Court, 154 *Revista Forense* 168 (1954).

(3/2.4). Consequently, the taxpayer is the individual or entity which holds title to the property. Title to real property situated in Brazil is acquired through a deed drawn up before a notary and registered with a special state office, the *Registro de Imóveis* (Registry of Real Property). Although it is, therefore, easy for the tax authorities to keep a record of real property owners and of transfers of ownership, administrative regulations in most states and municipalities require all individuals and entities acquiring real property to file a registration form with the appropriate tax office.

The owner of the property remains liable for the tax even though the property is rented. The Federal Housing Authority has ruled that it is no violation of the rent control provisions if the rental exceeds the prescribed ceiling by virtue of the addition of the real property tax to the stipulated rent.[5]

Even though an individual or entity occupies land without having legal title thereto, real property taxes may be assessed against the occupant under some state court decisions.[6] These decisions, however, are limited to cases involving the uncontested occupancy of land whose owner is unknown. They do not stand for the general principle that real property taxes are imposed on the beneficial owner of real property as distinguished from its legal owner.

3/2.3   Persons Exempt from Real Property Taxes

The following enjoy immunity from taxation under Art. 31 of the Constitution and are not, therefore, liable to real property taxes:

a. FEDERAL, STATE, AND MUNICIPAL GOVERNMENTS. The constitutional immunity that federal, state, and municipal governments enjoy has been extended by a federal statute [7] to decentralized autonomous federal, state, or municipal organizations known as *autarquias,* but not to corporations owned by a government.[8]

b. CHURCHES OF EVERY DENOMINATION. The exemption of church buildings used exclusively for worship is clearly recognized. Its application

---

[5] Regarding the influence of rent control on tax assessments, see 3/2.7c below.

[6] São Paulo State Court of Appeals, 154 *Revista dos Tribunais* 95 (1954); 157 *Revista dos Tribunais* 110 (1945); Minas Gerais State Court of Appeals, 133 *Revista Forense* 472 (1951). Consistent with such decisions the courts have also held that lack of legal title is no excuse for failure to pay the tax; São Paulo State Court of Appeals, 101 *Revista Forense* 528 (1945). And as a consequence, the courts have decided that payment of the tax, even if over an extended number of years, is not prima facie evidence of title; São Paulo State Court of Appeals, 150 *Revista dos Tribunais* 236 (1944).

[7] Decree-law No. 6,016 of November 22, 1943. See Sousa, *Compêndio* (2d ed. 1954), Par. 49.

[8] Supreme Court, 2 *Revista de Direito Administrativo* 231 (1945); 32 *Revista de Direito Administrativo* 67 (1953); Court of Appeals for the Federal District, 39 *Revista de Direito Administrativo* 247 (1955).

to other buildings owned by churches or religious institutions is more doubtful but is usually granted by a special statute of the taxing government, unless the property is used for income-producing purposes.

c. POLITICAL PARTIES. The buildings used by political parties for their headquarters are exempt from real property taxes.

d. BENEVOLENT AND EDUCATIONAL INSTITUTIONS. Real property belonging to benevolent and educational institutions organized under the laws of Brazil which devote their entire income to furthering their declared objects are exempt from real property taxes. Local statutes occasionally impose certain restrictions, e.g., that educational institutions must provide free tuition for a specified number of students designated by government school authorities, or that benevolent institutions which maintain hospitals must allocate a specified number of beds to patients designated by government relief agencies. The validity of such restrictions, which are not expressed in the Constitution, has not been tested.

e. OTHER EXEMPTIONS. In addition to the constitutional immunities just described, further exemptions are usually granted in greater or less degree by local statutes. An example is the exemption often granted by municipalities, for a specified number of years, for factory buildings owned and occupied by industries newly established in their territory. A federal statute exempts forests from all taxation.[9]

3/2.4   Base of the Tax in General

Although the Constitution is not explicit in this respect, a real property tax is generally defined as a tax on the ownership of unimproved or improved real property, including, in the latter case, the buildings. By definition the tax is not imposed on the exploitation of the land, on the business conducted on the premises, or on the income or profits derived from such exploitation or business.[10]

3/2.5   Base of the State Tax on Rural Real Property

a. DETERMINATION OF BASE. The base of the state tax on rural property is generally the capital value of the land itself, exclusive of all natural

[9] Code of Forestry, Decree No. 23,793 of January 23, 1934, Art. 17, interpreted to cover not only the direct taxation of forests as such, but also the use of their capital value as a basis for real property or other taxation. Regarding mineral deposits, see 19/4.2

[10] Under the Constitution of 1934 and the Charter of 1937 the taxation of income from land and buildings was allocated to the municipalities as distinct from the general income tax attributed to the Federal Union. Parliamentary debate relating to the pertinent provisions of the 1946 Constitution clearly indicates that it was the intent of that Constitution to confer full taxing powers on income from all sources to the Federal Union and to define the real property tax as a tax on the ownership of real property.

and man-made accretions, such as trees, crops, roads, buildings, etc. Although the statutes occasionally take natural or artificial accretions into account, such inclusions do not necessarily render a real property tax unconstitutional. Rather, the test is whether the capital value of the additions to the land is taken into account in a way which converts the tax into one on the exploitation of the land or on the product or income derived from it.

b. VALUATION. Capital value for the purposes of the tax is the fair market price which the property will command if offered for sale under normal conditions. This value is determined by an appraisal made by the tax authorities and may be contested by the taxpayer either in an administrative appeal or before the courts. Tax authorities in all state capitals and in most larger towns conduct such appraisals in accordance with appropriate technical methods, and they may be revised every year. However, there is usually no definite statutory rule regarding the frequency of appraisals and of subsequent revisions.

The most usual method of determining fair market price is through Harper's formula:

$$V = v\sqrt{\frac{aS}{N}}$$

when "v" is the value of the frontage of the property per meter, "a" is the frontage length in meters, "S" the total area in square meters, and "N" the average depth of the property. The value of "v" is determined by multiplying the value of one square meter by "N," and "N" is a standardized variable adopted on the theory that if the depth is in excess of a given ratio (usually 3:1) to the frontage, it tends to reduce the value of the property. The value per square meter for this formula is taken from tables of standardized figures for each district of the state, such tables being established from prices of actual transactions in each given area and revised usually every year. In preparing such tables, attention is also given to the characteristics of each individual piece of property; for instance, that it is level, rocky, a corner lot, or irregular in shape. Outside the larger cities, methods of appraisal vary widely, and they are not, in general, as reliable as the above method.

Since real property taxes are assessed once a year, a higher appraisal of the property made in the course of the year and applied to the installment of tax payable in the second half of the year has been held to be illegal.[11]

3/2.6   Base of Municipal Tax on Unimproved Urban Real Property

The base of the municipal tax on *unimproved* urban real property is the same as that of the state tax just discussed. Since the Constitution defines

[11] São Paulo State Court of Appeals, 184 *Revista dos Tribunais* 257 (1950).

the tax as one on unimproved real property, and since there are other municipal taxes on improved urban real property (specifically including the value of the land beneath the buildings), the capital value of buildings may never be included in the base of the municipal tax on unimproved urban real property. For the relevant definition of the term "building," see 3/2.7b below.

Whenever, on a single tract of land, the area of unimproved property exceeds a stipulated percentage of the area covered by buildings, the unimproved portion is subject to the tax on unimproved real property.

3/2.7   Base of Municipal Tax on Improved Urban Real Property

a. DETERMINATION OF BASE. As stated before, the municipal tax on unimproved urban real property is computed on capital value, and the municipal tax on improved urban real property is computed on rental value. The latter tax is therefore sometimes described as "a tax on capital value as measured by rental value."

b. ITEMS EXCLUDED FROM TAX BASE. The base of the municipal tax on *improved* urban real property never includes any of the items listed in Art. 43(3) of the Civil Code (3/2.1 above, item 3). The most important of these items for tax purposes is machinery affixed to an industrial building. To include the capital value of such machinery in the base of a tax on the ownership of the building would convert the tax into one on the industrial activity carried on in the building. This would not necessarily follow if the capital value of other items of property which are permanently kept in a building for its beautification or convenience, such as furniture, art collections, and the like, were included in the base; in practice, however, such items, although constituting real property under the provisions of Art. 43 of the Civil Code, are never regarded as such for tax purposes.

The definition of the term "building" for the purposes of the tax on improved urban real property is always understood to be limited to buildings which are suitable for permanent human occupancy. This definition, therefore, excludes any temporary constructions such as amusement parks, circus or carnival tents, as well as other constructions which, however permanent, are not designed for human occupancy, such as walls, fences, monuments, radio or television towers, water tanks and the like. Land occupied by such structures is therefore subject only to the municipal tax on unimproved land.

c. VALUATION. The rental value for the purpose of the municipal tax on improved real property is determined from the lease, unless the government regards the stipulated rent as inadequate. In this case, it may determine the rental value of the premises through an appraisal.[12] The same rule applies if there is no written lease, if the building is occupied or otherwise used by its owner, or if the owner grants the use of the property to another rent-free. In some cities a combination of rental value and capital value is used to determine the base of the tax.[13] The rules concerning periodic revisions of appraisals to determine the capital value (3/2.5) also apply to appraisals for rental value; there are, however, court decisions holding that appraisals for rental value cannot be revised unless rent control ceilings are changed.[14] These decisions appear to be inconsistent with the definition of the tax as one on rental value as distinguished from one on the actual income from rents. Other courts have held under this definition that ceilings under the rent control provisions are no bar to a tax assessment on the basis of rental values which exceed the allowable maximum rentals.[15]

3/2.8 City Planning through Real Property Taxes

By local ordinance, cities and towns sometimes use real property taxes as a means of city planning. For example, they may institute penalty rates for land occupied by structures which are regarded as unsuitable in that location, for untended vacant lots, for abandoned buildings in a state of decay, or for tenements, warehouses, or factories located in areas which have become residential districts. Conversely, tax exemptions or reductions are sometimes granted for buildings of exceptional artistic value, for landscaped gardens, for buildings housing private art galleries open to the public, etc. Similar exemptions or reductions may also be granted to stimulate desirable new construction; in this case, certain time limits are usually provided for the completion of the buildings. Specific exemptions have been granted by a federal statute [16] for the construction and operation of new hotels; however, most municipalities have refused to comply with that statute on the ground that it infringes upon the constitutional taxing power of the states and municipalities.[17]

[12] The principles set forth under 3/2.5 above governing appraisals of capital value also apply to appraisals of rental value.

[13] As an example, in 1956 the tax rate in the City of São Paulo was 10% of rental value if the building was rented or used by its owner for business purposes, or 8% if the building was used by its owner for residential purposes; but in either case not less than 0.4% of capital value.

[14] Court of Appeals for the Federal District, 74 *Arquivo Judiciário* 145 (1945), 103 *Revista Forense* 80 (1945); Paraná State Court of Appeals, 133 *Revista Forense* 193 (1951).

[15] Supreme Court, 13 *Revista de Direito Administrativo* 113 (1948); Rio Grande do Sul State Court of Appeals, 123 *Revista Forense* 203 (1949).

[16] Decree-law No. 6,761 of July 31, 1944.

[17] Exemption denied under the federal statute but granted under a similar local statute by São Paulo State Court of Appeals, 208 *Revista dos Tribunais* 497 (1953).

3/2.9   Rates and Computation of the Tax

Real property taxes are usually assessed for the entire year, but the tax is payable in either semiannual or quarterly installments.

a. STATE TAX ON RURAL REAL PROPERTY. The rates of the state tax on rural real property are usually low. The basic rate may be as low as 0.24% and is never higher than 2%. However, there may be substantial rate increases (as high as 200% of the basic rate in the State of Rio Grande do Sul) based upon the ratio of uncultivated to total area of a property; conversely, rate reductions may be granted for intensively cultivated property.

The methods of application of the basic rate from one state to another present much too great a diversification to be treated in detail here. The rates are sometimes graduated according to the nature or area of the land, its geographical location, or its exploitation or produce (agriculture, pasture, etc.). All that can be attempted here is a list of the most common methods of applying the basic rate.[18] Following that list, the states are arranged alphabetically, each with the number corresponding to its method of taxation.

1. Percentage rates graduated according to capital value.
2. Percentage rates graduated according to area.
3. Percentage rates graduated according to capital value but differentiated according to geographical location.
4. Percentage rates graduated according to capital value but differentiated according to type of exploitation.
5. Percentage rates graduated according to capital value combined with area, but differentiated according to type of exploitation.
6. Single percentage rate on capital value.
7. Fixed rates according to area but differentiated according to type of exploitation.

Alagôas	1	Paraná	4
Amazonas	3	Pernambuco	1
Bahia	4	Piauí	6
Ceará	3	Rio de Janeiro	2
Goiás	5	Rio Grande do Norte	2
Maranhão	2	Rio Grande do Sul	5
Mato Grosso	2	Santa Catarina	1
Minas Gerais	4	São Paulo	6
Pará	7	Sergipe	1
Paraíba	2		

b. MUNICIPAL TAX ON IMPROVED REAL PROPERTY. The rates of the municipal tax on improved real property vary widely from one city to

[18] Based on data privately obtained from the Committee for Economic and Financial Studies of the Ministry of Finance, Rio de Janeiro. The State of Espírito Santo does not impose a rural real property tax, nor does the Federal District, since its entire area is defined as urban or suburban.

another, but they are usually higher in the largest cities, where they range from 6% to 10% of rental value. In Rio de Janeiro, the rate is 10%; in São Paulo, the rate on business property or leased property is 10%, while the rate on a residence occupied by the owner is 8%.

3/2.10 Fees Levied on Real Property

Most states and municipalities follow the practice of assessing fees either on the ownership or exploitation of real property on substantially the same bases as those of the real property taxes themselves. It has often been argued that such fees assume the character of real property taxes and are therefore unconstitutional, but the courts have shown a marked tendency to uphold their validity.

a. MUNICIPAL WATER AND SEWERAGE FEES. Municipal fees for water and sewerage or for the construction and maintenance of paved streets are frequently assessed on rental value, which also constitutes the base of the tax on improved real property. No constitutional problem arises in this case because both the fees and the tax in question are imposed by the municipality. In this situation the rates of the fees and of the tax are cumulative and there is no relationship between the service rendered and the basis upon which the fee is assessed. In practical effect, therefore, the fees simply become additions to the real property tax,[19] though the collections therefrom are usually earmarked for a specific purpose.

b. MUNICIPAL STREET PAVEMENT FEES. Street paving fees, even when computed on rental value, usually have different rates according to the nature of the paving and sometimes according to the location of the street. The differences in rates and the fact that the fees ultimately fall on rental value have been cited to support the contention that the fee actually constitutes a tax and that, as such, it is discriminatory. The Supreme Court rejected both contentions, holding that since the paving of streets is of general interest to the community, a payment exacted in connection therewith is properly called a fee; and that since the owners of property located on the newly paved streets derive a direct benefit, the fee can legally be assessed on the value of those properties on the ground that it is increased by the public work done.[20]

c. STATE AND MUNICIPAL ROAD FEES. Fees for building and maintaining roads are assessed by both the states and the municipalities, and are

---

[19] In some cases, e.g., in the City of São Paulo, water fees are assessed at a basic rate on rental value, plus a variable monthly rate depending on consumption. It seems clear that only the latter rate has the true characteristics of a fee. The fact that the basic rate is assessed annually and collected together with the property tax tends to stress the fact that it is an addition to it.

[20] Supreme Court, 122 Revista Forense 416 (1949), 22 Revista de Direito Administrativo 66 (1950).

usually measured by the capital value of the real property bordering the road or connected with it.[21]

The constitutional validity of fees collected by a municipality for the building and maintenance of roads has also been contested as conflicting with the state real property tax. However, the Supreme Court sustained the constitutionality of these fees on the same grounds as those advanced to uphold the street pavement fees.[22]

3/3. Inheritance and Gift Taxes

3/3.1 In General

In the taxation of transfers of property, the distinction which is usually adopted is the economic one between gratuitous transfers and transfers for a consideration. The former are usually subjected to estate (or inheritance) and gift taxes and the latter, to transfer taxes. The presentation of the various transfer taxes in this volume conforms to this economic distinction. Accordingly, the discussion of the taxes imposed on gratuitous transfers (inheritance taxes and gift taxes) is included in this chapter, while the taxes on transfers for a consideration are summarized in Chapter 4.

Inheritance and gift taxes are imposed only at the state level. The Constitution of Brazil, in defining the taxing powers of the states, distinguishes according to the legal nature of the transaction through which title to the property is acquired by the transferee, i.e., between transfers causa mortis and those inter vivos. Thus, Art. 19(II) of the Constitution reserves to the states the right to tax "the transfer of property (i.e., movable and immovable property) causa mortis," and Art. 19(III), the right to tax the transfer of "immovable property inter vivos and its contribution to the capital of a company," thus including gifts with other transfers. Notwithstanding the distinction adopted by the federal Constitution, the tax laws of the states recognize the close relationship existing between transfers by gift and transfers by reason of death, and apply the same rules, and, in particular, the same tax rates to both. It will appear from the following, however, that the formal

[21] Under the Constitutional Charter of 1937, the federal government intervened in this matter through a Presidential Order stating that the annual amount of the fee could in no case exceed 1/10th of 1% of the property value as determined for the purposes of the state tax on rural real property. Subsequent to the Constitution of 1946, the court declared this limitation to be no longer applicable because a federal order could not interfere with matters of local legislation; see São Paulo State Court of Appeals, 204 *Revista dos Tribunais* 586 (1952); 221 *Revista dos Tribunais* 423 (1954).

[22] Supreme Court, 2 *Revista de Direito Administrativo* 710 (1945); 4 *Revista de Direito Administrativo* 196 (1946); 168 *Revista dos Tribunais* 755 (1947); 121 *Revista Forense* 410 (1949).

approach of the Constitution is reflected in certain rules which are in
conflict with the true economic nature of the taxes discussed here.

3/3.2   Jurisdiction

The jurisdiction of the various states in the matter of inheritance and
gift taxes is regulated by the federal Constitution according to the nature
of the property transferred.

Transfers of tangible real property inter vivos or of tangible property
(real or personal) causa mortis are subject to the jurisdiction of the state
in whose territory the property is located at the time of the transfer
(Const. Art. 19 §2). Transfers of intangible property by reason of death
come under the jurisdiction of the state where the property (including
securities and credits) is "liquidated or transferred to the heirs" (Const.
Art. 19 §3). The courts have construed this rather indefinite language
to refer to the state of the decedent's last domicile, unless the transfer is
subject to recording formalities in addition to the proceedings of the
probate court, in which case tax jurisdiction belongs to the state in which
the recording is made.[23]

The following is a summary of various representative state tax laws.

3/3.3   The Taxpayer

a. GENERAL RULE. The statutory taxpayer is always the transferee of the
property, i.e., the heir, legatee, or donee.[24]

b. EXEMPT PERSONS. Exemptions from gift and inheritance taxes may be
based on the person of the taxpayer, or the nature or value of the property
transferred; regarding the latter, see 3/3.5. Exemptions based on the
person of the taxpayer are comparatively uniform in the various states.
Apart from those covering gifts and bequests to persons of very limited
means,[25] the following exemptions apply.

1. Gifts and bequests to federal, state, or municipal governments, to churches
   of every denomination, to charitable and educational institutions,[26] and to

[23] The recording agency may be a government office such as the Registry of Real
Property (as in the case of the transfer of rights in real property) or a corporation
or other business entity (as in an assignment of nominative shares or participations).

[24] Under the rules of the civil law, which are reflected in the constitutional provisions cited at 3/3.1, the property of the decedent passes immediately upon his death
to his heirs or legatees according to their shares (intestate or testamentary). Accordingly, the estate as such is not considered a transferor on whom the tax might be
imposed. The rule cited in the text applies to the inheritance tax even if the
decedent leaves only one heir or legatee (because of the graduation of the tax
according to the degree of family relationship, see 3/3.7), and it applies likewise to
the gift tax.

[25] E.g., to individuals not subject to income tax because of insufficient income.

[26] In some states, this exemption is subject to certain restrictions, such as the
allocation of a certain number of hospital beds to patients designated by the relief

political parties, under the general immunity from taxation granted by Art. 31 of the federal Constitution.

2. Under the rules of the civil law governing community property marriages, each spouse owns an undivided one-half share in the other's property existing at the time of the marriage or acquired thereafter. Under this form of property settlement there is, upon the death of one spouse, no acquisition of property by the surviving spouse to the extent of this undivided share, but merely a division of what was formerly joint property. The state statutes, however, usually treat this exclusion as an exemption in favor of the surviving spouse.

3. The statutes further list among the exemptions bequests to the executor or administrator of the estate which are within the limits of his statutory commission.[27]

3/3.4 Tax Base

A comparison of the constitutional provisions cited at 3/3.1 makes it apparent that the scope of the inheritance tax, as contemplated by the law, is much wider than that of the gift tax. While the latter tax applies solely to transfers of real property, the inheritance tax applies to those of movable as well as real property.

In practice, however, the impact of the inheritance tax is largely limited to those types of property which, because of mandatory registration, are subject to effective government control. The outstanding example is real property. Items of movable (tangible or intangible) property which can be so controlled are nominative securities, patents, copyrights, and, to a lesser extent, bank deposits and automobiles. Fiscal control is practically impossible in the transfer of bearer securities, which therefore constitute the chief means of tax evasion, and it is very difficult for valuables such as jewelry, antiques, etc., which are often privately divided among the heirs and not declared as part of the decedent's estate.[28]

Intangible property falls under the general definition of the term "property" in the Civil Code and is subject to the tax.[29] Intangible movable property (Civil Code Art. 48) includes "authors' rights," and this term is understood to cover patents as well as copyrights.

The inheritance tax is computed on the fair market value of the distributive share of each heir or legatee, which is determined after all liabilities of the estate, including court costs and administrative and funeral expenses have been settled. The gift tax is computed on the fair

agencies or of a certain number of scholarships to students selected by the educational authorities. The Constitution itself does not impose any restrictions.

[27] Under the rules of the Civil Code, an executor or administrator who is not an heir is entitled to commissions of not more than 5% of the net value of the estate.

[28] It must be remembered in this connection that the ownership of tangible movable property is transferred by delivery and that possession is presumed to be lawful unless proved otherwise.

[29] Regarding intangibles which are real property by statutory definition (Civil Code, Art. 44), see 19/3.1.

market value of the property donated. Regarding determination of fair market value, see 3/3.6.

3/3.5 Exempt Transfers

Exemptions based on the nature or value of the property transferred are of considerably lesser importance than those granted to certain persons (3/3.3b), and they show wider differences from one state to another. The more usual exemptions are as follows:

1. An inheritance tax is not imposed if the total net value of the estate (assets minus liabilities) does not exceed a certain minimum amount, usually Cr$ 10,000. It will be noted that this exemption is based on the net value of the entire estate, although the tax is computed on the value of the distributive shares of each heir or legatee (3/3.7). Because the exemption is granted for reasons of administrative convenience rather than as a relief measure for the benefit of the taxpayers, it is inapplicable if the net value of the estate is greater than the minimum figure.
2. Inheritances, bequests, and gifts of "authors' rights," as defined above, are exempt from the inheritance tax. This exemption is usually based on Art. 203 of the federal Constitution which forbids direct taxation of such rights.
3. Deposits in savings banks (*caixas econômicas*) below a certain amount are usually exempt for reasons of administrative convenience.

3/3.6 Valuation of Transferred Property

The fair market value of property transferred by gift or inheritance is determined by an appraisal made in accordance with the principles listed below. The assets of an estate are appraised only after all claims either by or against the estate have been settled.

The appraisal of real property acquired by gift is made according to the rules which apply to the real property transfer tax (19/6.3). Gifts of personal property are not subject to tax, as already indicated.

The assets of an estate are appraised by experts appointed by the probate court. Real property is appraised in the same manner as for purposes of the real property transfer tax (19/6.3). There are no fixed standards for the appraisal of personal property, in view of its variety, except for listed securities, which are valued at their quoted price on the effective date if such a price exists. Appraisals for purposes of inheritance or gift taxes differ in certain respects from those made in connection with transfers for a consideration, although the object in both cases is to determine fair market value. The courts have pointed out that the transfers discussed here are not made to realize a profit, nor, in the case of transfers causa mortis, are they voluntary. They have, on these grounds, stressed the need for applying more lenient methods of valuation for purposes of gift and inheritance taxes than in connection with transfers for a consideration.[30]

The value of property for gift tax purposes is determined as of the date of the gift. Whether, for purposes of the inheritance tax, fair market value should be determined as of the date of death or the date of the appraisal is not finally settled. Earlier decisions preferred the date of appraisal as the one on which the assessment is made.[31] The trend of the more recent decisions, however, is clearly in favor of the date of death, on the ground that under Art. 1572 of the Civil Code the title to property passes immediately from the decedent to his heirs or legatees upon the decedent's death.[32]

There usually is a substantial time interval between the decedent's death and the appraisal of the property and collection of the tax. The states have made several attempts, not always successful, to remedy this situation in order to avoid the difficulties inherent in appraisals made long after the effective date and to speed up their tax collections. In invoking the rule of the Civil Code that probate proceedings must be instituted within thirty days after the date of death, some states have tried to collect additions to the inheritance tax if this rule was not observed; this method, however, was declared unconstitutional on the ground that a state cannot impose penalties for violation of a federal law.[33] On the other hand, the statute of the State of Santa Catarina, which requires payment of the tax within 90 days after death (regardless of whether the estate is settled by then), was upheld as being within the state's power to regulate its taxes.[34]

3/3.7 Tax Rates

Both the inheritance tax and the gift tax are computed on the net fair market value, determined as indicated above, of the property passing to each individual beneficiary. The rates are graduated according to a combination of two factors; namely, (a) the net value of the assets received by the beneficiary, and (b) the degree of family relationship

[30] São Paulo State Court of Appeals, 220 *Revista dos Tribunais* 217 (1954); 222 *Revista dos Tribunais* 298 (1954); 228 *Revista dos Tribunais* 238 (1954).

[31] São Paulo State Court of Appeals, 193 *Revista dos Tribunais* 903 (1951); 211 *Revista dos Tribunais* 318 (1953); 218 *Revista dos Tribunais* 565 (1953); 220 *Revista dos Tribunais* 221 (1954).

[32] São Paulo State Court of Appeals, 224 *Revista dos Tribunais* 307 (1954); 232 *Revista dos Tribunais* 249 (1955); 235 *Revista dos Tribunais* 501 (1955); 238 *Revista dos Tribunais* 276 (1955); 229 *Revista dos Tribunais* 289 (1954). In the last-cited decision, the court points out that if property is appraised as of a date subsequent to the decedent's death, the tax will cover an increment in value which occurred after the taxable event.

[33] Supreme Court, 128 *Revista dos Tribunais* 675 (1940).

[34] Santa Catarina State Court of Appeals, 64 *Arquivo Judiciário* 319 (1942); Supreme Court, 42 *Revista de Direito Administrativo* 68 (1955).

or the absence thereof between the decedent or donor on the one hand and the beneficiary on the other.[35]

Most states apply increased tax rates to transfers in favor of heirs, legatees, and donees residing abroad. In the state of São Paulo, this increase amounts to 20% of the tax. The courts have upheld the validity of the addition provided that there is no discrimination between nonresident Brazilians and nonresident foreigners.[36] The object of the state law in these situations has been described as being to impose a final tax on property which will presumably leave the state and escape further taxation rather than to penalize absenteeism. While this reasoning would seem applicable only to movable property, neither the laws nor the courts make a distinction between movable property and real property in this respect.

The table of rates reproduced on page 76 is the one which is presently in force in the state of São Paulo.[37] It is shown here as a fairly representative example of the structure of inheritance and gift taxes existing in all Brazilian states; the rates in the state of São Paulo are, however, somewhat higher than those in other states.

3/3.8   Administration

There is no separate revenue administration of the inheritance tax. Under the civil law of Brazil, estates are settled before a probate court and all controversies regarding the inheritance tax are decided in the same judicial proceedings. Consequently, the administrative procedures described in the introductory chapter of this report (1/5.) do not apply to the inheritance tax and the administrative courts or boards of review or appeal have no jurisdiction as far as this tax is concerned.

The civil law allows a period of 30 days from the date of death to institute probate proceedings before the court which has jurisdiction over the last domicile of the decedent, or, if he was a nonresident, in whose district real property of the decedent is located. The proceedings are opened by the surviving spouse or an heir, who must file the will and a death certificate with the court; if there is no will, a motion must be made that all heirs not already represented be notified.[38]

[35] This method is in accordance with Art. 19(II) of the federal Constitution which describes the tax on transfers by reason of death as an inheritance, rather than an estate, tax. Notwithstanding the constitutional mandate, two or three northern states have experimented with a mixed system of rates, i.e., a percentage rate of the entire net value of the estate (estate or capital tax) plus graduated rates on the net value of the assets passing to each heir or legatee (inheritance or transfer tax). Whether the courts will uphold such systems is as yet unknown.

[36] Supreme Court, 70 *Arquivo Judiciário* 173 (1944).

[37] State Code of Taxation approved under Decree No. 22,022 of January 31, 1953, Book V, Appendix I.

[38] Any interested party, which may be a creditor or the Treasury Department, may make this motion if the surviving spouse or heirs do not make it within the 30-day period.

Table 6: *Rates of inheritance tax in State of São Paulo.*

Family Relationship	Net value of assets [a]									
	20	50	100	250	500	1,000	2,500	5,000	10,000	Over 10,000
Descending or ascending lines	2%	4%	6%	8%	10%	12%	14%	17%	20%	25%
Spouses	8	10	12	15	18	21	24	27	30	35
Brothers	25	28	31	34	37	40	43	46	49	52
Uncles or nephews	28	31	34	37	40	43	46	49	52	55
1st degree cousins	31	34	37	40	43	46	49	52	55	58
Other cousins	34	37	40	43	46	49	52	55	58	61
Strangers	37	40	43	46	49	52	55	58	61	64

[a] Thousands of cruzeiros.

Notes to the Table

1. The tax is not graduated and all property falling into a given bracket is taxed at the rate applying to that bracket. Example: If a son receives a gift, bequest, or inheritance of a net value of Cr$ 30,000, the tax is 4% on Cr$ 30,000 and not 2% on the first Cr$ 20,000 plus 4% on the excess of Cr$ 10,000.

2. If an heir receives his share of the estate and, in addition thereto, a bequest, the net values of both are combined to determine the applicable rate.

3. Similarly, the net values of different kinds of property transferred (real property, securities, automobiles) are added together.

4. The 1% addition to the real property transfer tax in favor of state housing agencies (19/5.2) also applies to transfers by gift or by reason of death if the net capital value of the real property transferred exceeds Cr$ 100,000.

If assets of the estate are distributed to an heir or legatee in excess of his share, the distributee is required to make an equalization payment to the estate. In some states, this transaction is considered to be partly in the nature of a sale by the estate to the heir or beneficiary (inasmuch as the value of the asset distributed exceeds the recipient's share) and the real property transfer tax is imposed on the value of the "sold" portion if the asset transferred is in the nature of real property.

Since the property of a decedent passes immediately to his heirs or legatees by operation of law (3/3.6), the decree of the probate court which specifies the distribution of the estate has merely declaratory effect. In its decree, the court incorporates the assessments of the inheritance tax which are issued by the state tax authorities against each heir or legatee according to his distributive share. Controversies in reference to appraisals made are decided by the probate court, and other controversies by the state district court which has jurisdiction in fiscal matters. In either case, the aggrieved party has the right of appeal to the state court of appeals.

The inheritance tax is paid by the heir or legatee after issuance of the

decree of the court ordering the distribution. Physical possession of
the property is transferred by the executor or administrator and the
required entry in the real property register is made only after the tax is
paid.[39]

State statutes provide for interest or a fine or both if the inheritance
tax is not paid within a certain time limit after issuance of the court
decree, so that the payment of the tax cannot be deferred by failure to
take possession of the property.

Assessment and collection of the gift tax follow the procedure applicable to the real property transfer tax (19/6.).

[39] A copy of the decree of the court and proof of payment of the inheritance tax
must be filed with the Registry of Real Property.

CHAPTER 4

TAXES ON TRANSACTIONS

4/1. **Description of Taxes on Transactions**
    4/1.1   Scope of Chapter
    4/1.2   Relative Importance of Taxes on Transactions
    4/1.3   Impact of Taxes on Transactions
4/2. **Sales Tax**
4/3. **Export Tax**
4/4. **Customs Duties**
4/5. **The Federal Excise (Consumption) Tax**
4/6. **The "Impôsto Unico"**
4/7. **Stamp Taxes**
4/8. **The Municipal Business Tax**
4/9. **The Real Property Transfer Tax**
4/10. **The Tax on Exchange Remittances**

4/1. Description of Taxes on Transactions

4/1.1 Scope of Chapter

The purpose of this chapter is to present a concise summary of all the taxes on transactions in Brazil in order to provide a perspective of the complicated structure of "indirect" taxes which exists at the federal, state, and municipal levels. The more important taxes of this type are analyzed in detail in Chapters 15 through 19, except the tax on exchange remittances (4/10.) which is discussed briefly in this chapter and not taken up again in the later chapters of this work.

4/1.2   Relative Importance of Taxes on Transactions

Taxes on transactions are the principal source of government revenue in Brazil (see 1/2.3 and Table 2). At the federal level, their combined yield is greater than that of the income tax, which is the most important single source of revenue (1/6.2). The most important federal taxes on transactions are the federal excise, or consumption, tax (4/5.; 16/2.); the federal stamp tax (4/7.; 17/2.), and the excise on certain products such as gasoline and electricity known as *impôsto unico* (4/6.; 16/3.).

At the state level, the principal tax, both from the point of view of its importance to the taxpayer and of public revenue, is the sales tax (4/2.; 15/1.). Taxes of relatively limited importance are the export taxes (4/3.; 15/6.), the stamp taxes (17/3.), the real property transfer tax (4/9.; 19/1.), and certain minor excise taxes, such as the so-called agricultural and industrial exploitation taxes imposed by most states except São Paulo.

Transaction taxes are also the most important source of municipal revenue. The principal local tax of this type is the business tax (4/8.; 18/1.). There are, also, local license and amusement taxes (1/6.4; 18/4.).

The combined effect of these taxes, even without including import duties (1/2.6), indicates the extent to which economic activity in Brazil is subject to indirect taxation.

4/1.3   Impact of Taxes on Transactions

The impact of taxes on transactions can be illustrated by the example of an article which is produced and consumed in Brazil. The mere entry of most commodities into the commerce of the country will subject them to the federal excise tax. In addition thereto, successive state sales taxes and possibly percentage increases thereof, or fees, will become due each time an article changes hands. Furthermore, federal, state, and municipal stamp taxes will apply, depending on the nature of the transaction. The cumulative effect of these taxes will usually be to add a considerable amount to the price paid by the ultimate consumer.

If an article is imported for use in Brazil, it is subject to import duties and to the federal excise tax. In the case of fuels, lubricants and electricity, the *impôsto unico* is substituted for the import duties and the federal excise tax. Import documents are subject to the federal stamp tax. In addition thereto, state sales taxes (together with additions or fees) apply each time the imported article is sold.

An article which is produced in Brazil for export is subject to the federal excise (consumption) tax unless it is exported directly by the manufacturer. The *impôsto unico* applies in lieu of the federal excise tax if the exported product is one of those which are covered by that tax. The article is subject to the export tax of the state in which it is produced, and possibly to that of the state from which it is exported. State sales taxes also apply because it is held that the export tax and the sales tax are imposed on different grounds and that they are therefore not mutually exclusive. Finally, federal stamp taxes are due on contracts and documents drawn in connection with the export.

In addition to the taxes listed in the foregoing paragraphs, business as such is subject to municipal business taxes.

4/2. Sales Tax

The sales tax is reserved to the states as an "exclusive" tax. The rates must be uniform within a state regardless of the nature, origin, or destination of the goods. Interstate sales are the subject of constitutional provisions and federal legislation, especially with a view to reconciling conflicts between producer states and consumer states. The sales tax can be collected by the producer state at the time the goods are shipped out of the state. Any balance of tax resulting from a markup of the price made by the manufacturer's agent or branch in a different state also belongs to the producer state.

According to the Constitution, the sales tax may be imposed on sales in which the seller is a merchant (the term includes manufacturers and producers); this rule looks exclusively to the characteristics of the seller. Most states, however, also impose the tax if only the buyer is a merchant, and this practice is not considered unconstitutional. It can be stated, therefore, that the tax applies if either party to a sale is a merchant. Unlike the rule of the commercial law, the purpose of the sale is immaterial and the tax therefore applies to sales made by a merchant which are not in the regular course of his business as well as to purchases by a merchant of goods not intended for resale. Some states also impose a sales tax or an equivalent tax (such as the "transaction tax" in the State of São Paulo) if neither the seller nor the buyer is a merchant.

Only sales of movable property are subject to the tax. The tax falls due only upon delivery, which may be either actual or constructive. Consignments are treated as sales for purposes of the tax.

The tax is computed on the invoice price plus incidental selling expenses. Discounts are deductible unless they are conditioned upon certain time limits. Whether the sales tax base should include government bonuses paid to Brazilian exporters on the foreign currency they surrender and premiums payable to the Bank of Brazil by Brazilian importers is not finally settled.

The rate of the sales tax varies among the different states and federal areas. With the exception of the State of Amazonas, which levies the tax (at the rate of 8%) only on the first sale of the product, the tax is payable in all jurisdictions on each of the various sales of a product. The lowest tax rate (1.25%) applies in the federal territories and the highest (4%) in the Federal District; in the states, except Amazonas, the average rate is between 2½% and 3%. Additions to the tax (sometimes called "fees") apply in a number of states.

4/3. Export Tax

The export tax is imposed by the states as an extension of the sales tax to cover commodities exported for sale abroad, and it should therefore not be considered as an integral part of the complicated structure of exchange control, customs duties, and international trade policy. The Constitution reserves the export tax to the states and seeks to prevent interference with national foreign trade policy through a limitation of the tax rate to 5% ad valorem; the rate may, in certain cases, be increased to up to 10%. In order to prevent the use of the tax as a barrier to inter-state commerce, the Constitution restricts its imposition to shipments of goods produced in the state to foreign countries.

The application of the export tax has encountered constitutional prob-lems in cases where merchandise produced in one state is transferred to another for shipment abroad. This practice is sometimes unavoidable, as in the case of the nonmaritime states. At other times, merchandise is channeled through a state which does not impose an export tax in an attempt to evade the export tax levied by the producer state. Another problem arises if merchandise produced in one state is processed or improved in another before export; in this situation, both states usually claim the export tax on the ground that the merchandise was "produced" in their territory. In order to counteract attempts at tax evasion, most states imposing an export tax demand payment of the tax on all goods produced or processed in their territory when they leave the state, and refund the tax later upon proof that the merchandise was in fact not exported.

The State of São Paulo, while not imposing an export tax under that name, collects a stamp tax on goods produced in the state for export. The rate of this tax is always kept equal to that of the state sales tax.

4/4. Customs Duties

Customs duties on imports are related to the system of excise taxation in Brazil. However, these duties differ from the federal excise, or con-sumption, tax (4/5.) and the special federal excise tax, or *impôsto unico*, on fuels, lubricants, and electricity (4/6.), in that the customs duties are supplemented by the system of exchange and import regulations (1/2.7). Under the proposed revision of the present tariff described briefly in

Chapter 1 (1/2.6), imported articles, which are now the object of specific rates of duty, will incur ad valorem charges which will be integrated with the premiums for foreign exchange now paid by importers at exchange auctions (1/2.7b).

4/5. The Federal Excise (Consumption) Tax

The federal excise tax is imposed on practically all goods which are manufactured in, or imported into, Brazil, except those which are subject to the *impôsto unico* (4/6.). The tax is an "exclusive" federal tax.

Although the tax is known as the consumption tax (*impôsto de consumo*) it is imposed on the manufacturer or importer, who is personally liable for its payment. He may pass the tax on to his customers.

The bases and rates of the tax are defined according to different principles in 29 schedules or lists of manufactured articles which are attached to the Federal Excise Tax Act. In most cases the rates on imported articles are the same as those applying to similar domestic products.

The tax falls due at the moment when the goods leave the factory or enter through customs; it is, therefore, not dependent upon a sale. Administrative control is very strict, and the manufacturer or importer may become liable for heavy fines for violations which are sometimes difficult to avoid in view of the complicated and frequently changing rules. Failure to pay the tax, which often is the result of a changed interpretation of the law, may result in its forced absorption by the manufacturer or importer, since it is generally impossible to recover the tax from the customer once the merchandise has been shipped. Brazilian products which are exported directly by the manufacturer are exempt from the tax.

4/6. The "Impôsto Unico"

According to the Constitution, the production, distribution, and consumption of fuels and lubricants, and the export and import thereof, are subject to a single federal tax (*impôsto unico*) in place of all other federal, state, and municipal taxes or customs duties. The Constitution further provides that domestic minerals and electric power shall be subject only to this one tax. Under these provisions, a single federal tax (*impôsto unico*) has been imposed on fuels, lubricants, and electricity. Federal, state, and municipal taxes on mining still exist, but their combined burden is limited to a definite amount under federal law.

To the extent that the *impôsto unico* applies, it takes the place of the federal excise tax (for domestic petroleum products and electric power) and the customs tariff (for imported products). In view of the exclusive character of the *impôsto unico*, all taxes which the states and municipal-

ities have tried to impose on oil companies have been declared unconstitutional except the municipal business taxes (18/2.4g).

4/7. Stamp Taxes

Stamp taxes, in the proper sense of the term (as distinguished from
various other taxes which are paid by affixing stamps), are those which
are imposed on certain transactions evidenced by documents. Depending on whether a particular transaction is regulated by federal, state, or
municipal law, stamp taxes are levied at all three levels of government.

A multiplication of stamp taxes on the same transaction is prevented
by the rule that each of the three governments may impose the tax only
on transactions which are within its particular jurisdiction or which
take effect in its territory. Since civil and commercial transactions are
governed by federal law, the scope of the federal stamp tax might be
considerably wider than that of state or municipal taxes of this kind
except that the Constitution exempts from the federal stamp tax transactions which are subject to an exclusive state or municipal tax (e.g., the
sales tax).

The federal tax on legal documents takes the form of a fixed fee per
page, irrespective of the value of the transaction. The federal tax on
private written agreements, on the other hand, is proportionate and
measured by the value of the contract (the rate is 0.6%, or Cr$ 6 per
Cr$ 1,000 of value).

The stamp tax is also imposed on loans, on transfers of securities, on
the authorized capital of business entities, on distributions of capital, and,
at a special rate, on installment contracts. While the federal stamp tax
as such is not a heavy burden on commerce, violations of the rules may
result in heavy fines, and compliance often requires a disproportionate
amount of time and effort.

4/8. The Municipal Business Tax

The business tax is reserved to the municipalities as an "exclusive"
tax and it constitutes their main source of revenue. It is defined as a tax
on the individual or entity carrying on any commercial, industrial, or
professional activity in the widest sense. Since it is in the nature of a
franchise tax rather than an income tax, it applies whether or not a profit
is realized. Federal legislation has been proposed to deal with the
problem of apportionment of the tax where a business is carried on in
more than one municipality. Thus far, this problem has been resolved
only in a few instances and on a local basis (City of São Paulo and
State of Bahia).

The methods of assessing the tax vary greatly from one municipality
to another. In municipalities which are unable to administer more

complicated methods of assessment, the tax is simply computed as an addition to the state sales tax. In most cases the tax is assessed on a dual basis, i.e., as a fixed percentage of the rental paid for the use of the business premises, combined with a fixed amount or a percentage of the annual turnover. Other factors are often considered. New industries are frequently exempted from the tax for a limited time.

4/9. The Real Property Transfer Tax

The real property transfer tax is an "exclusive" state tax which applies to transfers of real property for a consideration. It must be distinguished from two other state taxes, namely, the inheritance and gift taxes on gratuitous transfers of real property, and the sales taxes on sales and exchanges of movable property. Transfers of rights in real property and the contribution of such property to the capital of a legal entity, as well as its distribution to shareholders or partners upon liquidation, are within the scope of the real property transfer tax. On the other hand, mortgages and other liens are not considered real property for the purposes of this tax.

The real property transfer tax is imposed on the transferee. It is measured by the fair market value of the property at the time of the transfer, which is determined by an appraisal. While the tax rate varies in the different states, the average rate is 10%, except that a lower rate applies in some states to contributions of real property to the capital of a corporation or partnership. The mandatory public registration of real property and of transfers thereof throughout Brazil has resulted in a highly efficient administrative control of the tax.

4/10. The Tax on Exchange Remittances

The Constitution provides for an "exclusive" federal tax on the remittance of funds abroad (Art. 15[V]). The tax is imposed on actual or constructive remittances made in payment for imported merchandise, expenditures incurred abroad by importers, and living expenses of persons residing abroad. This enumeration, however, is not exhaustive, as the law states that the tax is also due on any other remittance of funds abroad for any purpose.[1]

Exemption from the tax is provided for remittances made for the following purposes:

1. Amortization of the foreign debt of a Brazilian government (federal, state, or local) and interest payments thereon;
2. Repayments of foreign capital invested in Brazil and of interest, dividends, or profits accruing on such capital;
3. Importation of essential food;

[1] Law No. 156 of November 27, 1947.

4. Importation of fuel, lubricants, printing paper, and books;
5. Diplomatic and consular affairs, on the basis of reciprocity;
6. Exchange obligations between authorized banks.

The rate of the tax was originally 5%. It was increased to 8% by Law No. 1,433 of September 15, 1951, and later raised to 10% by Law No. 2,308 of August 31, 1954. The two increases in the rate were earmarked for the renovation of the Brazilian navy and for the Federal Electric Power Fund, respectively.

Exchange transactions are strictly regulated by the Bank of Brazil under the authority conferred by Decree No. 24,268 of May 19, 1934. Only authorized banks may carry out exchange operations and they are responsible for the payment of the tax. The penalty for illegal exchange dealings is a fine of 20 times the amount of the transaction, not merely of the defaulted tax.

PART II

ANALYSIS OF THE INCOME TAX

The following presentation of the income tax law of Brazil follows the uniform system adopted by the World Tax Series. This method of presentation does not necessarily follow the system of the Brazilian law. The reader is advised to refer to Chapter 2 for a brief survey of the Brazilian income tax system as a whole.

CHAPTER 5

CLASSES OF TAXPAYERS

5/1. Resident Individuals

    5/1.1   Taxation by Assessment

    5/1.2   Withholding of Income Tax at the Source

5/2. Resident Corporations

    5/2.1   Determination of Residence

    5/2.2   Tax Effects of Corporate Residence

           a. Taxation by Assessment

           b. Withholding of Income Tax at the Source

    5/2.3   Classification of Corporations and Other Entities

    5/2.4   Registration

    5/2.5   Status of Corporations for Tax Purposes

5/3. Other Resident Taxpayers

    5/3.1   Partnerships

    5/3.2   "Sociedade Em Conta de Participação"

    5/3.3   Limited Liability Companies

    5/3.4   Individuals and Sole Proprietorships Engaged in Business

    5/3.5   Decedents' Estates

    5/3.6   Bankrupt's Estate

5/4. Nonresidents

    5/4.1   Who Is a Nonresident Individual

    5/4.2   Tax Effects of Individual's Nonresidence

    5/4.3   Income of Nonresident Individuals Subject to Taxation at the Source under Other Provisions of the Law

5/4.4 Change of Residence
a. Transfer of Residence from Foreign Country to Brazil
b. Transfer of Residence from Brazil to a Foreign Country
5/4.5 Temporary Visitors
5/4.6 Definition of Nonresident Corporation
5/4.7 Tax Effects of Corporation's Nonresidence
5/4.8 Status of Branches
5/4.9 Other Nonresident Taxpayers

5/5. Tax-Exempt Individuals
5/5.1 In General
5/5.2 Foreign Diplomatic Representatives
5/5.3 Authors, Professors, and Journalists
5/5.4 Clerics

5/6. Tax-Exempt Entities
5/6.1 Entities Exempt Because of Their Purpose
5/6.2 Cooperatives
5/6.3 Who Determines Exemption
5/6.4 Loss of Exemption
5/6.5 Nonresident Entities Exempt by Reciprocity
5/6.6 Exemption Because of Insufficient Income

5/1. Resident Individuals

5/1.1 Taxation by Assessment

All individuals who are residents of, or domiciled in, Brazil and who have net annual income in excess of Cr$ 60,000 computed in accordance with the law are subject to income tax regardless of their nationality, sex, age, marital status, or occupation (Reg. Art. 1, as modified by Law No. 2,862, Art. 19). This provision refers to the tax collected by way of assessment, which is composed of two separately computed taxes, a schedular tax and a complementary tax.

Residents of a foreign country who have been physically present in Brazilian territory for 12 consecutive months or more are treated as residents for purposes of the income tax. These persons, therefore, are subject to the schedular and the complementary taxes and are required to file a return in the year following that in which they complete 12 months of residence in Brazil. They are treated, for tax purposes, exactly like residents of Brazil.

Conversely, taxation by assessment does not apply to individual residents of Brazil (including citizens) who have been absent from the country for more than 12 consecutive months for purposes other than foreign studies or government service.[1] These persons, although they may still be domiciliaries of Brazil, are no longer residents for income tax purposes.

It is evident, therefore, that residence or nonresidence of an individual, for purposes of the income tax law, depends solely on the objective fact of continuous physical presence in, or continuous physical absence from, the country during a period of at least 12 months. The nationality of the taxpayer, his intent, and the reasons for his presence in, or absence from,[2] Brazil are immaterial.

For the rules applying in the case of a change of status from resident to nonresident and vice versa during the taxable year, see 5/4.4.

5/1.2   Withholding of Income Tax at the Source

Withholding of income tax at the source applies to certain types of income of resident individuals and is based on the mere objective fact that income of a certain type is paid to the recipient. The characteristics and personal circumstances of the taxpayer are immaterial. Consequently, there is no minimum amount of income below which the tax does not apply, and there are no personal and family allowances, except in the case of the tax withheld on wages and salaries (8/1.5).

The categories of income subject to withholding of tax at the source in the case of resident individuals are salaries and wages (8/1.5) and income from bearer securities (9/2.2a). Regarding the tax imposed on gains on the sale of real property realized by individuals, which in Brazilian terminology is also called a withholding tax, see 9/8.2.

5/2.   Resident Corporations

5/2.1   Determination of Residence

Under Brazilian law, a corporation's residence for tax purposes is determined by its domicile. Generally, a corporation is domiciled at the place where it has its seat, i.e., where its management is located. The nationality of the corporation, i.e., the place where it was formed or organized, is immaterial, as is the nationality or residence of its shareholders.

A foreign corporation has a tax domicile in Brazil, and consequently is taxed by assessment, if it is doing business in Brazil through a permanent establishment or permanent agency located in the country. If it

[1] Reg. Art. 73, Reg. Art. 97(1), and Reg. Art. 97 §2(d).
[2] Except in the situations covered by the provisions cited in note 1 above.

has more than one branch there, its residence is at its principal Brazilian establishment.[3]

5/2.2 Tax Effects of Corporate Residence

a. TAXATION BY ASSESSMENT. Corporations are subject to taxation by assessment only if they are residents of Brazil. The Income Tax Regulations create a fundamental difference in the taxation by assessment of corporations and of individuals. The income of individuals is classified under different schedules, each with its particular deductions and uniform tax rate. The amount of income under any schedule is immaterial; the classification, and therefore the tax rate, is based solely on the nature of the income. For the progressive complementary tax, however, the tax rate is based solely on the amount of income, regardless of its source or nature.

The income of corporations, on the other hand, is classified as "business income" without further differentiation, and this income is subjected to a flat tax rate (15% on the first Cr$ 500,000 of taxable income and 20% on the excess).

b. WITHHOLDING OF INCOME TAX AT THE SOURCE. The tax on income from bearer securities received by corporations resident in Brazil is subject to withholding at the source. This subject is discussed in detail in 9/2.3.

5/2.3 Classification of Corporations and other Entities

A corporation is a "juridical person of the private law," a term which is defined in the Civil Code of Brazil.[4] In conformity with the uniform terminology of the World Tax Series, the term "legal entities," or "entities," will be used to designate juridical persons.

Besides corporations, the term "legal entity" includes all civil and mercantile companies and foundations and, for income tax purposes, all (incorporated or unincorporated) entities which are regulated by the private law, regardless of where they were formed or organized and of whether they are registered (Reg. Art. 27). The definition includes all the various forms of business organization, except as otherwise noted in 5/3.2 below. It excludes public corporations, especially the federal government, the states, and the municipalities. Foreign governments are exempt from the provisions of the income tax law only if an equivalent exemption is granted to the Brazilian government by the foreign country.

The rules governing the determination of residence (5/2.1) and the tax effects of that residence (5/2.2) are the same for other legal entities as they are for corporations.

---

[3] A foreign corporation may not operate in Brazil without authorization by the federal government, Corp. Law, Art. 64. This provision, however, is of no significance for income tax purposes (11/3.2).

[4] *Código Civil*, Art. 16.

5/2.4   Registration

Although all business entities are required to be listed with the Commercial Registry (*Junta Comercial* or *Registro do Comercio*) of the place where their principal seat of business is located, the application of the income tax laws is in no way dependent on this registration (Reg. Art. 27 §2). The failure of the taxpayer to register as required by law results in taxation on the basis of estimated profits (6/9.2).

5/2.5   Status of Corporations for Tax Purposes

Corporations and all other legal entities are taxpayers and, as such, obliged to file returns, to pay income tax on their business profits, and to comply with the other fiscal obligations imposed by law. It should be particularly noted that while the principles of taxation applying to the various forms of organization included in the term "juridical persons" are the same, those regulating the taxation of the profits in the hands of their shareholders, owners, and partners are not uniform. The profits of a corporation are taxed to the shareholder only if and when such profits are distributed to him.

5/3.   Other Resident Taxpayers

5/3.1   Partnerships

Under Brazilian law, a partnership [5] is a taxable entity. The determination of the taxable income of a commercial partnership and the computation of the tax payable thereon follow the rules applicable to the business income of entities set forth in Chapter 7. Regarding the special rate of tax applicable to professional partnerships, see 12/2.6 under [2].

In addition to the taxation of the partnership as such, each partner is taxed on his distributive share of the partnership profits if and when this share is actually distributed to the partner or credited to his account on the books of the partnership. This income must be reported by the partner in his return for the year following that of the credit or distribution. It is classified as income from capital taxable under Schedule F and it is therefore subject only to complementary tax (9/2.1a). The reason for this rule is that the income has already been subjected to the proportionate tax imposed on the partnership under Reg. Art. 44, which is the equivalent of the schedular taxes imposed on individuals. Consequently, it is subjected only to the complementary tax in the hands of the partner. [6]

[5] *Sociedade em nome coletivo* or *sociedade em nome com firma,* and its variations such as the *sociedade em comandita simple* and *sociedade em comandita por ações.*

[6] Sousa, §31; Reinach, "O Impôsto de Renda No Sistema Tributário do Brasil," *Serviço Social,* vol. 4 No. 33 (São Paulo, 1944) p. 24.

5/3.2 Sociedade Em Conta de Participação

The *sociedade em conta de participação* (partnership on participation account [7]) is not regarded as an entity for income tax purposes and therefore not taxed as such. Each participant in the venture is taxed under Schedule H [8] on his distributive share of the profits realized.

5/3.3 Limited Liability Companies

For tax purposes, limited liability companies (1/4.2f) are treated exactly like corporations.

5/3.4 Individuals and Sole Proprietorships Engaged in Business

The business income of all taxpayers is subject to uniform rules of taxation which are laid down in the part of the Income Tax Regulations dealing with entities (Reg. Arts. 27 *et seq.*). In order to apply these rules to sole proprietorships and to individuals who, acting in their own name, are continuously [9] engaged in transactions of a civil [10] or commercial nature for profit, the law (Reg. Art. 27 §1) employs the fiction that these taxpayers are entities for income tax purposes.[11] It follows that there is a fundamental difference between the taxation of individuals engaged in business and those who are not so engaged.

The owner of an individual business is obliged to file two income tax returns, one as an entity and one in his individual capacity. He must in the latter return report (under Schedule F) the entire profit shown in the return filed by him as an entity and pay the complementary tax thereon, whether or not such profit was withdrawn by him during the year. The legal theory governing this rule is that the profit, whether withdrawn or

---

[7] The characteristics of this form of a partnership, or joint venture, were explained at 1/4.2d above.

[8] Regarding Schedule H (the miscellaneous classification of the Income Tax Regulations) see 10/4.1 below. The applicable schedular tax rate is 5%, Reg. Art. 25.

[9] Occasional acts of commerce do not result in the application of the rules on the taxation of business income, CC, *Rev.* 1954 No. 81.

[10] This term refers to transactions which are regulated by the civil as distinguished from the commercial law. The most important type of the former are the selling or renting of real property since commercial operations, as defined in the Commercial Code, are restricted to movable property. It should be noted, however, that the nature of income as commercial income may also be determined by the form of organization under which the taxpayer's business is carried on. All transactions of a corporation are deemed to be of a commercial nature and are governed by the commercial law.

[11] This rule is commonly referred to in Brazil as the "assimilation" of the status of sole proprietorships and of individuals engaged in business to that of an entity. It has also been stated (Sousa, §27-A) that these taxpayers assume, for income tax purposes, the status of a corporation with a single shareholder. It should be remembered, however, that it is the sole purpose of this "assimilation" to apply the rules on the taxation of business income, and that individuals and sole proprietorships are not otherwise considered as "entities."

not, is at the disposal of the proprietor at any time. The result, however, is that a taxpayer doing business as an individual is subject to a heavier tax burden than the shareholder of a corporation, who is taxed only on actual distributions of profits and not on amounts appropriated to a reserve or otherwise withheld from distribution.

The "assimilation" of individual firms is automatic in the case of those which are registered with the *Junta Comercial*. A sole proprietorship (*firma individual*) is of a purely formal nature, i.e., it exists as such only when registered; if unregistered, it is an individual. In the case of individuals whose business is not listed in the Commercial Register, the classification depends on the evaluation of the facts by the fiscal authorities.[12]

5/3.5 Decedents' Estates

The income tax of a decedent's estate is generally computed in the same manner and on the same basis as that of an individual taxpayer (Reg. Art. 45 §3).

The first Cr$ 60,000 of the annual net income of an estate are not subject to tax in the year in which the death of the decedent occurred and in the following year.[13]

If the annual net income of the estate for a subsequent year during which the estate is in the process of administration exceeds Cr$ 60,000, the rate of the complementary tax is 3% for the first Cr$ 60,000 of net income; the net income in excess of Cr$ 60,000 is taxed at the graduated progressive rates applying to individuals.[14]

5/3.6 Bankrupt's Estate

The estate of a bankrupt is not a taxable entity and income accruing while the estate is in the hands of the receiver remains untaxed.[15] This result is based partly on the formal ground that the Income Tax Regulations do not provide for taxation of a bankrupt's estate,[16] and partly on the

---

[12] The following activities, among others, have been held to constitute the conduct of a business with the result that the rules on the taxation of entities apply: buying and selling of real property if done continuously, DIR, *Rev.* 1943 No. 628; the business of a consulting engineer who works independently on specific assignments and furnishes materials, CC, *Rev.* 1948 No. 890; otherwise, if he does not furnish materials, DIR, *Rev.* 1943 No. 220; agents acting for the account of third parties are not taxed as entities, CC, *Rev.* 1951 No. 969; it will, however, be assumed that the agent acted for his own account unless he proves that he bought merchandise for others, CC, *Rev.* 1947 No. 291. Further examples in Sousa, §27-A and Rezende, Note 114.

[13] Reg. Art. 48. If, therefore, the death of the decedent occurs in 1957, the exemption of Cr$ 60,000 applies both to the year 1957 (for which the final return of the decedent is filed) and to the year 1958 (which becomes the base year for the 1959 return to be filed by the administrator of the estate).

[14] Reg. Art. 48 Sole §.   [15] CC, *Rev.* 1946 No. 478.

[16] Especially not in Chapter 3 of the Income Tax Regulations dealing with special cases of income taxation.

ground that it is not the purpose of bankruptcy proceedings to realize profits, but to collect and distribute the assets of the bankrupt for the benefit of his creditors.

Any deficiencies in income tax owed by the bankrupt become due immediately upon the opening of bankruptcy proceedings,[17] and a discharge or settlement with the creditors is dependent upon prior liquidation of any open liability for income tax.[18]

5/4. Nonresidents

5/4.1 Who Is a Nonresident Individual

The question of residence or nonresidence of an individual, for purposes of the Brazilian income tax, is determined solely on the basis of the objective fact of continued physical presence in, or absence from, the country for a period of 12 consecutive months, irrespective of the nationality of the taxpayer, his intention, and the reasons for his presence or absence (5/1.1).

A Brazilian citizen who remains absent from the country for more than 12 months becomes a nonresident for income tax purposes and subject to withholding of tax on his income from sources in Brazil.[19] A foreigner whose stay in Brazil exceeds 12 months becomes a resident and subject to taxation by assessment on the basis of an income tax return to be filed by him.

An individual domiciled abroad who is doing business in Brazil through a permanent establishment or agency located in the country becomes a resident for income tax purposes; see 11/3.1.

5/4.2 Tax Effects of Individual's Nonresidence

Individuals who are nonresidents of Brazil and not engaged in business in the country are not subject to taxation by assessment; they are taxed by way of withholding at the source on their income derived from sources in Brazil. The rate of the withholding tax is 20% (Reg. Art. 97[1]), or 25% in the case of income from royalties (Reg. Art. 97[2]). The tax is, in general, computed on gross income.

An exception to this rule exists in the case of income from real property (Reg. Art. 97 §5). See 9/4.2.

Regarding the determination of taxable income in the case of a nonresident, see 6/1.3.

---

[17] Reg. Art. 91.

[18] Reg. Art. 126.

[19] Reg. Art. 97(1), except individuals domiciled in Brazil who are absent from the country for reasons of government service or foreign studies, Reg. Art. 73 and Reg. Art. 97 §2(d).

5/4.3   Income of Nonresident Individuals Subject to Taxation at the Source under Other Provisions of the Law

The types of income listed under 5/1.2 are subject to taxation at the source even if realized by an individual who is a resident of Brazil. The Income Tax Regulations provide for situations where income of this nature is realized by nonresidents, in order to prevent a duplication of withholding or excessive withholding of income tax.

Under Art. 97 §4 of the Income Tax Regulations, the tax on income of a nonresident which was already subjected to taxation at the source [20] is withheld only to the extent required to raise the total amount of tax to 20%, the withholding rate generally applied to nonresident individuals.[21]

The Income Tax Regulations do not cover the situation in which the withholding rate applying to resident individuals is in excess of the 20% rate generally prescribed for income realized by nonresidents of the country.[22] Considering that it is not the intent of the statute to favor nonresidents over residents in the matter of tax withholding, and that the facts giving rise to withholding of tax under Reg. Art. 96 (payment of income to bearer) are quite independent of those under Reg. Art. 97 (payment of income to a nonresident), it appears that the higher rates apply to residents and nonresidents alike.[23]

An important exception to the statutory rules discussed exists by virtue of administrative and judicial practice in the case of profits from the sale of real property (9/8.2). Such profits realized by a resident individual are subject to taxation at the source at the flat rate of 10% under Reg. Art. 92. The decisions hold that the 10% tax collected at the source is the only tax due on this type of gain and that there will be no additional withholding of income tax, even if the gain is realized by a nonresident individual.[24]

5/4.4   Change of Residence

a. TRANSFER OF RESIDENCE FROM FOREIGN COUNTRY TO BRAZIL. If an individual transfers his residence from a foreign country to Brazil, it must be distinguished whether or not he had income from Brazilian sources before becoming a resident of the country.

If he has such income, it is and continues to be subject to withholding

[20] Under the provisions of Reg. Arts. 96(1) and (2).

[21] At the present time, only interest on government securities made out to bearer is subject to a resident withholding rate of less than 20%; see 9/1.6.

[22] Effective January 1, 1957, the withholding rates are 21% on interest from bearer bonds, and 28% on dividends from bearer shares and certain other distributions; see 9/1.6; 9/2.2.

[23] No decisions which would clarify this question have been published at this time.

[24] DIR, *Rev.* 1950 No. 613; 1951 No. 1175; CC, *Rev.* 1951 No. 1107. See Sousa, §46.

of tax at the source under Reg. Art. 97, notwithstanding the physical presence of the individual in Brazil, until the end of the calendar year in which the change of residence occurs.[25] The individual becomes subject to taxation as a resident in the calendar year following the year of that change (Reg. Art. 60).[26] He must file an income tax return on or before April 30 of the following year, and this return must include his entire income during the year of the change of residence, which becomes the base year for the purposes of this return. (Reg. Art. 60 §1.) It should be noted that the total income of the year of the change, including that already taxed by withholding at the source, must be included in the return, and that no part of the withholding tax paid is credited against the tax due on the basis of the return or refunded to the taxpayer.[27] Applicable abatements and deductions, not operative on taxes withheld at the source, may be offset by the taxpayer against the gross income reported in his return.[28]

If the taxpayer first receives income from Brazilian sources when he is physically present in Brazil, withholding of tax at the source begins as soon as he receives income. Whether it continues until the *date* on which the taxpayer completes 12 months of residence in Brazil, or until the end of the *year* into which that date falls (the year in which the taxpayer completes 12 months of residence) is somewhat doubtful under the decisions.[29]

For purposes of taxation by assessment, the individual becomes a taxpayer in the year following the year of the change of residence (Reg. Art. 61). He must, therefore, include the income realized by him between the date of his arrival in the country and the end of the year of the change in the return to be filed by him on or before April 30 of the next succeeding year (Reg. Art. 61 §1). No part of the tax withheld at the source

[25] DIR, *Rev.* 1942 No. 194; 1949 Nos. 396, 412 and 482.

[26] This rule applies even if the taxpayer has not completed 12 full months of physical presence on April 30 of the year following the year of the change.

[27] CC, *Rev.* 1954 No. 416. This result is a logical consequence of the base-year system discussed in 6/3.1, under which the tax paid *during* a particular year is also the tax *for* such year, and only measured by the income of the preceding year (the base year: in this case, the year of the change of residence). If, however, the withholding of tax should continue during the taxable year (the year following the one in which the taxpayer became a resident of Brazil), this portion of the withholding tax will be credited or refunded, DIR, *Rev.* 1942 No. 194; 1949 No. 518.

[28] Reg. Art. 60 §1; Reg. Art. 22.

[29] The rulings of the Income Tax Division in the Ministry of Finance on this point are contradictory. See, on the one hand, DIR, *Rev.* 1945 No. 223 and, more recently, decision of the Income Tax Division dated July 16, 1954, No. 291.514/53 (individual held to have become resident of Brazil as of the date on which he completed 12 months' stay in Brazil). On the other hand, DIR, *Rev.* 1945 No. 290 (individual arriving in Brazil in 1944 held to have become resident of Brazil in 1946, the year following the one in which he had been physically present in the country for more than 12 months; therefore first return required to be filed for 1946, based on the income of calendar year 1945, and withholding at the source to continue until December 31, 1945). The decision is criticized by Rezende, Note 201.

is credited against the tax due under the return nor is it refunded to the taxpayer.

b. TRANSFER OF RESIDENCE FROM BRAZIL TO A FOREIGN COUNTRY. A resident of Brazil who transfers his residence to a foreign country or remains abroad for a continuous period of at least 12 consecutive months becomes a nonresident for income tax purposes.[30] On the question of whether this change becomes effective in the year in which the taxpayer establishes a foreign residence (or completes 12 months of absence from the country) or in the next succeeding year, the decisions are in conflict.[31]

Example
    An American citizen who has had income from Brazilian sources subject to withholding tax between January 1 and October 20, 1954, settles in Brazil on that date and has further income for the balance of the year 1954. He continues to live in Brazil until 1956 when he returns to the United States.

  1. The taxpayer is obliged to file a tax return on or before April 30, 1955, reporting his Brazilian income for the calendar year 1954 including the income realized between January 1 and October 20, 1954, on which income tax was already withheld. He may, however, offset the applicable schedular deductions against such income. The taxpayer is further entitled to the abatements (personal allowance, allowances for dependents, and certain deductions) for purposes of the complementary tax. The tax withheld on the portion of the income included in the return will not be refunded.[32]
  2. Regarding the fiscal obligations of the taxpayer in connection with his departure from Brazil in 1956, the following rules apply:
     If the taxpayer leaves Brazil on or before April 30, 1956, the filing date of the 1956 income tax return, he must file this return reporting his income for the year 1955 and pay the tax thereon in order to obtain the tax clearance certificate without which no passport or exit permit is issued (Reg. Art. 134). The payment of the tax includes the full amount of tax due on the taxpayer's income for the year 1955, including installments which otherwise would fall due later.[33] If, on

[30] It would seem that completion of twelve months' absence from Brazil, and not establishment of a foreign residence, should be the decisive factor.
[31] See on the one hand, DIR, *Rev.* 1943 No. 301; 1951 No. 748 (no return due to be filed in the year following that of the change, based on the income of the latter year); on the other hand, DIR, *Rev.* 1949 No. 412 (change becomes effective after 12 months; therefore a resident of Brazil who left the country on May 30, 1946, held obliged to file returns for 1946 and 1947, based on the income of 1945 and 1946, respectively. If the taxpayer continues to have income from sources in Brazil, withholding at the source becomes effective from January 1, 1947 on.) See also Rezende, Notes 3 and 201.
[32] Regarding the foregoing, see decision of the Income Tax Division of July 16, 1954, No. 291.514/53.
[33] Regarding the time when the return must be filed and the tax be paid, see 13/1.1 below. Persons leaving Brazil must appoint a resident to act as their representative before the Income Tax Division. The Division construes such representation to imply personal liability of the representative for any deficiencies in tax. Reg. Art. 195 Sole § does not seem to justify these requirements.

the other hand, the taxpayer abandons his Brazilian residence after April 30, he will have filed his 1956 return and he remains liable merely for the still unpaid portion of the tax computed on the return.

In either case, the fiscal obligations of the taxpayer for the year 1955 will be fully satisfied at the time he leaves Brazil. The income of the taxpayer for the year of his departure, however, remains in effect completely untaxed, regardless of whether such income was received before or after the date the taxpayer gave up his residence in Brazil. This peculiar result follows from the "base-year" concept [34] underlying the Brazilian income tax system, according to which the return filed (and the tax paid) *in* a particular year is also the return (and tax) *for* such year; the liability of the taxpayer is merely *measured* by the income of the preceding year. With the payment of the tax computed on the return of the taxpayer filed *in* 1956 (although computed on the basis of 1955 income), therefore, the liability of the taxpayer *for* the year 1956 is fully discharged. He is not required to file a tax return in 1957 reporting his income for 1956 (received either before or after the date of his departure) and if he should continue to receive income after leaving Brazil, the payor of the income is not required to withhold tax thereon; if the payment of income continues, the obligation to withhold tax becomes effective again only from January 1, 1957, on.[35]

5/4.5 Temporary Visitors

A temporary visitor whose sojourn in Brazil covers a period shorter than 12 consecutive months is a nonresident for income tax purposes and subject to withholding of tax at the source on all his income from Brazilian sources.[36] After completing a continuous period of 12 months in the country — regardless of his intent and the purpose of his stay — the individual automatically becomes a resident of Brazil for income tax purposes. Whether this change becomes effective in the year in which the individual completes 12 full months of physical presence in Brazil, or in the next succeeding year, is doubtful under the decisions.[37]

5/4.6 Definition of Nonresident Corporation

A corporation which has its domicile outside Brazil is considered a nonresident for income tax purposes. The domicile of a corporation is at the place where it has its seat, i.e., where its principal establishment and the center of its management are located.

5/4.7 Tax Effects of Corporation's Nonresidence

A nonresident corporation is not subject to taxation by assessment unless it is doing business in Brazil through a permanent establishment or

[34] A fuller explanation of this concept, in its proper context, is given in 6/3.1.
[35] See decision of the Income Tax Division of July 1954, No. 291.514/53.
[36] DIR, *Rev.* 1950 No. 602.
[37] See decisions cited in footnote 29 in 5/4.4a.

permanent agency located in the country (see 5/2.1, 11/3.1, and 11/3.3). It is, however, subject to withholding of tax on all its income from sources in Brazil. The rates of the withholding tax are the same as those applying to nonresident individuals (5/4.2).

For the determination of taxable income realized by a foreign corporation, see 11/3.1.

5/4.8 Status of Branches

Particular rules of taxation apply to the Brazilian branch of a foreign legal entity. The branch, being established in Brazil, is considered an entity for income tax purposes and is subject to tax like an independent entity organized under Brazilian law. Since it is, on the other hand, an integral part of the foreign organization, it is held that the profits of the branch are realized by its home office as soon as such profits are determined and that they become subject to taxation by withholding at the source at that moment, in addition to the tax collected by way of assessment.[38]

For details of income determination and specific rules regarding the taxation of the Brazilian branch of a foreign entity, see 11/3.3.

The profits realized by the Brazilian branch of a foreign company or corporation, to the extent that such profits are reinvested in the industrial equipment of the branch, are exempt *from the withholding tax under Reg. Art. 97.*[39]

5/4.9 Other Nonresident Taxpayers

The rules governing the taxation of nonresident corporations apply to other nonresident entities. Regarding the definition of nonresidence, see 5/4.6. All nonresident entities are subject to withholding of income tax at the source on their income from sources in Brazil at the rates applicable to nonresident individuals (5/4.2).

5/5. Tax-Exempt Individuals

5/5.1 In General

Under Brazilian law (Reg. Art. 1 cited at 5/1.1 above), no class or group of individuals is as such exempt from income tax. The law merely

[38] DIR, *Rev.* 1943 No. 684; 1944 No. 420; CC, *Rev.* 1943 No. 551; 1949 No. 759; 1950 No. 39; 1951 No. 116; Min. of Fin., *Rev.* 1944 No. 490-B; Federal Court of Appeals, *Rev.* 1950 No. 563; Supreme Court of Brazil, *Rev.* 1947 No. 805; 1950 No. 431. Regarding the origin of this rule, see Sousa, "O Impôsto sobre a Renda das Sociedades Estrangeiras," *Estudos de Direito Tributário* (São Paulo, 1950), p. 11, and in *Revista Fiscal*, July 15, 1951; see also Rezende, Note 283.

[39] Reg. Art. 97(2)(c). The profits are *not* exempted, however, from the regular income tax imposed on legal entities under Reg. Art. 44; the purpose of the law is merely to avoid the double taxation of branch profits in this particular instance. For a fuller discussion of the taxation of branch profits, see 11/3.3.

recognizes an exemption of certain types of income in a very limited number of cases. If an individual benefiting from one of these exemptions has other income which is not specifically exempt from tax, he is taxed on such income under the general rules.

5/5.2 Foreign Diplomatic Representatives

Foreign diplomatic representatives accredited in Brazil and their personnel are exempt from income tax on their remuneration on the basis of reciprocity. The exemption does not extend to Brazilian nationals.[40]

5/5.3 Authors, Professors, and Journalists

Authors' royalties and the remuneration (salaries and retirement pensions) of teachers, professors, and journalists are exempt from income tax. Constitution of Brazil, Art. 203; Income Tax Reg. Art. 24 §3.

5/5.4 Clerics

The decisions [41] recognize an exemption of the emoluments of Catholic priests and other clerics. This exemption is based on the view that these receipts do not constitute income in the economic sense.

5/6. Tax-Exempt Entities

5/6.1 Entities Exempt Because of Their Purpose

Benevolent, philanthropic, charitable, religious, educational, cultural, scientific, artistic, literary, recreational, and athletic organizations and foundations; and professional associations and syndicates organized to further the interests of their members are exempt from taxation (Reg. Art. 28). See Art. 31 of the Constitution (1/3.5).

5/6.2 Cooperatives

Cooperatives organized under either the civil or the commercial law are included in the list of tax-exempt organizations named in Reg. Art. 28. Also listed are various types of agricultural cooperatives, farm credit associations, consumers' cooperatives, associations building homes for their members, publishing companies whose products are distributed exclusively among their members or intended solely for advertising on behalf of the cooperative society or association, and associations insuring their members against labor accidents.

[40] DIR, *Rev.* 1952 No. 732; Rezende and Viana, *Consolidação das Leis do Impôsto de Renda* (Rio de Janeiro, 1955), Note 17.
[41] DIR, *Rev.* 1953 No. 285; *Rev.* 1954 No. 26; CC, *Rev.* 1954 No. 183. The older practice took the opposite view.

5/6.3   Who Determines Exemption

The exemption is granted by the Income Tax Division in the Ministry of Finance upon application of the entity and proof by it of:

1. The fact that the entity is organized and registered in accordance with the applicable law.
2. The purpose and character of its activities, the nature of its resources and the conditions under which they are obtained.
3. The fact that the profits of the entity are applied to the full extent in promoting its declared object.

5/6.4   Loss of Exemption

The associations, societies, and foundations listed under 5/6.1 above will lose the exemption if they compensate their directors or distribute profits to their members in any form. Cooperatives (5/6.2) lose the exemption if they distribute dividends to their members. However, the payment of fixed interest or dividends up to 12% per annum on the paid-in capital of the association in accordance with existing cooperative legislation will not affect the exemption (Reg. Art. 28 Sole §).

5/6.5   Nonresident Entities Exempt by Reciprocity

Foreign airlines and steamship companies are exempt from Brazilian income tax if the country of their nationality grants a corresponding exemption to similar Brazilian companies (Reg. Art. 30). The exemption may be provided for in a convention between the two countries affected; otherwise, it is granted by simple administrative act of the competent authority in Brazil. Whether the exemption extends to income of the foreign home office of the exempt organization which, under general rules would be subject to taxation at the source, is doubtful.[42]

5/6.6   Exemption Because of Insufficient Income

All entities regardless of their form of organization (including corporations, sole proprietorships, partnerships, etc.) whose *gross* annual income does not exceed Cr$ 150,000, are exempt from income tax.[43] This exemption applies automatically if the gross income for any particular year does not exceed the statutory minimum; it is not dependent on compliance

---

[42] For exemption: DIR, *Rev.* 1951 Nos. 636 and 1162. Against exemption: CC *Rev.* 1949 No. 20. See Rezende, Note 121.

[43] This exemption was introduced into Brazilian income tax law by Law No. 2,354 of November 29, 1954. The exemption of entities with gross annual income not exceeding Cr$ 150,000 has been compared with that of individuals with net annual income not exceeding Cr$ 50,000 (now Cr$ 60,000), see Sousa, §26-C. Individuals with income of less than the minimum amount are not taxpayers according to Reg. Art. 1, and the same would seem to be true for entities with insufficient income.

with the formal requirements set forth under 5/6.3, above (Reg. Art. 28[d]).

The exemptions in favor of certain entities referred to in 5/6.1–5/6.6 do not extend to those who receive income of any kind from the exempt organization (Reg. Art. 31).

CHAPTER 6

.... :

PRINCIPLES OF

INCOME DETERMINATION

6/1. Concept of Taxable Income

6/1.1 Definition
6/1.2 Resident Individuals
   a. Schedular Income
   b. Principles of Schedular Deductions
   c. Income for Complementary Tax
   d. Abatements Under the Complementary Tax
   e. Nonincome Items and Tax-Exempt Items
6/1.3 Nonresident Individuals
   a. Concept of Income
   b. Tax-Exempt Income
6/1.4 Entities

6/2. Books and Records

6/2.1 General Rules
6/2.2 Required Books

6/3. Accounting Periods

6/3.1 Base Year and Taxable Year
6/3.2 Change of Accounting Period from Calendar Year to Fiscal Year Basis
6/3.3 Change from Fiscal Year to Calendar Year
6/3.4 Change from One Fiscal Year to Another
6/3.5 Change of Accounting Period in the Case of Reorganizations
6/3.6 Commencement of Operations
6/3.7 Termination of Operations

6/4. Accounting Methods — Cash Basis and Accrual Basis

    6/4.1   Individuals

        a. Receipts

        b. Disbursements

    6/4.2   Entities

6/5. Valuation of Assets

    6/5.1   Inventories

    6/5.2   Receivables

    6/5.3   Securities

    6/5.4   Fixed Assets

6/6. Reserves

    6/6.1   Reserves and Provisions

    6/6.2   Statutory Regulation of Reserves

6/7. Head Office and Branch Office Accounting

    6/7.1   Centralized and Decentralized Accounting

    6/7.2   Local Branch of Nonresident Entity

6/8. Attribution Rules

    6/8.1   In General

6/9. Alternative Methods of Determining the Tax Base

    6/9.1   Taxation on the Basis of Presumed Profits

    6/9.2   Taxation on the Basis of Estimated Profits

6/1. Concept of Taxable Income

6/1.1 Definition

The taxable income of individuals — other than business income — is the difference between gross income and statutory allowances.[1] The taxable income of entities (including individuals engaged in business) is the amount of business profits for the year, as adjusted for tax purposes.[2] In the usual situation, actual profits form the basis of taxation, but "presumed" profits or "estimated" profits are substituted for actual profits under certain circumstances.[3]

While deductions and allowances are a matter of statutory grace, the Income Tax Regulations nowhere define the term "gross income" nor is their underlying concept of income based on any particular economic

[1] "Schedular deductions" for purposes of the schedular tax, Reg. Art. 18, "abatements" (family allowances and certain deductions) for purposes of the complementary tax, Reg. Art. 21.

[2] Reg. Arts. 27 and 32.

[3] Regarding these alternate bases of taxation, see 6/9.1 and 6/9.2 below.

theory. It may be stated, in general, that it is the intent of the law to limit the impact of the income tax to recurrent receipts from a productive source (capital, labor, or a combination of both), giving consideration to the fact that certain expenditures are of necessity incurred in order to earn the income. It follows from this concept that receipts which are not in the nature of a recurrent return from an income-producing activity [4] or which are not in the nature of income at all (payments representing a return of capital, etc.) are not included in gross income; and it follows further that the law, while not expressly defining gross receipts and gross income, is aware of the difference and uses the latter concept as the starting point in the determination of taxable income.

Within this general framework, the determination of taxable income proceeds along somewhat different lines in the case of resident individuals, resident entities, and nonresident taxpayers (individuals and entities).

6/1.2 Resident Individuals

The income tax imposed on resident individuals is composed of a schedular and a complementary tax.

The rates of the schedular taxes under the different schedules vary between 1% and 10% (for details, see 12/1.1). No schedular tax is provided for under Schedules F and G; the importance of these schedules lies in the classification of income for purposes of the complementary tax.

The applicable rate of schedular tax depends solely on the type of schedular income, irrespective of its amount. The rates of the complementary tax, on the other hand, are progressive and based on the amount of income subject to the tax, regardless of its character. There is no liability either for schedular or for complementary tax if the net annual income of an individual does not exceed Cr$ 60,000 (see c, below).

a. SCHEDULAR INCOME. Taxable income under each applicable schedule is gross schedular income less specific schedular deductions.

The types of income classified under the various schedules are as follows:

1. Schedule A: Interest from (nominative) government securities.
2. Schedule B: Interest from other sources and certain other income from capital.
3. Schedule C: Compensation for personal services as an employee.
4. Schedule D: Compensation for independent personal services.
5. Schedule E: Income from real property.
6. Schedule F: Income from distributions by entities, business income of individuals, and foreign income.
7. Schedule G: Income from agriculture.
8. Schedule H: Income from gainful occupations not includible under another schedule.

[4] Regarding gains realized by individuals from the sale of real property, see 9/8.2.

The law does not include a schedule for business income of individuals, for the reason that income of this type is subject to uniform rules of taxation regardless of who earns the income (see 5/3.4). The business income of a partnership, a sole proprietorship, or of an individual engaged in business is taxed in the same manner as that of an incorporated entity. In the case of individual proprietors or partners, the tax imposed on the business takes the place of the schedular taxes applicable to other types of income; in addition to this tax, the owner or partner is liable in his individual capacity for the complementary tax under Schedule F.

b. PRINCIPLES OF SCHEDULAR DEDUCTIONS. While the specific deductions applicable to the various categories of income vary, the following general rules apply to all deductions claimed under any one of the schedules (Reg. Art. 12):

1. Only deductions which are specifically allowed by the law can be claimed.[5]
2. Only expenses actually paid are deductible. This rule in effect prohibits the use of the accrual basis in the case of expenditures.
3. Expenses deducted under one schedule cannot be deducted again under a different schedule. If the same deduction applies to income taxable under different schedules, it may not be apportioned between them.[6] The taxpayer must elect under which schedule he wants to take the deduction.
4. Deductions will only be allowed in the amount claimed if, in the opinion of the assessing authority, they are proved and justified.[7] Otherwise, the deductions will be estimated.
5. Deductions which are not in proportion to the gross schedular income reported or which are not allowable under the law may be disallowed without a hearing of the taxpayer.
6. Deductions disallowed for failure of proof or justification cannot be claimed again after the time for an administrative appeal has expired (13/4.2a).
7. Deductions claimed for rent, commissions, brokerage, salaries, wages, bonuses, etc., are only allowable if the amounts paid as well as the names and addresses of the payees are indicated in the tax return.
8. Deductions not listed in the taxpayer's return (or listed in a lesser amount) cannot be claimed or increased after the taxpayer has received a notice of assessment, or notification that an assessment ex officio has been initiated (regarding assessments ex officio, see 13/2.2). Prior to such notices, the taxpayer is entitled to claim new deductions or increase deductions previously taken by filing a petition for amendment.[8]

The various classes of gross schedular income, the specific deductions pertaining to each type and the tax rate applicable to the net schedular

[5] CC, *Rev.* 1951 No. 161; Rezende, Note 53.
[6] Rezende, Note 55.
[7] This does not necessarily imply that written evidence must be presented in support of every deduction claimed. Reasonable expenses necessary in connection with earning the income will be allowed, and the standards of proof demanded will vary with the type of gross income involved. CC, *Rev.* 1951 No. 542; Rezende, Note 56.
[8] See 13/6.1.

income so determined are analyzed in Chapters 7–10, according to types of income.

c. INCOME FOR COMPLEMENTARY TAX. The sum total of net schedular income under all schedules applicable to a particular taxpayer for a given taxable year becomes gross income for purposes of the complementary tax. It follows that only income which is classifiable under one of the eight schedules enters into the computation of the complementary tax.

Taxable income for purposes of the complementary tax is the sum total of net schedular income under all applicable schedules less certain statutory allowances and deductions called abatements. (See d, below.) It should be clearly understood, however, that only taxpayers with annual net income in excess of Cr$ 60,000 are subject to the individual income tax, and this is true for both the complementary tax and the schedular tax. There is no liability for income tax whatever if either the net schedular income is not in excess of Cr$ 60,000 or if, although larger, it is reduced to Cr$ 60,000 or less after application of the statutory abatements. Individuals with less than the minimum income are not considered taxpayers according to Art. 1 of the Income Tax Regulations. Obviously, the income subject to complementary tax must be determined in order to decide in any given case whether an individual is subject to schedular *and* complementary tax.

Where the exclusion applies because the statutory minimum income is not reached, the particular individual is not obliged to pay an income tax for the year in question; this does not imply an exemption from any and all fiscal obligations such as the requirement to file a return,[9] and to give information therein regarding payments made to third parties.

d. ABATEMENTS UNDER THE COMPLEMENTARY TAX. The abatements for purposes of the complementary tax are partly in the nature of allowances for dependents and partly in the nature of deductions. They include the following (for details see 12/1.2b):

1. Allowances for dependents (Cr$ 50,000 for the spouse, Cr$ 25,000 for each child).
2. Interest on personal debts of the taxpayer.
3. Life insurance premiums.
4. Extraordinary losses.
5. Charitable contributions.

e. NONINCOME ITEMS AND TAX-EXEMPT ITEMS. The following items do not enter into the computation of gross income under any one schedule (Reg. Art. 11 §2): [10]

---

[9] A return must be filed if *gross income* is in excess of Cr$ 60,000, Reg. Art. 63 §1(a).

[10] Since gross income for purposes of the complementary tax is defined as the sum total of the net schedular income under all applicable schedules, the exclusion of certain receipts for purposes of the schedular tax results automatically in their exclusion for purposes of the complementary tax also.

1. Insurance amounts paid by reason of the death of the insured.[11]
2. The value of property acquired by gift or inheritance.[12]
3. Insurance premiums refunded for any reason including the cancellation of the policy.
4. The rental value of improved real property if occupied by the owner thereof.[13]
5. Amounts received by employees as indemnification upon the rescission of an employment contract.
6. Pensions and retirement pay received in certain cases of illness.
7. Authors' royalties and the remuneration and retirement pensions of professors, teachers, and journalists.[14]

The exemptions do not extend to interest and other increments of the principal received tax-free under 1, 2, 3, 5, and 6 above.

6/1.3 Nonresident Individuals

a. CONCEPT OF INCOME. Whether the concept of taxable income, as applied to nonresident individuals, has the same meaning as in the case of residents, or whether it is more extensive, is not free from doubt. If the first interpretation is the correct one, only such items as would constitute taxable income in the hands of a resident will be subject to taxation if realized by a nonresident; if the latter interpretation prevails, the few statutory exemptions discussed below will constitute the only limitation on the taxation of nonresidents. There are statements in the decisions to the effect that a nonresident is taxed on all his income from Brazilian sources, regardless of its nature.[15] The range of income held to be taxable to a nonresident includes royalties, salaries, commissions,[16] fees for services rendered abroad, interest, dividends, and various benefits, gratuities, bonuses, pensions, and annuities. On the other hand, it may well be argued that the foregoing enumeration does not include any item which would not be taxable in the hands of a resident, and that the law probably does not intend to tax nonresidents on items of gain which do not fall into the general concept of income under its system. The following items have been held *not* to constitute taxable income to nonresidents: remittances in payment of imported merchandise (as constituting gross re-

---

[11] Regardless of whether payment is made in a lump sum or in the form of an annuity, Rezende, Note 50. But amounts paid in addition to the capital (interest, participations in the profits of the insurance company, etc.) are taxable, Reg. Art. 11 §3.

[12] I.e., the capital transferred. Income accruing on such capital is taxable, Reg. Art. 11 §3; Rezende, Note 50-A.

[13] Consequently, expenses in connection with real property occupied by the owner thereof (taxes, interest, etc.) are not deductible.

[14] Constitution of 1946, Art. 203; Income Tax Reg. Art. 24 §3.

[15] DIR, *Rev.* 1948 No. 457 and 1949 No. 682.

[16] Except commissions exempt under the provisions of Reg. Art. 97 §2(a) and (b); see 6/1.3b.

ceipts, not gross income or profits, of the foreign vendor); [17] remittances in payment of premiums on insurance contracted abroad (as constituting gross receipts, not gross income or profits, of the foreign insurer);[18] gain on the sale of real property by a nonresident vendor was held not taxable under Reg. Art. 97 because this provision refers to income, whereas the gain on the sale is a capital gain; [19] gains on the sale of securities, because such gains would not be taxable to a resident taxpayer.[20]

The correct view would seem to be that, while items of income do not necessarily have to meet the requirements of any one of the schedular classifications applying to residents in order to constitute taxable income if realized by a nonresident, they must at least come under the traditional concept of gross income or profits in order to be the object of taxation. If this is so, it is apparent that the area of doubt will be limited to a few rare and extraordinary cases. Within this area, the determining factor will probably be whether the receipts in question are in the nature of gross income or profits as distinguished from gross receipts, or payments on capital account.

It has been held that the exemption in favor of authors' royalties [21] does not apply to nonresidents and that therefore such payments, if remitted abroad, are subject to the withholding tax on nonresidents under Reg. Art. 97.[22] The validity of these rulings, however, is doubtful.[23]

b. TAX-EXEMPT INCOME. The following items of income realized by non-residents are specifically exempted from the requirement of withholding of income tax at the source (Reg. Art. 97, §2); they are, consequently, not subject to income tax at all:

1. Commissions paid by exporters of any Brazilian products to their agents abroad.
2. Commissions paid by Brazilian shipping lines to their agents abroad, for any services rendered by the latter.

The income of individuals domiciled in Brazil who are absent from the country for reasons of government service or foreign studies is not

---

[17] CC, *Rev.* 1949 No. 675; Sousa, §46.

[18] CC, *Rev.* 1951 No. 158; see also *Rev.* 1952 No. 621. These decisions are criticized by Gilberto de Ulhoa Canto in 13 *Revista de Direito Administrativo* 477 on the ground that the risk is located in Brazil and therefore the insurer's income from premiums is earned in Brazil.

[19] DIR, *Rev.* 1951 No. 1175; CC, *Rev.* 1951 No. 1107.

[20] DIR, *Rev.* 1943 No. 239. The ruling of the Income Tax Division in *Rev.* 1949 No. 594 (capital gains of nonresidents resulting from a reorganization) is to the contrary; see criticism of this decision by Rezende, Note 283.

[21] See 5/5.3.

[22] DIR, *Rev.* 1948 No. 457; 1951 No. 352.

[23] Especially in view of the constitutional exemption in favor of authors' royalties (Constitution of Brazil, Art. 203) and the fact that nationality is not a material factor under the Income Tax Regulations (Reg. Arts. 1 and 97). On the other hand, it might be pointed out that the Constitution of Brazil (Art. 141) guarantees equal rights to citizens and *resident* foreigners.

exempt from tax, but merely from the withholding provisions applicable to nonresidents; these individuals are obliged to report their taxable income in a return to be filed with the foreign representative of the Brazilian Treasury.[24]

6/1.4 Entities

In the case of entities, the Income Tax Regulations provide three different bases of the tax, namely, actual profits, presumed profits, and estimated profits. The term "entities" includes partnerships, sole proprietorships, and individuals engaged in business.

Taxation on the basis of actual profits is the method of taxation which applies in the large majority of cases. A detailed analysis of this method is given in Chapter 7.

For a discussion of the other two methods of taxation (presumed profits and estimated profits), see 6/9.1 and 6/9.2.

6/2. Books and Records

6/2.1 General Rules

Taxation on the basis of actual profits is the usual method of taxing business income. The starting point for computing taxable income is the book income with certain adjustments for tax purposes listed below. Art. 32 of the Income Tax Regulations prescribes that the actual profits of entities shall be determined annually on the basis of their balance sheet and profit and loss account. Under Reg. Art. 34, the actual profits must be proved by books of account which are kept in the language of the country, in Brazilian currency,[25] and in the form prescribed by the commercial and fiscal law. The books must show all transactions of the taxpayer in Brazilian territory as well as the profits thereof from year to year.[26]

It follows from the above provisions that the maintenance of proper books and accounting records is an indispensable condition of taxation on the basis of actual profits. A violation of the precepts of Reg. Art. 34, i.e., the failure of a legal entity to keep books or to keep them in adequate form, will invariably result in taxation on the basis of estimated profits (Reg. Art. 34 and 6/9.2 below).

[24] Provided that they receive the income through this agency. Reg. Art. 73.

[25] The Income Tax Regulations promulgated in 1955 introduced an important innovation to the effect that taxpayers are no longer permitted to keep their accounts in foreign currency. Formerly such accounts were permitted, especially in the case of foreign public utility companies. The conversion to cruzeiros must be made in the first return filed after the effective date of the law (January 1, 1955). Reg. Art. 206. Whereas the law does not give an indication as to the proper rate of exchange (see on this question, 11/2.4) it states (Reg. Art. 206 Sole §) that book profits resulting from the conversion shall not be included in taxable income.

[26] Reg. Art. 34 §1.

Neither the income tax law nor the commercial law referred to in Art. 34 of the Income Tax Regulations prescribes any particular system of accounting. It is left to the taxpayer to select the system which is best suited to its particular situation, provided that it discloses all individual business transactions with clarity and individuality. The principle which is evident from the administrative and judicial decisions is clearly that only a system which presents all business events in full detail will be acceptable for income tax purposes.

The rules of the Income Tax Regulations in reference to the books to be kept apply to the Brazilian branches [27] of a foreign enterprise (Reg. Art. 141 §9); the same is true regarding the books prescribed by the commercial law.[28]

The maintenance of a few books of original entry is prescribed in part by the Income Tax Regulations, and in part by the commercial law.

6/2.2   Required Books

The "indispensable" books, which are absolutely required under the commercial law,[29] are the journal and the press-copy letter book.

The journal must contain a precise and detailed record of all business transactions entered into by the taxpayer, especially in regard to all receipts and disbursements either for the account of the firm or of third parties; it must show all credit instruments issued, accepted, or endorsed by the taxpayer, and it must include a summary of the last balance sheet.[30] The copy letter book represents a file of all letters sent out by the taxpayer together with the invoices, statements of account, and other data which accompanied those letters.

In addition to the journal and the press-copy letter book, all entities must maintain the following books and have them legalized (stamped) by the authorities:

1. Cash sales register.
2. Sales tax stamps register.
3. Press-copy invoice book.
4. Register of customers' signed accounts.
5. Inventory register.
6. Purchase register.

[27] "Filiais," "sucursais," "agências." These terms all refer to divisions of the same legal entity. The words have no precise legal definition but are in common usage as denoting branches of lesser importance, in the order named.
[28] Corp. Law, Art. 68, prescribes that all activities of foreign companies exercised in Brazil are subject to the laws of Brazil.
[29] Commercial Code, Arts. 11–14.
[30] Monthly entries in the journal in summarized form are acceptable, provided there are subsidiary records disclosing the detail of all transactions and that these detailed records observe the rules of Arts. 12 and 14 of the Commercial Code. See Rezende, Note 126.

In addition to the foregoing, corporations are required to keep the following books and have them legalized:

1. Register of nominative shares.
2. Transfer register of nominative shares.
3. Minute book of shareholders' general meetings.
4. Register of shareholders attending general meetings.
5. Minute book of directors' meetings.
6. Minute book of the meetings of the fiscal committee.
7. Register of participating certificates.
8. Register of transfer of participating certificates.

The entries in the books must be made according to commercial usage and in chronological order. Blank spaces, erasures, interlineations and other corrections are prohibited (Commercial Code Art. 14).

The books must be bound and the pages numbered consecutively. They must be stamped and legalized on every page.[31] Under the provisions of Art. 13 of the Commercial Code, the legalization of books was the function of the commercial courts but since such courts have ceased to exist, books are legalized by the Commercial Registry which is a state recording office existing in the capital of each state.[32]

It should be noted that the Commercial Code dates back to 1850 and that its obviously obsolete provisions in the matter of bookkeeping are observed in a purely formal manner. The required books are kept, but they are kept merely as copies of accounts maintained in accordance with more modern methods. As an example, only letters which are of particular importance or which may have to be presented as evidence in the courts will be reproduced in the press-copy letter book. In practice, at least a formal compliance with the antiquated rules is essential to prevent a rejection of the taxpayer's return and taxation on the basis of estimated profits, and this formal observance of the provisions of the Commercial Code is all that is required.

The inventory book and purchase register referred to above are required by Art. 141 of the Income Tax Regulations. The provision is applicable to entities resident in Brazil whose capital is in excess of Cr$ 50,-000,[33] and to the Brazilian branch of a foreign corporation regardless of the amount of capital employed in Brazil. A looseleaf system of cards in lieu of these books is acceptable. The books or cards must be registered with and legalized by the authorities listed in the law. The inventory book must list all inventories of raw material, goods in process, and

---

[31] Books which are not legalized are nonexistent for income tax purposes and the tax is assessed on the basis of estimated profits, CC, *Rev.* 1951 No. 502.

[32] Civil societies (partnerships of lawyers, physicians, accountants, etc.) are not subject to commercial legislation; their books must be registered and authenticated by the income tax offices as provided in Reg. Art. 22 §3; DIR, *Rev.* 1951 No. 742.

[33] Regardless of the volume of business transacted; see Rezende, Note 342.

finished products produced or purchased by the taxpayer. Freight and cartage, insurance, and customs duties are part of the cost of merchandise and as such must be entered in the purchase book.[34]

6/3. Accounting Periods

6/3.1 Base Year and Taxable Year

The income tax returns of individuals and entities must be filed between January 1 and April 30 of every year. The year in which the return is due to be filed and the tax is payable is the taxable year. The tax paid *during* any taxable year is also the tax *for* such year. It is measured, however, by the income of a preceding period of twelve consecutive months which is called the base year. As an example, the income tax return of a taxpayer for taxable year 1955 is filed on or before April 30, 1955, but it is based on the income of calendar year 1954 or, in the case of a taxpayer reporting on the basis of a fiscal year, the income of the fiscal year ending in 1954.

In the case of an entity, the base year may be either the calendar year immediately preceding the taxable year, or a fiscal year ending on any day of that calendar year (Reg. Art. 38). In the case of individual taxpayers, the base year is always the calendar year immediately preceding the taxable year; individuals, as distinguished from entities, are not allowed to report their income on the basis of a fiscal year (Reg. Art. 22).

In general, the income tax return must cover a full calendar or fiscal year. A return covering a period of either more or less than 12 months may be required in the case of a change in the taxpayer's accounting period. Such a change may be made without authorization by the government. If it is made, the return will be based on the actual profits realized by the taxpayer between the date of the balance sheet accompanying the last income tax return filed and the most recent balance sheet prepared. Annualization of income is not required.

6/3.2 Change of Accounting Period from Calendar Year to Fiscal Year Basis

The financial statements of a company and the returns based thereon may include a period of more or less than 12 months.[35] In the case of a change from calendar year to fiscal year, a short business year (one

---

[34] DIR, *Rev.* 1949 No. 140.

[35] Before Law No. 2,354 of November 29, 1954, a return had to cover a period of neither more nor less than 12 calendar months in practically every case. Under this rule a taxpayer could avoid taxation of some income by changing his accounting period. It was the purpose of the amending provisions to preclude such possibilities for the future.

which covers a period of less than 12 months) will result, and this is the base period for purposes of the return.[36]

Example 1

A corporation changes in 1954 from the calendar year basis to a fiscal year ending June 30. Its last return (based on calendar year 1953) was filed on or before April 30, 1954.

The return of the taxpayer for the year 1955 (due April 30, 1955) will be based on the six-month period ended June 30, 1954; beginning with 1956, the returns will be based on a full fiscal year ending June 30.

6/3.3   Change from Fiscal Year to Calendar Year

Example 2

A corporation changed in 1953 from a fiscal year ending February 28 to the calendar year basis. Its 1954 return, based on the year ended February 28, 1953, was filed April 30, 1954.

The corporation is required to include in its return for the year 1955 the income of the 22-month period from March 1, 1953, to December 31, 1954. The return should be accompanied by two sets of financial statements covering the periods from March 1 to December 31, 1953, and from January 1 to December 31, 1954, respectively.

6/3.4   Change from One Fiscal Year to Another

The principles discussed under 6/3.2 and 6/3.3 above apply (depending on whether the change is made to a preceding or succeeding month of the calendar year, respectively).

Example 3

Corporation X has reported its income on the basis of a fiscal year ending June 30, and its last return on this basis was filed April 30, 1954, covering the year ended June 30, 1953. It decides in 1954 to change to a fiscal year ending April 30. The returns of the corporation for the years 1955 and 1956 should cover the following periods:

1955 return: Period from July 1, 1953, to either April 30, 1954, or June 30, 1954, according to the dates of the statements prepared.

1956 return: Period beginning either May 1, 1954, or July 1, 1954, and ending April 30, 1955.

6/3.5   Change of Accounting Period in the Case of Reorganizations

The principles set forth in 6/3.2–6/3.4 above apply in the case of reorganizations, e.g., the incorporation of a single proprietorship,[37] or the merger or consolidation of several entities with different fiscal years.[38]

[36] For purposes of control, entities are now required to file financial statements and supporting information for the *two* last business years with their returns in the case of a change of accounting period, Reg. Art. 38 §2. Regarding the information to be submitted, see 13/1.2a.

[37] DIR, *Rev.* 1943 No. 363.

[38] DIR, *Rev.* 1947 No. 457.

6/3.6   Commencement of Operations

The first return of a legal entity is based on the income realized between the date when operations commenced and December 31 of that year (Reg. Art. 62).[39] An entity which begins and terminates its activities in the same calendar year is obliged to file a return when it ceases its operations [40] and to include therein the results of the period during which it was in existence (Reg. Art. 62 §1). Annualization of income is not required.

The Income Tax Regulations further provide (Art. 62 §2) that an entity which fails to prepare financial statements for the first year during which it is in existence, will be taxed on the basis of presumed profits according to the rules applying to this method under Reg. Art. 40.[41] Whether this provision applies generally to the first year of operations of legal entities, or only to those which begin and terminate their activities in the same year,[42] is doubtful. Although there is strong authority for the first-mentioned interpretation,[43] the second would seem to be preferable. Taxation on the basis of presumed profits normally is an elective method which is quite favorable to taxpayers qualified to make the election. That a taxpayer not qualified to elect this method should be at liberty to enforce its application by his failure to prepare financial statements for the initial period of business is an incongruous result. The incongruity is emphasized by the fact that a failure of this kind normally results in estimation of profits, a method which is designed to protect the interests of the government and which is entirely unfavorable from the taxpayer's point of view.[44]

To the extent that the tax is based on presumed profits for the first year of operations, the method applies to all entities including those which are not qualified to elect it.[45] Taxable income, under this method,

[39] This provision constitutes an exception to the general rule that a return must be based on a full twelve month period of operations.

The Income Tax Regulations do not provide for the case in which a legal entity adopts a fiscal year at the beginning of its operations. It appears that in this situation a return must be filed in the year succeeding that of the formation of the company covering the results from the date of formation until December 31, and that in the next following year, the procedure will be the same as that which applies in the case of a change from calendar to fiscal year.

[40] Reg. Art. 62 §1 requires that the return be filed "immediately." This requirement is generally interpreted in the light of Reg. Art. 52, i.e., that the return must be filed within 30 days from the date on which the liquidation of the company is terminated. Sousa, §40; Rezende and Viana, *Consolidação*, Note 205-A.

[41] See discussion of this method in 6/9.1.

[42] Expressed differently, the question is whether the scope of Reg. Art. 62 §2 is determined by Reg. Art. 62 first section, or Reg. Art. 62 §1.

[43] DIR, *Rev.* 1943 No. 687; *Rev.* 1948 No. 651; CC, *Rev.* 1955 No. 170; Rezende, Note 205.

[44] See discussion of this method in 6/9.2.

[45] Corporations, limited liability companies, branches of foreign entities, and other

is deemed to be equal to 8% of the annual gross receipts (Reg. Art. 40). If the taxpayer had not actually started its business operations during the initial period and not realized any receipts, it would seem obvious that an income tax should not be assessed. Some older decisions, however, took the view that an income tax might be computed in this situation on estimated profits, i.e., a percentage of assets or capital.[46]

6/3.7 Termination of Operations

A legal entity must file two income tax returns during the final period of its existence. One is the usual return based on the income of the preceding fiscal or calendar year. The other return must include the income from the beginning of the current business year until the date of dissolution (Reg. Art. 52; 9/9.2). In the case of this latter period, the base year and the taxable year are identical.

A company which cannot elect to be taxed on the basis of presumed profits and fails to prepare financial statements at the end of the final period of its activities is subject to taxation on the basis of estimated profits under Reg. Art. 34 §4.[47]

6/4. Accounting Methods — Cash Basis and Accrual Basis

6/4.1 Individuals

The Income Tax Regulations prescribe the use of the cash basis of reporting income for individual taxpayers in regard to nonbusiness income (for individuals engaged in business, see a, below). The application of this method, however, differs depending on whether a receipt or a disbursement is involved.

a. RECEIPTS. Reg. Art. 22 §1 requires the inclusion in gross income of all items which during the base year were legally at the disposition of the taxpayer, including those originating in a prior year. This rule in effect prescribes the inclusion of constructive receipts in gross income besides actual receipts during the base period.

All items of income actually received in cash during the base period must be included even if they pertain to a different year such as prepaid rent [48] or interest accrued over several years.[49] On the theory of constructive receipt, the crediting of income by the debtor is the equivalent of the

taxpayers whose capital exceeds Cr$ 100,000 or whose annual gross income exceeds Cr$ 500,000, Reg. Art. 33 and its §1. See Rezende, Note 205; Rezende and Viana, *Novo Regulamento do Impôsto de Renda* (Rio de Janeiro, 1955), Note 190.

[46] DIR, *Rev.* 1947 No. 655; *Rev.* 1948 No. 151. See criticism of these decisions in Rezende, Note 205.

[47] DIR, *Rev.* 1951 No. 677. See Rezende, Note 185-E.

[48] DIR, *Rev.* 1944 No. 191. See Rezende, Note 103.

[49] DIR, *Rev.* 1949 No. 424; CC, *Rev.* 1951 No. 273.

payment thereof unless the debtor is insolvent; again, it is immaterial whether the income credited in a particular base year was earned in that year or not. In the matter of dividends paid on nominative shares [50] it has been held [51] that a dividend is at the disposition of the shareholder at the end of the business year for which it is declared by the corporation, provided that the payment of the dividend is decided upon by the general meeting of shareholders.[52] The same holds true for directors' fees.[53] The profits of entities (including partnerships) become income of the owners or partners only if and when they are credited or distributed to them.[54] An exception to this rule is recognized in the case of sole proprietorships whose profits are considered to be always at the disposition of the owner; the latter must therefore include these profits in his taxable income of the year in which they are earned, regardless of any credit or withdrawal.[55]

In the case of income from foreign sources, it seems to be the administrative practice to abandon the principle of constructive receipt and to require the taxpayer to include only income actually received in Brazil during the base period.[56]

Receipts which are returned by the taxpayer are not includible in taxable income. This rule applies even if the receipt is returned in the year following the base year, provided that the tax is not yet assessed at the time the refund is made (CC, *Rev.* 1949 No. 988).

[50] Dividends paid on bearer shares are subject to taxation at the source; see 9/2.2.

[51] CC, *Rev.* 1948 No. 837; 1949 No. 779; 1950 No. 144; 1951 Nos. 514 and 1039.

[52] This meeting will, of course, be held after the end of the business year. The general meeting of the shareholders alone has authority to approve the financial statements submitted by the directors (Corp. Law, Art. 98). Therefore, the financial statements for any given business year and any dividends proposed by the directors acquire legal existence only as and when they are approved by the general meeting. Consequently the dividend is legally at the disposition of the shareholders only as of the date of such approval. The decisions, however, generally hold (but with occasional doubts) that the approval by the general meeting is retroactive to the end of the business year for which the dividend is declared and that, therefore, the tax on the dividend is due as of the end of such year. See DIR, *Rev.* 1951 No. 372; CC, *Rev.* 1951 No. 619. Whether the approval of the dividend always has retroactive effect or only if the meeting is held within the statutory period of four months (Corp. Law, Art. 98, Sole §) is not entirely clear. See CC, *Rev.* 1951 No. 514. The Income Tax Division is opposed to the theory of "retroactivity" which leads to taxation of the dividend at the (usually lower) tax rates of the preceding year. See Rezende, Note 103. The provision of Art. 211 of the present Income Tax Regulations intends to put an end to the controversy by stating that the rates under the present law are applicable to income taxable after January 1, 1955, *even though previously produced.*   [53] CC, *Rev.* 1950 No. 144.

[54] This does not include tax-paid amounts credited by a company to a reserve account, CC, *Rev.* 1949 No. 735 (credits to a tax reserve); the rule is different if reserves, although accumulated in various years, are distributed to the members, CC, *Rev.* 1950 No. 5. Amounts transferred to a reserve for the increase of the capital of a limited liability company, charged to profit and loss in proportion to the participations of the members, are taxable income to the latter, *Rev.* 1950 No. 110; 1951 No. 155.   [55] See Rezende, Note 103.

[56] See 11/2.2 and rulings cited there.

b. DISBURSEMENTS. The treatment of disbursements differs from that of receipts in that only expenses actually paid during the base year are recognized as deductions for purposes of the schedular tax and as abatements for purposes of the complementary tax.[57] Thus, in computing deductions and abatements, constructive payments are not recognized, and credits are not the equivalent of payment.[58]

6/4.2   Entities

Whereas the income tax law clearly prescribes the use of the cash basis for individual taxpayers, it does not contain any provisions regulating the accounting basis of income reported by entities.[59] The fundamental principle laid down in Reg. Art. 34 is that taxable income will be determined on the basis of the books of the company, which must clearly reflect the results of its activities in Brazilian territory from year to year, and which must be kept as prescribed by the commercial and fiscal law.

This principle evidently does not clearly prescribe the use either of the cash receipts and disbursements basis or of the accrual basis of accounting. Reg. Art. 37 (a), which states that an expense must have been "realized" in the course of the business year to qualify as a proper deduction, also contributes little to the specific problem under review. In actual practice, the use of the accrual basis is required as regards items of income, and it is permitted regarding expenses. The rule, in effect, is that income is taxable when earned, whether it is collected or not, and that the deduction of expenses which represent a definite and enforceable liability of the taxpayer will be permitted even if payment thereof is not made before the end of the base year, provided that they are properly entered in the books at that time.[60]

Enterprises engaged in the building of highways, railroads, and similar construction work extending over more than one taxable year must include the entire profit from a particular job in their taxable income of the year of completion (Reg. Art. 56).

6/5.   Valuation of Assets

6/5.1   Inventories

According to Art. 141 of the Income Tax Regulations [61] which states the rules for the valuation of inventories, the values of the various items

[57] This principle is stated in Reg. Art. 12 §1 (schedular tax); the cited provision is incorporated by reference in Reg. Art. 20 (complementary tax).

[58] CC, *Rev.* 1951 No. 965; Rezende, Note 102.

[59] The term includes sole proprietorships and individuals engaged in business, see 5/3.4.

[60] CC, *Rev.* 1955 No. 190. Regarding the deduction of bonuses paid to employees, see 7/2.3; regarding deduction of taxes, see 7/2.7.

[61] The provision is applicable to entities with capital in excess of Cr$ 50,000.

must be reflected in the inventory book maintained by the taxpayer.[62]

The inventories of raw materials and goods in process of a taxpayer engaged in manufacturing must be listed at cost (Reg. Art. 141 §3). Finished products and merchandise bought for resale, however, should be listed at the lower of cost (of production or acquisition) or market, and this provision applies to manufacturing as well as trading businesses (Reg. Art. 141 §4).

The cost of a manufactured product includes the elements of raw material, direct labor, and overhead;[63] in the case of merchandise bought for resale, expenses directly incurred in connection with the purchase, such as freight, cartage, and customs duties, are added to the cost.[64] Goods of the same kind bought at various times and at different prices may be valued on the basis of average cost as well as under the first-in, first-out method. The use of a standard cost system is permitted.[65] Whether the valuation of inventories by way of a percentage mark-down from sales prices ("retail method of inventory valuation") is acceptable under Brazilian practice is very doubtful.[66] In no case may estimated figures be substituted for the actual cost of production.[67]

The Income Tax Regulations do not define the term "market," except by indicating that the market value of merchandise traded on an exchange is the exchange price on the balance sheet date (Reg. Art. 141 §4).

Blanket reductions of the values shown in the inventory are prohibited (Reg. Art. 141 §5). This rule merely prohibits arbitrary write-downs of inventories on account of their actual or anticipated decline in value; it does not conflict with the substitution of an actual market price for a higher cost price.

The use of valuation reserves to provide for the decline in value of inventories is permitted for book purposes; these reserves may not, however, be deducted in computing taxable income (Reg. Art. 141 §5).

The rules of the Corporation Law [68] regarding the valuation of inventories are identical with those of the Income Tax Regulations just discussed, except that valuation at cost or market, whichever is lower, is prescribed for all merchandise including raw materials and presumably goods in process. There is no apparent reason for this discrepancy between the commercial law and the income tax statute.

---

62 The physical inventory must be taken as of the effective date of the balance sheet, DIR, *Rev.* 1948 No. 543.

63 See Rezende, Note 342-B.

64 Rezende, Note 342-A.

65 DIR, *Rev.* 1949 No. 487. The Income Tax Regulations do not require or permit the use of any particular method or methods of valuation. The methods enumerated in the text have been used by taxpayers and accepted by the Division. The acceptability of the last-in, first-out method is doubtful.

66 Admitted by CC, *Rev.* 1952 No. 791; not admitted by DIR, *Rev.* 1951 No. 765.

67 DIR, *Rev.* 1951 No. 1010.

68 Corp. Law, Art. 129 Sole §(b).

By express provision of the Corporation Law,[69] an excess of the market or sales value of inventory items over their cost (of production or acquisition) may not be distributed to the stockholders as a dividend because it does not constitute a realized profit, nor may this increased value be reflected in the computation of reserves based on a percentage of the profits.

6/5.2 Receivables

Receivables which are barred by the statute of limitations may not be included among the assets of the firm. Receivables which are of doubtful collectibility must likewise be excluded unless there is a suitable reserve [70] against such items on the books (Corp. Law, Art. 129 Sole §[c]).

6/5.3 Securities

Shares of corporations and other securities held in the portfolio of the firm must be valued at actual cost.[71] The deduction of a valuation reserve, while permissible or even required under the commercial law and accepted accounting principles, is not permitted for income tax purposes. A loss deduction is allowed only after the loss has been actually realized through a sale or other disposition of the securities (7/2.6).

6/5.4 Fixed Assets

Fixed assets used in the business of the taxpayer must be valued at historical cost, and the taxpayer may not use a higher appraisal value for depreciation purposes. For movable property subject to decline in value through use or the passage of time, suitable reserves for depreciation and amortization must be provided (Corp. Law Art. 129 Sole §[a]).[72]

Depreciation of real property is not allowed for income tax purposes.

The Corporation Law (Art. 130 §2) further provides that, if the reserve for depreciation or amortization exceeds the cost of the related asset, the excess reserve must be distributed to the shareholders in the form of a cash dividend.

6/6. Reserves

6/6.1 Reserves and Provisions

Brazilian income tax law draws a distinction between "provisions" (*provisões*) and "reserves" (*reservas*) in the technical sense of the term.

---

[69] Corp. Law, Art. 129 Sole §(a).

[70] Notwithstanding the wording of the statute (*reserva equivalente*), the law does not require a reserve in the full nominal amount of such receivables.

[71] Corp. Law, Art. 129 Sole §(b).

[72] See discussion of the depreciation deduction in 7/3.1–7/3.6.

"Provisions" are amounts which constitute deductible expenses within the limits set by the law; included in this classification are provisions for bad debts,[73] for depreciation,[74] depletion [75] and amortization, and the special reserves of insurance and capitalization companies.[76] All other amounts which a corporation or company appropriates from surplus or current profits and credits to a reserve account must be restored to profits for income tax purposes.[77]

The rules of the income tax law regarding reserves apply to all legal entities, except individual proprietorships, even though the latter assume the status of entities under the income tax law. Individual proprietorships cannot have reserves in the proper sense because their profits, regardless of how they are treated on the books, are always at the disposition of the owner, and they are taxed accordingly.[78] Partnerships, on the other hand, can have reserves the same as incorporated entities.

Under established judicial practice, the Brazilian branch of a foreign corporation or company is an integral part of the foreign organization and cannot have reserves of its own. The profits of the branch are deemed to be distributed to its home office as soon as such profits are determined, i.e., as of the balance sheet date.[79] It is a very important consequence of this principle that the Brazilian branch of a foreign corporation is not subject to the 4% charge on reserves (see 7/8.2) and, in particular, the 30% tax on excess reserves (see 7/8.3).

6/6.2   Statutory Regulation of Reserves

Every corporation organized in Brazil is obliged to credit an amount of 5% of its annual net profits to a statutory reserve before it makes any other appropriation of profits, in order to ensure the integrity of its capital. This appropriation ceases to be mandatory as soon as the accumulated reserve equals 20% of the share capital; like other reserves, it may be increased through voluntary appropriations until the total of *all* reserves is equal to the full amount of the paid-in capital stock.[80]

Except for certain special reserves required of insurance and capitalization companies, the law prescribes only the statutory reserve just referred to. The bylaws of the company may provide for other reserves to be set up, and they may regulate the order in which profits are to be allocated to such reserves.[81]

The appropriations discussed above are reserves in the technical sense of the term as applied in Brazilian income tax law. Therefore, the

---

[73] Reg. Art. 37(c).   [74] Reg. Art. 37(d).   [75] Reg. Art. 37(f).
[76] Reg. Art. 37 §1(a).   [77] Reg. Art. 43 §1(f)–(m).
[78] See DIR, *Rev.* 1952 No. 85; Rezende, Note 281-B.
[79] The rules of taxation applying to these branches are discussed in 11/3.3.
[80] If the capital is impaired through losses, appropriations of profits must be resumed until the reserve is restored, Corp. Law, Art. 130.
[81] Corp. Law, Art. 130 §1.

amounts appropriated to any one of these reserves, including the one required by statute, are not deductible for income tax purposes.

The total annual profits of a corporation may never be transferred to reserve accounts.[82] This rule does not imply that an annual distribution of dividends is required under Brazilian corporation law; its purpose is merely to safeguard the maintenance of a free balance of undistributed profits.[83]

The total of all reserves must not exceed the amount of the paid-in capital stock of the corporation,[84] and in this context the term "reserves" includes surplus. Any amount in excess of this limit must be distributed to the stockholders as either a cash dividend or a stock dividend, or be utilized by the corporation to cover unpaid subscriptions to its capital stock. In all these situations, the shareholder realizes taxable income.

An increase of the reserves (including surplus) beyond the statutory limit of the paid-in capital stock results in the imposition of a tax of 30% on the excess. The 30% tax is incurred only if the general meeting votes to add the whole or a part of the annual profits to reserves or undistributed surplus, when, as a result of such addition, their total exceeds the paid-in capital. If the general meeting decides to distribute this surplus, or to capitalize it, the 30% tax is avoided.

For the 4% charge (in the nature of an enforced loan) on reserves, see 7/8.2.

For the 30% tax on excess reserves, see 7/8.3.

6/7. Head Office and Branch Office Accounting

6/7.1 Centralized and Decentralized Accounting

The maintenance of a centralized accounting system is optional. It is, therefore, entirely permissible to maintain separate accounting records for a branch [85] and to compute its profits independently. Whether or not the accounting system is centralized, the results of the branch must be consolidated with those of the head office (Reg. Art. 34 §2), and a single income tax return filed by the latter.[86] The filing of separate returns for head office and branch is not permitted.[87]

---

[82] Corp. Law, Art. 130 §1.

[83] See Sousa, §33(B)(b).

[84] Corp. Law, Art. 130 §2.

[85] The books of the branch must be legalized by the proper authority, the same as the books of the head office, DIR, *Rev.* 1951 No. 332.

[86] If a decentralized system of accounting is used, separate financial statements of the branch must be included in the information to be filed with the return under the provisions of Reg. Art. 38.

[87] If two separate income tax returns are filed by the head office and the branch, one based on actual profits and the other on presumed profits, the returns will be consolidated. See decisions quoted in Rezende, Note 128. The tax will in this situation be computed on estimated profits.

6/7.2 Local Branch of Nonresident Entity

For the taxation of the Brazilian branch of a foreign corporation or company, see 11/3.3.

6/8.   Attribution Rules

6/8.1 In General

Reg. Art. 1 Sole § states the rule that whoever has the possession of property as if the property belonged to him is taxed on the income from such property. The interpretation of this rule in judicial and administrative practice includes both the case in which the taxpayer is in possession of the property under a claim of right and the very different one in which the taxpayer acts as a trustee or agent for another but does not disclose the identity of his principal to third parties.

The principle of the cited section of the Income Tax Regulations has been applied to the following situations:

A taxpayer alleged that he had assigned the rental income from urban real property to his sons by way of an anticipated distribution of his future estate; the real property continued to be owned by the taxpayer and no formal contract existed between him and the sons regarding the alleged advancement, as required by law. It was held that the taxpayer remained liable for income tax on the rents (Ministry of Finance, *Rev.* 1950 No. 710).

A partner who assigns part of his partnership share to a third party but does not disclose the assignment and continues to collect the profits pertaining to his full share is taxable as regards these distributions (DIR, *Rev.* 1948 No. 147).

A taxpayer who fails to prove that money deposited by him in a bank belongs to another is taxable on the interest on the deposit (CC, *Rev.* 1950 No. 147); similarly, if shares actually owned by a bank are held in the name of an individual because the bank is prevented by law from owning shares in its own name, the individual is subject to income tax on the dividends paid and other distributions made on the shares (CC, *Rev.* 1954 No. 274).

The holder of a power of attorney whose authority is limited to administering property and to negotiating (even if he may exercise the power for his own benefit) is not taxed on the income from the property. If, however, the right to the income which he collects is assigned to him, he becomes liable for income tax on the collections (DIR, *Rev.* 1947 No. 565).

In the case of a usufruct, the usufructuary is taxed on the income from the property transferred to him (CC, *Rev.* 1948 No. 76). If the usufruct is terminated by the death of the usufructuary, the owner to whom the property reverts is not liable for tax on the income therefrom as long as the usufruct is not declared to be terminated in appropriate legal proceedings and the owner has not regained possession of the property. He first reports the income in the year following the one during which these events happen (DIR, *Rev.* 1948 No. 463).

6/9. Alternative Methods of Determining the Tax Base

6/9.1 Taxation on the Basis of Presumed Profits

Taxation on the basis of presumed profits is a privilege which the law accords to certain legal entities at their election. Corporations, limited liability companies,[88] other entities with capital exceeding Cr$ 100,000 or with annual gross income exceeding Cr$ 500,000,[89] and Brazilian branches or agencies of foreign entities [90] may not exercise this option (Reg. Art. 33).[91] The "presumed profits" which form the basis of taxation under this method are defined as an amount equal to 8% of the gross income (if in excess of Cr$ 150,000) realized during the base year.[92] No deductions of any kind are permitted. The term "gross income" includes all receipts of the taxpayer from any source regardless of whether they result from transactions for the taxpayer's own account or from compensation for services rendered, and regardless of whether the transactions are normal and usual in the taxpayer's business or foreign to its object and purpose (Reg. Arts. 40 and 42).

To the presumed profit determined as outlined above, the regular tax rates under Reg. Art. 44 are applied.

The amount of the sales and receipts which form the basis of taxation of presumed profits can be determined and proved only from the books of the taxpayer (Reg. Art. 41). If no books are kept or the existing books are unacceptable to the tax authorities, neither actual nor presumed profits can serve as the basis of taxation and the tax will be computed on the basis of estimated profits, discussed immediately below.

The election to be taxed on the basis of presumed profits is made in the income tax return of the taxpayer for the year to which the election applies and it is irrevocable for that year (Reg. Art. 33 §2).

88 CC, *Rev.* 1954 No. 412. For an exceptional case of the taxation of a limited liability company on the basis of presumed profits (office and records destroyed by fire shortly before the end of the business year), see CC, *Rev.* 1949 No. 178.

89 The amount of *profits* realized is immaterial.

90 These are always taxed on the basis of actual profits, Reg. Art. 33 §1.

91 Under an amendment to Reg. Art. 33 by Law No. 2,354 of November 29, 1954, agricultural companies of any type whose gross annual income is not in excess of Cr$ 1,000,000 may elect to be taxed on the basis of presumed profits. Reg. Art. 33 §3.

92 Reg. Art. 41 uses the term *"ano civil"* exclusively. It follows that the taxpayer must report on the basis of the calendar year. When the presumed profits are based on gross proceeds from sales, the income is determined from the sales register for the preceding calendar year.

Regarding the application of this method of taxation to a company which begins and terminates its operations in the same calendar year, see 6/3.6 above.

6/9.2   Taxation on the Basis of Estimated Profits

Unlike the system of taxation on the basis of presumed profits, taxation on the basis of estimated profits is not a privilege available to certain taxpayers, but an alternative method provided by law to protect the interests of the government when legal entities either keep no books of account or keep such deficient ones that no adequate determination of taxable income is possible (Reg. Art. 34 §4).

The statutory requirements in regard to the books and records to be maintained by an entity are set forth in 6/2.1 and 6/2.2. It should be noted in particular that these requirements apply to the full extent to the Brazilian branch of a foreign entity (Reg. Art. 34 §4).

It is hardly possible to list in this study the great number of factual situations, reproduced in many hundreds of administrative and judicial decisions, in which the books and records of a taxpayer were rejected by the income tax authorities as insufficient and unacceptable. Apart from omissions and falsifications made with obviously fraudulent intent,[93] any system of bookkeeping which violates the basic requirements of clarity, accuracy, and particularity of the entries or which is not supported by the required documentation is liable to be rejected unless the violations are of very minor consequence. It should be stated again that the rules of the Commercial Code regarding the books and records to be kept by a business are incorporated by reference in the income tax law and that therefore any failure to observe the formal rules of the commercial law is just as fatal as a violation of those of its provisions which deal with the substance of the records to be kept. Examples of some of the violations of formal provisions which lead to an estimation of profits, regardless of whether any distortion of income actually resulted, are:

1. The failure of the taxpayer to have his books legalized by the Commercial Registry *before* entries are made therein.[94]
2. Failure to transcribe the financial statements or a summary thereof into the journal.[95]
3. The maintenance of a mechanical (looseleaf or punch card) bookkeeping system (CC, *Rev.* Nos. 155, 482, and 505). Accounting systems of this type unless supplemented by the required books (6/2.2)

---

[93] Concealment of sales will result in rejection of the books, CC, *Rev.* 1951 No. 1387. Credits to a partner for alleged contributions to the company (*suprimentos*) are taxed to the company if the origin of the money is not proved, CC, *Rev.* 1950 Nos. 551, 552, 666, 668; 1951 No. 1391; 1954 No. 118.

[94] CC, *Rev.* 1946 No. 606; 1948 No. 636. Nonlegalized books are considered as nonexistent at law, CC, *Rev.* 1951 Nos. 502 and 836.

[95] CC, *Rev.* 1949 Nos. 657, 799, 803, 1049; *Rev.* 1951 No. 872.

are unacceptable for income tax purposes because they dispense with
the detailed recordings in a book of original entry as prescribed by the
Commercial Code.

A taxpayer who refuses to present his books for an audit or who fails
to substantiate his allegation that they were lost or destroyed will be
taxed on the basis of estimated profits.[96] How long a taxpayer must preserve the books for income tax purposes is not entirely free from doubt.[97]

In the discretion of the assessing authorities, who will consider the
nature of the business, profits will be estimated to equal any one of the
following amounts (Reg. Art. 34 §4):

1. 30% of the book value of the total assets as of the last balance sheet
   date.[98]
2. 15% to 50% of the capital of the firm. For the purposes of this provision,
   "capital" includes the paid-in capital plus the reserves and surplus, the
   profits credited to *sócios* (partners or owners) as well as the amount of
   their contributions or advances to the firm (CC, *Rev.* 1951 No. 477).
3. 15% to 50% of the gross income determined as for the purposes of the
   tax on presumed profits.[99]

It is the practice of the government under 2 and 3 above to impose the
minimum rate of 15% in the first year of the violation and to raise that
rate by 5% for each year during which it continues.[100] It has been held,
however, that taxation on the basis of estimated profits (although a sanction applied to enforce compliance with the statutory rules) is not a
penalty, and that therefore the rates must be chosen in a way which
approximates the presumptive actual income of the taxpayer as closely
as possible (CC, *Rev.* 1951 No. 477).

To the estimated net income as calculated under one of the three bases
outlined above, the regular tax rates under Reg. Art. 44 are applied.

The taxation of the partners or owners (under Schedule F) on the
profits distributed or deemed to be distributed to them by the entity
follows the rules applicable to distributions of actual profits (9/2.1);[101]
as far as taxation of these individuals is concerned, estimated profits are
substituted for actual profits of the entity.

[96] CC, *Rev.* 1949 No. 621. Circumstances beyond the control of the taxpayer are
given consideration.

[97] According to CC, *Rev.* 1950 No. 62, the mandatory books must be preserved for
twenty years.

[98] Reg. Art. 34 §4 enumerates the following assets: *ativo imobilizado* (fixed
assets); *disponivel* (cash); *realizavel a curto e a longo prazo* (accounts receivable,
inventory, loans, investments, etc.).

[99] Reg. Art. 40 §§ 1 and 2; 6/9.1.

[100] See CC, *Rev.* 1951 No. 391; *Rev.* 1954 Nos. 73 and 227; numerous other decisions quoted in Rezende, Note 129.

[101] CC, *Rev.* 1955 No. 163.

CHAPTER 7

BUSINESS INCOME

7/1. Gross Profit

7/1.1 In General — Determination of Income
7/1.2 Income from Capital Transactions
7/1.3 Occasional Income from Commercial or Industrial Transactions

7/2. Deductions

7/2.1 General Principles
7/2.2 Rent
7/2.3 Salaries and Other Compensation for Services Rendered
7/2.4 Interest
7/2.5 Repairs, Maintenance, and Construction Expenses
7/2.6 Worthless Assets
7/2.7 Taxes
7/2.8 Insurance
7/2.9 Bad Debts
7/2.10 Charitable Contributions
7/2.11 Other Business Deductions
       a. Advertising and Entertainment Expenses
       b. Travel Expenses
7/2.12 Employees' Participations in the Profits of the Firm
7/2.13 Participation in Profits by the Government
7/2.14 Participations in Profits by Holders of Participating Certificates

7/3. Depreciation

7/3.1 General Rule

7/3.2 Depreciation Methods

7/3.3 Depreciation Rates

7/3.4 Obsolescence

7/3.5 Amortization of Leasehold Improvements

7/3.6 Amortization of Intangibles

7/4. Business Losses

7/4.1 Deductible Losses

7/4.2 Loss Carry-over

7/4.3 Losses of Partnerships and Individual Proprietorships

7/4.4 Losses of Domestic Branch of Foreign Entity

7/4.5 Currency Exchange Losses

7/5. Nondeductible Expenses

7/5.1 Capital Expenditures

7/5.2 Certain Payments to Owners and Officers of Firms and Companies

    a. Certain Withdrawals by Owners or Partners

    b. Compensation to Nonresident Directors

    c. Interest Paid to Owners or Partners

7/5.3 Reserves

7/5.4 Indemnifications Provided by the Labor Law

7/6. Additions to Income

7/6.1 Distributions or Appropriations of Profits not Previously Taxed

7/6.2 Surplus from Revaluation of Fixed Assets

7/6.3 Profits on the Sale of Assets

7/7. Exclusions from Income

7/7.1 Distributions of Profits Already Taxed to the Distributing Entity

7/7.2 Income from Bearer Securities

7/7.3 Insurance on the Life of an Owner or Partner

7/8. Special Taxation of Reserves

7/8.1 In General

7/8.2 Temporary Levy of 4% on Reserves (Compulsory Loan)

7/8.3 Taxation of Excess Reserves of Corporations

7/1. Gross Profit

7/1.1   In General — Determination of Income

The Income Tax Regulations do not give a definition of taxable income other than by stating that entities [1] shall be taxed on their actual profits as shown from year to year in the balance sheet and statement of profit and loss (Reg. Art. 32). According to Reg. Art. 37, actual profits constitute the difference between the amount of gross profit and certain specifically listed deductions (see 7/2. and 7/3.). The figure so arrived at is subject to certain adjustments for tax purposes which are enumerated in Reg. Art. 43.[2]

It follows that the starting point in the computation of the taxable income of an entity is the amount of gross profit rather than gross income, and it is for this reason that the Income Tax Regulations contain no definition of gross income of entities or rules on the computation of the cost of goods sold. The amount of gross profit is determined primarily from the books of the taxpayer. The maintenance of a reliable bookkeeping system is therefore an indispensable requirement of taxation on the basis of actual profits, and the statutory rules in the matter of books and records must be carefully observed (see 6/2.).

The basis of the taxation of entities under Brazilian income tax law is the economic profit as reflected in the books of account, with the additions, deductions, and adjustments specifically prescribed by the law. Any gain which improves the financial and economic situation of the taxpayer and which is properly incorporated in its books forms part of gross income for tax purposes. On this ground, premiums paid to a corporation on shares of stock issued by it are included in the taxable income of the corporation,[3] and the same result has been reached in the case of income from a forgiveness of indebtedness.[4]

The taxable income of an entity determined as outlined above is subject to the proportionate tax rates of Reg. Art. 44 (see 12/2.3). The nature and composition of the income are of no importance, and it is immaterial how the same income would be taxed to an individual (not engaged in business) under the various schedular classifications. Moreover, the requirement that all income of an entity is subject to uniform rules of taxation results of necessity in the taxation of certain income

---

[1] The term "entities" includes sole proprietorships and individuals engaged in business, see 5/3.4.

[2] See 7/5., 7/6., 7/7.

[3] CC, *Rev.* 1949 No. 1043; 1951 No. 469; 1954 No. 422. The decisions are based on Reg. Art. 43 §1(f) (utilization of reserve funds) discussed in 7/6.1. The rule is different if the contribution by the shareholders is credited to capital, DIR, *Rev.* 1949 No. 684.

[4] CC, *Rev.* 1947 No. 141; 1948 No. 781. This type of income is excluded from the gross income of an individual under Reg. Art. 11 §1(a).

which is either not taxed or taxed under special rules in the case of an individual.

Regarding the rule that only income from Brazilian sources is taxable to an entity, see 11/2.3.

7/1.2   Income from Capital Transactions

Capital gains are included in the taxable income determined as outlined in 7/1.1 above. Gains from the sale of real property realized by individual taxpayers receive special and preferential tax treatment under Reg. Art. 92 (9/8.2). Gains from the sale or other disposition of securities or other capital assets (unless such transactions constitute a business) are not taxed to individuals. Both types of gain, however, are part of an entity's business income and are taxed to it under the general rules.[5]

7/1.3   Occasional Income from Commercial or Industrial Transactions

Individuals not regularly engaged in trade or business who earn occasional income from commercial or industrial sources are taxed on it under Schedule H (miscellaneous income) [6] rather than under the rules pertaining to business income. The applicable schedular tax rate is 5% (Reg. Art. 25).

Capital gains of these individuals, however, are not considered commercial or industrial profits.[7]

7/2. Deductions

7/2.1   General Principles

In conformity with the principle that taxable income is represented by book income with certain adjustments, the Income Tax Regulations do not contain a detailed catalogue of allowable deductions. They permit instead the deduction of all expenses which are connected with the income-producing activity, i.e., which are necessary for the creation of the income and the maintenance of the productive source,[8] and which were incurred in the course of the base year (Reg Art. 37[a]). This general provision is supplemented by a brief list of individually named deduc-

---

[5] Regarding gains from the sale of real property, see DIR, *Rev.* 1947 No. 426; 1951 No. 360; 1952 No. 687; Rezende, Note 273. The fact that the sales price of real property sold at a gain is immediately reinvested in the purchase of other real property does not affect the taxation of the gain. CC, *Rev.* 1951 No. 392.

Regarding gains from the sale of corporate shares or quotas of a limited liability company, see DIR, *Rev.* 1947 No. 566; 1948 No. 154; CC, *Rev.* 1951 Nos. 588 and 1290; Rezende, Note 122.

[6] Reg. Art. 10(e). See 10/4.1 below.

[7] Rezende, Note 46-G.

[8] I.e., the capital and the fixed assets, Sousa, §34(A).

tions. Although some of the most usual items of expense (rent, salaries, etc.) are not specifically listed, their deductibility is clearly covered by the general provision of Reg. Art. 37(a); the specific provisions in reference to individually named deductions are, therefore, primarily in the nature of definitions and limitations. Consequently, the statement frequently found in administrative decisions that only the deductions enumerated in the law can be claimed for income tax purposes does not exclude those which meet the general requirements of Reg. Art. 37(a). The allowable deductions, nondeductible expenses, and the additions to income required under the law are discussed below.

All deductions claimed are subject to proof and justification and both requirements will be examined by the assessing authorities (Reg. Art. 12 §3).[9] This rule, which is stated by the Income Tax Regulations in connection with schedular deductions, is expressly incorporated by reference in the provisions of the law dealing with abatements for purposes of the complementary tax [10] and it is likewise applicable to the deductions claimed by entities in order to arrive at net business income.

Where the law itself defines the type and measure of evidence to be submitted by the taxpayer in support of certain deductions,[11] the question remains whether the administrative authorities are entitled to demand proof which goes beyond the statutory requirements. The Federal Court of Appeals has repeatedly stated, although only by way of dicta, that the Administration is not entitled to demand such further proof.[12]

Since the taxpayer is required to keep books of account (6/2.1 et seq.), an expense may be claimed as a deduction only if it is properly recorded in the books. Expenses which are not so recorded will not be allowed as deductions upon a later audit of the taxpayer's return, even if all other statutory requirements of the deduction are fully met.[13]

After the statutory notice of assessment has been issued, or the process of assessment ex officio (13/2.2) has been initiated, the taxpayer is not permitted to amend the return filed in order to claim a deduction not previously taken or to increase one formerly claimed in a lesser amount (Reg. Art. 63 §4). The disallowance of a deduction results in a fine. In order to avoid the fine and at the same time to preserve his right to contest the disallowance, a taxpayer should not claim a doubtful deduction in the return, but should file, together with the return, a petition of

---

[9] The term "justification" refers to the nature of the expense, i.e., the question whether it is an allowable deduction at all; and the term "proof" to the question whether the expense was in fact incurred by the taxpayer.

[10] Reg. Art. 20.

[11] As in the case of deductions claimed by individual taxpayers for interest, Reg. Art. 20(a); for life insurance premiums, Reg. Art. 20(b); or for charitable contributions, Reg. Art. 20(d).

[12] Rev. 1951 No. 732; 1952 No. 6.

[13] Regarding deductions not reflected in the financial statements, see CC, Rev. 1951 No. 612; Rezende, Note 134.

amendment in which the deduction is substantiated and claimed (see 13/4.1).

Every deduction must be taken in the proper year; a deduction which is not so claimed is lost forever. If, for example, a taxpayer fails to deduct depreciation allowable in a particular year because it was a loss year or because the deduction would for other reasons not have resulted in a tax benefit, it will not be possible for him to transfer this deduction to a later year (CC, *Rev.* 1946 No. 693).

7/2.2   Rent

Rent for the premises in which the business of the taxpayer is carried on and for equipment used in the business is deductible under the general provision of Reg. Art. 37(a). The expense is deductible even if paid to the owners or partners of the firm, provided that the latter include the amount of rent received in their taxable income. If there is a discrepancy between the rental as listed in the lease and the amount of rent actually paid, the latter will determine the allowable deduction, whether it is higher or lower than the contractual figure (CC, *Rev.* 1951 Nos. 577 and 1026).

Regarding rentals arranged for between an individual business firm and its owner, see 9/4.1a.

7/2.3   Salaries and Other Compensation for Services Rendered

Compensation paid for services rendered is deductible under the general provision of Reg. Art. 37(a).

Bonuses and gratuities paid to employees are additional compensation for services and deductible as such unless they are in excess of the statutory limits indicated at 8/1.2. In order to be deductible, the amounts must be paid during the taxable year (CC, *Rev.* 1952 No. 237) or credited to the employees individually and so entered in the books; if charged in the aggregate to a special account, they are held to constitute a reserve rather than an expense, and the deduction is denied (CC, *Rev.* 1945 No. 293).[14]

Commissions paid or credited to third parties are deductible.[15] The payment of commissions to the owners of the firm will usually be in the nature of an anticipated distribution of profits. The fact that the owners of the paying concern also hold an interest in the firm to which the commissions are paid will not disqualify the deduction (DIR, *Rev.* 1948 No. 590).

Payments made to an employee upon his resignation from the firm are

---

[14] Bonuses credited to employees must be paid before April 30 of the following year to be deductible. CC, *Rev.* 1955 Nos. 178 and 186.
[15] CC, *Rev.* 1944 No. 375; 1948 No. 414.

likewise deductible. The same payments made to a retiring partner, however, are included in the income of the company (and subject to complementary tax in the hands of the recipient) as a distribution of profits.[16] For a discussion of other payments which are nondeductible, see 7/5.

7/2.4 Interest

Interest on debts incurred in connection with the development of the business is deductible under Reg. Art. 37(b).

The administrative decisions permit the deduction of interest paid on deposits and bona fide loans made by the owners of the business but require that a fixed rate of interest be agreed upon in order to prevent a secret distribution of profits.[17] Likewise, interest paid on a current account between the firm and the owner or partner is deductible. Interest paid by the Brazilian branch of a foreign corporation to the home office abroad is deductible; like other income of the foreign company, it is subject to taxation at the source (11/3.1). If the interest charge results from a loan contracted abroad by the foreign home office, it is deductible only if the loan is secured by property of the Brazilian branch (DIR, *Rev.* 1945 No. 267).

7/2.5 Repairs, Maintenance, and Construction Expenses

Expenditures made by the taxpayer for repairs and maintenance, incurred to keep the property in normal and efficient operating condition or to restore it to such a condition, are deductible under the general expense allowance of Reg. Art. 37(a).

The deduction of capital expenditures is not allowed. The borderline, however, between deductible expenses and nondeductible capital expenditures is somewhat vague under the decisions. In general, the cases distinguish between ordinary expenses of conservation and maintenance which are deductible and improvements which add to the value of the property and may not be deducted.[18] Expenses for the installation of machines are deductible (CC, *Rev.* 1952 No. 136). The classification as "installation expenses" which are currently deductible has been applied to substantial installation work done on business premises (CC, *Rev.* 1949 No. 740).

The designation of an expenditure in the books of the taxpayer is immaterial; the determining factor is whether or not the expenditure adds to the value of the property.

---

16 Decisions in Rezende, Note 135.

17 DIR, *Rev.* 1944 No. 117. See Sousa, 34(B)(a).

18 CC, *Rev.* 1946 Nos. 71, 592, 593; 1951 No. 1258 (with annotation by Rezende); 1952 No. 317 (individual firm).

7/2.6 Worthless Assets

The Income Tax Regulations do not allow a deduction of a reserve for
loss of value of securities or for fluctuations in their value.[19] Only when a
loss is actually realized through a sale of the securities can it be deducted.

7/2.7 Taxes

All taxes which are imposed upon the taxpayer and constitute an expense of the base year are deductible from gross income. The deduction
includes expenses incurred by the taxpayer in connection with the payment of the tax [20] and additions to the tax for late payment.[21]

It should be noted that the deduction includes the income tax imposed
on entities [22] but not the 15% addition to the tax which is in the nature of
an enforced loan rather than a tax.[23] The income tax which is deductible
in any particular taxable year is the tax paid during the preceding business
year (the base year) which is computed on the basis of the income of the
next preceding year.[24] The deductibility of the income tax imposed on
entities affects its effective rate which, therefore, is always less than the
nominal rates of 15% or 20%.

Only taxes which are imposed upon the taxpayer are deductible. This
excludes the deduction of taxes which are merely withheld by the payor
of certain income but which are imposed upon the recipient thereof, such
as the income tax withheld on dividends distributed on bearer shares [25]
or on payments of income to nonresident individuals and corporations
domiciled abroad [26] including the income tax paid by the Brazilian branch
of a foreign corporation for the account of the latter.[27] For the same
reason, the special tax on remittances abroad (1/6.2e) is not deductible by
the entity making the remittance (CC, *Rev.* 1950 No. 469). Real property
taxes paid by a company on property rented by it may be deducted by
the company as being in the nature of additional rent. If a tax which
must be withheld by the payor is actually absorbed by him (as in the case
of dividends on bearer shares declared "tax-free"), the amount of the tax
constitutes additional taxable income to the payee (CC, *Rev.* 1952 No.

[19] CC, *Rev.* 1946 No. 429; *Rev.* 1949 No. 99.
[20] CC, *Rev.* 1950 No. 65.
[21] CC, *Rev.* 1954 No. 52.
[22] DIR, *Rev.* 1943 No. 270. Individuals cannot deduct the income tax paid by
them. CC, *Rev.* 1954 No. 112.
[23] Rezende, Note 135; see 12/2.4a.
[24] As an example, the income tax which is deductible on the return for taxable year
1956 (base year 1955) is the tax paid in and for the year 1955 which is computed on
the income of 1954.
[25] CC, *Rev.* 1950 No. 123; 1951 Nos. 190 and 505; Ministry of Finance, *Rev.* 1951
No. 741; CC, *Rev.* 1952 Nos. 527, 929; DIR, *Rev.* 1952 No. 691.
[26] CC, *Rev.* 1945 No. 226.
[27] DIR, *Rev.* 1948 No. 121; CC, *Rev.* 1951 No. 380.

663) and is subject to withholding.[28] The payment by an entity of the income tax imposed on its owners constitutes an additional distribution of profits which is taxable to the recipients as well as the distributing entity (CC, *Rev.* 1954 No. 555).

Whether only taxes actually paid during the base year are deductible from gross income or whether it is sufficient for the deduction if the liability for the tax is accrued on the books under proper accounting procedures is not entirely free from doubt, especially in regard to income taxes.[29] It seems well established that an income tax assessed constitutes a proper expense of the year of assessment even if actual payment thereof is made during the next succeeding year;[30] on the other hand, a tax reserve set up at the end of a business year to provide for the tax liability for such year is not a deductible expense; the deduction must be taken in the year in which the tax is paid and the amount of the payment charged against the reserve.[31]

The fact that a tax is contested does not affect its deductibility; the taxpayer does not have to wait for a final decision on his protest or appeal to claim the deduction.[32]

7/2.8 Insurance

Premiums on insurance covering the assets of the business are deductible under the general provision of Reg. Art. 37(a).

Premiums on insurance contracts covering the life of the owner or a partner of an entity other than a corporation are deductible if the firm is the beneficiary under the policy,[33] but not if the insurance contract runs in favor of the surviving members of the firm. In the latter case, the insurance contract is regarded as a private agreement between the partners and the premiums paid by the entity on behalf of the insured partners are considered to be an additional distribution of profits.

Amounts paid by the insurance company by reason of the death of the insured are not includible in the taxable income of the entity which is the beneficiary under the policy.[34]

[28] CC, *Rev.* 1951 Nos. 505 and 1052; 1952 No. 663; DIR, *Rev.* 1952 Nos. 418, 433-Q and 691.

[29] See Rezende, Note 135; CC, *Rev.* 1951 No. 1025.

[30] CC, *Rev.* 1949 No. 788; 1951 Nos. 1025 and 1385.

[31] CC, *Rev.* 1947 No. 54; 1954 No. 284 and decisions quoted in the preceding footnote. However, the income tax actually paid during the year may be offset against the reserve, unless it was charged to profit and loss, CC, *Rev.* 1955 No. 56.

[32] CC, *Rev.* 1950 Nos. 27, 46, 65 and 160; 1953 No. 144; 1954 No. 373. The deduction of an unpaid and contested income tax was denied by the Tax Court, CC, *Rev.* 1954 No. 59. It appears from the case, however, that the administrative authorities had already conceded that the tax was not owed.

[33] DIR, *Rev.* 1943 No. 524.

[34] Reg. Art. 43 §2(e). See 7/7.3.

7/2.9 Bad Debts

The Income Tax Regulations allow the deduction of a reasonable provision [35] for bad debts originating from commercial or financial transactions, as distinguished from investments (7/2.6); the reasonableness of the charge is determined by the nature and amount of the outstanding receivables as well as by the character of the business (Reg. Art. 37[c]).

The administrative decisions generally place the maximum deduction at 10%, computed on the amount of receivables shown in the balance sheet at the end of the base year.[36] This does not mean that a deduction of 10% can be claimed without proof of loss in at least that amount. Only in very rare and exceptional cases have the decisions sanctioned an allowance in excess of 10% of receivables.

The decisions hold that a direct charge-off of receivables becoming uncollectible during the base year is permitted only in the absence of a bad-debt provision.[37] It seems, however, that a change from the reserve method of charging off bad debts to the direct charge-off method or vice versa is acceptable to the income tax authorities, provided that an existing excess reserve is adjusted through profit and loss at the end of the base year so that the amount of the provision does not exceed the allowable percentage of receivables which are outstanding at this point of time. The excess of uncollectible items over the amount of the reserve as set up at the beginning of the base year may be charged directly to profit and loss.[38]

Recoveries of bad debts previously charged off must be credited to profit and loss account in the year of recovery (CC, Rev. 1937 No. 321). The usual practice is to credit the recoveries to the provision account and to adjust the balance of the reserve through the profit and loss account at the end of the base year. The amount recovered must be included in income of the year of recovery whether or not the charge-off had resulted in a reduction of the income of the prior year. Brazilian income tax law does not recognize the "tax benefit" rule.

An excessive provision for bad debts is not only restored to income

[35] The losses on collection of receivables which are actually sustained during a base year must be charged to the provision account. At the end of the year the account is closed, the balance, if any, transferred to profit and loss, and a new provision set up for the following year, CC, Rev. 1942 No. 341.
If the account is held open, the balance therein must be adjusted to a figure corresponding with the allowable percentage of receivables shown in the balance sheet at the end of the base year. The corresponding book entries are to profit and loss account, debiting this account if the provision is increased and crediting it if the provision is decreased. See CC, Rev. 1949 No. 161; 1954 No. 296.
[36] CC, Rev. 1951 No. 279; 1954 Nos. 157 and 199; 1955 Nos. 158 and 159.
[37] CC, Rev. 1945 No. 248; 1946 No. 481; 1947 No. 387; 1949 No. 159.
[38] This practice seems to be accepted by the income tax authorities; see quotation from the Income Tax Bill proposed by the Income Tax Division in 1941 in Rezende, Note 136.

for purposes of the regular income tax, but is also considered a reserve subject to the 4% charge on reserves, which is in the nature of an enforced loan, and the 30% tax on reserves exceeding the amount of the paid-in capital of a corporation (7/8.).

7/2.10   Charitable Contributions

The Income Tax Regulations allow the deduction of donations and gifts made to philanthropic institutions which have legal status in Brazil (Reg. Art. 37[g]). The amount of the deduction is not limited. Entities, as distinguished from individuals,[39] are no longer required to file the receipt of the donee with their annual return.

Contributions for political purposes are not deductible.[40]

7/2.11   Other Business Deductions

a. ADVERTISING AND ENTERTAINMENT EXPENSES. Advertising expenses are deductible (DIR, Rev. 1944 No. 122). The same is true for entertainment expenses and presents made to maintain the goodwill of the employees or customers of the firm (CC, Rev. 1951 No. 328).

b. TRAVEL EXPENSES. Travel expenses are deductible if they are either proved or modest in relation to the turnover of the business.[41] It seems that the deduction is not allowed if the firm has an office or agent at the place of destination.[42]

7/2.12   Employees' Participations in the Profits of the Firm

Participating shares of employees in the profits of a business are excluded from the taxable income of the latter under Reg. Art. 43 §2(a). This provision refers to contractual agreements between a business enterprise and its employees under which the latter participate in the profits of the firm. The often-announced legislative regulation of this subject, which the Federal Constitution of 1946 provided for, has still not materialized.

7/2.13   Participation in Profits by the Government

The participating shares of the federal government or a state or municipal government in the profits of a business are excluded from the taxable income of the enterprise under Reg. Art. 43 §2(b).

[39] Reg. Art. 20(d).
[40] CC, Rev. 1951 No. 1093; 1952 No. 314.
[41] CC, Rev. 1946 Nos. 472 and 704; 1950 No. 398. See, on the other hand, CC, Rev. 1946 No. 561 (disallowing travel expenses amounting to 20% of gross profit and not proved) and Rev. 1954 No. 285 (business purpose of directors' foreign trip not proved).
[42] Sousa, §34(A)(j).

7/2.14   Participations in Profits by Holders of Participating Certificates

The question whether or not the portion of the profits of a corporation which is distributed to the holders of participating certificates reduces the taxable income of the corporation is unsettled; see 9/2.1e.

7/3.   Depreciation

7/3.1   General Rule

The Income Tax Regulations (Reg. Art. 37[d]) allow a deduction for physical depreciation of movable property employed in the business. The depreciation deduction is strictly limited to movable property. There is no deduction for depreciation of buildings or other improvements to realty.[43] The deduction is further limited to compensate for physical deterioration of the property. Obsolescence does not enter into the computation of depreciation, but it is reflected in the deduction referred to below under 7/3.4.

In determining the proper amount of depreciation, the actual historical cost of the asset and its useful life must be taken into account. Increases in book value on account of revaluation are not to be considered.[44]

Since depreciation is based only on the physical deterioration of the asset and is independent of profits, the taxpayer cannot omit the deduction in a year in which the deduction would not result in a tax benefit and claim a higher deduction in a later year.[45] It seems, however, that, if the taxpayer fails to claim depreciation, the undepreciated cost of the asset will be taken into account in determining a loss upon a sale or exchange.[46] Depreciation must be charged on the books to be deductible.

The law provides that the distribution of unused depreciation reserves to the stockholders or partners of the firm makes these funds taxable to the distributing entity. The transfer of depreciation funds to a free reserve has the same effect, unless a new depreciation reserve is formed out of these amounts before the end of the base year (see 7/6.1).

The fact that the lessee of movable property has stipulated to return the property in the same condition in which he received it does not

---

[43] This limitation must be understood, however, to refer only to property which is immovable by its nature such as buildings, etc., and not to property which becomes part of the realty under the rules of the civil law regarding accession, e.g., machines firmly attached to the floor of a building. See Sousa, §34(D)(e), and 3/2.1.

[44] CC, *Rev.* 1951 No. 1211; 1954 No. 565; DIR, *Rev.* 1948 No. 622. Depreciation must not exceed the book value of the asset nor be continued after its useful life is exhausted, CC, *Rev.* 1950 No. 253.

[45] CC, *Rev.* 1952 No. 80; see also DIR, *Rev.* 1942 No. 400. The latter ruling points out that failure to register actual depreciation results in misleading financial statements through the overstatement of asset values.

[46] CC, *Rev.* 1936 No. 477.

prevent the lessor from deducting depreciation at the usual rates to give effect to the passage of time.[47]

7/3.2   Depreciation Methods

Although the straight-line method of depreciation is the one most frequently used, it is not the only one which is permissible. The Income Tax Regulations do not prescribe the use of any particular method of depreciation, and the authorities will permit the use of any method that is properly and consistently applied.

7/3.3   Depreciation Rates

It is important to note that the Income Tax Regulations do not specify rates of depreciation for various kinds of property. The rates applied have been created entirely through long administrative practice.

The following rates are generally allowed (applying the straight-line method of depreciation):

1. Office furniture and machines (typewriters, dictaphones,
   adding and calculating machines, etc.) [48]   10%
2. Industrial and agricultural machines, equipment, tools, and
   accessories (except electrical installations) [49]   10%
3. Automobiles and other vehicles   20%
4. Electrical installations [50]   20%
5. Ships [51]   5%

It should be noted that the full annual depreciation rate may be used for the year during which the asset was acquired; as an example, a depreciation rate of 20% may be applied to the cost of a truck acquired in December.

Depreciation rates in excess of the standard rates have occasionally been accepted by the income tax authorities in cases where special circumstances prevailed (unusual strain,[52] work in several shifts,[53] exposure

[47] CC, *Rev.* 1949 No. 664.

[48] 20% disallowed for hotel furniture (CC, *Rev.* 1952 No. 323) but allowed for bed and table linen (CC, *Rev.* 1950 No. 394). College furniture: 15% allowed (CC, *Rev.* 1951 No. 943). Even where regulatory legislation requires specific higher rates of depreciation (as in the case of insurance companies, which must charge off depreciation of 20%) such legislation does not affect the rates allowed for tax purposes (CC, *Rev.* 1952 Nos. 211 and 345; 1955 No. 193).

[49] CC, *Rev.* 1954 Nos. 53 and 262.

[50] CC, *Rev.* 1955 No. 60.

[51] CC, *Rev.* 1955 Nos. 97 and 125. A rate of 20% was allowed in the case of a wooden hull, CC, *Rev.* 1952 No. 530. It was formerly questioned whether depreciation is allowable at all because under the rules of the commercial law a ship is regarded as real property having its situs at the port of registration.

[52] 20% allowed on account of excessive vibration (nail factory); CC, *Rev.* 1952 No. 661.

[53] 15%: CC, *Rev.* 1951 No. 1273; or even 20%: CC, *Rev.* 1952 No. 145; 1954 Nos. 367 and 387. The criterion used does not seem entirely reliable (only 15% allowed

to corrosives in a chemical factory,[54] etc.). It should be pointed out, however, that a taxpayer exceeding the usually accepted rates of depreciation without prior authorization by the government does so at his peril and may incur a very heavy tax liability. Excess provisions for depreciation are counted among the reserves which, if more than the paid-in capital of a corporation, are subject to a penalty tax of 30% (7/8.). Furthermore, excessive depreciation claimed in one year and disallowed for that year will not be allowed as a deduction in subsequent years.

7/3.4 Obsolescence

Under Reg. Art. 37(e) (as amended by Law No. 2,354 of November 29, 1954, Art. 17) the taxpayer is allowed to deduct from gross income the cost of machinery and equipment which has fallen into disuse or become obsolete. The deduction is reduced by the amount of accumulated depreciation on the old machinery or equipment, and by the obsolescence reserve established prior to 1946.[55] Amounts received upon the sale of the obsolete or discarded items do not reduce the deduction but must be included in gross income (Reg. Art. 37[e]).

This deduction replaces the former one [56] for the full cost of new machinery and equipment acquired to replace obsolete or discarded items of the same kind.[57] The basis of the replacement asset is determined only by its own cost and useful life and there is no connection with the basis of the asset replaced or the gain or loss realized upon the sale thereof.

7/3.5 Amortization of Leasehold Improvements

If, at his own expense, the lessee installs buildings or other improvements on rented premises which become the property of the lessor upon the expiration of the lease, the lessee may amortize the cost of the improvements over the term of the lease and deduct a proportionate part

despite proof that factory worked twice the normal time; CC, *Rev.* 1952 No. 624).

A rate of 30% was allowed for shoe factory equipment in CC, *Rev.* 1953 No. 79. It seems from the wording of the decision, however, that the obsolescence factor was considered with respect to the particular equipment under review (molds).

[54] 20% allowed in CC, *Rev.* 1950 No. 50.

[55] Until December 31, 1946, the allowance for depreciation was reflected in two deductions (each at the standard rate of 10%), one covering physical depreciation and the other the obsolescence factor. As long as the prior deduction for the full cost of replacement machinery and equipment applied (see text) the deduction was required to be reduced by the depreciation on the items replaced and by the obsolescence reserve accumulated thereon until 1946. For this reason, the latter reserve was required to remain on the books "frozen" as of December 31, 1946, and this is the reserve referred to in the text.

[56] This deduction was introduced by Law No. 154 of November 25, 1947; it was in force until December 31, 1954.

[57] Regarding the abuse in connection with the deduction formerly allowed, see Sousa, *Compêndio*, 1st ed. (1952), §124-E.

of the cost in each taxable year.[58] The value of the improvements repre-sents taxable income to the lessor.[59]

The unamortized balance of the expenditures made by the lessee for the improvement or adaptation of rented premises may be deducted by him upon the termination of the lease, if the improvements become the property of the lessor and the latter is not required to compensate the tenant therefor.

7/3.6   Amortization of Intangibles

The question of the amortization of intangibles has not been given more than cursory attention in the published decisions and legal literature, and the sources of authority are extremely scarce. With this limitation, it may be stated that amortization of patents is recognized as a deduction for income tax purposes, whereas amortization of commercial or indus-trial trademarks is not.

A patent of invention under Brazilian law has a life of fifteen years, after which the invention becomes public property.[60] On the ground of this definite time limitation, the decisions hold that the capital investment in a patent may be amortized over its life, and that the annual amortiza-tion charge is an allowable deduction for income tax purposes.[61] A commercial or industrial trademark, business name, shop name, or symbol may be registered under Brazilian law for ten years, and the registration may be renewed indefinitely for successive ten-year periods.[62] Because the protection of a trademark can be so extended, it loses its value not through the mere passage of time but through other factors (nonuse or abandonment), while a trademark which is kept alive may become more valuable in the course of time. On these grounds, the decisions deny the deduction of amortization.[63]

[58] DIR, *Rev.* 1948 No. 150. See also CC, *Rev.* 1949 No. 87; 1951 No. 328. Al-though the principle stated in the text represents the established practice of the Tax Court (see DIR, *Rev.* 1947, No. 288), some later decisions of the same authority seem to imply that the tenant may deduct the entire expense in the year in which it was made in lieu of amortizing it over the term of the lease. See in particular, CC, *Rev.* 1951 No. 963 and Rezende, Note 135.

[59] DIR, *Rev.* 1948 No. 150. The decision leaves doubt whether the income is measured by the full value of the improvements at the time they are made or by their depreciated value upon the expiration of the lease. Likewise, the year in which this income is reportable by the lessor is doubtful.

[60] Decree-law No. 7,903 (*Código da Propriedade Industrial*) of August 27, 1945, Art. 39.

[61] CC, *Rev.* 1948 No. 75; DIR, *Rev.* 1948 No. 126; to the same effect, Rezende, Note 137, and annotation to *Rev.* 1948 No. 75.

[62] Decree-law No. 7,903, Art. 138.

[63] The deduction was allowed (at an annual rate of 10%) in CC, *Rev.* 1946 No. 601 and in DIR, *Rev.* 1948 No. 126 (the latter decision is not clear regarding the applicable rate of amortization). These older and very summary rulings are superseded by the decisions of the Tax Court in *Rev.* 1948 No. 75 and 1954 No. 284 which disallow the deduction on the grounds set forth in the text. To the same effect, Rezende, *loc. cit.*

Patents and trademarks may be among the assets which are contributed to a corporation upon its formation as part of its statutory capital. It is clear that the valuation of these intangibles is entirely in the discretion of the incorporators and that the tax authorities have no power to prevent or correct a possible overvaluation for tax purposes.[64]

7/4. Business Losses

7/4.1 Deductible Losses

The Income Tax Regulations do not specifically deal with the question of deductible business losses sustained by legal entities, except as regards losses from uncollectible accounts.[65] Since, however, the taxable income of entities is determined on the basis of their book income computed according to acceptable principles of commercial accounting, losses sustained by them in trade or business, in transactions entered into for profit, or resulting from casualties or accidents reduce their taxable income, provided such losses are properly reflected in the books.

7/4.2 Loss Carry-over

The loss sustained in one business year (base year) may be carried forward to, and utilized to reduce or eliminate the taxable income of, the next three business years, provided that current reserves or accumulated profits and those of the succeeding years are insufficient to absorb the loss (Reg. Art. 43 §§3 and 4).[66] The loss that can be carried forward is the excess of allowable deductions over gross income of the loss year, i.e., the book loss computed with the deductions allowed by Reg. Art. 37, but before the tax adjustments required under Reg. Art. 43 (see below). Besides losses from business operations, casualty losses affecting the business assets enter into the computation of the loss.[67]

The reserves or accumulated profits to which the statute refers include surplus [68] existing at the end of the loss year. As an example, a loss of Cr$ 100,000 sustained in 1955 may not be carried forward to subsequent years if the taxpayer's balance sheet shows surplus of Cr$ 100,000 or more as of December 31, 1955; if there is surplus of Cr$ 60,000, only the unabsorbed balance of the loss, or Cr$ 40,000, may be carried forward to, and will constitute a loss deduction for, the three subsequent years.

The taxpayer is not bound to apply the loss in the order of the years

[64] Corp. Law, Arts. 5 and 6.
[65] Reg. Arts. 37(c) and 38(e); see under Bad Debts (7/2.9), above. Casualty losses of individuals constitute an abatement for purposes of the complementary tax (Reg. Art. 20[c]); regarding this subject, see 12/1.2b5.
[66] Although the statute speaks of "nonexistence" and not of "insufficiency" of reserves or surplus, it seems clear that the latter meaning is intended, and this interpretation was adopted by the income tax authorities. See DIR, *Rev.* 1951 No. 1018; CC, *Rev.* 1954 No. 307; 1955 No. 174.
[67] CC, *Rev.* 1951 Nos. 795 and 1258.
[68] Both earned surplus and capital surplus.

following the loss year (exhausting the income of the first succeeding year before offsetting that of the second year and so forth); he may apply the loss or a portion thereof against the income of any one of the three succeeding years as he sees fit.[69] The functioning of the loss deduction may be illustrated by the following example:

A corporation shows the following results for the years 1948 through 1954; it had no surplus of any kind at the end of 1947:

1948	(Loss)	Cr$ (200,000)
1949	(Loss)	(450,000)
1950	(Loss)	(300,000)
1951	Profit	300,000
1952	Profit	200,000
1953	Profit	400,000
1954	Profit	500,000

The losses of the years 1948 to 1950 may be carried forward as follows:

The 1948 loss can be applied only against 1951 income, 1951 being the third succeeding taxable year; the loss for the year 1949, against the income of the years 1951 and 1952. If the 1948 loss was carried forward to 1951, reducing the income of that year to Cr$ 100,000, only Cr$ 300,000 of the total loss of Cr$ 450,000 for 1949 can be applied against the income of the years 1951 and 1952, and the unused balance of Cr$ 150,000 is lost and cannot be used to offset income of the year 1953. The loss for 1950 can be carried forward to the years 1951, 1952, and 1953; if, however, the income of the years 1951 and 1952 was eliminated by the carry-over of the 1948 and 1949 losses, the 1950 loss can be applied only against 1953 income.

The three-year limitation on the loss carry-over clearly indicates that the unabsorbed portion of the loss carried over to any taxable year cannot be used to create a new loss for that year (the year *to which* the loss is carried over) which in turn might be carried forward to the following three years. In the above example, a portion of Cr$ 150,000 of the 1949 loss remained unabsorbed by the income of the years 1951 and 1952; this unabsorbed balance cannot be utilized to create a constructive loss for the year 1952 which might be carried over to 1953, 1954, and 1955.

It is important to note that the income to which the loss of any one of the three preceding years is applied is the "actual profit," i.e., the book income computed with the deductions allowed under Reg. Art. 37 but before making the adjustments for tax purposes prescribed by Reg. Art. 43 and discussed below in 7/5., 7/6., and 7/7.[70]

[69] DIR, *Rev.* 1951 Nos. 759, 760 and 795. For individual firms see DIR, *Rev.* 1951 No. 651.

[70] This follows clearly from the wording of Reg. Art. 43 §3, the statutory source of the deduction. See CC, *Rev.* 1954 No. 307 (the net operating loss of a prior year cannot be applied against revaluation surplus of the current year which must be included in taxable income of that year under Reg. Art. 43 §1[h]).

The following example will demonstrate this principle:

Example 1

The gross income of Corporation A for the year is Cr$ 180,000, which includes dividends of Cr$ 100,000 from Corporation B. The total expenses for the year are Cr$ 150,000 of which Cr$ 50,000 are nondeductible.

The book income of the company for the year is Cr$ 30,000 (total income of Cr$ 180,000 less total expenses of Cr$ 150,000).

For income tax purposes, the company shows a loss of Cr$ 20,000, as follows:

Deductible expenses	Cr$ 100,000
Less Income subject to tax (Cr$ 180,000 less dividends of Cr$ 100,000 nontaxable under Reg. Art. 43 §2(c); see 9/2.3 below)	80,000
Tax Loss	Cr $ 20,000

Since there is an economic gain rather than a loss, the loss carry-over provisions do not apply.[71]

It would seem that under general principles of Brazilian income tax law, the loss of a prior year can be carried over to a subsequent year only if the loss is currently reflected in the financial statements of the company for the loss year and that a later correction of the balance sheet resulting in a loss will not be accepted for tax purposes.[72]

7/4.3 Losses of Partnerships and Individual Proprietorships

The net operating loss deduction is available to all entities, but it is not available to individuals.[73] Since partnerships and individual proprietorships constitute entities for income tax purposes, they can utilize the deduction.

The profit or loss of a sole proprietorship is attributed to the owner thereof by operation of law, regardless of any book entries or actual distribution (see 5/3.4.). Consequently, the owner of a sole proprietorship reports the current income of the business in his individual income tax return (under Schedule F) as computed by the entity, i.e., reduced by the loss carry-over from prior years, if any.[74]

[71] To the same effect, DIR, *Rev.* 1951 No. 1018 (revaluation of assets includible in taxable income under Reg. Art. 43 §1[h] does not affect the loss carry-over).

[72] See CC, *Rev.* 1951 No. 1258. The decision is not entirely clear in this respect.

[73] CC, *Rev.* 1952 Nos. 546 and 849.

[74] DIR, *Rev.* 1951 No. 651; CC, *Rev.* 1955 No. 484, *reversing* CC, *Rev.* 1952 No. 849. This view conforms with the wording of Reg. Art. 8 which requires the inclusion, in the individual's income tax return, of the "profits *subject to the proportional tax in the hands of the juridical person*"; see Rezende, Annotation to the decision of the Tax Court in *Rev.* 1952 No. 849; Rezende-Viana, *Consolidação das Leis do Impôsto de Renda*, Note 173-B.

The profits or losses of a partnership, as distinguished from a sole proprietorship, become those of the partners only by an actual distribution, i.e., the payment or credit of the profit to the partners, or the charge of the loss against their accounts. The administrative practice, however, is to the effect that the proration of the loss of a partnership among the partners destroys the net operating loss carry-over of the partnership, and that the net operating loss deduction is preserved only if the losses of prior years are kept in suspense.[75] If this rule is observed, each partner will report in his individual income tax return (under Schedule F) his share of the current partnership income, reduced by a proportionate part of the partnership's loss carry-over from prior years.

7/4.4   Losses of Domestic Branch of Foreign Entity

The application of the net operating loss deduction in the case of the Brazilian branch of a foreign entity is not entirely free from doubt. The branch is subject to a double imposition of income tax on its profits, namely, the assessed income tax applicable to all legal entities under Reg. Art. 44, and the withholding tax on nonresident taxpayers (imposed on the foreign organization but collected from its Brazilian branch) under Reg. Art. 97. The question here is whether the net operating loss of the branch (sustained in any one of the three preceding years) may be carried forward and utilized to reduce or eliminate the current year's income for purposes of the assessed income tax under Reg. Art. 44, or the withholding tax under Reg. Art. 97, or both.

The rulings of the Income Tax Division [76] hold, in principle, that the net operating loss deduction is available to the Brazilian branch of a foreign organization, apparently for purposes of both the assessed tax under Reg. Art. 44 and the withholding tax under Reg. Art. 97; they state, however, that the deduction is lost if and when the profit of the current year is either credited or remitted to the foreign home office; whether this loss of the deduction affects only the withholding tax under Reg. Art. 97 or both it *and* the assessed tax under Reg. Art. 44 is not clear.[77]

As far as the withholding tax under Reg. Art. 97 is concerned, both decisions cited are difficult to reconcile with the fundamental principle of Brazilian income tax law that the profits of the branch are those of the foreign organization as soon as determined, i.e., as of the balance sheet date, and that they belong to the latter by operation of law, i.e.,

---

[75] DIR, *Rev.* 1951 No. 795. The decision is criticized by Rezende, Note 173-C.

[76] DIR, *Rev.* 1951 Nos. 776 and 786.

[77] The decision in *Rev.* 1951 No. 776, *supra*, holds that the withholding tax under Reg. Art. 97 becomes due in the situation indicated; according to the decision in *Rev.* 1951 No. 786, *supra*, both the income tax under Reg. Art. 44 *and* the withholding tax under Reg. Art. 97 are imposed in the same situation. Rezende, Note 173-C, considers the principles expressed in either decision as being without legal foundation.

without the necessity for any actual credit or remittance on the part of the branch.[78]

On the basis of the principle stated, it might be argued that the net operating loss deduction is never available for purposes of the withholding tax under Reg. Art. 97 as long as the foreign organization as a whole, on which the withholding tax is legally imposed (although it is collected from its Brazilian branch), does not show a loss for the year in question; conversely, it might be argued that the deduction should apply if the Brazilian branch sustains a loss, because only the profits or losses of the branch are material for Brazilian income tax purposes, and that the treatment of these profits or losses on the books of the branch should have no effect on existing tax liabilities.

The actual present handling of the question by the income tax authorities appears to be to the effect that the net operating loss deduction is available to the branch for purposes of the assessed income tax under Reg. Art. 44, but that it cannot be invoked for purposes of the withholding tax under Reg. Art. 97.[79]

The net operating loss deduction which is available to the branch is presumably not limited by the existence on the books of the branch of "reserves or profits in suspense" [80] (including surplus) because, in contemplation of law, a branch is an integral part of the foreign entity and cannot have funds and reserves of its own.

7/4.5 Currency Exchange Losses

A loss sustained by an entity which results from a decline of either the Brazilian or a foreign currency between the date of a transaction and the date it is liquidated is a deductible expense when the obligation is paid and the loss actually realized.[81] Reserves set up to provide for losses of this kind are not deductible and must be restored to profits for income tax purposes.[82]

---

[78] See Rezende, Note 283, who points to the inconsistency of the decisions cited with the principle stated in the text. Some older administrative rulings, quoted by Rezende for the proposition that the deduction does not affect the withholding tax (DIR, *Rev.* 1943 No. 684; 1944 No. 103) do not seem to be in point because these decisions were promulgated before the net operating loss deduction was introduced into Brazilian income tax law by Law No. 154 of November 25, 1947.

[79] See Ministry of Finance, *Rev.* 1954 No. 487, *reversing* CC, *Rev.* 1949 No. 277. But see CC, *Rev.* 1955 No. 349.

[80] Reg. Art. 43 §3; see 5/4.8 and 11/3.3.

[81] CC, *Rev.* 1954 No. 319.

[82] A loss of receivables resulting from the devaluation of a foreign currency may be considered in computing the provision for bad debts, but the limits of this deduction (10% of total receivables outstanding at the end of the year, see 7/2.9) must be observed. If this provision proves insufficient upon later realization of the exchange loss, the balance of the loss is deductible at that time, DIR, *Rev.* 1951 No. 1187 (see also Rezende, Note 439, regarding an obvious error in the cited decision).

7/5. Nondeductible Expenses

7/5.1 Capital Expenditures

Amounts expended in the acquisition of capital assets are not a proper deduction for income tax purposes, even though charged to profit and loss (Reg. Art. 43 §1[a]). The allowance formerly available for the cost of machinery and equipment acquired as a replacement for worn-out or obsolete assets of the same kind has been eliminated and replaced by a deduction for the depreciated cost of the asset which is replaced.[83]

7/5.2 Certain Payments to Owners and Officers of Firms and Companies

The law imposes restrictions on the deduction of compensation paid by entities to their owners, partners and certain elected officers if such payments are either in excess of the statutory limits or are not recorded in the books of the paying concern as regulated by the statute. The disallowed compensation or portion of the compensation is taxed to the recipient as income from capital under Schedule F, as distinguished from the allowable portion which is taxed to the recipient under Schedule C as compensation for services.[84]

In detail, the following payments are nondeductible (Reg. Art. 43 §1[b] and [c]).

a. CERTAIN WITHDRAWALS BY OWNERS OR PARTNERS. Withdrawals by owners or partners of the firm or company which are not charged to the general expense account or to a subsidiary account or which, although so charged, are not for services rendered or do not represent fixed monthly compensation agreed upon for such services (Reg. Art. 43 §1[b] and Reg. Art. 8[b]).[85] Furthermore, compensation which is in excess of the statutory limits is nondeductible to the extent set forth below (Reg. Art. 43 §1[c]; Art. 5 §§2–5):[86]

1. Annual payments to the administrative officers of a corporation or other entity exceeding either Cr$ 120,000 for each participant or 20% of the paid-in capital of the entity for all participants (Reg. Art. 5 §2).[87]

[83] Reg. Art. 37(e) as amended by Law No. 2,354 of November 29, 1954, Art. 17. The details of the presently available deduction are discussed in 7/3.4.

[84] Regarding taxation of compensation for services as an employee, see 8/1.

[85] The following payments have been held to be nondeductible as in the nature of distributions of profits: compensation based on the profits of the firm (CC, *Rev.* 1943 No. 725); commissions (CC, *Rev.* 1945 No. 124); likewise, legal fees paid to a partner (CC, *Rev.* 1950 No. 549).

[86] The quoted limitations only apply to remuneration for services; dividends or other benefits paid to the recipients in their capacity as shareholders are not taken into account, CC, *Rev.* 1950 No. 254; Sousa, §35-B.

[87] The administrative practice originally was to interpret this provision to mean that the second limitation (20% of the paid-in capital) applied in the case of each individual participant. See DIR, *Rev.* 1942 No. 180. This interpretation has been aban-

2. Annual payments to the members of the fiscal and administrative committee of any entity exceeding either Cr$ 60,000 for each participant or 20% of the paid-in capital of the entity for all participants (Reg. Art. 5 §2).[88]

3. Remuneration for services paid to the owner of a sole proprietorship or a partner of a commercial or industrial partnership or limited liability company [89] exceeding Cr$ 30,000 per annum, if the capital share *of the recipient* is Cr$ 150,000 or less; 20% of the capital share *of the recipient* or Cr$ 120,000, whichever is less, if the capital share *of the recipient* exceeds Cr$ 150,000 (Reg. Art. 5 §1[I][c] and §3).[90]

4. In the case of a partner without capital investment in the firm (*sócio de indústria*), payments for services rendered which are not in accordance with the terms of the partnership agreement or which, although stipulated in the agreement, either do not constitute fixed compensation for services or exceed an amount of Cr$ 10,000 per month. Also disallowed are payments in any amount which are not charged to expense (either the general expense account or a subsidiary account) on the books of the firm (Reg. Art. 5 §4).

5. Bonuses to employees,[91] however designated, which exceed Cr$ 120,-000 per year for any one beneficiary (Reg. Art. 5 §5).

In all cases above, only the excessive portion of the compensation, or the part thereof not entered as required in the books of the firm, is nondeductible (Reg. Art. 5 §6).

b. COMPENSATION TO NONRESIDENT DIRECTORS.   No part of any compensation for services or profit shares paid to corporate directors who are nonresidents of Brazil is deductible (Reg. Art. 43 §1[d]). This provision is not operative at present because the Corporation Law prohibits the appointment of directors who are not residents of Brazil.[92]

c. INTEREST PAID TO OWNERS OR PARTNERS.   Interest paid to owners or partners on their contributions to the capital of the firm is not deductible (Reg. Art. 43 §1[e]).[93]

7/5.3   Reserves

For the discussion of the difference between deductible "provisions" and nondeductible "reserves" in the proper sense, see 6/6.1. All amounts

doned in favor of the one stated in the text (CC, *Rev.* 1945 No. 158; 1951 Nos. 285-A, 972). See Rezende, Note 22.

[88] See footnote 87.   [89] CC, *Rev.* 1954 No. 158.

[90] This limitation has been interpreted to refer to the amount of the *registered* capital share of the partner of a limited liability company, as distinguished from the *paid-in* capital in the case of directors (see [1] above), CC, *Rev.* 1955 No. 38.

[91] This provision does not refer to a company's owners and officers, whose remuneration (including bonuses) is dealt with in §§2 and 3 of Reg. Art. 5 ([1] and [3] above), CC, *Rev.* 1952 Nos. 595, 627, 787, and 792; 1955 No. 46. On the other hand, the total remuneration paid to partners of a limited liability company is regulated by Reg. Art. 5 §3, even if the recipients are also officers of the firm, CC, *Rev.* 1955 No. 109.   [92] Corp. Law, Art. 116.

[93] Such interest may be included in the organization expenses of a corporation provided it does not exceed 6% per annum.

which a legal entity appropriates from surplus or current profits and credits to a reserve must be restored to profits for income tax purposes (Reg. Art. 43 §1[f]).

The purpose and designation of the reserves are entirely immaterial. The fact that a particular reserve may be required by prudent business practice or even be prescribed by the commercial law does not affect its taxability. Examples of taxable reserves are the amount of undistributed profits,[94] the legal reserve of corporations required by Article 130 of the Corporation Law, premiums on new shares issued which were credited to a special reserve fund,[95] tax reserves,[96] reserves for liabilities to employees under the labor law,[97] reserves for fluctuations in the value of securities held,[98] additions to obsolescence reserves after January 1, 1947,[99] etc.

Art. 43 §1(k) of the Income Tax Regulations expressly prohibits the deduction of inventory valuation reserves. The reason given for this rule, namely, that declines in the value of inventories are automatically given effect at annual intervals through the periodic valuation at the lower of cost or market,[100] does not seem valid as far as inventories of raw materials or goods in process are concerned. For these inventories, the Income Tax Regulations (Art. 141 §3) prescribe cost as the only basis of valuation; cost or market, whichever is lower, is the statutory basis of valuation only in regard to finished products.[101] It follows that in the event of a general decline in the price level of some product or article, adjustment for the lower price may be made only in the price of the finished product, which often will not be collected in the same accounting period. A company finding itself at the end of the year with large stocks of raw materials or natural products whose price has greatly declined after the date of their acquisition will not be permitted to value these inventories at the prevailing lower market prices and will thus be compelled to overstate its assets as well as its profits for that year.

7/5.4   Indemnifications Provided by the Labor Law

Under Reg. Art. 43 §1(m),[102] the amount of a reserve set up by a company to provide for indemnities prescribed by the labor law is not deductible in computing taxable income. The reason for the disallowance

---

[94] Reg. Art. 43 §1(f).

[95] CC, *Rev.* 1951 No. 469; the rule is different if the contribution of the shareholders is credited to capital, DIR, *Rev.* 1949 No. 684.

[96] CC, *Rev.* 1947 No. 54; 1949 No. 788; 1955 No. 56.

[97] Reg. Art. 43 §1(m). See 7/5.4.

[98] CC, *Rev.* 1946 No. 429; 1949 No. 99; 1954 No. 370; 1951 Nos. 1025 and 1385.

[99] Reg. Art. 43 §1(l).

[100] Sousa, §35(I); CC, *Rev.* 1947 No. 661 (but see CC *Rev.* 1950 No. 263).

[101] Reg. Art. 141 §4.

[102] This provision was added by Law No. 2,354 of 1954, Art. 6, Sec. II, which embodies the older case law on the subject.

is that appropriations of profits for this purpose are in the nature of a reserve for contingencies. If and when the liability of the employer to make payments of this type becomes fixed, the amounts actually expended constitute a proper deduction for income tax purposes.

7/6. Additions to Income

7/6.1 Distributions or Appropriations of Profits not Previously Taxed

Profits from any source not previously taxed become taxable income of an entity if they are used to increase its capital (Reg. Art. 43 §1[g]), or any of its reserves (Reg. Art. 43 §1[j]), or if they are distributed to the partners or shareholders in any form (Reg. Art. 43 §1[i]).

As a practical matter, only amounts transferred from a "provision" account (i.e., from the provision for depreciation, amortization, depletion, bad debts, etc.) could have legally remained untaxed.[103] The requirement under discussion, therefore, applies primarily to the complete or partial dissolution of one of these accounts.[104]

A corporation may increase its capital either by raising the nominal value of the outstanding shares or by distributing a stock dividend.[105] Either one constitutes a taxable event for the corporation, as does an increase in the value of the quotas of a limited liability company.[106]

The capitalization or distribution of previously untaxed amounts is a taxable event because these dispositions in effect terminate the former use of these funds which enjoyed exemption from income tax. It follows that funds on which income tax has already been paid are not taxed again to the entity when these funds are appropriated to increase its capital.[107]

For the same reason, an increase in capital which is financed by actual contributions of the partners or shareholders does not give rise to the imposition of a tax on the entity (DIR, *Rev.* 1949 No. 648). An increase in the capital of the Brazilian branch of a foreign entity through retention of profits is not a taxable event, because the profits or reserves from which the funds transferred to capital originate are necessarily tax-paid amounts.[108]

[103] Sousa, §35-G.

[104] Regarding an increase of capital and distribution of a stock dividend with funds taken from the depreciation provision, see CC, *Rev.* 1948 No. 235; for transfers from other formerly untaxed amounts, see DIR, *Rev.* 1948 No. 828; CC, *Rev.* 1950 No. 131. For the issuance of new shares in a reorganization financed with tax-paid funds, see DIR, *Rev.* 1948 No. 603.

[105] It is questionable whether this includes a stock split; illustrative example in CC, *Rev.* 1951 No. 1051.

[106] See decision of the Federal District Court for the Federal District in *Rev.* 1946 No. 354.

[107] DIR, *Rev.* 1948 No. 603; 1951 No. 1164; CC, *Rev.* 1950 No. 199.

[108] DIR, *Rev.* 1952 Nos. 92 and 97. The reasoning of the decisions is based on the principle that the profits and reserves of the branch are imputed to the foreign organization as of the date of their determination by operation of law and therefore imme-

The amounts transferred to capital or reserves must be included in taxable income of the year in which the transfer occurred.[109]

If reserves are newly created, they become subject to the special levy of 4% (in the nature of a compulsory loan) which is imposed on all reserves (7/8.2), and they are counted among the total reserves whose increase beyond the amount of the paid-in capital of a *corporation* results in the imposition of a tax of 30% on such excess reserves (7/8.3).

For the tax situation of the partners and shareholders of entities in the case of the increases in capital or reserves and the distributions discussed in the foregoing, see 9/2.1d.

7/6.2   Surplus from Revaluation of Fixed Assets

If a legal entity revalues its assets, the surplus arising from the revaluation must be added to its taxable income for the year of revaluation (Reg. Art. 43 §1[h]). In order to facilitate a more realistic presentation of asset values in the financial statements of business entities which gives effect to the progressive decline of monetary values, the income tax law successively adopted various tax incentives in order to encourage a revaluation of assets. Thus, revaluations undertaken between June 27, 1946, and December 31, 1947,[110] were entirely exempt from income tax. Revaluations performed between January 1, 1952, and June 30, 1953, were favored with a greatly reduced tax rate.[111] Revaluations of assets since July 1, 1953, are again subject to the general rule of Reg. Art. 43 §1(h).[112]

While the present law subjects revaluations to the full income tax rates both to the entity and to the owners, partners, or shareholders, it provides for a deferment of the tax imposed on the entity for up to four years from the year of revaluation, so that the revaluation surplus becomes taxable

diately subject to the withholding tax on nonresidents under Reg. Art. 97. The true reason would seem to be that the branch is deemed incapable of having its own reserves in the proper sense of the term, since it is an integral part of the foreign organization. Therefore all profits and "reserves" of the branch are subject to the regular income tax on entities under Reg. Art. 44; the additional imposition of the withholding tax under Reg. Art. 97 on the branch profits seems immaterial in this context. See annotation by Rezende, No. 46-G, to the ruling of the Income Tax Division in *Rev.* 1952 No. 97.

[109] DIR, *Rev.* 1949 No. 394; 1951 No. 469.

[110] I.e., during the effective period of Decree-law No. 9,407 of June 27, 1946. See Reg. Art. 43 §5.

[111] The statutory sources are former Reg. Art. 96 §3 as amended by Law No. 1,474 of November 26, 1951, and Law No. 1,772 of December 18, 1952. Only assets acquired up to December 31, 1946, were the object of the cited provisions which imposed a number of important restrictions as a condition of their application. The rate of tax imposed on the increase in value was 10%, payable by the entity in twenty-four monthly installments and deductible by it. This tax of 10% was in lieu of all taxes ordinarily imposed on the entity *and* on the owners or shareholders in connection with a revaluation.

[112] This rule also applied to revaluations between January 1, 1948, and December 31, 1951.

income not later than in the fifth year (base year) thereafter. As an example, a write-up of assets performed in base year 1954 must be included in taxable income of one of the following years up to base year 1959.[113] It is a condition of this temporary deferment of tax that the increase in the book value of the asset be balanced on the credit side of the financial statements by a corresponding revaluation reserve (Reg. Art. 43 §1 [h][I]).

The provisions of Reg. Art. 43 §1(h) apply to reorganizations accompanied by a revaluation of the assets of the transferor entity.[114] If, upon a revaluation in connection with a reorganization, the value of the shares (or capital quotas) of the shareholders (or partners) is increased, the individuals so benefited are subject to the complementary tax on this increase.[115]

Regarding revaluations of assets under Law No. 2,862 of September 4, 1956, and the special tax thereon, see 14/4.

7/6.3   Profits on the Sale of Assets

Profits on the sale of assets are likewise includible in taxable income under Reg. Art. 43 §1(h). The profit on the sale is measured by the difference between the sales price and the book value of the assets (cost less depreciation) at the time of the sale. There is no deferment of tax regarding this portion of taxable income.

This provision would seem rather superfluous in the case of most entities, because the gain realized by them on the sale of any of their assets (stock in trade or capital assets) will always form part of the actual profits. It is, however, of practical significance in the sale of real property by individual proprietorships, which are treated like entities for income tax purposes (5/3.4). Gain on the sale of real property sold by a sole proprietorship is taxed as part of its business income under Reg. Art. 44 and not at the special rates applied to such gains if realized by an individual taxpayer (9/8.2).[116] Likewise, a gain on the sale of securities forms part of the business income of a sole proprietorship, whereas such gains are not taxed at all if realized by an individual who is not engaged in business.

If a company sells shares of another corporation below their nominal value to the members of the company in proportion to their capital shares,

---

[113] Apparently, the taxpayer may select the year in which to report this income or distribute it over several years; the tax rates of the year of inclusion apply. See Rezende, Note 173-C.

[114] CC, *Rev.* 1949 No. 274 (incorporation of sole proprietorship) and *Rev.* 1951 No. 612 (reorganization of corporation).

[115] See CC, *Rev.* 1949 No. 864. In the case of bearer shares, the tax under Reg. Art. 96 must be withheld by the corporation.

[116] DIR, *Rev.* 1948 No. 405; see also CC, *Rev.* 1951 No. 1287.

the sale is in the nature of an anticipated distribution of profits (DIR, *Rev.* 1949 No. 651). The gain to the members, measured by the difference between the sales price of the shares and their face value, is taxed to them as a dividend, and the loss sustained on the sale by the distributing company is not recognized for income tax purposes.

7/7.   Exclusions from Income

7/7.1   Distributions of Profits Already Taxed to the Distributing Entity

Profits which were subjected to income tax under Reg. Art. 44 in the hands of the entity which distributes these profits in the form of a dividend or otherwise, are not includible in the taxable income of the recipient entity, provided that payment of the tax is duly proved (Reg. Art. 43 §2[c]). See discussion under 9/2.3.

The gain on the sale of shares of other corporations is clearly income not previously taxed and is therefore includible in the business income of the selling corporation.[117]

7/7.2   Income from Bearer Securities

Under the Brazilian system of taxation, all income from securities made out to bearer is taxed at the source, and the tax liability in respect of such income is fully satisfied by payment of the withholding tax. Consequently, dividends received on bearer shares and interest received on bearer bonds held in its portfolio are not included in an entity's taxable income and need not be reported in its income tax return (Reg. Art. 43 §2[d]). The theory of the law is that since the tax withheld at the source is imposed on the recipient of the income and not the payor who merely acts as withholding agent, the recipient shall not be burdened with a second tax on the same income.[118]

This exemption, however, applies only for the benefit of the recipient entity; it does not carry over to the owners of the latter. If Company A, which holds bearer shares of Company B, receives a dividend from B and in turn distributes this dividend to its own (A's) shareholders, the distribution is subject to tax in their hands. The method of taxation follows the general rules, i.e., if the shares of Company A are bearer shares, A will withhold 28% tax under Reg. Art. 96(3)(a) for the account of the shareholders;[119] if the shares are nominative, the shareholders will include the dividend in their income tax returns under Schedule F (Reg. Art. 8[c]).[120]

---

[117] CC, *Rev.* 1949 No. 203.
[118] See DIR, *Rev.* 1947 No. 649; and Rezende, Note 173.
[119] DIR, *Rev.* 1951 No. 620.
[120] CC, *Rev.* 1951 No. 827; 1952 Nos. 855 and 986; 1955 No. 26; see 9/2.1

7/7.3   Insurance on the Life of an Owner or Partner

If a partnership or limited liability company [121] is the beneficiary under a policy insuring the life of one of its partners or owners, amounts paid by the insurance company by reason of the death of the insured are not includible in the taxable income of the entity (Reg. Art. 43 §2[e]). The premiums paid by the entity are a proper deduction for income tax purposes (7/2.8). The treatment of life insurance is therefore the same in the case of an entity as it is in the case of an individual taxpayer, if the entity is the beneficiary under the policy.

7/8.   Special Taxation of Reserves

7/8.1   In General

In addition to the inclusion of reserves in taxable income for purposes of the regular income tax, the law [122] provides for special taxes on reserves as set forth below.[123]

7/8.2   Temporary Levy of 4% on Reserves (Compulsory Loan)

Art. 3(b), Law No. 1,474 of November 26, 1951, imposed a special charge of 3% on the reserves of a legal entity to be collected during the five taxable years from 1952 through 1956 (base years 1951 through 1955). The collection of this charge was extended for 10 years, i.e., until taxable year 1966 (base year 1965) by Law No. 2,973 of November 26, 1956, which also increased its rate to 4%.

The 4% charge is imposed on the total of all reserves, surplus, and undistributed profits which appear in the financial statements of the company.[124] The statutes [125] except only the legal reserves of corporations [126] (6/6.2) and the special reserves of insurance and capitalization companies. However, they follow the distinction between reserves and pro-

---

[121] The statements made in the text do not apply to the shareholders of a corporation (even a closely held corporation) or to employees and officers of a corporation.

[122] Art. 3, Law No. 1,474 of November 26, 1951, as modified by Law No. 2,973 of November 26, 1956.

[123] The temporary tax privileges applicable in the case of increases of capital (before July 1, 1953) by way of utilization of reserves accumulated to December 31, 1951 (Law No. 1,474 Art. 1 §§2–4 and Law No. 1,772 of December 18, 1952) are omitted as obsolete. See Sousa, §47.

[124] Law No. 1,474 Art. 3 §2(III); Regulations promulgated by Decree 30,812 of May 2, 1952, Art. 4 §5; Law No. 2,973, Art. 1 §3. It follows that only reserves included in the balance sheet for the end of the base year are included, not reserves which were formed and dissolved in the same base year, Rezende, Note 165.

[125] Law No. 1,474 Art. 3(b); Decree 30,812, Art. 4 §1(b); Law No. 2,973, Art. 1 §3.

[126] Corporation Law, Art. 130. A similar reserve set up by a limited liability company will be subject to the charge because it is not required by law, CC, *Rev.* 1954 No. 453.

visions (6/6.1), and the contribution will not be imposed on provisions for depreciation (7/3.1–7/3.3), amortization (7/3.5, 7/3.6), bad debts (7/2.9), and depletion (10/1.2), so long as such provisions are within the statutory limits.[127]

The statutory provisions are entirely clear in stating that the levy under discussion is imposed on all entities *except* individuals who for income tax purposes assume the status of entities.[128] Since the profits of a sole proprietorship are always at the disposition of the owner, a separation of the profits on the books of the firm and their allocation to reserves, undistributed profits, etc., has no effect for income tax purposes.[129]

The same principle applies to the Brazilian branch of a foreign entity, which, as an integral part of the foreign organization, has, strictly speaking, no reserves or undistributed profits of its own which could be the object of a special contribution.[130]

There has been some uncertainty whether the contribution is assessed on the same reserves from year to year or only on new reserves or increases of existing reserves. The weight of authority and the administrative practice favor the latter interpretation.[131]

The contribution is in the nature of a compulsory loan and is to be refunded beginning with the sixth year after collection, together with a premium.[132] It is collected as a separate (fifth) installment following the last installment of the regular income tax.[133]

7/8.3 Taxation of Excess Reserves of Corporations

The income tax law adds a sanction to the rule of the Corporation Law that the reserves of a corporation may in no event exceed the amount of the paid-in capital stock.[134] If this rule is violated, a tax of 30% is imposed on the excess. The tax is intended to counteract the practice of letting surplus accumulate in the corporation, rather than distributing it to the shareholders, to avoid the imposition of the complementary tax on corporate distributions classified under Schedule F.

The tax is imposed on the shareholders, but the corporation must withhold the tax and pay it within 30 days after the general meeting of the shareholders approving the increase in the reserves.

[127] The charge will be imposed on the excess of a reserve for income tax over the amount of tax debited to the reserve (rather than to profit and loss account) during the base year, CC, *Rev.* 1954 No. 402.

[128] Reg. Art. 27 §1; see 5/3.4.

[129] Rezende, Note 165.

[130] Rezende, *loc. cit.*

[131] Sousa, §30(B); Rezende, *loc. cit.*

[132] Law No. 1,474, Art. 3 §3; Law No. 1,628 of June 20, 1952; Decree 30,812, Art. 4 §11; Law No. 2,973, Art. 1 §3.

[133] It is in this respect exactly like the addition to the income tax discussed at 12/2.4a and it is regulated in the same statute.

[134] Law No. 1,474 of 1951, Art. 2; Reg. Art. 99; Corp. Law, Art. 130 §2.

By express provision of the statute, the tax applies only to corporations and not to other entities such as limited liability companies (DIR, *Rev.* 1952 No. 88), partnerships, or individual firms treated like corporations for income tax purposes. The tax is independent of, and levied in addition to, the regular income tax (Reg. Art. 99).

Whereas the prohibition of the Corporation Law applies only to excessive statutory reserves, the penalty tax attaches to reserves of all kinds without distinction, including accumulated surplus, undistributed profits,[135] and excessive provisions for depreciation, amortization, depletion, and bad debts.[136]

The capitalization of the excess reserves or their distribution to the shareholders does not give rise to the income tax on the shareholders usually resulting from such transactions. The 30% tax is in lieu of all income taxes imposed on the shareholders in connection with corporate distributions.[137] If the shares on which the distribution is made are nominative, the shareholder is entitled to credit a proportionate part of the 30% tax paid by the corporation on his behalf against his personal income tax.[138] If the shares are made out to bearer, the tax paid by the corporation is in lieu of the 28% tax [139] otherwise withheld by the corporation on such distributions.

The liability for the tax arises as soon as the general meeting of shareholders passes a resolution approving an increase of the reserves beyond the statutory limit; it is not affected by a reversal of this decision.[140]

---

[135] DIR, *Rev.* 1952 No. 770; CC, *Rev.* 1955 No. 189; Sousa, §47; Rezende, Note 165.

[136] DIR, *Rev.* 1952 No. 93; CC, *Rev.* 1955 No. 189. The term "excessive" is used in a dual sense in this context. Provisions for depreciation, amortization, depletion, and bad debts are termed "reserves" only to the extent that they exceed the proper limits of such provisions as determined by administrative practice. Only this excess over the deductible amounts is combined with the other reserves to determine whether the total is greater than the amount of the paid-in capital stock; this latter excess, if any, is the basis of the tax on the excess reserves.

Rezende, Note 165, points to the danger of establishing excess provisions for depreciation, etc., in view of the uncertainty resulting from the failure of the income tax statute to fix the proper limits of these deductions. On the other hand, it should be remembered that the determination of these provisions is not final unless and until it is approved by the general meeting, which is held after the end of the base year; the resolutions date back to the balance sheet date (see CC, *Rev.* 1955 No. 190). It should, therefore, be possible at that time to establish with reasonable certainty whether there is an excess of reserves which would be subject to the 30% tax.

[137] Reg. Art. 99 Sole §; Law No. 1,474, Art. 2 §2.

[138] Reg. Art. 24 §7; Law No. 1,474, Art. 2 §3. The computation of the amount to be credited may present some difficulty. As an example, a corporation has excess reserves of Cr$ 100,000 on which it pays the 30% tax, or Cr$ 30,000. The corporation distributes the excess reserves in the form of a cash dividend and A who owns 50% of the stock receives Cr$ 35,000. Apparently A reports income of Cr$ 50,000 under Schedule F and takes a credit of Cr$ 15,000 (50% of Cr$ 30,000) against his personal income tax. See Rezende, Note 165.

[139] Reg. Art. 96(3) as amended by Law No. 2,862, Art. 25.

[140] Rezende, Note 165.

Since the tax is imposed on the shareholders, it is not deductible by the corporation.

The excess reserves are taxed only once; if the reserves are further increased in a later year by another resolution of the general meeting of the shareholders, the tax falls only on the new increase, not on the excessive amount already taxed in the prior year.

Whether the 15% addition to the income tax, in the nature of a compulsory loan (12/2.4a), is payable also on the 30% tax on excess reserves is doubtful. It seems, however, that the income tax authorities insist on the collection of this addition. On the other hand, Reg. Art. 210 §1, which enumerates the statutory sources of the various taxes subject to the 15% addition, makes no reference to Reg. Art. 99, which imposes the 30% tax.

CHAPTER 8

INCOME FROM

PERSONAL SERVICES

8/1. Compensation for Services as an Employee

    8/1.1 In General

    8/1.2 Gross Income

          a. Employees

          b. Officers, Partners, etc.

    8/1.3 Deductions

          a. Travel Expenses

          b. Office Expenses

          c. Dues

          d. Contributions to Employees' Benefit Funds

    8/1.4 Tax Rate

    8/1.5 Withholding at Source on Wages and Salaries

          a. Employees

          b. Corporate Officers and Directors, Owners and Partners of a Business

8/2. Income from Professional Services and Other Independent Work

    8/2.1 In General

    8/2.2 Gross Income

    8/2.3 Deductions

    8/2.4 Blanket Deduction

    8/2.5 Tax Rate

8/3. Income-Spreading Provisions

    8/3.1 In General

    8/3.2 Wages and Salaries

    8/3.3 Professional Fees

8/1. Compensation for Services as an Employee

8/1.1 In General

The income discussed in this section is that earned by an individual for services rendered as an employee. For purposes of the schedular classification, compensation for the services of the owner of an individual business, a partner, or a member of the fiscal and administrative committee of a corporation is treated like income from employment. Regarding the tax situation of foreign employees rendering services in Brazil, see 11/3.4c.

8/1.2 Gross Income

a. EMPLOYEES. Income from compensation for services rendered by an employee is classified under Schedule C, regardless of the nature and description of the services, the designation of the remuneration (salaries, wages, profit participations,[1] per diems, bonuses, gratuities, expense and representation allowances,[2] etc.), and the characteristics of the employer (i.e., whether a government agency, a private firm, a corporation, or an individual).

The form of the contract under which the services are rendered is entirely immaterial, provided only that an employer-employee relationship exists; whether it does or not is determined by the labor law. The Income Tax Regulations (Art. 5 §1[II]) expressly include pensions and retirement pay resulting from an employment contract and the remuneration of traveling salesmen (Reg. Art. 5 §1[a]). The income from independent professional services (e.g., those of a lawyer, physician, engineer, etc.) is classified under Schedule C rather than Schedule D if the services are rendered under a fixed retainer agreement (CC, *Rev.* 1951 No. 242/243).

A voluntary bonus paid by the employer is taxable to the employee under Schedule C to the extent that the annual amount of the bonus does not exceed Cr$ 120,000; any excess is taxed under Schedule F (see under b[5], below).

b. OFFICERS, PARTNERS, ETC. The compensation paid to the members of the fiscal and administrative committee of a corporation or to corporate officers,[3] and the "salaries" of the owner of an individual business or the partner of a commercial or industrial partnership are likewise included

---

[1] Also commissions earned by an employee. Commissions of an independent broker, agent, or manufacturer's representative come under Schedule D. The difference is important not only because of the tax rate, but also because of the applicable deductions.

[2] The employee must include the amounts reimbursed in gross income (Reg. Art. 11 §1[c]) and then deduct the amounts actually disbursed (Reg. Art. 14[a]); the same is true for social security payments deducted by the employer.

[3] Called "directors"; see 1/4.2g.

under Schedule C, provided that the amounts paid or credited to these individuals are not in excess of certain statutory limits and are duly entered in the books of the firm.

The principle determining the tax treatment of these types of compensation was discussed in connection with the deduction allowable to the company or corporation in computing its business income (7/5.2): if the compensation paid does not exceed the monetary limits of the statute and meets its accounting requirements, it is deductible by the paying entity and taxed to the recipient under Schedule C as compensation for services. If it exceeds the statutory limits, the excessive portion is not deductible by the payor and is taxed to the recipient as income from capital under Schedule F (Reg. Art. 5 §6). If the accounting requirements of the statute are violated, no part of the compensation is deductible by the payor, and all of it is taxed to the recipient under Schedule F.

In detail, the following payments to administrative officers of a corporation or company and to the members of the fiscal and administrative committee of a corporation are included in the taxable income of the recipients under Schedule C:

1. Annual payments to the members of the fiscal and administrative committee of any company or corporation not exceeding Cr$ 60,000 for *each* participant, or 20% of the paid-in capital of the company or corporation for *all* participants (Reg. Art. 5 §2);

2. Annual payments to the administrative officers of any company or corporation not exceeding Cr$ 120,000 for *each* participant, or 20% of the paid-in capital of the company or corporation for *all* participants (Reg. Art. 5 §2);[4]

3. Payments to the owner of an individual firm or a partner of a commercial or industrial partnership of Cr$ 30,000 per year, if the capital share *of the recipient* does not exceed Cr$ 150,000; 20% of his capital share, if it is larger than Cr$ 150,000; but in no event more than Cr$ 120,000 per year (Reg. Art. 5 §3).

4. In the case of a partner without capital investment in a firm, the amount of compensation includible under Schedule C is limited to Cr$ 10,000 per month (Reg. Art. 5 §4).

5. Amounts received as a bonus, however designated, cannot exceed an amount of Cr$ 120,000 per year for any employee (Reg. Art. 5 §5).

The types of compensation referred to in numbers 3 and 4 above must be expressed in fixed monthly amounts, and they must be charged either to general expense or to a subsidiary expense account on the books of the company (Reg. Art. 5 §1[I][c] and §4). The amounts paid must be for services rendered by the individual in the capacity of an owner or

---

[4] CC, *Rev.* 1951 No. 972. DIR, *Rev.* 1942 No. 180 had ruled the limit to be 20% of capital but not more than Cr$ 60,000 (or Cr$ 120,000, respectively) for *each* participant. See criticism by Rezende in footnote to the 1942 decision, reproduced in *Anotações* (1st ed.) p. 38; passing reference in *Anotações* (2d ed.) Note 22.

partner of the firm.[5] Commissions paid to an owner or partner are excluded from taxation under Schedule C.[6] The bonuses referred to in number 5 above are voluntary payments by the employer which must be distinguished from the contractual profit participations discussed at 7/2.12; the latter are taxed to the recipient under Schedule F. Bonuses paid to owners, partners, the administrative officers of a company or to the members of its fiscal and administrative committee are likewise not covered by Reg. Art. 5 §5 (number 5 above), because the total remuneration of these individuals (including bonuses) is subject to the limitations indicated in numbers 1–4 above.[7]

It should be noted that income from the forgiveness or cancellation of indebtedness in consideration of services rendered is taxable under Schedule C if the services are those of an employee (Reg. Art. 11 §1[a]).

For allocation of income from salaries and wages to more than one taxable year, see 8/3.2 below.

8/1.3 Deductions

The following deductions, and only these, are allowed against Schedule C income under Art. 14 of the Regulations.

a. TRAVEL EXPENSES. Traveling expenses include the cost of transportation and the board and lodging of the employee, expenses for freight and cartage of articles required for the trip, and rent for premises used for exhibition purposes.

Under the decisions,[8] the expense of domestic or foreign travel of employees, corporate officers, or members of the fiscal and administrative committee of a corporation is deductible only if it is necessarily incurred in the proper exercise of the functions of the employee and thus constitutes an indispensable requirement for earning his income. While the employee who claims the deduction will have to prove the necessity of the expense, the decisions are not uniform as to the proof required to substantiate its amount.[9] In order to deduct the expense, the employee's trip must be to some destination other than either his home or the place where he is employed.[10] No deduction is allowed for the cost of commuting to the place of business if the officer or employee resides in a different locality for his own convenience.[11]

---

[5] Compensation for legal services rendered to the firm by one of its members is not taxed under Schedule C; CC, *Rev.* 1950 No. 549; see Rezende, Note 20.

[6] CC, *Rev.* 1945 Nos. 23 and 124; 1950 Nos. 31, 41, 152; 1951 Nos. 409, 597, 1317.   [7] See Note 91 at 7/5.2.

[8] CC, *Rev.* 1952 Nos. 605, 974; 1953 Nos. 137, 363, 483, 533, and 557; 1954 No. 150.

[9] Compare CC, *Rev.* 1951 No. 1053; 1953 No. 483 (proof of expense required) and CC, *Rev.* 1953 No. 439; 1954 No. 292 (expenses which are modest in comparison with the employee's income allowed without strict proof).

[10] CC, *Rev.* 1952 No. 974.   [11] CC, *Rev.* 1948 No. 5A.

Amounts received by an officer, partner, or employee as reimbursement for traveling and similar expenses must be included in his taxable income under Schedule C (Reg. Art. 11 §1[c]); the amounts actually expended by him are deductible.

b. OFFICE EXPENSES. This deduction is only available to certain tax-payers such as public officials, traveling salesmen, etc., who are required to pay their own office expenses (including expenses of correspondence) out of their compensation (CC, *Rev.* 1950 Nos. 369 and 371).

c. DUES. Membership dues paid to scientific associations and expenses for the purchase of or subscriptions to journals, periodicals, and technical books are deductible. Expenses in connection with the purchase or rental of materials, instruments, or other equipment are likewise deductible under this heading so long as they are indispensable for the exercise of a technical profession or occupation.[12]

d. CONTRIBUTIONS TO EMPLOYEES' BENEFIT FUNDS. The mandatory con-tributions collected by employees' benefit funds, such as the Institutes of Social Security, are deductible under this heading.[13] The same is true for the syndicate tax,[14] but premiums under group life insurance policies are not deductible.

Expenses not specifically allowed by the Regulations cannot be de-ducted, even if they are necessary to earn or collect the salary.[15]

8/1.4   Tax Rate

The rate of the schedular tax under Schedule C is 1% (Reg. Art. 25).

8/1.5   Withholding at Source on Wages and Salaries

a. EMPLOYEES. Withholding of income tax at the source on salaries and wages became effective in Brazil on January 1, 1955.[16]

The types of compensation subject to withholding are those which are classified under Schedule C and include commissions, per diems,

[12] DIR, *Rev.* 1943 No. 120-A. In practice, the deduction is allowed without further proof if it is not in excess of 5% of gross schedular income; if a larger deduc-tion is claimed, the excess over 5% is subject to proof, CC, *Rev.* 1945 No. 463; 1946 No. 215; 1954 Nos. 153, 385, and 514; 1955 No. 35. See Sousa, §9 and Rezende, Note 63.

[13] The Institutes of Social Security also collect voluntary contributions towards an increase of the regular pensions, which are treated like insurance premiums.

[14] This tax represents union dues instituted by the federal government in the form of a salary tax, the collection of which is delegated to the unions themselves. The unions may collect voluntary dues besides this tax.

[15] CC. *Rev.* 1952 No. 378; Rezende, Note 59.

[16] The provisions of Law No. 2,354 of November 29, 1954, which introduced this innovation, were incorporated in Reg. Art. 98(2). They were amended by Law No. 2,862 of September 4, 1956, Arts. 20, 21. The new provisions became effective January 1, 1957.

and other variable payments. The employer is required to withhold income tax for every month in which the compensation paid or credited to the employee or worker is more than Cr$ 5,000. If the monthly compensation exceeds Cr$ 10,000, withholding is required in respect of the portion between Cr$ 5,000 and Cr$ 10,000 computed after deducting the monthly social security contributions and the syndicate tax (8/1.3d).[17]

In computing the withholding tax, full consideration is given to the personal exemption and the family allowances of the employee, which are prorated on a monthly basis.[18] The applicable amounts are listed in a new withholding table which supersedes the one in effect for 1955 and 1956.[19] Payment of the tax must be made during the month following the one in which it was withheld.[20] Compensation for services paid in advance must be allocated to the months to which it pertains and the withholding tax is computed and paid accordingly (Law No. 2,862, Art. 20 §5).

The employee must give a statement of his family status and dependents to his employer who forwards a copy thereof to the Income Tax Division. The statement is valid for one year and withholding proceeds according to the employee's family situation on January 1. The employer is not responsible for the correctness of the statement.[21]

The tax liability of an employee whose only income is from salaries or wages of not more than Cr$ 10,000 in any one month, received from one employer, is fully satisfied by withholding at the source, and the employee is not required to file a return.[22] If the salary or wages exceeded Cr$ 10,000 during any one month of the base year, if the employee received compensation for services from more than one employer, or if he had other income during the base year, he is required to file a return,[23] provided that his annual gross income from all sources is more than Cr$ 60,000.[24] In this case, the employee will credit the tax withheld against the total tax computed on his return.[25]

---

[17] Law No. 2,862, Art. 20 and its §3. This rule constitutes an important departure from the prior law under which the withholding provisions were entirely inapplicable if the monthly compensation exceeded Cr$ 10,000.

[18] Law No. 2,862, Art. 20, §1. This represents another important reform of the prior law which gave insufficient consideration to the family situation of the employee and often resulted in a withholding tax where no tax (or a lesser one) would have been due under Schedule C.

[19] Law No. 2,862, Art. 20 §2.

[20] Reg. Art. 102 §4.

[21] Reg. Art. 98 Sole §.

[22] Reg. Art. 63 §1(b) as amended by Law No. 2,862, Art. 21.

[23] Reg. Art. 63 §9 as amended by Law No. 2,862, Art. 21 Sole §.

[24] While there is liability for income tax only if the *net* annual income of an individual exceeds Cr$ 60,000 (Reg. Art. 1 as modified by Law No. 2,862 Art. 19), a return must be filed if *gross* annual income is more than Cr$ 60,000 (Reg. Art. 63 §1[a] and Law No. 2,862, Art. 19 §2).

[25] Reg. Art. 24 §6.

b. CORPORATE OFFICERS AND DIRECTORS, OWNERS AND PARTNERS OF A BUSI-
NESS. The withholding provisions set forth above apply to corporate
officers and to the members of the fiscal and administrative committees of
corporations and companies as well as to owners of sole proprietorships
and partners of commercial or industrial enterprises. The compensation
of these persons [26] (whether fixed or variable) is subject to withholding
at the source according to the rules set forth under (a) above.

8/2. Income from Professional Services and Other Independent Work

8/2.1 In General

This section covers the taxation of compensation for independent
services, including professional and certain business services. As far as
commercial services are rendered by an entity, the income therefrom is
business income and is taxed according to the rules which apply to that
classification (7/1.1).

8/2.2 Gross Income

Income from professional services and from other independent work,
including the income from personal services other than those rendered by
an employee, is classified under Schedule D. In detail, the law (Reg. Art.
6) lists the following types of income:

1. Fees for professional services, including those of a physician, engineer,
   lawyer, accountant, dentist, and others of a similar nature. It should be
   noted, however, that the administrative decisions regard a doctor, lawyer,
   accountant, etc., receiving a fixed monthly retainer (independent of the
   volume of work done for the particular client) as an employee for income
   tax purposes. Consequently, a fixed monthly retaining fee is taxed as a
   salary under Schedule C rather than as a professional fee under Schedule
   D.[27] It follows that if a professional man receives a fixed retainer or
   retainers from one or several clients but not from others, the retainer is
   taxed under Schedule C and the fees under Schedule D.[28]
2. Income from the rendering of services of a *noncommercial* nature. An
   individual exercising a *commercial* activity is treated for income tax
   purposes like a legal entity.
3. The remuneration of agents, representatives, and other persons who,
   although participating in commercial transactions, do not carry them out
   for their own account.[29]

[26] Regarding the determination of the individual income tax on this type of compensation, see 8/1.2b; regarding the deduction available to the corporation or company, see 7/5.2.
[27] CC, *Rev.* 1949 No. 862; 1951 No. 242/243; 1954 No. 549; and, especially, 1951
No. 1036. See also Sousa, §10, and Rezende, Note 17.
It would appear that withholding applies because it is settled that professional
services on a retainer basis are classified as Schedule C income for taxation by assessment, even though there is not, strictly speaking, an employer-employee relationship
as otherwise required under Schedule C; see Sousa, *loc. cit.*
[28] CC, *Rev.* 1954 Nos. 62 and 549.   [29] CC, *Rev.* 1949 No. 1063.

4. Remuneration and expense reimbursements received by persons exercising auxiliary judicial functions such as notaries, public officials and others, to the extent that they are not compensated from public funds.

5. Brokerage and commissions earned by brokers, auctioneers, and forwarding agents.

6. The income from contracts for work and labor, such as contracts for the services of an independent architect, builder, engineer, contractor, etc., whether the services are in the nature of designing or construction. It should be carefully noted, however, that the contract must be for services only. If materials are furnished, the income is treated as derived from a commercial activity by an individual proprietorship and taxed under the rules applying to entities and not under Schedule D (5/3.4).[30]

Interest on fees and other compensation classified under Schedule D is likewise taxed under this schedule, as is income from a forgiveness or cancellation of indebtedness in consideration of services rendered which are classified under Schedule D.[31]

For allocation of professional fees to more than one taxable year, see 8/3.3 below.

8/2.3 Deductions

The deductions allowed under Schedule C (8/1.3) are applicable to Schedule D income. In addition to those deductions, the following are permitted by the statute (Reg. Art. 15):

1. Advertising expenses;

2. Rent, water, light, power, and telephone expenses for the premises in which the professional activity is exercised;

3. Premiums for fire and other insurance covering the installations used in the income-producing activity;

4. Compensation for services of employees;

5. Rent or maintenance expense of vehicles used by doctors or their personnel;

6. Employers' contributions to employees' social welfare organizations;

7. Litigation fees and court costs which are collected with the fees;

8. Taxes incurred in connection with the exercise of the profession (except income tax);

9. Reasonable amounts for depreciation of the cost of the initial investment in professional equipment, determined on the basis of the cost of acquisition of the installations and their expected life (Reg. Art. 15 §1[a]). The administrative decisions limit this deduction to a maximum of 10% of the cost per year;[32]

10. The profit shares distributed to third parties, provided that their names and addresses and the amounts paid to them are indicated in the taxpayer's return (Reg. Art. 15 §1[b]).

[30] Sousa, §10 and §27.
[31] Reg. Art. 11 §1(a); Reg. Art. 4 §3; Rezende, Note 48.
[32] CC, *Rev.* 1945 No. 391, and 1949 No. 479. See also Sousa, §10; Rezende, Note 76 (10%, at most 20%).

If the taxpayer conducts the professional activity in a rented residence, he may deduct 20% of the rental paid, provided that no other deduction is claimed by him for outside office rent (Reg. Art. 15 §2). If the activity is conducted in the taxpayer's own home, a proportionate part of the expenses for light, power, water, etc., may be deducted.[33]

In the case of taxpayers who have income from both Schedules C and D — for instance, a physician with both a private practice and a salaried position in a hospital, or a lawyer who receives fixed retainers from some clients and individual fees from others — deductions applying to both types of income may be taken only once, and the taxpayer must elect whether to take them under Schedule C or Schedule D. The law makes no provision for an allocation of these deductions on the basis of gross schedular income. Since the tax rate under Schedule D is twice as high as the rate applied to Schedule C income, it will usually be to the advantage of the taxpayer to claim the deductions under Schedule D rather than Schedule C.

8/2.4 Blanket Deduction

Because the exact amount of the deductions allowed under Schedule D will in many instances be difficult to prove, the administrative practice is to sanction a blanket deduction of 40% computed on gross Schedule D income. This blanket deduction, however, cannot be claimed by the taxpayer as a matter of right, and it does not relieve him of the burden of substantiating his expenses.[34] It is for the government to decide on the basis of the detailed information presented by the taxpayer whether the application of the 40% rule is justified in the individual case. If the taxpayer can fully prove his expenses, they will be allowed as a deduction even if they are in excess of 40% of gross income.[35]

8/2.5 Tax Rate

The rate of the schedular tax under Schedule D is 2% (Reg. Art. 25).

8/3. Income-Spreading Provisions

8/3.1 In General

The Income Tax Regulations provide for the allocation of compensation for services rendered during more than one year, but paid in a single

---

[33] Rezende, Note 72, suggests the application of the 20% deduction of Reg. Art. 15 §2 (see text). See also CC, *Rev.* 1947 No. 421.

[34] Ministry of Finance, *Rev.* 1950 Nos. 632 and 708; CC, *Rev.* 1950 No. 82. See Rezende, Note 67. The blanket deduction of 40% cannot be substituted for itemized deductions claimed in the return after the taxpayer has received a notice of assessment, CC, *Rev.* 1954 No. 166. See also item 8 in 6/1.2a.

[35] CC, *Rev.* 1954 Nos. 113 and 448; 1955 No. 150; and numerous other decisions quoted by Rezende, *loc. cit.*

year, over the base years in which the services were rendered. Although the applicable provisions are of no practical effect as far as the schedular tax with its fixed rates is concerned (except in the case of a change in tax rates over the years), they are of considerable importance regarding the complementary tax, which is computed at graduated rates. The conditions on which the application of the relief provisions depends must be proved by the taxpayer who wants to avail himself of them.[36]

8/3.2 Wages and Salaries

Under Art. 23(d) of the Income Tax Regulations, salaries and wages received in one amount pursuant to a judicial or administrative decision may be allocated in equal amounts to the base years to which they apply.

8/3.3 Professional Fees

If compensation taxable under Schedule D — such as that of a lawyer, physician, engineer, etc. — for services rendered during more than one year is paid in a lump sum, the amount of compensation may be allocated to the base years in which it was earned (Reg. Art. 23[a]).

[36] CC, *Rev.* 1955 No. 17.

CHAPTER 9

....

INCOME FROM CAPITAL

9/1. Interest Income

9/1.1   Resident Individuals

9/1.2   Interest on Nominative Government Securities
a. Gross Income
b. Deductions
c. Tax Rate

9/1.3   Interest on Other Nominative Securities
a. Gross Income
b. Deductions
c. Tax Rate

9/1.4   Miscellaneous Interest Taxable under Schedule B
a. Interest on Deposits, Debts, and Loans
b. Implied and Presumed Interest
c. Profits from Discount Operations

9/1.5   Interest Classified under Other Schedules

9/1.6   Interest on Bearer Securities

9/1.7   Resident Entities

9/1.8   Nonresidents

9/2. Income from Dividends and Other Distributions

9/2.1   Distributions to Resident Individuals Taxable under Schedule F
a. Sole Proprietorship and Partnership Profits
b. Cash Dividends on Nominative Shares
c. Stock Dividends
d. Distributions Not in the Nature of Profits and Dividends

      e. Distributions to Holders of Participating
        Certificates
      f. Revaluation

9/2.2 Distributions to Resident Individuals Taxed at
the Source

      a. Cash Dividends and Other Cash Distributions
        on Bearer Shares
      b. Stock Dividends on Bearer Shares
      c. Distributions to Holders of Capitalization
        Bonds
      d. Distributions on Participating Certificates

9/2.3 Distributions to Resident Entities

9/2.4 Distributions to Nonresident Individuals and
Entities

9/3. Annuities, Pensions, and Life Insurance

9/3.1 Individuals

9/3.2 Entities

9/4. Income from Rent

9/4.1 Real Property Rentals — Resident Individuals
and Entities

      a. Gross Income
      b. Deductions
      c. Tax Rate

9/4.2 Real Property Rentals — Nonresidents

9/4.3 Income from Subleasing Real Property and
from Renting Movable Property

      a. Resident Individuals
      b. Resident Entities
      c. Nonresidents
      d. Compensation for the Use of Foreign
        Motion Pictures

9/5. Income from Royalties

9/5.1 Royalties from Licensing Patents, Processes,
Formulas, and Copyrights

      a. Resident Individuals
      b. Resident Entities
      c. Nonresidents

9/5.2 Royalties from Licensing Industrial and
Commercial Trademarks

      a. Resident Individuals
      b. Resident Entities
      c. Nonresidents

9/6. Presumptive Income

9/6.1   In General

9/7. Taxation at Source of Income from Capital

9/7.1   Income from Capital Taxed at Source to Residents

9/7.2   Income from Capital Taxed at Source to Nonresidents

9/8. Capital Gains

9/8.1   General Rule

9/8.2   Gains on the Sale of Real Property
   a. Basis
   b. Determination of Gain
   c. Tax Rate
   d. Payment of the Tax

9/9. Liquidation and Reorganization

9/9.1   In General

9/9.2   Liquidation of Business Entities

9/9.3   Change in the Legal Form of a Business — Effect on Existing Tax Liabilities
   a. Succession
   b. Transformation
   c. Continuation of the Business of a Dissolved Entity

9/9.4   Change in the Legal Form of a Business Not a Taxable Event

9/9.5   Gains from the Redemption of Securities
   a. Resident Individuals
   b. Resident Entities
   c. Nonresidents

9/1.   Interest Income

9/1.1   Resident Individuals

All income from interest received by individuals is subject to schedular and complementary tax, except interest income from bearer securities, which is taxed at the source as indicated below. The classification of interest income among the various schedules differs with the nature of the income.

9/1.2   Interest on Nominative Government Securities

a. GROSS INCOME.   Interest on federal, state, and municipal bonds is subject to income tax under Schedule A regardless of when the securities were issued.[1] The rule that income from securities made out to bearer is not subject to schedular tax applies to interest on government securities, so that only income from nominative government bonds is taxed under Schedule A (Reg. Art. 3).

Certain government securities are exempt from the income tax. The exemption must be specifically stated in the law which authorizes the issuance of the securities or in another federal law.[2] The number of securities so exempted is very limited.[3]

b. DEDUCTIONS.   The only deductions allowed against Schedule A income are expenses for commissions and brokers' fees incurred in connection with the purchase or sale of the securities and the collection of interest therefrom (Reg. Art. 13).

c. TAX RATE.   The rate of the schedular tax under Schedule A is 3% (Reg. Art. 25).

9/1.3   Interest on Other Nominative Securities

Interest income from nominative securities, except those issued by a government agency, is taxed under Schedule B (Reg. Art. 4).

a. GROSS INCOME.   The interest income included in Schedule B is mainly that derived from loans and bank accounts.

If the purchaser of securities pays for the interest accrued to the date of the sale and later collects the full amount of the interest coupon, a proportionate part of the interest is included in the gross income of both the seller and the buyer of the securities (Reg. Art. 4 §6).

---

[1] It was argued in the early days of the Brazilian income tax that a bond is a contractual obligation, the income from which can not be unilaterally reduced by the government through taxation. This issue is obsolete today. See Sousa, §7. It was also argued that federal taxation of income from state and municipal bonds was unconstitutional. Now the Federal Constitution of 1946 (Art. 15 §3) expressly provides that such income may be taxed, provided that the rate of tax is not higher than the tax rate on federal bonds.

[2] Sousa, §7.

[3] The ruling of the Income Tax Division in *Rev.* 1944 No. 497, cited in Sousa, *loc. cit.*, lists the following:

1. All foreign public indebtedness of Brazil.
2. The securities issued by the *Reajustamento Econômico* (Decrees No. 23,535 of Dec. 1, 1933, and No. 24,233 of May 5, 1934).
3. Federal securities issued in connection with the *Revolução Constitucionalista* of 1932 in São Paulo (Decree No. 21,717 of Aug. 10, 1932).
4. Federal loans issued under Decrees No. 14,946 of Aug. 15, 1921, and No. 19,412 of Nov. 19, 1930.

b. DEDUCTIONS. The only deductions allowed against Schedule B income are expenses for commissions and brokers' fees incurred in connection with the purchase or sale of securities and with the collection of interest therefrom (Reg. Art. 13).[4]

c. TAX RATE. The rate of the schedular tax under Schedule B is 10%. This is by far the highest schedular tax rate under the Brazilian income tax law, which tends to favor income from personal work over that derived from capital.

9/1.4   Miscellaneous Interest Taxable under Schedule B

The following types of interest or payments in the nature of interest are taxed under Schedule B (Reg. Art. 4).

a. INTEREST ON DEPOSITS, DEBTS, AND LOANS. Interest on cash deposits (on term or at sight) for any purpose is taxed under Schedule B. The law specifically lists deposits to secure the performance of a contract or to guarantee the fulfillment of professional duties or the proper exercise of public offices. It also includes interest paid or credited on current accounts, commercial credits in the nature of loans, and interest on the sales price of real property.

Finally, Reg. Art. 4 refers to all interest on debts or cash loans, regardless of the form of the contract, the guaranty of performance given, or the nature of the instrument or agreement. This covers interest on debts determined by judicial decision and on practically every agreement under the commercial and civil law.

b. IMPLIED AND PRESUMED INTEREST. If the parties have stipulated for an increment in the nature of interest,[5] without, however, calling it interest, the assessing authorities will determine the amount of interest on the basis of the character of the instrument or agreement and the prevailing interest rate (Reg. Art. 4 §1). This provision will also be applied if the creditor, having been requested by the fiscal authorities to give information on interest resulting from debts or loans, fails to give this information or reports less interest than he actually received.

Amounts paid by an insurance company in excess of the face value of a policy (whether such payments are made in the form of a nonrecurrent bonus or an annuity) are taxed under Schedule B (Reg. Art. 4 §5[a]). This covers the situation in which an insurance company grants to a policyholder who has carried his policy for a stated number of years a participation in its annual profits. Such excess payments are in the na-

---

[4] CC, *Rev.* 1948 Nos. 15 and 883; 1951 No. 238; Rezende, Note 58.

[5] The provision is aimed in particular at indebtedness in the form of promissory notes, which, under Brazilian law, cannot bear interest. The amount of interest is, therefore, usually merged with the principal.

ture of interest since they are compensation for the use of capital, and they are taxed accordingly. The face amount of an insurance policy paid by reason of the death of the insured is not included in gross income (Reg. Art. 11 §2[a]).

c. PROFITS FROM DISCOUNT OPERATIONS. Profits from discount operations are clearly in the nature of interest and they are taxed accordingly (Reg. Art. 4 §5[c]).

9/1.5 Interest Classified under Other Schedules

Interest from sources other than those described above is classified according to the nature of the transaction from which it results (Reg. Art. 4 §3). As an example, interest on overdue rent is treated as income from real property and taxed under Schedule E (9/4.1a). Interest on back wages or salaries partakes of the nature of compensation for services and is taxed to the recipient under Schedule C (8/1.2); interest on income from an occasional sale on the installment basis is taxed as miscellaneous income from transactions entered into for profit under Schedule H (10/4.1).

The foregoing principle does not apply in the case of a novation, i.e., the conversion of an original debt for compensation or rent, etc., into a loan. Here, the interest is taxed under Schedule B like other loan interest (Reg. Art. 4 §4).

9/1.6 Interest on Bearer Securities

It will in most cases be impossible for the fiscal authorities to establish the identity of the owner of securities made out to bearer. The income tax law, therefore, provides for the withholding of tax at the source on all income from bearer securities; this income is not subject to taxation by assessment and is not to be included in the income tax return of the recipient.

The Income Tax Regulations differentiate several types of interest on bearer bonds and apply different tax rates to them. Within each category the tax rate is proportionate, i.e., fixed and unchanging regardless of the size of the income; and it is computed on *gross* income without any deductions (Reg. Art. 96 §2). The rates reproduced below are those of the withholding tax applying to resident individuals and entities.[6]

1. 6% upon interest on federal, state, and municipal bonds, except those which enjoy exemption from income tax under a federal statute (Reg. Art. 96[1]).
2. 21% upon interest on debentures or other bonds made out to bearer and issued in connection with loans contracted for either within or without

[6] Regarding the withholding tax imposed on the interest income of nonresidents and foreign entities, see 9/1.8.

the country by Brazilian companies or by foreign companies operating in Brazil (Reg. Art. 96[2][b], as amended by Law No. 2,862 of September 4, 1956, Art. 25).

9/1.7   Resident Entities

Every kind of interest, except that on bearer securities, received by a legal entity is taxed as part of its business income and subject to the uniform rate of tax applied to such income under Reg. Art. 44.

Interest received by an entity on bonds or other securities made out to bearer is taxed by withholding at the source, and the rates of the tax are the same as those applying to individual holders of such securities (7/7.2; 9/1.6). Not being subject to taxation by assessment, the interest is not to be included in the income tax return of the recipient entity.

9/1.8   Nonresidents

All interest income derived from sources in Brazil by nonresident individuals or entities is subject to withholding of income tax at the source.

The rate of withholding is 20% (Reg. Art. 97[1]) and the tax is computed on gross income (Reg. Art. 97 §5).

If the income is of a type which requires withholding of tax at the source in the case of residents also, but at a lower rate than that applying to nonresidents,[7] an additional amount of tax sufficient to bring the total up to 20% must be withheld (Reg. Art. 97 §4). If the regular withholding rate is higher than 20%, as in the case of interest on bearer bonds (9/1.6), the higher rate applies (5/4.3).

9/2.   Income from Dividends and Other Distributions

9/2.1   Distributions to Resident Individuals Taxable under Schedule F

Distributions received by shareholders of corporations or members of limited liability companies and the profits accruing to partners and owners of sole proprietorships are classified under Schedule F, which imposes no schedular tax. These items are therefore subject to complementary tax only. As far as the following statements refer to distributions on securities (dividends on corporate shares, etc.), they apply to nominative securities only. Distributions on bearer securities are taxed at the source under Reg. Art. 96; see 9/2.2. The following distributions are taxed to individuals under Schedule F.

a. SOLE PROPRIETORSHIP AND PARTNERSHIP PROFITS. The profits of sole proprietorships and partnerships constitute Schedule F income to the owners and partners. Sole proprietorship profits become income of the

---

[7] I.e., at the rate of 6% on interest from government securities payable to bearer (Reg. Art. 96[1]); see 5/4.3.

owner as soon as they are determined (6/4.1a), while partnership profits must be credited or distributed to the partner to be includible in his income (5/3.1). Both kinds of profits also are subject to the assessed tax in the hands of the entity which earned them (Reg. Art. 8[a]).[8]

b. CASH DIVIDENDS ON NOMINATIVE SHARES. Cash dividends and extra payments distributed to the holders of nominative shares are includible under Schedule F (Reg. Art. 8[c]). Constructive dividends are taxed in the same way as actual dividends.[9]

c. STOCK DIVIDENDS. Dividends to the holders of nominative shares paid in the stock of the corporation making the distribution are income under Schedule F (Reg. Art. 8[d]). The value for tax purposes of all shares distributed as a stock dividend (including those discussed in 9/2.1d[2] below) is their *par value* (DIR, Rev. 1942 No. 305).

d. DISTRIBUTIONS NOT IN THE NATURE OF PROFITS AND DIVIDENDS. Distributions made out of surplus originating from one of the following sources are includible in Schedule F income (Reg. Art. 8[d]).

1. From the capitalization of any funds which were previously not taxed, such as the provisions for amortization, depreciation, and revaluation of assets.[10]
2. From an increase in the capital of the distributing corporation by means of funds taken from any source.[11] This increase of capital may take the form of raising either the number of outstanding shares or the par value of the shares already issued and outstanding.[12]

[8] It is immaterial whether this entity is taxed on the basis of actual, presumed, or estimated profits. Regarding these various methods of taxing entities, see 6/1.4, 6/9.1, and 6/9.2.

[9] CC, *Rev.* 1949 No. 651 (sale of securities by a corporation to its shareholders below book value); see also Federal District Court in *Rev.* 1950 No. 622; 1951 No. 1343. The decision of the District Court in *Rev.* 1950 No. 622 was reversed by the Federal Circuit Court of Appeals, *Rev.* 1952 No. 886. (It should be noted that the appellate court considers the par value rather than book value of the securities sold to the shareholders.)

[10] That this "utilization" renders previously untaxed funds taxable to the distributing corporation was explained in 7/6.1. As to the distinction between provisions (representing amounts not previously taxed) and reserves (amounts previously included in taxable income), see 6/6.1. Current Brazilian accounting practice requires that when a "provision" is capitalized or distributed, it must as a preliminary step be converted into a "reserve." This purely formal requirement arises from the fact that "provisions" are appropriated to specific purposes, such as depreciation, etc., whereas "reserves" are part of the free surplus.

[11] While the question whether or not these funds were previously taxed to the distributing company is immaterial as far as the imposition of the complementary tax on the distributee is concerned, this difference is important for the distributing corporation, which will not be taxed again upon the distribution of profits which were already included in its taxable income.

[12] DIR, *Rev.* 1944 Nos. 148 and 161. While these decisions deal with bearer shares, the principle stated therein is evidently applicable to nominative shares. Rezende, Note 39-A.

3. From a revaluation of the assets of the distributing corporation, or the sale of a part of these assets without an impairment of its capital.[13]

In every case of the distribution of a stock dividend, the value thereof which must be included in the taxable income of the recipient is represented by the *par value* of the new shares distributed, and surplus attaching to the shares is disregarded.[14]

e. DISTRIBUTIONS TO HOLDERS OF PARTICIPATING CERTIFICATES. Pro rata portions of profits and other benefits distributed to the holders of participating certificates [15] and similar securities are taxable under Schedule F (Reg. Art. 8[e]).

Participating certificates do not form part of the share capital of a corporation; the holders of these certificates are, therefore, creditors rather than equity holders of the corporation issuing these securities. Whether or not the portion of the profits distributed to the holders of participating certificates reduces the taxable income of the corporation is doubtful.[16]

f. REVALUATION. The benefits accruing to the owners or partners of entities which result from an increased valuation of the assets in the event of incorporation or the formation of a new company are taxable under Schedule F (Reg. Art. 8[f]).

The cited provision covers the cases of a merger [17] and a consolidation.[18] In either case, the assets of the companies which are parties to the reorganization [19] must be reappraised. If upon the exchange the shareholders receive shares of a total par value in excess of the total par value of the shares surrendered by them, this excess is taxable as a gain under Schedule F. It is the theory of the law that as a result of the appraisal of the assets, which the law prescribes in the case of a merger, consolidation, or the formation of a new company, the

---

[13] CC, *Rev.* 1952 No. 116. The qualifying words "without impairment of capital" merely exclude the sale of assets at a figure below the book value of the assets.

[14] DIR, *Rev.* 1942 No. 305.

[15] Participating or founders' certificates (*partes beneficiárias* or *partes de fundador*) are negotiable securities without par value which confer on their holders a contingent right to share in the annual profits of the issuing company up to a limit of 10%; Corp. Law, Art. 31. The participation may be in the form of fixed interest. The company may sell the certificates for cash or issue them to founders, shareholders, or third parties in consideration of services rendered.

[16] The decisions of the Tax Court in this question are conflicting and the issue cannot be regarded as settled. *For Deduction:* CC, *Rev.* 1953 No. 353 (if certificates issued for services rendered, but not if issued as negotiable securities); 1954 No. 249. Both decisions quoted have been appealed to the Ministry of Finance. *Against Deduction:* CC, *Rev.* 1952 No. 769; 1954 No. 538 (appealed to District Court); 1955 No. 12. The latter decisions represent the trend of the administrative practice.

[17] *Fusão*, regulated in Corp. Law, Art. 153.

[18] *Incorporação*, regulated in Corp. Law, Art. 152.

[19] I.e., the company to be absorbed (in the case of a merger) or the companies to be consolidated (in the case of a consolidation).

par value of the shares of the participating corporations or of a newly formed corporation will be equal to the value of the corporate assets. For this reason, only the par value of the shares is considered and surplus attaching to the shares is disregarded.

Example 1

Corporation A has 1,000 shares of a par value of Cr$ 100 each issued and outstanding. The surplus of the corporation amounts to Cr$ 150,000, or Cr$ 150 per share.

The shareholders of Corporation A decide to organize new Corporation B with a capital of Cr$ 200,000, divided into 1,000 shares of a par value of Cr$ 200 each. The only assets transferred to B at the present time by the shareholders of A are 500 shares of A, which Corporation B received in exchange for all of its capital stock. The shareholders of A realize a gain upon the exchange of Cr$ 150,000, measured by the excess of the *par value* of the B shares received (Cr$ 200,000) over the *par value* of the A shares surrendered (Cr$ 50,000). The surplus of Cr$ 75,000 attaching to the 500 shares of A is not considered in computing the gain upon the exchange.

In the case of the incorporation of a sole proprietorship or a partnership, the gain to the transferors is measured by the excess, if any, of the par value of the shares issued by the new corporation over the appraised value of the assets transferred.[20]

9/2.2   Distributions to Resident Individuals Taxed at the Source

a. CASH DIVIDENDS AND OTHER CASH DISTRIBUTIONS ON BEARER SHARES. Cash dividends paid to the holders of bearer shares of corporations and all extra payments on such shares are subject to taxation at the source. The withholding rate is 28%.[21]

The tax is computed on gross income (Reg. Art. 96 §2). It must be paid by the corporation within 30 days from the date of publication, in the official gazette, of the resolution of the general meeting of the shareholders approving the payment of the dividend (Reg. Art. 102 §2).[22]

This is probably the most important of the withholding provisions from

[20] The newly formed corporation does not realize taxable income upon the transfer of the assets, DIR, *Rev.* 1947 No. 791.

Reg. Art. 8(f) is a rather cryptic provision which, moreover, has no exact counterpart in the article of the Income Tax Regulations dealing with bearer securities (Reg. Art. 96). Most reorganization gains, however, are represented either by new shares issued or by an increase in the par value of existing shares and thus qualify either under Reg. Art. 8(d), if the shares are nominative (see d., above), or under Reg. Art. 96(3)(c), if they are made out to bearer (see 9/2.2b, below).

[21] Reg. Art. 96(3)(a) as amended by Law No. 2,862, Art. 25. The applicable tax rate is that of the year of distribution, whether the profits distributed were earned in the current or a prior year, CC, *Rev.* 1954 No. 182. The rate of 28% is effective from January 1, 1957, on.

[22] This rule applies without exception, even if payment of the dividend is made at a later time, CC, *Rev.* 1955 Nos. 134 and 169. Late payment of the tax results in a penalty (CC, *Rev.* 1954 No. 172); see 13/7.3.

the practical point of view. If the shareholdings of an individual are very substantial, it will obviously be to his advantage to have them in the form of bearer shares, subject to a uniform tax rate of 28%, rather than in the form of nominative shares, the dividends from which are subject to complementary tax computed at graduated rates.

b. STOCK DIVIDENDS ON BEARER SHARES. The value of new shares and of other benefits [23] distributed to the holders of bearer shares is subject to taxation at the source. The withholding rate is the same as the one applying to the distribution of a cash dividend (Reg. Art. 96[3][c] as amended). The value of the new shares distributed is determined by their par value, and no other valuation is required or even permitted.

A stock dividend represents taxable income to the shareholder in either one of the following situations:

1. If any existing funds of the corporation are capitalized and distributed in the form of a stock dividend. The generic term "funds" includes both amounts which were previously taxed (accumulated surplus and "reserves" in the technical sense) and those not previously subjected to income tax (i.e., provisions).
2. If the funds which are capitalized and distributed originate from a revaluation of the assets of the corporation or from the sale of a part of its assets "without impairment of capital," i.e., at a price at least equal to the book value of the assets.

The rules listed above cover the capitalization and distribution to the shareholders, in the form of a stock dividend, of any funds in the hands of the entity, whether such funds were previously taxed to it or not. They cover the capitalization and distribution of excess provisions for amortization, depreciation, bad debts, etc., as well as a distribution of reserves in the proper sense of the term, i.e., appropriations of surplus on which the corporate income tax was previously paid. The only difference, taxwise, as far as the distributing company is concerned, is that the distribution of amounts not previously taxed constitutes a realization of income and results in the imposition of the business income tax (under Reg. Art. 44) upon the amount distributed.[24] The distribution of a reserve has no such effect, because the amount appropriated to the reserve became subject to tax at the time the reserve was created (Reg. Art. 43 §1[f]). To the distributee, the tax consequences of the distribution are the same, since the tax is withheld at the source in both cases.

The rules on distributions of this type are the same as the ones applying in the case of similar distributions to the holders of nominative shares

[23] Such as an increase in the par value of the shares by means of a transfer from surplus or reserves, CC, *Rev.* 1954 No. 85.

[24] This amount is includible in the taxable income of the distributing entity of the year in which the distribution was made (7/6.1).

(9/2.1c). The fact that the wording of the statutory provisions [25] is not exactly the same is immaterial. However, while the rules are the same, the applicable tax rates are different. In the case of distributions on nominative shares, the complementary tax with its graduated rates applies; in the case of distributions on bearer shares, a fixed tax rate of 28% is imposed on the recipient, regardless of the amount of the distribution.

c. DISTRIBUTIONS TO HOLDERS OF CAPITALIZATION BONDS. Distributions to the holders of capitalization bonds [26] out of the profits of the issuing company are taxed by way of withholding at the source (at the rate of 15%) because capitalization bonds are bearer securities, and the tax is computed on gross income (Reg. Art. 96[2][c] and its §2).

d. DISTRIBUTIONS ON PARTICIPATING CERTIFICATES. Income tax is withheld on distributions of profits and other benefits distributed to the holders of participating certificates [27] made out to bearer (Reg. Art. 96[3][b]). The rate of withholding is 28% (Law No. 2,862, Art. 25) and the tax is computed on gross income (Reg. Art. 96 §2).

9/2.3 Distributions to Resident Entities

The Income Tax Regulations provide that distributions representing profits which have already been subjected to the proportionate tax in the hands of the distributing entity shall not be taxed again to the entity receiving the distribution, provided that the payment of the tax by the distributing entity can be proved (Reg. Art. 43 §2[c] and [d]). This rule, which covers dividends on both nominative and bearer shares, and distributions of profits by entities other than corporations, in effect establishes a full exemption of this income in favor of all entities receiving such distributions, including partnerships and sole proprietorships.[28] The entity receiving the distribution will, therefore, exclude it in computing its taxable income.[29]

---

[25] Reg. Art. 8(d)(I) and (II) (nominative shares) and Reg. Art. 96(3)(c)(I) and (II) (bearer shares).

[26] A capitalization bond is a bond issued by a capitalization company, the face value of which is paid by the purchaser in installments over an extended period during which the bond bears no interest. Capitalization companies usually grant to the bondholders a participation in their profits when the bonds have been outstanding for a certain time, and this is the profit described in the text as taxable to the bondholder under Reg. Art. 96(2)(c).

Regarding the taxation of gains from the redemption of capitalization bonds prior to their maturity, see 9/9.5a3. These securities are always made out to bearer.

[27] Regarding the characteristics of these securities, see note 15 *supra;* regarding the treatment of income from nominative securities of this kind, see 9/2.1e.

[28] The owner of the sole proprietorship must include the distribution in his personal income tax return under Schedule F, CC, *Rev.* 1951 No. 1099; Rezende Note 37.

[29] DIR, *Rev.* 1951 No. 994. The same rule applies if the shares are redeemed at a price in excess of their cost to the entity receiving the redemption price, DIR, *Rev.*

It should be carefully noted, however, that, in the case of distributions on bearer shares, the exemption applies only to the proportionate tax imposed on business income under Reg. Art. 44, not to the withholding tax of 28% under Reg. Art. 96(3)(a).[30] If Corporation A receives a dividend on bearer shares of Corporation B, A will exclude the dividend from its business income for purposes of the assessed income tax on entities under Reg. Art. 44, but B is required to withhold 28% of the dividend for A's account. If the shares of Corporation A are also bearer shares, and A in turn distributes the dividend received to its own shareholders, it must withhold tax again for its shareholders' account.[31]

9/2.4   Distributions to Nonresident Individuals and Entities

All income from dividends and from other distributions made by legal entities received by nonresident individuals and entities is taxed at the source. The general rate of the withholding tax applying to nonresidents is 20% (Reg. Art. 97[1]), and this rate applies except where the law requires withholding of tax at a higher rate, on the same type of income, in the case of resident taxpayers.[32] The tax is computed on gross income (Reg. Art. 97 §5).

The application of the various withholding rates may be summarized as follows: [33]

1. *Subject to withholding at the rate of 20%:*

   Distributions on nominative shares, including cash dividends (9/2.1b), stock dividends (9/2.1c), and certain other distributions (9/2.1d).

   Distributions to holders of nominative participating certificates (9/2.1e). Certain reorganization gains (9/2.1f).
   Distributions to holders of capitalization bonds (9/2.2c).

2. *Subject to withholding at the rate of 28%:*

   Dividends (in cash or in stock) and other distributions on bearer shares (9/2.2a and 9/2.2b).

   Distributions to holders of participating certificates made out to bearer (9/2.2d).

1952 No. 81. The excess of the redemption price over the cost of the shares is considered a realization of profits of the distributing company which were already subjected to the proportionate tax in its hands.

[30] DIR, *Rev.* 1947 No. 649; 1950 No. 291; 1951 No. 827; CC, *Rev.* 1951 No. 620.

[31] It is clear that while the *rate* of the two withholding taxes is the same, the *amounts* thereof are different; A will withhold 28% of the net amount received from B which in turn is 72% of the full amount of B's profits distributed, so that the shareholders of A will receive 51.84% (72% of 72%) of the original amount of the profits of B.

[32] See 5/4.3.

[33] The tax rates listed are those effective January 1, 1957 (Law No. 2,862 of September 4, 1956, Art. 25). See note 21, *supra.*

9/3.   Annuities, Pensions, and Life Insurance

9/3.1   Individuals

Pensions and retirement pay arising out of an employment contract are, by express provision of Reg. Art. 5 §1(II), treated as compensation for services rendered and taxed to the recipient under Schedule C.[34]

The payment of the amount of an endowment policy to the insured or the beneficiary named by him, either in a lump sum or in the form of an annuity, is not subject to income tax (DIR, *Rev.* 1935 No. 46). The same is true for the face amount of a life insurance policy paid by reason of the death of the insured (Reg. Art. 11 §2[a]). Gain is recognized, however, upon the conversion of an endowment policy into a straight life insurance policy. The gain is measured by the difference between the total amount of the premiums paid under the converted policy and the face amount of the new policy acquired upon the exchange (CC, *Rev.* 1942 No. 423), and it is taxed under Schedule B.

Although the premiums paid under a life insurance policy are, within certain limits, deductible for purposes of the complementary tax (Reg. Art. 20[b]),[35] those paid on a single-premium endowment policy are not.

Regarding the tax treatment of amounts paid by an insurance company in excess of the face value of the policy (taxed under Schedule B), see 9/1.4b.

9/3.2   Entities

Amounts paid by an insurance company to an entity by reason of the death of an owner or partner are not includible in the taxable income of the company (Reg. Art. 43 §2[e] and 7/7.3).

9/4.   Income from Rent

9/4.1   Real Property Rentals — Resident Individuals and Entities

a. GROSS INCOME. Rental income from real property (whether urban or rural) is taxed to a resident individual under Schedule E (Reg. Art. 7). However, if the lease should include any movable property, the total income from it is taxed as miscellaneous income under Schedule H (schedular tax rate 5%) rather than as real property income under Schedule E (schedular tax rate 3%) (Reg. Art. 10 Sole §). Interest on overdue rent is likewise taxed under Schedule E (Reg. Art. 7 Sole §[a]).

If the use of improved city real property is let gratuitously, the rental value of the property is income taxable under Schedule E to the owner — not to the party who occupies the building (Reg. Art. 7 Sole §[b]).

---

[34] Straight annuities not in connection with an employment contract are not in use in Brazil.

[35] For details, see computation of the complementary tax at 12/1.2b[3].

If a business firm is located in premises belonging to its individual owner, the latter must include the rental value in his income under Schedule E; the firm deducts the same amount under general expenses.[36]

The income received by resident entities from renting real property is includible in their business income and subject to the assessed income tax under Reg. Art. 44. The deductions allowable to arrive at net rental income are the same as those available to a resident individual.

b. DEDUCTIONS. The following deductions are allowed under Schedule E, *if borne by the owner of the real property* (Reg. Art. 16):

1. Federal, state, and municipal taxes and charges which are imposed on the real property or its use, except fines and additional charges for late payment.

2. Maintenance expenses of improved real property, but not in excess of 10% of the rental declared (Reg. Art. 16 §2).[37]

3. Commissions for collection of rent. This deduction is limited to 5% of the rental declared (Reg. Art. 16 §2).[38]

4. Fire insurance premiums.

5. Ground rent in the case of emphyteusis.[39]

6. Owners of apartments may deduct proportionate shares of the aggregate expense paid by them for light, electric power, and the salaries of janitors and elevator attendants (Reg. Art. 16 §1[a]).

7. Owners of apartment buildings may deduct expenses for air conditioning, light, electric power, heating, and cooling of water, and the salaries of janitors and elevator attendants (Reg. Art. 16 §1[b]).

8. The owners of homes located in private housing developments may deduct the expenses listed under 6 and 7.

Only the foregoing expenses which are specifically listed in the statute are deductible.[40]

[36] DIR, *Rev.* 1948 No. 737. The criticism of this decision by Rezende, Note 35 (to the effect that if a particular rental is arranged for, this and not the rental value of the premises should be used) does not seem justified.

[37] It seems that this percentage will be allowed irrespective of proof of a larger amount and that the rulings of the Tax Court denying a deduction in excess of the statutory limit, even though higher actual expenditures are proved (CC, *Rev.* 1949 No. 94; 1951 No. 1283; 1952 No. 224), should be interpreted to this effect. See, however, the contrary ruling of the Tax Court in *Rev.* 1951 No. 1405 and Rezende, Note 87.

[38] Here again it is doubtful whether the statutory deduction can be claimed irrespective of proof of a larger amount or whether it constitutes only the upper limit of the allowable deduction. Considering that the Income Tax Regulations specify both the 10% and the 5% deduction in one and the same provision, there does not seem to be any justification for adopting different interpretations. See, however, Rezende, Note 87.

[39] Emphyteusis is an incorporeal right in real property in the nature of an easement, with the right in the lessee to alienate the estate or pass it to his heirs by descent, and the reservation of an annual rent to the transferor. Under Brazilian law, only noncultivated land or land intended for improvement may be given in emphyteusis and the right is always in perpetuity, Civil Code of Brazil, Arts. 678 *et seq.*

[40] Therefore, mortgage interest paid on the real property which produces the rental income is not allowed as a schedular deduction, CC, *Rev.* 1946 No. 626; Rezende,

c. TAX RATE. The rate of the schedular tax under Schedule E is 3% (Reg. Art. 25).

9/4.2 Real Property Rentals — Nonresidents

Rental income derived by nonresident individuals and entities from real property situated in Brazil is, like other income realized by these taxpayers, subject to withholding of tax at the source. The rate of the withholding tax is 20% (Reg. Art. 97[1]).

It is important to note that while the withholding tax on nonresidents is in all other cases based on gross income, the amount of real property rental income subject to withholding is computed with the deductions allowed to resident individuals and listed under 9/4.1b above (Reg. Art. 97 §5).

9/4.3 Income from Subleasing Real Property and from Renting Movable Property

a. RESIDENT INDIVIDUALS. Income from the subleasing of real property and from the renting of movable property is taxed under the miscellaneous classification of Schedule H (Reg. Art. 10[b] and [c]). The same classification applies if real property is leased by an individual together with movable property (9/4.1a).

The deductions allowable are the same as under Schedule E (9/4.1b and Reg. Art. 17). A sublessor may deduct the rental he pays to the lessor.

The schedular tax rate applicable to Schedule H income is 5% (Reg. Art. 25).

b. RESIDENT ENTITIES. The income discussed here forms part of the business income of resident entities and is taxable under Reg. Art. 44. The expenses incurred are deductible as business expenses.

c. NONRESIDENTS. As stated in 9/4.2 above, a nonresident lessor of real property located in Brazil (individual or entity) is taxed by way of withholding at the source on the basis of *net* rental income under the rule of Reg. Art. 97 §5. Since this provision speaks in general terms of income from real property, it would seem to cover income from subleasing immovable property as well as straight rental income.

d. COMPENSATION FOR THE USE OF FOREIGN MOTION PICTURES. A special rule defines the taxable income of nonresident producers, distributors, or agents of foreign motion pictures in Brazil as 30% of the amounts paid, credited, or remitted to them or to a third party, or otherwise used for

Note 78. It is an abatement for purposes of the complementary tax, subject to limitations if the land is used for agricultural purposes taxable under Schedule G.

their account (Reg. Art. 97 §3). The income so determined is taxed at the source at the usual rate of 20% applying to nonresident taxpayers under Reg. Art. 97 §1. In practical effect, therefore, the tax on this type of income is fixed at 6% of the gross rental which is paid or otherwise made available to the foreign party entitled thereto.

9/5. Income from Royalties

9/5.1 Royalties from Licensing Patents, Processes, Formulas, and Copyrights

a. RESIDENT INDIVIDUALS. Profits derived by the holder of patents of invention or manufacturing processes by means other than their direct exploitation are taxed to him under Schedule D, the same as income from independent professional services (Reg. Art. 6[g]; and see 8/2.1–8/2.5). The provision covers, in particular, royalties received by the holder of the right from a party manufacturing under a license agreement. The income from direct exploitation of the rights discussed here, whether realized by the holder of the right or a licensee, is considered to be derived from an industrial or commercial activity and taxed as business income.[41] Authors' royalties are exempt from income tax.[42]

The applicable schedular tax rate is 2% (Reg. Art. 25). The deductions available are those allowed against Schedule D income under Reg. Art. 15 (8/2.3) as far as applicable.

b. RESIDENT ENTITIES. Royalties received by entities from licensing the rights discussed here fall into the general category of business income and, as such, are subject to taxation under Reg. Art. 44.

c. NONRESIDENTS. Royalties from the licensing of patents, processes, and formulas derived by nonresident individuals and entities from sources in Brazil are subject to withholding of income tax at the source at the rate of 25%, computed on the gross amount of the royalties (Reg. Art. 97[2] and its §5).[43]

9/5.2 Royalties from Licensing Industrial and Commercial Trademarks

a. RESIDENT INDIVIDUALS. Profits derived by the holder of industrial and commercial trademarks by means other than their direct exploitation are taxed to him under Schedule H, the miscellaneous classification which applies to income from transactions for profit not included under one of the other schedules (Reg. Art. 10[d]).

---

[41] Sousa, §27.

[42] Constitution of 1946, Art. 203; Reg. Art. 24 §3.

[43] DIR, *Rev.* 1950 Nos. 410 and 594; 1952, Nos. 104-D and 681; CC, *Rev.* 1952 Nos. 349 and 658; 1953 No. 399. Regarding taxation of royalties of nonresident authors, see 6/1.3 above.

The applicable schedular tax rate is 5% (Reg. Art. 25).

The deductions available are those allowed against income from independent professional services under Schedule D (Reg. Art. 17 and 8/2.3).

b. RESIDENT ENTITIES. Royalties received by entities from licensing industrial or commercial trademarks constitute business income taxable under Reg. Art. 44.

c. NONRESIDENTS. The rules on taxation of royalties from patents, etc., set forth under 9/5.1c above, apply (Reg. Art. 97[2] and its §5). They apply likewise to mining royalties.[44]

9/6. Presumptive Income

9/6.1 In General

The few instances in which a tax is levied on presumptive income are discussed in connection with the specific types of income to which the tax applies.

Regarding the presumptive income of individuals from the gratuitous letting of improved urban real property, see 9/4.1a.

Regarding the election of certain entities to be taxed on the basis of presumed profits, see 6/9.1.

9/7. Taxation at Source of Income from Capital

9/7.1 Income from Capital Taxed at Source to Residents

The withholding provisions applying to income from capital are discussed in detail throughout this chapter in relation to the particular types of income and the individuals and entities which receive it. Reference to those discussions follows.

Regarding gains to resident individuals from the sale of real property, see 9/8.2.

Regarding income to resident individuals and entities from bearer securities, see under the following headings.

Interest income to resident individuals from bearer securities: 9/1.6.

Interest income to resident entities from bearer securities: 9/1.7.

Cash dividends and other distributions to resident individuals on bearer securities: 9/2.2a.

Stock dividends to resident individuals on bearer securities: 9/2.2b.

Distributions to the holders of capitalization bonds: 9/2.2c.

Distributions to the holders of participating certificates made out to bearer: 9/2.2d.

Cash dividends and other distributions to resident entities on securities made out to bearer: 9/2.3.

[44] DIR, *Rev.* 1947 No. 399; Rezende, Note 283.

Gains to resident individuals from the anticipated retirement of capitalization bonds: 9/9.5a3.

Gains to resident individuals from the redemption of bearer securities: 9/9.5a4.

Gains to resident entities from the redemption of bearer securities: 9/9.5b.

9/7.2   Income from Capital Taxed at Source to Nonresidents

As explained in 5/4.2 and 5/4.7, the tax on the income of nonresident individuals and entities from Brazilian sources is withheld at the source. The details concerning this withholding tax on income from capital are given throughout this chapter in relation to each type of income. Reference to those discussions follows.

Interest income to nonresident individuals and entities from bearer securities: 9/1.8.

Distributions to nonresident individuals and entities on bearer securities: 9/2.4.

Rental income to nonresident individuals and entities from real property: 9/4.2.

Income to nonresident individuals and entities from subleasing real property and from the renting of movable property: 9/4.3c.

Income to nonresident individuals and entities from renting foreign motion pictures: 9/4.3d.

Royalty income to nonresident individuals and entities from licensing patents, processes, and formulas: 9/5.1c.

Royalty income to nonresident individuals and entities from licensing industrial or commercial trademarks: 9/5.2c.

Royalty income of nonresident authors: 6/1.3.

Gains to nonresident individuals and entities from the redemption of securities: 9/9.5c.

9/8.   Capital Gains

9/8.1   General Rule

With the exception of gains on the sale of real property discussed below, individuals are not taxed on capital gains under Brazilian income tax law. This refers in particular to gains on the sale of shares and other securities, unless such sales constitute a business.[45] Corporations and other entities [46] include capital gains in business income subject to taxation under Reg. Art. 44.

[45] DIR, *Rev.* 1951 Nos. 800 and 826; CC, *Rev.* 1952 No. 472 (shares); DIR, *Rev.* 1949 No. 472; 1952 No. 695 (quotas of limited liability company); CC, *Rev.* 1951 No. 914 (any securities). See also 10/4.1a.

[46] Including sole proprietorships and individuals engaged in business who for income tax purposes assume the status of legal entities.

9/8.2 Gains on the Sale of Real Property

Gains realized by an individual on the sale of real property are subject to a tax computed under special rules (Reg. Art. 92); under the Brazilian system of taxation, this tax is assimilated to a withholding tax.

The tax applies only if the *vendor* is an individual; [47] whether the *vendee* is a natural person or a legal entity is immaterial. Estates in process of administration are treated like individuals for the purpose of this provision.[48]

The imposition of the tax further presupposes a *sale;* an expropriation of real property under the right of eminent domain is a sale, although a forced sale (DIR, *Rev.* 1950 No. 377). In the case of an exchange of one lot of real property for another, the provision applies only to the extent that money is received on the transaction by one of the parties.[49]

Certain transactions which constitute sales in the economic but not in the legal sense come under the provision here discussed, such as the transfer of real property in payment of a debt,[50] and the contribution of real property to the capital of a corporation or other commercial company by a shareholder or associate.[51]

Only gains on the sale of tangible real property as defined in Art. 43 of the Civil Code [52] are subject to the tax. Intangible rights treated as immovable property under Art. 44 of the Civil Code are excluded.

Sales of rural real property of a value not exceeding Cr$ 100,000 are exempt from the tax here discussed (Reg. Art. 93).[53] Sales of all rural real property were exempted until December 31, 1950.[54]

a. BASIS.   The basis [55] of real property acquired by purchase is its cost. If the property was acquired through an exchange for other real property, the property received takes the basis of the property given in exchange if no money passed upon the transfer. If, however, money was paid upon the transfer, the basis of the property acquired is equal to the basis of the property given in exchange plus the amount of the money paid.

In the case of real property acquired through inheritance, the administrative practice has long been settled to the effect that the basis of the property is not its cost to the decedent, but its appraised value as determined in the course of the settlement of the estate for purposes of the

---

[47] Such gains are taxed to entities as part of their business income, Sousa, §§35-H and 43.

[48] DIR, *Rev.* 1948 Nos. 473 and 485; Rezende, Note 273.

[49] DIR, *Rev.* 1951 No. 1174. See Sousa, §43.

[50] DIR, *Rev.* 1947 No. 503; 1948 No. 773. See Rezende, Note 273-A.

[51] DIR, *Rev.* 1947 No. 744; 1949 Nos. 381 and 801; Federal Court of Appeals, *Rev.* 1952 No. 433-C. See Rezende, *loc. cit.*

[52] For a discussion of this provision, see 3/2.1.

[53] CC, *Rev.* 1954 No. 563; see 3/3.6.   [54] Reg. Art. 92 §1.

[55] I.e., the amount which is compared with the sales price in order to determine the gain or loss on the sale.

state inheritance taxes and the distribution of the estate to the heirs and legatees.[56]

This rule has now been expressly incorporated in the law by Reg. Art. 92 §5.[57]

The provision just cited also determines the basis of real property acquired by gift as equal to the value of the property for purposes of the state gift tax (3/3.6).

b. DETERMINATION OF GAIN. The tax is levied on the gain, i.e., the difference between the basis of the property including improvements — usually cost — and its sales price (Reg. Art. 92 §1).

If real property is contributed to a corporation or limited liability company upon its organization, the gain is measured by the difference between the cost of the property to the shareholder or partner and its appraised value at the time of the contribution. Such an appraisal is prescribed by the Corporation Law in the case of a contribution of property to the capital of a corporation; it is not required if the contribution is made to a limited liability company or other association. In the latter case, the tax would, in theory at least, fall on the excess of the value at which the property contributed is accepted by the company, over its cost to the contributing partner. Since the former value is purely in the discretion of the partners it is, of course, easy to avoid a tax on the gain. The Income Tax Regulations do not require an appraisal of property for purposes of determining its basis in the case of a contribution to capital.

The following items are deducted from the sales price in order to determine the taxable gain:

1. The real property transfer tax (Chapter 19) paid by the seller at the time of his *acquisition* of the property (Reg. Art. 92 §1[a]).
2. The cost of improvements placed on the property by the seller, and the interest on loans contracted for the purpose of improving the property (Reg. Art. 92 §1[b]).
3. Sales commissions paid by the seller (Reg. Art. 92 §1[c]).

The term "improvements" in the case of urban or rural real property includes all accretions in value arising from capital investments made by

---

[56] DIR, *Rev.* 1946 Nos. 336 and 359; *Rev.* 1947 No. 678; *Rev.* 1948 Nos. 33, 111, 171, 462, and 877; *Rev.* 1949 Nos. 521 and 685; *Rev.* 1951 No. 680 (with comments by Castro Viana); CC, *Rev.* 1954 No. 202. On the other hand, the Federal Court of Appeals held (34 *Revista de Direito Administrativo* 67) that there could be no taxable gain on the sale of real property acquired through inheritance because there was no element of cost to the seller, since his acquisition of the property was gratuitous.

[57] This new provision was added by the Administration on the occasion of the republication of the Income Tax Regulations under Decree No. 36,773 of January 13, 1955. It has no statutory basis and extends the scope of §1 of Reg. Art. 92 which is of statutory origin and expressly states that the tax falls on the difference between the sales price of the property and its *cost* to the seller. The constitutionality of Reg. Art. 92 §5 has been questioned on the ground that the Income Tax Regulations are in the nature of an administrative pronouncement and as such cannot widen the scope of the statutory law which they reproduce. See Sousa, §43.

the owner.[58] The term therefore includes not only buildings and similar constructions, but also planted trees, crops, etc. Only the natural growth of the soil is not considered as an improvement.[59]

The law (Reg. Art. 92 §2) provides for certain percentage reductions of the gain depending on the period during which the property was held. These percentages are applied to the difference between the cost of the real property including the improvements made thereto by the seller on the one hand, and the gross sales price (before deducting transfer tax and selling commissions) on the other.

The applicable percentages are as follows:

1. 10% if the property is sold within 2 years from the date of acquisition.
2. 15% if the holding period is more than 2 but not more than 5 years.
3. 25% if the holding period is more than 5 but not more than 10 years.
4. 30% if the holding period is in excess of 10 years.

The net gain computed as indicated above constitutes the amount subject to the tax.[60]

c. TAX RATE. The tax rate is 10% (Reg. Art. 92). In view of the percentage reductions applied, the effective tax rate will always be less than 10% of the actual gain on the sale. The addition to the tax in the nature of a compulsory refundable loan (12/1.3b) applies.

d. PAYMENT OF THE TAX. The seller of the property is responsible for the payment of the tax, and he must report the details of the transaction on the proper return form furnished by the government (Reg. Art. 95). The tax must be tendered by the seller when he files the return. Notaries and federal and state registrars exercising the functions of a notary are subject to penalties for authenticating a sale unless the payment of the tax is proved to them by means of the tax receipt (Reg. Art. 94); they may not record deeds with a value higher than that shown on the tax receipt (Reg. Art. 94 §3). A return on the prescribed form setting forth the details of

---

[58] DIR, *Rev.* 1948, Nos. 434 and 826; Rezende, Note 273-B.

[59] This interpretation is further supported by the wording of Reg. Art. 92 §1, which by its terms excludes only intangible real property (as defined in Art. 44 of the Civil Code, i.e., rights which are considered real property only by a legal fiction, such as mortgages, inalienable government bonds, and rights of inheritance in an estate in process of administration). The exclusion of these rights in §1 of Reg. Art. 92 would seem to indicate that all items which are real property by their nature and not only by legal fiction are included provided they arise from a capital investment made by the owner.

[60] The factors determining this figure, i.e., cost, sales price, and allowable deductions, must be proved by the seller. A judicial appraisal of the improvements is acceptable as proof of their value, Reg. Art. 92 §§3 and 4. If the seller is unable to submit the required evidence at the time the tax is due, the information furnished by him will be accepted, subject to proof within 60 days from the date of payment, and this period may be extended, Reg. Art. 92 §§6 and 7. If the deductions or holding period are not proved, they will be disregarded in the computation of the tax.

the transaction must likewise be filed by the vendor even if the sale has not resulted in a taxable gain. (This is called a "negative report.")

Payment of the tax does not foreclose the right of the tax authorities to verify the correctness of the return and payment. As a result of the assimilation of the tax here discussed to a withholding tax, the five-year statute of limitations does not apply (Reg. Art. 191; 13/6.2).

9/9. Liquidation and Reorganization

9/9.1 In General

"Reorganization" is not at present recognized in Brazil as a separate area of the income tax law, although rearrangements of the structure of business enterprises, exchanges and redemptions of securities, and other transactions commonly associated with this term frequently occur. The statutory rules on the subject are extremely limited and often so closely connected with matters discussed elsewhere in this report that their separate treatment would not be practical. In these instances, appropriate cross references will be made. The subjects discussed in this section are: the liquidation of business entities (9/9.2), changes in the legal form of a business both with respect to existing tax liabilities (9/9.3) and the creation of new ones (9/9.4), and the treatment of gains from the redemption of securities (9/9.5).

9/9.2 Liquidation of Business Entities

A business entity in the process of liquidation is subject to income tax under the general rules (Chapter 7) until the liquidation is terminated (Reg. Art. 51). The partners or members of an entity without independent legal existence (such as a partnership) remain liable for the unliquidated fiscal obligations (including fines and penalties) assessed against the entity (Reg. Art. 53). The company is obliged to file two income tax returns during the year in which its liquidation is terminated, one covering the preceding business year (base year) according to the general rules (13/1.2) and the other for the final period of liquidation (Reg. Art. 52; 6/3.7).[61]

9/9.3 Change in the Legal Form of a Business — Effect on Existing Tax Liabilities

Art. 54(a) through (c) of the Income Tax Regulations covers the various situations in which only the legal form of a business is changed, but the business itself is continued under the modified form. The general principle of the law is that changes of this nature have no

[61] The latter return must be filed within 30 days from the date on which the liquidation is terminated, Reg. Art. 52 Sole §; see DIR, *Rev.* 1955 Nos. 299 and 545.

effect on existing income tax liabilities,[62] and the successor or successors assume these liabilities by operation of law.

The terms used by the Regulations to classify the various organizational changes are not always clearly defined and their areas of application are somewhat uncertain. These uncertainties are, however, of little practical significance because the tax consequences of the different organizational changes are the same, regardless of their classification.[63]

In detail, Reg. Art. 54 classifies changes in the form of a business under the following headings.

a. SUCCESSION. The term "succession," as used in Reg. Art. 54(a) [64] refers to the transaction by which the successor company acquires the assets and assumes the liabilities of the predecessor company, continuing the business of the latter. It includes the cases of a merger (*fusão*), consolidation (*incorporação*),[65] and under some decisions, the continuation of the business of a sole proprietorship by a partnership or limited liability company.[66]

The following do not constitute successions:

1. The acquisition of a sole proprietorship by another sole proprietorship without full assumption of the predecessor's assets and liabilities.[67] Likewise, the purchase of the assets of a dissolved company does not constitute a succession.[68]

2. The distribution of the assets of a dissolved entity to the owners, partners, or shareholders who use the assets to form new companies.[69]

3. The sale of the shares or participations of a commercial company.[70]

b. TRANSFORMATION. Reg. Art. 54(b) refers to the "transformation" of a firm or company into another of any type whatever. The term "transformation" thus covers, in a very general manner, the continuation of an

---

[62] If the change occurs in the course of the year, the income of the old and the new firm during the same base year are combined in one return. Unless both firms kept proper books during the portions of the base year when they were in existence, the profits for the entire period are determined by estimate (6/9.2); CC, *Rev.* 1952 No. 650.

[63] Regarding changes of the accounting period in the case of reorganization, see 6/3.5.

[64] Reg. Art. 54(a) actually speaks of "succession in the form prescribed by the existing laws." There is no regulation of this transaction, however, either in the commercial law or the tax laws. Consequently, the term is employed according to its use in accepted commercial parlance; see Rezende-Viana, *Consolidação das Leis do Impôsto de Renda* (1955) (hereinafter cited as "Rezende-Viana, *Consolidação*"), Note 189; CC, *Rev.* 1952 No. 152; 1954 Nos. 96 and 196.

[65] See Rezende-Viana, *Consolidação*, Note 188.

[66] Provided that at least one of the members of the old firm becomes a member of the new one, CC, *Rev.* 1952 Nos. 277 and 839; 1954 No. 273. These cases would seem to be more adequately covered by the term "transformation" (see [b] below).

[67] Rezende-Viana, *Consolidação*, Note 189.

[68] *Ibid.;* CC, *Rev.* 1954 No. 96; 1955 No. 24.

[69] Rezende-Viana, *Consolidação*, Note 189.

[70] *Id.*, Note 188.

existing business under a different form of organization. The more important examples are:

1. The incorporation of a sole proprietorship [71] or its continuation in the form of a limited liability company.[72]
2. The incorporation of a partnership or a limited liability company.[73]
3. The incorporation of the Brazilian branch of a foreign corporation.[74]
4. The formation of a partnership by two sole proprietorships.[75]

C. CONTINUATION OF THE BUSINESS OF A DISSOLVED ENTITY. Reg. Art. 54 speaks of the continuation of the business of a dissolved entity by a surviving partner, by an estate (either under the same firm name or a different one), or by a sole proprietorship. This term applies if a commercial organization or its business is carried on either by the estate of the deceased owner, by a partner of the old firm (in the form of a single proprietorship), or, finally, by an entity in which at least one of the owners of the old firm becomes a member.[76]

9/9.4 Change in the Legal Form of a Business Not a Taxable Event

With the exception noted below, the changes in the legal form of a business listed at 9/9.3 do not give rise to income tax liabilities, even if the owners, partners, or shareholders change, or if their proportionate shares or participations do not remain the same. In particular, the incorporation of an individual business, a partnership, a limited liability company, or the Brazilian branch of a foreign corporation is not a taxable event.

Income tax liabilities both of an entity which is a party to a reorganization and of its owners, partners, or shareholders may, however, result from a revaluation of assets which is undertaken in connection with the reorganization. The Corporation Law [77] prescribes such revaluations in the case of mergers and consolidations. The income tax liabilities resulting from a revaluation of assets may be briefly summarized as follows:

1. The entity whose assets are revalued must include the reappraisal surplus in taxable income, with an option to defer the payment of the tax thereon for four years (Reg. Art. 43 §1[h]; see discussion at 7/6.2).

[71] CC, *Rev.* 1947 No. 8; 1948 No. 93; 1951 No. 428; 1952 No. 501.
[72] CC, *Rev.* 1952 No. 839.
[73] CC, *Rev.* 1950 No. 704; 1951 No. 892; 1952 No. 260; 1955 No. 448.
[74] CC, *Rev.* 1953 No. 461.
[75] CC, *Rev.* 1951 No. 877; 1952 No. 984.
[76] Rezende-Viana, *Consolidação*, Note 190; see CC, *Rev.* 1952 No. 277; 1955 Nos. 10, 196, 275.
[77] Arts. 152, 153. The law does not, however, prescribe that the appraisal be performed or reviewed by the government, so that the determination of values is entirely in the hands of the interested parties.

2. The benefits accruing to the owners, partners, or shareholders from a revaluation of assets made in connection with a merger, consolidation, or the formation of a new company are subject to complementary tax if the shares or participations held by these individuals are nominative (Reg. Art. 8[f]; see discussion at 9/2.1f). If, as a result of the revaluation of assets, new shares are distributed to the holders of *bearer* shares, these distributions are subject to withholding of tax at the source (Reg. Art. 96[3]; see discussion at 9/2.2b). The present withholding rate is 28%, computed on the par value of the new shares distributed.

9/9.5   Gains from the Redemption of Securities

a. RESIDENT INDIVIDUALS

1. Nominative shares.   Under Art. 15 of the Brazilian Corporation Law, a corporation is not permitted to trade in its own shares or even to retain such shares as treasury stock. The statute permits a corporation to repurchase its shares only for the purpose of either cancelling or reissuing them and this only in the following three cases.

1. The case in which a corporation, utilizing undistributed profits or unappropriated reserves, repays either to all its shareholders, or to some of them determined by lot, the value of their shares which are subsequently cancelled (*resgate*) (Corp. Law, Art. 16).

    The corporation has a choice between reducing its capital or keeping it unimpaired by increasing either the number of the remaining shares or their par value.[78]

2. The redemption of the shares of a dissenting stockholder who withdraws from the corporation(*reembôlso*).

    A shareholder can withdraw from the corporation only in certain specific situations which are defined in the Corporation Law.[79] The shares owned by the retiring shareholder must be reissued by the corporation. If a buyer cannot be found for them, the shares must be cancelled.[80] The option to increase the par value of the shares which is open to the corporation in the case discussed under (1) above (*resgate*) is not available here.

3. The repurchase by a corporation of its shares (*compra*). A repurchase is permitted only as a step to reduce the capital and only if the market price of the shares does not exceed the amount to be repaid to the shareholders (see below). The repurchased shares must be cancelled (Corp. Law, Art. 19).

In all three cases above, the price to be paid by the corporation for each share is its stated value, i.e., the value arrived at by dividing the total net assets of the corporation, as shown in its last balance sheet

[78] Corp. Law, Art. 16 Sole §. The provisions of Reg. Art. 8(d) and Reg. Art. 96(3)(c), which impose a tax on an increase in the number or the par value of shares, do not apply in this situation, which merely amounts to an equalization of the remaining capital with the number of outstanding shares.

[79] Corp. Law, Arts. 107 and 105(a), (d), (e) and (g).

[80] Corp. Law, Art. 17. The law does not put a time limit on the cancellation or reissuance of the shares.

approved by the general meeting of shareholders, by the number of outstanding shares (Corp. Law, Art. 107).

The Income Tax Regulations deal specifically with the computation of the gain realized by a shareholder upon the redemption of shares only in the situations described under (1) and (2) above (*resgate* and *reembôlso*). In these cases, the gain is measured by the excess of the redemption price over the cost of the shares to the shareholder, or over their par value if the shares were originally issued to him (Reg. Art. 4, §5[b]).

The gain to the shareholder is taxed under Schedule B.[81] It is, therefore, subject to schedular tax at the rate of 10% (Reg. Art. 25) and to the progressive complementary tax.

The Regulations do not specifically refer to gains realized by a shareholder upon the repurchase of his shares by the corporation (*compra*, see [3] above), which would seem capable of producing a taxable gain similar to the ones resulting from the transactions described under (1) and (2) above.

If a corporation redeems shares through distributions of property, the basis of the property in the hands of the shareholder is equal to the par value of the shares surrendered by him.[82] The shareholder, therefore, does not realize a gain or loss on the exchange. The corporation realizes a gain only if and to the extent that the par value of the shares received upon the exchange exceeds the book value of the assets distributed.

A situation different from those discussed under (1)–(3) above is presented if a corporation amortizes its shares out of available surplus (*amortização*). Art. 18 of the Corporation Law defines the amortization of shares as a transaction by which the corporation, out of available funds and without impairment of its capital, repays to all the shareholders, or to some of them, such amounts as the shareholders would be entitled to if the corporation were presently liquidated.

The former controversy about whether these distributions to the shareholders constitute a tax-free return of capital has now been settled by statute.[83] The distributions are taxed as dividends under the rules set forth at 9/2.1b. and 9/2.2.a, depending on whether the shares are nominative or made out to bearer.

The repayment of the book value of the shares out of available surplus does not affect the status of the shareholder as such, because the shares are not surrendered to the corporation for retirement. In the event that

---

[81] Reg. Art. 4 §5(b). According to Sousa §8, distributions through retirement or redemption of shares should be taxed to the recipient shareholder under Schedule F rather than Schedule B as representing anticipated distributions in liquidation.

[82] DIR, *Rev.* 1956 Nos. 85 and 89. Reg. Art. 198, according to which income received in property is measured by the value of the property at the time of receipt, is apparently not applicable; see DIR, *Rev.* 1948 No. 582.

[83] Law No. 2,862 of September 4, 1956, Art. 26.

the corporation is liquidated, a shareholder whose shares were previously amortized is entitled only to his proportionate part of the surplus existing at the time of liquidation and not to further payments on the par value of the shares.[84]

Apart from the situations indicated, gains realized by an individual from transactions in shares or other securities are not taxed under Brazilian law provided that they do not constitute business income.[85]

2. Nominative participating certificates and similar securities. Gains realized by individual holders upon the redemption of nominative participating certificates and similar nominative securities are taxed as income from capital under Schedule F and subject to complementary tax only (Reg. Art. 8[e]).

3. Anticipated redemption of capitalization bonds. Gains in excess of Cr$ 1,000 resulting from the anticipated retirement, by means of a lottery, of capitalization bonds are subject to taxation at the source at the rate of 15% computed on gross income.[86]

4. Bearer Shares. The Income Tax Regulations do not contain a specific provision regarding the taxation of distributions in redemption of bearer shares as they do in the case of redemption of nominative shares (9/9.5a1). They merely state, in a negative way, that such distributions do not constitute income from lotteries subject to taxation at the source at the rate of 30% (Reg. Art. 96 [5]). While there is general agreement that it is not the intent of the law to exempt these distributions from income tax altogether, the question of the proper method of taxing them must be regarded as unsettled.

It has been argued that the provisions of the Regulations dealing with the redemption of nominative shares should be applied by analogy,[87] notwithstanding the fact that these rules deal with schedular income and are obviously intended for nominative shares only.[88] On the

---

[84] For this reason, the rule of Law No. 2,862, Art. 26 Sole §, that the shareholder shall not be subject to income tax on distributions in liquidation up to the par value of his shares, appears superfluous.

[85] DIR, *Rev.* 1951 No. 914; 1955 No. 1,030; Sousa, §8. Such profits constitute business income if realized by a legal entity which is required to enter the transaction in the books, but not if they constitute occasional transactions of an individual who is not required to keep books. See 10/4.1a and note 20 at 6/1.3 (nonresident individuals).

[86] Reg. Art. 96(2)(a) and Art. 96 §2. The nature and characteristics of this type of savings bond are explained in note 26 at 9/2.2c. The numbers of all bonds in process of installment payment participate in lotteries which are held from time to time and the winning numbers are redeemed in full. The excess of the redemption payment over the total amount of installments paid (except for the first Cr$ 1,000 of the excess) is the taxable gain.

[87] Rezende, Notes 16-B and 281, advances the argument that the holder of bearer shares identifies himself on the occasion of their redemption and thus justifies the action of the government in treating him as if he were the owner of nominative shares.

[88] Reg. Art. 4 §5(b). This in effect would result in the imposition of the schedular

other hand, it has been held that the provision of the Regulations dealing with the anticipated retirement of capitalization bonds [89] furnishes the appropriate statutory basis of taxation.[90]

The amortization of bearer shares out of available surplus of the corporation is taxed as a dividend (9/9.5a1).

b. RESIDENT ENTITIES. Gains from the redemption of shares or other securities which are held by a corporation or other entity [91] are excluded from its business profits taxable under Reg. Art. 44 to the extent that the gains represent profits already subjected to tax in the hands of the distributing entity.[92] If shares are redeemed, it is immaterial for purposes of the tax on business income under Reg. Art. 44 whether they are nominative or made out to bearer.

In the event that the shares or other securities redeemed are made out to bearer, however, the distributing entity must withhold income tax at the source for the account of the distributee (Reg. Art. 96 [3]; see 9/2.3). The withholding tax is presently levied at the rate of 28% [93] computed on the gross amount of the distribution.[94]

For redemption of shares through distributions of property, see 9/9.5a1.

c. NONRESIDENTS. In the case of nonresidents (individuals or entities), gains from the redemption of nominative securities are taxed by withholding at the source at the rate of 20%, computed on the gross amount of the distribution (Reg. Art. 97(1) and Art. 97 §5). In the case of bearer securities, it seems that the withholding rate of 28% (see b. above) will apply because the distributing entity is in no position to establish the identity of the owner of the securities. For redemption of shares through distributions of property, see 9/9.5a1.

tax of 10% applicable to Schedule B income, plus a complementary tax depending on the amount of total income.

[89] Reg. Art. 96(2)(a), discussed at 9/9.5a3.

[90] DIR, *Rev.* 1950 No. 185. The decision deals with the redemption of shares of a dissenting shareholder (*reembôlso*). This viewpoint is decidedly more favorable to the shareholder than Rezende's opinion, resulting as it does in the imposition of a withholding tax of 15% (with exemption for the first Cr$ 1,000) under Reg. Art. 96(2)(a).

[91] The gain is measured by the difference between the cost of the securities (if higher than their par value) and the amount of the distribution. On the books of the recipient this gain must be shown separately from the par value of the securities; DIR, *Rev.* 1955 Nos. 618, 974.

[92] Reg. Art. 43 §2(c) and (d); see 7/7.1; 9/2.3; see DIR, *Rev.* 1955 No. 779 with annotation by Rezende.

[93] Reg. Art. 96(3)(a) as modified by Law No. 2,862, Art. 25.

[94] This rule, which completely disregards the cost of the securities to the holder, is understandable if it is considered that there is no effective way to verify this cost in the case of bearer certificates.

CHAPTER 10

INCOME FROM SPECIAL ACTIVITIES
AND FROM MISCELLANEOUS SOURCES

10/1. Natural Resource Extraction

    10/1.1   In General

    10/1.2   Depletion of Mines, Other Natural Deposits, and Forests

10/2. Agriculture

    10/2.1   In General

    10/2.2   Individuals

        a. Gross Income

        b. Deductions

    10/2.3   Entities

10/3. Other Activities Subject to Special Treatment

    10/3.1   Income of Financial Institutions and Public Utility Companies

    10/3.2   Deductions Allowed Insurance, Capitalization, and Public Utility Companies

        a. Deductions for Technical Reserves of Certain Companies

        b. Deduction for Amortization of Investment of Public Utility Companies

10/4. Income from Miscellaneous Sources

    10/4.1   Resident Individuals

        a. Miscellaneous Income from Occupations and from Transactions Entered into for Profit — Schedule H

        b. Other Miscellaneous Income

10/4.2   Resident Entities
10/4.3   Nonresidents

10/1.   Natural Resource Extraction

10/1.1   In General

Art. 15 (III) of the Constitution of Brazil reserves the taxation of minerals (including taxation of their production, distribution, consumption, export, and import) exclusively to the federal government. The constitutional provision [1] further calls for the introduction of a single federal tax on mining, in lieu of all existing federal, state, and municipal taxes, the proceeds of which are to be apportioned among the various governments.

Since no federal statute implementing the constitutional mandate has been enacted to date, the taxation of mining enterprises is still regulated by Art. 68 of the Mining Code.[2] This provision limits the aggregate amount of all federal, state, and local taxes imposed on a mining business for a given year to 8% of the value of the production of the mine during the preceding year. This ceiling of 8% does not include the income tax,[3] except in the case of gold mines which, by specific statutory provision, benefit from an over-all limitation of 8% in respect of all taxes including the income tax.[4]

Except for the limitation in the case of gold mines, the taxation of income from mining follows the general rules. The income from mining when received by individuals occasionally qualifies as miscellaneous (nonbusiness) income taxable under Schedule H,[5] but in the large majority of cases the operation of a mine constitutes a business, with the result that the status of the individual recipient, for income tax purposes, is assimilated to that of an entity taxable as a corporation.[6] The income of entities from mining operations is taxed under Reg. Art. 44, the same as other business income.[7]

[1] Constitution, Art. 15 §2.

[2] Decree-law No. 1,985 of January 29, 1940, as amended by Decree-law No. 5,247 of February 12, 1943 (*Diário Oficial* of February 15, 1943). See 16/3.

[3] Mining Code, Art. 68. See DIR, *Rev.* 1950 No. 600; CC, *Rev.* 1952 Nos. 474 and 534; Federal Court of Appeals, *Rev.* 1952 No. 427; 1953 No. 610.

[4] Mining Code, Art. 68 §2. See also CC, *Rev.* 1951 No. 453. The exemption extends to income from by-products (CC, *Rev.* 1951 No. 457; 1954 No. 530; DIR, *Rev.* 1952 No. 744) and even to income which is unrelated to the mining operations, such as bank interest and real property rentals, CC, *Rev.* 1954 No. 278.

Under general principles (Reg. Art. 31), the exemption or partial exemption of a mining enterprise does not benefit the owners thereof in respect of profits derived by them from the business. See Federal Court of Appeals in *Rev.* 1953 No. 257.

[5] Schedule G which covers farm industries (see 10/2.2a below) is not applicable. Sousa, §13. Regarding the tax under Schedule H, see 10/4.1.

[6] Reg. Art. 27 §1; see discussion under 5/3.4.

[7] See DIR, *Rev.* 1951 No. 1008 (income from exploitation of a sandpit by an indi-

10/1.2 Depletion of Mines, Other Natural Deposits, and Forests

The Income Tax Regulations (Art. 37[f]) allow a deduction for the amortization of capital invested in the exploitation of mines, other natural deposits, and forests. The investment includes the natural resource itself as well as buildings, other constructions,[8] machines, vehicles, and materials.[9] The deduction is in every case based on cost.

The extent of the allowable annual deduction is not specifically prescribed by the law, which merely states that the deduction must be reasonable and not in excess of the amount commonly accepted in similar situations. The rate of amortization is determined in each individual case by the Income Tax Division, which acts on the basis of data supplied by the Bureau of Mines in the Department of Agriculture.

The contents of the deposit are estimated by the Bureau of Mines in proceedings preparatory to the issuance of a mining permit. The time limitation for the concession is stated in the permit and based on the expected life of the mine, which in turn depends on the claimant's own estimate of the intensity of operations. In examining this estimate, the Bureau considers the equipment of the claimant. On the same basis, the claimant then secures from the Income Tax Division a determination of the applicable rate of amortization, which is, in effect, merely an approval of the data established by the Bureau of Mines. In principle, this forecast should be reviewed from time to time on the basis of the miner's experience or a change of equipment, but this is rarely done. In actual practice, the estimates of the Bureau of Mines are always kept low, with the result that the deposit is never exhausted when the concession expires. Since the Bureau then grants an extension of the concession, mining companies do not usually secure a revision of the amortization rate during the life of the concession.[10]

If an extension of the concession is granted because the original estimate

vidual owner taxable under Schedule H; extraction of clay and manufacture of tiles and bricks by the owner on the same premises taxable under Reg. Art. 44); DIR, *Rev.* 1947 No. 625 (diamond prospector who sells precious and semi-precious stones to authorized buyers held to operate a business and to be taxable under Reg. Art. 44). See Rezende, Note 46-A.

[8] This represents an exception to the general principle of Brazilian income tax law that depreciation of real property is not permitted (7/3.1); CC, *Rev.* 1950 No. 116; 1951 Nos. 945 and 1070.

[9] The capital subject to amortization is that invested in the development of mines, mineral deposits, and forests, which the Mining Code (Decree-law No. 1985 of 1940, Art. 11) defines as follows:

1. The property intended for operations which is of a permanent character such as constructions, machines, apparatus, and instruments.

2. Animals and vehicles used either above or below the surface.

3. The provisions necessary for mining operations during a period of 120 days.

[10] See Sousa, §34-F.

was too low, a new appraisal is made and the rate of amortization is redetermined.

10/2. Agriculture

10/2.1 In General

This section discusses the taxation of income from farming, livestock raising (also bee-keeping, silkworm culture, and the raising of fish), and from the processing of agricultural and animal products, including farm industries.

10/2.2 Individuals

a. GROSS INCOME. The income of individuals from agriculture and related sources is classified under Schedule G (Reg. Art. 9), which does not provide for a schedular tax. This type of income, therefore, is subject to complementary tax only.[11] If, however, raw materials processed in an agricultural industry are acquired from third parties rather than produced on the farm itself, the operation is deemed to be of a commercial nature, and the rules on taxation of business income (10/2.3) apply.

There are two methods of determining net income:

1. The taxpayer may elect to be taxed on the basis of actual net income (Reg. Art. 58). The election can be made only if the taxpayer keeps reliable books and records showing his gross income and expenses.[12] When several associates participate in the operation of an agricultural property, each one is taxed separately on his proportionate share of the income (Reg. Art. 58 §2).

2. If the taxpayer cannot prove his true income by means of his books and records, either because he keeps no books or because they are not acceptable to the fiscal authorities, the law substitutes an amount of 5% of the value of the property as the net schedular income on which the tax is computed. The same method is applied to taxpayers who do not elect to be taxed on actual net income. The property consists of the land and pastures, the buildings and other improvements, equipment, agricultural machines, permanent crops, work animals, and animals held for income (Reg. Art. 57 §1).

   If the value of the constructions, improvements, equipment, and agricultural machines cannot be exactly determined, the value of the property will be represented by the fair market value of the land as appraised for real property tax purposes plus 10% to cover all other items (Reg. Art. 57 §2). If the property is rented, the net income will be determined on the basis of the information available to the assessing authorities, but the value of the rented properties will be excluded (Reg. Art. 57 §3).

[11] The personal exemption for purposes of the complementary tax (apart from allowances for dependents, etc.) is Cr$ 60,000.

[12] The income tax law does not prescribe any particular books or methods of bookkeeping for these taxpayers as it does for entities. Any informal records which clearly disclose income and expenses are acceptable to the fiscal authorities, Sousa §13.

b. DEDUCTIONS. If net income is determined under method [1] above, the taxpayer may deduct all expenses actually incurred in producing the income. This includes interest on loans contracted in connection with the maintenance or development of agricultural property operated by the taxpayer. Capital expenditures and personal expenses of the taxpayer are not allowable deductions except the cost of agricultural products used by the taxpayer for his support (Reg. Art. 58 §1).

If the income is determined under method [2] above, no deductions of any kind are allowed (Reg. Art. 57 §4).[13]

10/2.3 Entities

The income of entities engaged in farming, livestock raising, etc., and the income of any taxpayer engaged in farm industry who buys rather than produces his raw materials is taxed under the rules applying to business income discussed in Chapter 7; the principles regulating bookkeeping and the determination of taxable income are fully applicable, as are the tax rates of Reg. Art. 44.

Agricultural companies of any type whose gross annual income does not exceed Cr$ 1,000,000 may elect to be taxed on the basis of presumed profits (note 91 at 6/9.1).

10/3.   Other Activities Subject to Special Treatment

10/3.1   Income of Financial Institutions and Public Utility Companies

The computation of the taxable income of financial institutions and public utility companies follows, in general, the rules which apply to other business entities.

10/3.2   Deductions Allowed Insurance, Capitalization, and Public Utility Companies

The following special deductions may be claimed in addition to those generally available.

a. DEDUCTIONS FOR TECHNICAL RESERVES OF CERTAIN COMPANIES. The technical reserves of insurance and capitalization companies [14] which are

---

[13] Interest paid on debts incurred in connection with the *acquisition* of agricultural property is deductible in the individual income tax return of the owner for purposes of the complementary tax, CC, *Rev.* 1951 Nos. 585 and 1355. See 12/1.2b [3].

[14] "Capitalization companies" (*sociedades de capitalização*) are a special form of savings institution operating thrift plans and issuing bonds which are redeemed by periodic lotteries, or repaid with interest upon their maturity. Regarding the treatment of gains on the redemption of such capitalization bonds, see 9/9.5a[3]. Capitalization companies are regulated by Decree No. 22,456 of February 10, 1933.

required by the laws regulating their activities [15] constitute a deduction for income tax purposes (Reg. Art. 37 §1[a]).

b. DEDUCTION FOR AMORTIZATION OF INVESTMENT OF PUBLIC UTILITY COMPANIES. Public utilities [16] are granted a special deduction for the amortization of capital invested by them in assets which, under the terms of the contract or decree by which a public corporation grants the concession, become the property of the latter upon the expiration of the concession without any compensation to the concessionaire (Reg. Art. 37 §1[b]).

10/4. Income from Miscellaneous Sources

10/4.1 Resident Individuals

a. MISCELLANEOUS INCOME FROM OCCUPATIONS AND FROM TRANSACTIONS ENTERED INTO FOR PROFIT — SCHEDULE H. Art. 10 of the Income Tax Regulations provides a miscellaneous classification (Schedule H) which covers "the income from all lucrative transactions not included in the foregoing schedules" (Schedules A through G). The provision cited lists six different types of such income, which are reproduced below. This enumeration, however, is merely illustrative and not intended to be exhaustive.

The wording of Reg. Art. 10 has given rise to considerable difficulties of interpretation. Administrative practice, confirmed by the views of the text writers, proceeds by a process of elimination.[17]

It seems fairly settled that income from personal work and services is not properly included in Schedule H, because, if done by an employee, it comes under Schedule C, and if done in an independent capacity, under Schedule D. Income from commercial services also is not properly classified under Schedule H, because the person or organization rendering such services (unless they are merely sporadic) assumes the status of a legal entity for income tax purposes (Reg Art. 27 §1; 5/3.4 above).

The types of income which are specifically listed in Reg. Art. 10 are, for the purposes of this description, classified under the various categories of income to which they belong. They are as follows:

1. Income from a *sociedade em conta de participação* (partnership on participation account): 5/3.2.
2. Income from renting movable property: 9/4.3.
3. Income from subleasing real property: 9/4.3.
4. Income from licensing industrial or commercial trademarks: 9/5.2.
5. Occasional income from commercial or industrial transactions: 7/1.3.

---

[15] Insurance companies are regulated by Decree-law No. 2,063 of March 7, 1940, Arts. 57–66, and capitalization companies by Decree No. 22,456 of February 10, 1933.
[16] Called "concessionaires of public services," Reg. Art. 37 §1(b).
[17] Rezende, Note 46-A.

The Income Tax Regulations also list under Schedule H "net profits from the assignment of rights of any kind" (Reg. Art. 10[f]). This very general clause has given rise to considerable controversy.[18] Any sale of property is a transfer of rights in the legal view. All capital gains realized by individuals would, under a literal interpretation of this provision, qualify as Schedule H income. The administrative and judicial decisions, however, exclude capital gains from taxation under Schedule H. They hold that, except where expressly provided for by the law (as in the case of gains from the sale of real property), gains realized on the sale of property (securities, etc.) are not taxable either under Schedule H or any other schedule of the income tax law. The important effect of this interpretation is that profits on the sale of shares, bonds, other securities,[19] patents,[20] trademarks,[21] manufacturing processes and formulas (CC Rev. 1954 No. 306), and other capital assets are not taxed to individuals unless they constitute business income and are as such entered in the books of an individual firm.

The following types of income have been held to be taxable under Schedule H: [22]

1. An assignment of rights acquired under a contract of sale.[23]
2. Compensation received for nonexercise of contractual rights (DIR, Rev. 1948 No. 875).
3. Damages for breach of contract (DIR, Rev. 1948 No. 392).

The tax rate under Schedule H is 5% (Reg. Art. 25). The deductions allowed under Schedule H are the same as those applying under Schedule D (8/2.3) or Schedule E (9/4.1b), depending on the nature of the income (Reg. Art. 17).

b. OTHER MISCELLANEOUS INCOME

1. Profits from "report" operations and sales of futures. "Report" operations [24] are taxed to a resident individual under Schedule B by express provision of the law (Reg. Art. 4 §5[d]). The same treatment applies to the sale of futures.[25]

2. Gains from certain lotteries. Lottery gains are taxed by way of withholding at the source, at the following rates:

1. 25% in the case of cash prizes in excess of Cr$ 1,000 from lotteries for exclusively philanthropic purposes, including those operated by the government (Reg. Art. 96 [4]).

18 Regarding the following, see Sousa §14.
19 DIR, Rev. 1949 No. 594; CC, Rev. 1945 Nos. 412 and 427; 1951 No. 914.
20 CC, Rev. 1946 No. 694; see Rezende, Note 33.
21 CC, Rev. 1946 No. 493; see Rezende, loc. cit.
22 Sousa, §14.
23 DIR, Rev. 1948 No. 873 and Rev. 1951 No. 739; CC, Rev. 1951 No. 1249.
24 A "report" operation is one in which a party buys shares for cash and at the same time resells the stock at a higher price for future delivery.
25 Such as coffee "futures" and other term sales.

2. 30% in the case of cash prizes in excess of Cr$ 1,000 from other lotteries, sporting events, and bets and drawings of any kind (Reg. Art. 96 [5]).[26]

10/4.2   Resident Entities

The income of the various types listed under 10/4.1 [27] constitutes business income in the hands of a legal entity. As such, it must be entered in its books and is taxed under Reg. Art. 44.

10/4.3   Nonresidents

Any income listed under 10/4.1 which is realized by a nonresident individual or entity is subject to withholding of income tax at the source. The withholding tax is computed on gross income (Reg. Art. 97 §5). The rate of the withholding tax is 20% (Reg. Art. 97[1] and its §5), unless a higher withholding rate applies to residents in respect of the same kind of income as in the case of lottery gains (9/2.4).

---

[26] The quoted provision expressly excludes income from the anticipated redemption of capitalization bonds (9/9.5a3) and from the redemption or amortization of corporate shares (9/9.5a1 and 9/9.5a4).

The fact that bonds and shares redeemed may be chosen by lot made it necessary to exclude such distributions explicitly from the application of the 30% tax.

[27] Except income from foreign sources, which is not taxed to entities, Reg. Art. 35; 11/2.3.

CHAPTER 11

....

INTERNATIONAL ASPECTS

OF INCOME TAXATION

11/1. Scope of Discussion and Definition of Terms
11/1.1 Scope of Chapter
11/1.2 Definition of Terms

11/2. Income of Residents from Foreign Sources
11/2.1 In General
11/2.2 Resident Individuals
11/2.3 Resident Entities
11/2.4 Exchange Rates Applying to Income from Foreign Sources

11/3. Income of Nonresidents from Sources in Brazil
11/3.1 In General
11/3.2 "Doing Business in Brazil"
11/3.3 Brazilian Branch of Foreign Entity
a. In General
b. Gross Income
c. Deductions
d. Mitigation of Double Taxation of Branch Profits — Exemption of Reinvested Profits from the Withholding Tax
e. Branch Versus Subsidiary
11/3.4 Income of Nonresidents Subject to Withholding of Tax
a. Licensing of Patents, Trademarks, Processes, etc.

     b. Services Rendered by a Foreign Entity to
      a Brazilian Firm
     c. Personal Services as an Employee
  11/3.5 Income of Nonresidents from Sales to Brazil
     a. Export Sales
     b. Sales of Capital Assets
     c. Sale of Patents, Trademarks, Inventions,
      Processes, Brand Names, Designs, and
      Copyrights

11/4. Tax Treaties
  11/4.1 No Income Tax Conventions

11/1. Scope of Discussion and Definition of Terms

11/1.1 Scope of Chapter

This chapter discusses the taxation of income derived by resident individuals and entities from sources outside Brazil and of income derived by nonresident individuals and entities from Brazilian sources.

11/1.2 Definition of Terms

Regarding the definition of the terms "resident" and "nonresident," see 5/1. (resident individuals), 5/2. (resident corporations), 5/3. (other resident taxpayers), 5/4.1 (nonresident individuals), 5/4.6 (nonresident corporations), and 5/4.9 (other nonresident taxpayers).

11/2. Income of Residents from Foreign Sources

11/2.1 In General

The principle of Brazilian law is that resident individuals are taxed on income from foreign sources, while entities are not. The detailed rules are set forth below.

11/2.2 Resident Individuals

All income received from sources abroad by individuals not engaged in business who are residents of Brazil is classified under Schedule F (Reg. Art. 8 Sole §). Since Schedule F does not provide for a schedular tax, this income is subject to complementary tax only.[1]

---

[1] Regarding the practical impossibility of enforcing this provision, see Sousa, §12; Rezende-Viana, *Consolidação*, Note 44.

The decisions and rulings are to the effect that only foreign income which is actually remitted from abroad is included under Schedule F.[2] This requirement is not met if the income is merely credited abroad;[3] likewise, income which is not transferable because of currency restrictions in the country of origin need not be included in Schedule F.[4] Whereas an entity domiciled in Brazil is not taxed on its income from foreign sources (see 11/2.3), such income if distributed to the owners or partners is subject to the complementary tax in their hands.[5]

By express provisions of the Income Tax Regulations, Schedule F includes all foreign income regardless of its character. Examples of taxable income of this type are dividends and other distributions on securities,[6] fees for services rendered,[7] or commissions remitted from abroad. The fact that such income may have been taxed in the foreign country does not affect its taxability in Brazil.[8] However, since only income which is actually remitted from abroad is taxed in Brazil, it would seem that foreign income may be reported net of all foreign taxes paid thereon.

The Income Tax Regulations do not contain any rules governing the determination of the source of income; the principle to be derived from the decisions and rulings is that all income remitted from abroad is subject to the complementary tax regardless of its origin. Consequently, the place where personal services are rendered or utilized, or where title to merchandise sold passes to the buyer is immaterial. It is required, however, that the receipts be in the nature of income as this term is used elsewhere in the Income Tax Regulations; the taxability of foreign income does not extend to gross receipts, or payments constituting a return of capital. (See 6/1.3.)

11/2.3   Resident Entities

The Income Tax Regulations do not include any general rules regarding the source of income and the treatment of foreign income of entities. Reg. Art. 35, however, deals with entities whose profits originate from activities exercised partly in Brazil and partly abroad. The cited provision defines such activities and states the rule that only the portion of the total profits which is allocable to Brazilian sources shall be subject to income tax. If the books of the taxpayer do not permit an allocation

[2] CC, *Rev.* 1954 No. 336-A (with critical annotation by Castro Viana); see Rezende, Note 103.

[3] DIR, *Rev.* 1943 No. 447; 1947 No. 561; 1948 No. 728.

[4] CC, *Rev.* 1944 No. 263.

[5] CC, *Rev.* 1949 No. 89; DIR, *Rev.* 1951 No. 778. This is in harmony with the principle of Reg. Art. 31 that the exemption of an entity from income tax does not extend to those who receive income from the entity in any manner or form.

[6] DIR, *Rev.* 1943 No. 379; 1947 No. 561.

[7] DIR, *Rev.* 1943 No. 447; CC, *Rev.* 1948 Nos. 239 and 321.

[8] CC, *Rev.* 1948 Nos. 239 and 321.

between domestic and foreign income, taxable income shall be deemed
to be equal to 20% of gross income (Reg. Art. 35 §2).[9]

The following transactions are considered to be performed partly within
and partly outside Brazil (Reg. Art. 35 §1):

1. Commercial transactions and other transactions entered into for profit
   which are initiated in Brazil and consummated abroad, or vice versa.
2. The extraction of raw materials in Brazil and their subsequent processing, sale, or utilization abroad, or vice versa.
3. Transportation and other communication services between Brazil and
   foreign countries.[10]

Article 35 of the Income Tax Regulations requires the elimination of
foreign income in transactions which have both a foreign and a domestic
element in order to arrive at the tax base. The provision deals with the
taxation of Brazilian, not foreign, income. The principle to be derived
from this rule is clearly that entities, as distinguished from individuals,
are not taxed on income from sources outside Brazil.[11] The same principle is evident from Reg. Art. 34, which deals with the determination
of the taxable income of entities resident in Brazil. According to Reg.
Art. 34 §1, the accounting system of an entity must disclose all its transactions as well as the profits derived from year to year from its activities
"in the national territory."

11/2.4. Exchange Rates Applying to Income from Foreign Sources

The conversion of foreign income into Brazilian currency is covered by
Reg. Art. 199. The provision states that receipts in foreign currency
which are paid, credited, or remitted to the taxpayer, or which are received by him or invested for his account, shall be converted into Brazilian currency at the rate of exchange prevailing on the date of payment,
credit, remittance, receipt or investment, or at the rate of exchange at
which the transaction giving rise to the income was actually carried out.

The provision of Reg. Art. 199 dates back to an earlier period when

[9] Gross income is determined in the same way as it is for purposes of the tax on
presumed profits (6/9.1), i.e., it includes all income from transactions carried out for
the taxpayer's own account as well as compensation for services rendered,
whether the activities from which the income results are normal or extraordinary in
the taxpayer's business (Reg. Art. 40 §§1 and 2). The statement in the text is based
on the amendments made to Reg. Art. 35 by Law No. 2,354 of Nov. 29, 1954. In the
older decisions, e.g., DIR, Rev. 1943 No. 680 and CC, Rev. 1945 No. 33, it was held
that if the taxpayer failed to keep books showing the income from Brazilian sources,
the latter would be estimated under Reg. Art. 34 as in other cases where a proper
determination of taxable income proved impossible through the fault of the taxpayer.
The new provision covers the situation dealt with in the cited decisions.
[10] The term "communications" includes international cable and telegraph companies, CC, Rev. 1951 No. 625; Rezende, Note 132. Regarding exemption of foreign
shipping companies and airlines on the basis of reciprocity, see 5/6.5.
[11] See DIR, Rev. 1951 No. 778.

there was only one official rate of exchange for the Brazilian cruzeiro. At the present time, a great variety of different exchange rates applies, according to the nature of the business transaction involved. In this situation, it would seem that only the last part of the statutory rule cited above is still of practical significance, i.e., that the rate of exchange which is applicable to a particular transaction under existing currency regulations will also be the one which governs for income tax purposes.[12]

11/3. Income of Nonresidents from Sources in Brazil

11/3.1 In General

Brazilian income tax law does not distinguish between nonresident individuals and nonresident entities, so that the rules set forth below apply to both types of taxpayers.

The income of nonresidents from sources in Brazil is subject to withholding of income tax at the source, as further explained in 11/3.4. It should be clearly understood, however, that only those individuals and entities who are not considered to be doing business in Brazil are nonresidents for income tax purposes. An individual or entity doing business in Brazil through a permanent establishment or a permanent agency located in the country becomes a resident for income tax purposes and is taxed like a domestic entity under Reg. Art. 44, besides being liable for the withholding tax under Reg. Art. 97. Regarding the term "doing business in Brazil," see 11/3.2; regarding the tax treatment of the Brazilian branch of a foreign entity, see 11/3.3.

11/3.2 "Doing Business in Brazil"

The term "doing business in Brazil" is not of statutory origin and derives its meaning entirely from the practical application it has found in administrative and judicial decisions.

Art. 64 of the Corporation Law [13] requires a foreign corporation [14] de-

---

[12] It should be noted that Reg. Art. 199 in its former version contained a sole paragraph stating that entities were obliged to convert financial statements expressed in foreign currency into Brazilian currency at the rate of exchange prevailing on the last working day immediately preceding the balance sheet date. The opening section of the article was identical with the one reproduced in the text and applied to individuals only. Reg. Art. 199 Sole Paragraph was deleted by Law No. 2,354 of 1954. Now that entities domiciled in Brazil are no longer permitted to carry their accounts in foreign currency (Reg. Art. 206, see 6/2.1), it is to be assumed that Reg. Art. 199 in its present version applies to both individuals *and* entities.

[13] The text of the provision reads as follows:
"Art. 64. No foreign corporation or company, regardless of its purpose, shall operate in the country either directly or through a branch, agency, or establishment representing it, unless it is authorized to do so by the federal government, provided, however, that no such authority is required, except as may be required by law, for a foreign corporation to hold shares of stock of a Brazilian corporation (Art. 60)."

[14] This provision, as its wording indicates, is also applicable to entities other than corporations.

siring to operate in Brazil to qualify by taking out a permit to operate in the country from the federal government. The lack of this qualification, however, is irrelevant under the express provision of Reg. Art. 27 §2, which states in effect that the rules of the Income Tax Regulations apply to registered and nonregistered entities alike. The important question is whether or not the foreign entity is in fact doing business in Brazil through a permanent establishment or a permanent agency located in the country.

The granting of (exclusive or nonexclusive) licenses, by a foreign organization to a Brazilian entity, to manufacture and sell certain products does not in itself constitute doing business in Brazil on the part of the foreign organization. The decision of the Tax Court in the first case of this type submitted to it [15] is largely based on the fact that the foreign organization and the Brazilian company were separate and distinct legal entities. In a later and more elaborate decision on the same issue,[16] the Tax Court adopted the distinction suggested to it between the "legal" and the "functional" activity of a corporation, the former being merely a manifestation of its existence as an independent entity, i.e., the capacity to be the subject of rights and obligations; whereas the latter term refers to the actual exercise of an activity, in a permanent manner, in the country of its origin or in a foreign country.[17] The rule of the case is that the foreign corporation, by entering into the license agreement, had done no more in Brazil than exercise its legal capacity to enter into contractual agreements, but that it had not "projected" itself into the country by carrying out a continuous business activity through an establishment of its own located in Brazil.

The principle to be derived from the decisions is that something more than a contractual agreement is required to consider a foreign entity as doing business in Brazil. There must be a permanent, or at least continuous, exercise of the functions for which the entity was organized; there must be a business activity as distinguished from merely contractual arrangements, and this activity must be carried on through a branch, agency, or other establishment existing in the country and subject to the control of the foreign entity. A foreign entity which carries on its activities in Brazil through an independent agent acting in his own name (even though acting on behalf of the foreign entity) or through a local subsidiary with independent corporate existence (even though owned 100% by the foreign entity) is not considered to be doing business in Brazil.

[15] CC, Rev. 1949 No. 85, reversing CC, Rev. 1947 No. 37.

[16] CC, Rev. 1952 No. 349.

[17] This distinction was developed by Miranda Valverde, Sociedades por Ações (2d ed., Rio de Janeiro, 1950) p. 320; Rubens Gomes de Sousa, Estudos de Direito Tributário (São Paulo, 1950) p. 19; Cesarino Junior, Sociedades Anônimas Estrangeiras (São Paulo, 1934) p. 99. The taxpayer's brief in the case cited in footnote 16 was later published: Ruy Barbosa Nogueira, "Atividade Jurídica e Atividade Funcional," 27 Revista de Direito Administrativo 412 (1952), reprinted in 200 Revista dos Tribunais 56 (1952) and in 155 Revista Forense 93 (1954).

11/3.3 Brazilian Branch of Foreign Entity

a. IN GENERAL. The unincorporated branch [18] in Brazil of a foreign firm or corporation is a taxable entity. The principles of taxation applied to it are basically the same as those applied to independent taxpayers in that only income from sources in Brazil is taxable to the branch and only expenses incurred in the country are deductible by it.[19]

The dual nature of an unincorporated branch as an entity doing business in Brazil on the one hand and as an integral part of the foreign firm or corporation on the other, results in subjecting the profits of the branch to a double tax. As an entity doing business in Brazil, the branch must file the usual income tax return and pay the tax imposed by Reg. Art. 44. The branch profits, however, are also subject to the 20% withholding tax under Reg. Art. 97(1)[20] on the ground that the Brazilian branch is an integral part of the foreign entity. The principle is that the profits or losses of the branch are attributed to the head office as soon as they are determined, i.e., as of the balance sheet date, regardless of how they are shown in the books of the branch and whether they are in fact remitted or credited to the head office or made available to it in any other form.[21] This principle, which has been enunciated in countless administrative and judicial decisions,[22] has the support of the highest courts of Brazil [23] and is now firmly embedded in its income tax law.

b. GROSS INCOME. The branch of a foreign organization is always taxed on the basis of actual profits. The option to be taxed on the basis of presumed profits, which under certain conditions is available to independent entities (Reg. Art. 40, see 6/9.1), does not apply (Reg. Art. 33 §1).[24]

While taxable profits for purposes of the withholding tax under Reg. Art. 97 are in general the same as those for purposes of the assessed in-

---

[18] The Income Tax Regulations use the terms *"filiais, sucursais, agências"* interchangeably. All these terms refer to a branch in the proper sense and not to a subsidiary. However, a number of decisions loosely apply the term *"filiais"* where there is clearly a parent-subsidiary relationship.

[19] The provisions regarding the computation of the actual profits are made expressly applicable by Reg. Art. 34 §3. In particular, the books must be kept in the language and currency of Brazil and in the form prescribed by the commercial and fiscal law.

[20] This tax must be paid within thirty days after publication of the annual accounts of the branch (Reg. Art. 102).

[21] DIR, *Rev.* 1943 No. 684; Rezende, Note 283. Regarding the origin of this rule see Sousa, "O Impôsto sobre a Renda das Sociedades Estrangeiras" in *Estudos de Direito Tributário* (São Paulo, 1950), p. 11.

[22] DIR, *Rev.* 1944 No. 420; CC, *Rev.* 1943 No. 551; 1949 No. 759; 1950 No. 39; 1951 No. 116; 1954 No. 102; Min. of Fin., *Rev.* 1944 No. 490-B.

[23] Federal Court of Appeals, *Rev.* 1950 No. 563; Supreme Court, *Rev.* 1947 No. 805; 1950 No. 431; see Sousa in *Revista Fiscal* of July 15, 1951.

[24] The branch is, however, liable to taxation of estimated profits (on the basis of its capital or assets) the same as an independent entity, if it does not keep books or if the books are inadequate. See CC, *Rev.* 1948 No. 805 and 1950 No. 327. The principles of taxation on the basis of estimated profits are discussed in 6/9.2.

come tax under Reg. Art. 44, one important difference is that the income subject to withholding tax cannot be reduced by amounts, such as dividends received, which have already been taxed in the hands of another entity (Reg. Art. 43 §2[c]; see 7/7.1; 9/2.3) or income on bearer securities on which tax has already been withheld at the source (Reg. Art. 43 §2[d]; see 7/7.2). The decisions hold that the origin of the income is immaterial for purposes of the withholding tax under Reg. Art. 97.[24a]

c. DEDUCTIONS.   Only expenses incurred in the national territory of Brazil are deductible. The deductions for amortization and depreciation are by express provision of the law restricted to movable property located in Brazil (Reg. Art. 37 §2).

The most important consequence of the limitation of branch deductions to those incurred in Brazil is that expenses attributable to the foreign head office are not deductible. Administrative and judicial practice has been to take a rather narrow view of the question of the proper allocation of expenses between head office and branch.

It is settled law that charges made by the head office to the branch for a proportionate part of its overhead expenses are not deductible by the branch.[25] Likewise, service charges made to the branch by the head office (or an affiliated firm) have been held nondeductible on the ground that the services were rendered abroad.[26] A deduction for commissions and brokers' fees paid by the branch to the head office was denied on the ground that charges of this kind are unacceptable between divisions of the same legal entity and can only serve the purpose of transferring the profit of the branch to the head office.[27]

If the foreign home office invoices merchandise to the branch, the latter can deduct only the cost which is shown on the original invoice; a later increase of the cost or adjustment of the original cost cannot be taken into account (Reg. Art. 37 §3).

It would seem that the disallowance of a branch deduction will of necessity result in taxation of the amount restored to branch income both under Reg. Art. 44 and Reg. Art. 97(1). However, while this principle has been clearly stated in a number of administrative and judicial decisions, it has not been followed in others.[28]

[24a] CC, *Rev.* 1952 No. 496; 1953 No. 460; DIR, *Rev.* 1955 No. 404.

[25] DIR, *Rev.* 1948 No. 400; CC, *Rev.* 1951 No. 211; 1954 No. 547. The fact that payment of the home office expenses was approved by the Bank of Brazil without proof of payment of the income tax is immaterial (CC, *Rev.* 1949 No. 796); similarly, the Bank of Brazil's opinion that no income tax was payable has been held to be without effect because the Bank is not the proper authority to interpret the income tax laws, CC, *Rev.* 1951 No. 138.

[26] CC, *Rev.* 1949 No. 290.

[27] CC, *Rev.* 1952 No. 664.

[28] Compare DIR, *Rev.* 1951 No. 688. Amounts reimbursed by the branch for printed matter, illustrated services, and photographs furnished by the head office, although recognized as a bona fide expense indispensable for carrying on the business

Regarding the availability of the loss deduction, see 7/4.4.

d. MITIGATION OF DOUBLE TAXATION OF BRANCH PROFITS — EXEMPTION OF
REINVESTED PROFITS FROM THE WITHHOLDING TAX. A certain mitigation
of the double taxation of branch profits is accomplished by the provision
of Art. 97 §2(c) of the Income Tax Regulations, which exempts the part
of the profits of the branch that is reinvested in its industrial equipment
in Brazil from the withholding tax under Reg. Art. 97.[29] A company claiming the benefit of this exemption must secure the approval of the income
tax authorities and submit all the facts necessary for the latter's decision.[30]

"Industrial equipment," for the purposes of this provision, includes only
tangible fixed assets required to increase production, such as machines,
equipment, and other physical installations; it does not include money or
credits.[31] The acquisition of an existing factory is not considered an extension of the industrial equipment of the taxpayer.[32] Likewise, the statutory requirements are not satisfied if the branch credits all its profits to
the home office abroad, which in turn makes a larger amount available
to the branch for the extension of its industrial capacity.[33] The later
withdrawal of the amounts appropriated in connection with the investment and their remittance to the foreign home office will destroy the
exemption.[34] The sale of an asset whose purchase gave rise to the exemption has the same effect, unless the sales price is reinvested in industrial
equipment.

e. BRANCH VERSUS SUBSIDIARY. The following points may be listed as constituting tax advantages of the Brazilian branch of a foreign entity over
a subsidiary organized under Brazilian law.

The special taxes on reserves, namely the 4% addition to the tax in the
nature of an enforced loan on all reserves of a legal entity (see 7/8.2)
and the 30% tax on reserves of corporations in excess of the paid-in capital
(see 7/8.3), do not apply to a branch which, as an integral part of its
main organization, is considered incapable of having reserves of its own.
The freedom of the branch from the 30% tax on excess reserves (essentially a tax on undistributed profits) may well determine the choice be-

of the branch, held not allowable as being incurred abroad and subject to the withholding tax under Reg. Art. 97. Whether the amount disallowed as a deduction is
restored to branch income for purposes of taxation under Reg. Art. 44 is not clear
from the decision, which is criticized on this ground by Rezende, Note 283.

[29] DIR, *Rev.* 1951 No. 996; 1952 No. 97; CC, *Rev.* 1952 No. 346. It has been held
that the privilege extends only to profits actually invested, not those intended to be
used for expansion and credited to a reserve for that purpose, DIR, *Rev.* 1949 No.
428. Regarding the difficulty resulting from the fact that a company is unlikely to
commit itself to large investments before it knows what the profits for the year will
be, see Rezende, Note 285-C.

[30] DIR, *Rev.* 1948 No. 427; 1949 No. 104.

[31] DIR, *Rev.* 1949 Nos. 360 and 467.

[32] DIR, *Rev.* 1950 No. 598.

[33] DIR, *Rev.* 1949 No. 399.   [34] DIR, *Rev.* 1951 Nos. 689 and 1184.

tween branch and subsidiary in a given situation, especially for a new venture organized with limited capital but expected to realize considerable profits in the foreseeable future. If this venture is organized in the form of a subsidiary, its surplus may soon exceed the amount of the paid-in capital stock.

Another result of the theory that a branch is incapable of having reserves of its own is that the operating losses of the branch for the three preceding years can be offset against the profits of the current year without having to be applied first against existing surplus or reserves (see 7/4.4).

The limitations on the deduction of the compensation of corporate officers and the members of the fiscal and administrative committee, etc. (7/5.2) do not apply to branches.

The capital of a branch is in general more flexible and easier to rearrange than that of an independent corporation.

The disadvantages of the branch, as distinguished from a local subsidiary organized under Brazilian law, are apparent from the discussion above. They are, briefly, the double taxation of branch profits and the limitations and restrictions which have to be observed in computing the taxable income of the branch. These limitations do not apply if the operations of the foreign corporation in Brazil are carried out through a local subsidiary organized under Brazilian law.[35] The independent legal existence of a subsidiary corporation formed in Brazil, even if wholly owned by foreign interests, is fully recognized in the decisions.[36] The subsidiary is taxed only on its own income under Reg. Art. 44 and the withholding tax under Reg. Art. 97 applies only to income either formally credited or actually distributed to the foreign parent or affiliate. The deduction of the normal and necessary business expenses which a Brazilian entity pays to its foreign parent company is allowed,[37] while the deduction of these expenses is denied to a branch (11/3.3c).

The advantages and disadvantages of a branch as compared to a local subsidiary can be evaluated only on the basis of the facts of the individual case. This would seem to be especially true regarding the question whether the freedom of the branch from the 30% tax on excess reserves outweighs the disadvantage of the imposition of the 20% withholding tax on all profits of the branch regardless of their distribution to the foreign home office. It is also evident that tax considerations are only one of the factors that will determine the form of business organization which is best suited to the individual situation.

[35] See Sousa, "O Impôsto sobre a Renda das Sociedades Estrangeiras," in *Estudos de Direito Tributário* (São Paulo, 1950), *passim*.

[36] Compare CC, *Rev.* 1949 No. 869.

[37] CC, *Rev.* 1951 No. 184. (Royalties for use of the firm name and manufacturing processes and formulas paid by the Brazilian company under contract with foreign affiliates holding the majority of its shares.)

11/3.4   Income of Nonresidents Subject to Withholding of Tax

All income derived by nonresidents from sources in Brazil is subject to withholding of tax at the source (Reg. Art. 97). The rate of the withholding tax is generally 20% (Reg. Art. 97[1]), except as regards royalties to which a withholding rate of 25% is applied (Reg. Art. 97[2]). If tax at a rate of less than 20% has already been withheld at the source because of the nature of the income (see 9/1.8), the nonresident withholding rate will be applied only as far as is necessary to bring the entire amount of tax withheld up to 20% (Reg. Art. 97 §4). If the resident withholding rate exceeds 20%, as in the case of interest on bearer bonds (21%) or dividends and other distributions on bearer shares (28%), the higher withholding rate applies (see 5/4.3; 9/2.4).

The withholding tax imposed on nonresidents is generally computed on gross income. An exception to this rule prevails regarding income of individuals from real property located in Brazil, which is computed with the deductions available to resident taxpayers under Reg. Art. 16 as listed at 9/4.1b (Reg. Art. 97 §5).

Although the withholding tax imposed on nonresidents is computed on gross income, it is not applied to payments which are in the nature of gross receipts or which constitute a return of capital. Furthermore, it is evidently the intent of the income tax authorities not to impose the withholding tax in cases where payments or credits to nonresidents cannot be clearly separated between income and capital. (See 11/3.5.)

The applicable withholding rate is that which is valid for the year in which the withholding takes place.[38]

Income from the following transactions is subject to withholding of tax at the source.

a. LICENSING OF PATENTS, TRADEMARKS, PROCESSES, ETC. Royalties received by nonresidents from the licensing of patents, trademarks, processes, etc., to a party domiciled in Brazil are subject to withholding of tax at the source at the rate of 25% [39] computed on gross income (Reg. Art. 97 and its §5).

Regarding the distinction between license agreements and sales, see 11/3.5c, below. If the right to use a patent is transferred for the entire period of its life or remaining life, but title to the patent remains in the transferor, it would appear that the transfer is still regarded as in the nature of a license as distinguished from a sale, and that the consideration paid by the transferee constitutes a royalty subject to withholding of tax.

b. SERVICES RENDERED BY A FOREIGN ENTITY TO A BRAZILIAN FIRM. If serv-

[38] CC, *Rev.* 1952 No. 658; 1954 Nos. 182, 217, and 219.
[39] The 15% addition to the tax in the nature of a compulsory loan applies, Reg. Art. 210 §1; 12/2.4a.

ices are rendered by a foreign entity to a Brazilian enterprise, such as the installation of factories or machines, or communication of technical information or "know-how," the foreign entity is not by reason of such activities alone considered to be doing business in Brazil, and it is therefore not subject to taxation by assessment as a resident under Reg. Art. 44. Whether the fees or other remuneration remitted or credited to the foreign company are subject to withholding of tax under Reg. Art. 97 depends on whether the services are rendered in Brazil or abroad; the withholding tax applies only in the first-named situation.[40] If the work is done in Brazil under the direct supervision of the engineers or technicians of the foreign firm, the services are clearly rendered in Brazil,[41] but not if the information is communicated through the mails, or by way of training employees of the Brazilian firm in the foreign country. The form in which the compensation is paid to the foreign firm [42] is immaterial as regards the question of tax liability.

C. PERSONAL SERVICES AS AN EMPLOYEE. The following examples will demonstrate the tax situation of foreign employees:

Example 1
If the employee is paid from abroad and the total period of his residence in Brazilian territory is less than 12 months, he is not subject to any income tax. If he stays for more than 12 months, he is liable to complementary tax (Reg. Art. 8 Sole §) on income from foreign sources (Schedule F). This liability is retroactive to the beginning of the 12-month period.

Example 2
If the remuneration of the employee is paid or credited by a firm domiciled in Brazil and the employee remains in Brazilian territory for less than 12 months, his salary is subject to withholding at the source under Reg. Art. 97 (1). If his stay exceeds 12 months, the employee becomes a resident of Brazil and obliged to file a return in which his salary will be included under Schedule C; in this case, the deductions under Reg. Art. 14 are available to the taxpayer (8/1.3).

11/3.5   Income of Nonresidents from Sales to Brazil

The profit from the sale of tangible or intangible property made by a nonresident not doing business in Brazil to a resident of the country is not subject to income tax for the reason that this type of profit is not considered to be derived from Brazilian sources. Moreover, there are strong administrative reasons in favor of nontaxability because it will hardly be possible for the local authorities to determine the profit ele-

[40] The withholding rate is 20%, Reg. Art. 97(1), and it is computed on gross income, Reg. Art. 97 §5. The 15% addition to the tax in the nature of a compulsory loan applies, Reg. Art. 210 §1; 12/2.4a.

[41] Compare CC, *Rev.* 1947 No. 142; 1954 No. 379; 1955 No. 79.

[42] E.g., in shares of the Brazilian corporation to which the services are rendered, CC, *Rev.* 1954 No. 379.

ment of transactions which are executed by a party not required to keep books and to file income tax returns in Brazil.[43]

While it is settled law that a nonresident is not taxed on the profit from sales made to a Brazilian buyer, the question whether a particular transaction constitutes a sale may present difficulties.

a. EXPORT SALES. The profit on the sale of merchandise exported to Brazil by a seller not doing business in the country through a permanent establishment or permanent agency located there, is not considered to be derived from Brazilian sources and is therefore not subject to income tax.

This rule also applies if a foreign entity sells merchandise through a subsidiary located in Brazil, assuming that the activities of the subsidiary are limited to soliciting orders and forwarding them to the parent company for acceptance and execution, and that the subsidiary does not directly participate in the sale through delivery of the merchandise, collection of the sales price, or in any other manner. The profit on the sale made by the parent company is not taxed in Brazil under the rule just discussed. The sales of the parent are not imputed to the subsidiary; the latter is taxed under Reg. Art. 44 only on its own income, such as commissions paid to it by the parent company for its services.[44]

b. SALES OF CAPITAL ASSETS. The profit on the sale of capital assets, such as securities, is not taxed to the foreign seller for the reason that the profit is not derived from Brazilian sources and because such profits are not taxed to a Brazilian seller unless they are realized in a business (see 7/1.2). Since the concept of taxable income is the same whether applied to residents or nonresidents (see 6/1.3a), nonresidents are not taxed on profits of this kind.[45]

The rule is different as regards sales of real property situated in Brazil. The profit on sales of this type is clearly derived from Brazilian sources and it is taxed to a resident individual under special rules (see 9/8.2). These rules — and not the general withholding provisions of Reg. Art. 97 — apply equally to a nonresident individual seller of Brazilian real property.[46]

[43] See DIR, *Rev.* 1943 No. 469; CC, *Rev.* 1949 No. 675.

[44] CC, *Rev.* 1949 No. 675; see comments to this decision in Rezende, Note 130. In an unusually liberal decision (*Rev.* 1952 No. 1), the Federal Appellate Court approved of an agreement under which a Brazilian corporation retained 30% of the sales price as a commission for its services in selling in Brazil the merchandise of a foreign affiliate and remitted 70% to the latter. It should be borne in mind, in evaluating this decision, however, that its object was mainly to affirm the discretionary right of the government to apportion estimated profits; the ruling in this particular case has not been generally followed. It is criticized by Castro Viana in Rezende, Note 130, as giving undue weight to the agreement of the parties by leaving the determination of the income taxable in Brazil to their discretion.

[45] DIR, *Rev.* 1943 No. 239; *contra*, DIR, *Rev.* 1949 No. 594.

[46] DIR, *Rev.* 1948 No. 140; 1950 No. 613; 1951 No. 1175; CC, *Rev.* 1951 No.

C. SALE OF PATENTS, TRADEMARKS, INVENTIONS, PROCESSES, BRAND NAMES, DESIGNS, AND COPYRIGHTS. While it is immaterial from the income tax viewpoint whether the object of a sale is in the nature of tangible or intangible property, transfers of the types of property discussed here have presented considerable difficulty regarding their proper classification as between a sale and a license agreement.

It is not questioned in Brazilian legal literature [47] that patents are in the nature of intangible personal property and as such may be the object of a sale or assignment.[48] It is further recognized that the essence of a sale is the transfer of all the rights of the seller in the thing sold, and that this complete transfer is entirely different from one limited as to time or use, in which the transferor retains title to the property and divests himself of his right to use the property only for a limited time. Even so, the Income Tax Division takes the position that every transfer of the rights under a patent from a foreign transferor to a domestic transferee is in the nature of a license agreement and that the consideration paid therefor constitutes royalties subject to withholding of tax at the rate of 25% under Reg. Art. 97(2).[49] The situation is not viewed differently if the parties stipulate that the consideration shall be paid in one lump sum irrespective of the extent of the use.

In evaluating this view, it must be borne in mind that the specific enumeration of royalties among the types of income subject to withholding at the source and the imposition of a higher withholding rate on royalty income than that generally applicable to income of nonresidents are of very recent origin [50] and that the new provision was clearly designed to counteract tax evasion practised by some Brazilian affiliates of foreign companies by way of transferring profits abroad tax-free under the guise of deductible royalties.[51] In view of this, it may be assumed

1107. The rationale of the last-cited decision is that the profit on the sale of real property is in the nature of capital rather than income and therefore not subject to the withholding tax of Reg. Art. 97 which applies to *income* of nonresidents.

[47] Gama Cerqueira, 1 *Tratado da Propriedade Industrial* (Rio de Janeiro, 1946) 138 *et seq.*; Clovis Bevilaqua, *Direito das Obrigações* (4th ed., Rio de Janeiro, 1936) 301; Carvalho de Mendonça, 6 *Tratado de Direito Comercial* (4th ed., Rio de Janeiro, 1947) 607.

[48] The difference between the two forms of transfer is immaterial for income tax purposes. The view expressed by Castro Viana (annotation to the decision of the Tax Court in *Rev.* 1953 No. 116) that a transfer of patent rights to one country but not to others is inconsistent with the notion of a sale as a complete transfer of the seller's rights, has not been accepted by the courts and the Administration.

[49] DIR, *Rev.* 1944 No. 97; 1955 No. 667; but see 1948 No. 775

[50] Reg. Art. 97(2) was introduced by Law No. 2,354 of November 29, 1954, Art. 30. The obligation to withhold income tax on royalties paid abroad was recognized in the older rulings and decisions; see DIR, *Rev.* 1950 Nos. 410 and 594; 1952 No. 681; CC, *Rev.* 1949 No. 663; and 1952 Nos. 349 and 658.

[51] Payments credited by a Brazilian subsidiary to its foreign parent for the licensing of an industrial process were held nondeductible in the absence of proof of actual use of the process, Federal Court of Appeals, *Rev.* 1952 No. 11; see also CC, *Rev.* 1950 No. 28.

that the income tax authorities will continue to classify compensation paid abroad for the use of intangible property as royalties.

The Tax Court, on the other hand, construes a permanent and final transfer of the transferor's rights in intangible property as a sale,[52] even if part of the price is paid in installments related to the extent of the use of the property, and consequently holds in favor of nontaxation of the consideration paid.

11/4. Tax Treaties

11/4.1 No Income Tax Conventions

Except for specific treaties with certain foreign countries providing for mutual exemption from income tax of shipping companies and airlines,[53] Brazil is not a party to income tax conventions with foreign countries for the avoidance of double taxation and the exchange of fiscal information.

[52] CC, *Rev.* 1946 Nos. 493 and 694; 1953 No. 116; 1954 No. 306. The first-named decision is criticized by Rezende-Viana, *Consolidação das Leis do Impôsto de Renda* (1955) Note 46-G. But see CC, *Rev.* 1950 No. 208, affirmed upon reconsideration, *Rev.* 1951 No. 187.

[53] Regarding exemption on the basis of reciprocity under Reg. Art. 30, see 5/6.5.

CHAPTER 12

COMPUTATION OF THE TAX

12/1. Individuals

12/1.1   The Schedular Tax Rates
12/1.2   Computation of the Complementary Tax
a. Income Subject to the Tax
b. Family Allowances and Deductions
1. Allowances for dependents
2. Medical and dental expenses
3. Interest on personal debts
4. Life insurance premiums
5. Extraordinary losses
6. Charitable contributions
c. The Rates of the Complementary Tax
12/1.3   Additions to the Tax
a. Additions to the Tax under the Law for the Protection of the Family
b. The Compulsory Loan
12/1.4   Withholding of Income Tax on Wages and Salaries
12/1.5   Individual Tax Computation Illustrated
12/1.6   Translation of Individual Income Tax Return

12/2. Entities

12/2.1   Determination of Income
12/2.2   Entities Exempt from Tax because of Insufficient Income
12/2.3   Regular Income Tax Rates
12/2.4   Additions to the Tax
a. The Compulsory Loan
b. Charge on Reserves

12/2.5   Tax Computation of Entities Illustrated
12/2.6   Preferential Tax Rates for Particular Enterprises
12/2.7   Translation of Income Tax Returns for Juridical
         Persons (Entities)

12/1.   Individuals

12/1.1   The Schedular Tax Rates

The proportional tax rates applying under the various schedules are as follows (Reg. Art. 25):

Schedule A   (Interest from nominative government securities):   3%
Schedule B   (Interest from other sources and certain other
             income from capital):   10%
Schedule C   (Compensation for personal services as an
             employee):   1%
Schedule D   (Compensation for independent personal services): 2%
Schedule E   (Income from real property):   3%
Schedule H   (Income from gainful occupations not includible
             under another schedule):   5%

No schedular tax is computed on income classified under Schedule F (income from distributions by entities, business income of individuals, and foreign income) and Schedule G (agricultural income). These types of income are, therefore, subject to complementary tax only.

No income tax — schedular or complementary — is payable if the net annual income of an individual does not exceed Cr$ 60,000.

Since business entities with gross annual income not exceeding Cr$ 150,-000 are exempt from income tax (Reg. Art. 28[d]; see 5/6.6; 12/2.2), the owner of an individual business is not required to include the net income of the proprietorship in his personal income tax return under Schedule F, unless its gross income reaches the statutory minimum. Any nonbusiness income which the proprietor may have is subject to schedular tax (under the applicable schedule) and complementary tax, provided that the annual net income from these sources exceeds Cr$ 60,000.

The schedular tax does not apply to income which is subject to withholding of tax at the source.

12/1.2   Computation of the Complementary Tax

a. INCOME SUBJECT TO THE TAX.   The complementary tax is a graduated tax and the income subject to it is the sum total of net income under all applicable schedules, less certain family allowances and deductions called abatements. It follows that only income which can be classified under one of the schedules is subject to the complementary tax. There is no tax liability if the net income subject to complementary tax does not exceed Cr$ 60,000; if it does exceed that amount, the first Cr$ 60,000 of net income are not taxed (Reg. Art. 26, as amended by Law No. 2,862, Art. 19).

The complementary tax does not apply to income which is subject to withholding of tax at the source.

b. FAMILY ALLOWANCES AND DEDUCTIONS. The Income Tax Regulations specifically list the family allowances and expenses which the taxpayer may deduct from gross income in order to arrive at net income subject to complementary tax. Allowances and deductions which are not expressly permitted by the law cannot be claimed.[1]

1. *Allowances for dependents.* At present the taxpayer is allowed Cr$ 50,000 for his spouse and Cr$ 25,000 for each minor or invalid child or other descendant,[2] or a daughter who is unmarried, or widowed without support, or deserted by her husband without the possibility of enforcing his support obligation (Reg. Art. 20[e], as amended by Law No. 2,862, Art. 22). The following rules apply:

1. During the existence of the marital relationship — regardless of whether the spouses file a joint return or separate returns [3] — the husband (as the head of the household) is entitled to claim the exemption in regard to the first Cr$ 60,000 of taxable income (see 12/1.2a) and the allowances for his wife and children. If the spouses file separate returns,[4] the first Cr$ 60,000 of the wife's income are subject to complementary tax at the minimum rate of 3% (Reg. Art. 20 [e][I]).
2. In case of divorce or annulment of the marriage, each spouse is entitled to the exemption in regard to the first Cr$ 60,000 of his or her taxable income and to the allowances for the children whom he actually supports (Reg. Art. 20 [e][II]).

Dependent children include legitimate and adoptive as well as legitimated and recognized children whose income is included in the return of the taxpayer or who have no income of their own (Reg. Art. 20 §2). Children between 21 and 24 years of age who attend school and who have

---

[1] E.g., individuals as distinguished from entities (see 7/2.7) may not deduct income tax paid by them, or losses from the sale of real property (CC, *Rev.* 1951 No. 875).

[2] Provided that the descendant is not supported by his parents.

[3] The filing of a joint return is mandatory if the spouses live under the community property system, Reg. Art. 67; even under this system, however, the wife may file a separate return with respect to her income from personal work and certain other income, Reg. Art. 67 §2. See 13/1.1c.

[4] The filing of separate returns is optional if the spouses have adopted the system of separation of property, Reg. Art. 67 §1, and in the cases referred to in the preceding footnote. See 13/1.1c.

no income of their own are treated like minors for the purpose of the allowance (Reg. Art. 20 §3).

The taxpayer is further entitled to an allowance for supporting his parents, other relatives in the ascending line, or brothers or sisters, provided that a support obligation exists under the provisions of the civil law (Civil Code of Brazil, Arts. 396–405), and that the beneficiary is incapable of self-support. The taxpayer must prove the payment of the amounts claimed as an allowance. The allowance is limited to Cr$ 10,000 for each beneficiary, or to such amount as may be determined by judicial sentence (Reg. Art. 20[g] and its §4).

Finally, the taxpayer may claim an allowance of Cr$ 6,000 for each destitute child he is raising and educating, if he does not meet the legal qualifications for adopting the child under the provisions of Arts. 368 and 369 of the Civil Code (Reg. Art. 20[h]).

2. *Medical and dental expenses.* Medical and dental expenses incurred by the taxpayer either for himself or for his dependents listed under (1), above, constitute an allowance for purposes of the complementary tax. The payments made to physicians and dentists must be specified in the taxpayer's return as to their amount and the name and address of the payee, and they must be proved to the satisfaction of the assessing authority (Reg. Art. 20[f]).

The allowance for medical expenses includes hospitalization expenses incurred by the taxpayer for himself, his spouse, minor children, and unmarried daughters (Reg. Art. 20[i]).

The Income Tax Regulations do not impose a limitation on the amount of the allowance.

3. *Interest on personal debts.* Interest on personal debts of the taxpayer is deductible for purposes of the complementary tax (Reg. Art. 20[a]). The taxpayer must prove actual payment of the interest; crediting it is generally not sufficient. An exception applies under Reg. Art. 20 §1 in respect of interest on current accounts maintained between the taxpayer and a legal entity, e.g., a bank.[5] In this case, interest charged to the taxpayer is deemed to be actually paid by him as of the date of the charge, if the taxpayer's account shows a credit balance, or as of the date of the deposit made by the taxpayer to cover a debit balance in the account.

The interest deduction does not extend to the amortization of borrowed capital.[6]

To obtain the deduction for interest paid, the taxpayer must give the names and addresses of the parties to whom it was paid on the informa-

[5] See CC, *Rev.* 1955 No. 48.

[6] Sousa, §17; CC, *Rev.* 1951 Nos. 965, 1017, 1331; 1952 Nos. 138 and 352; 1954 No. 340. Rezende, Note 92. Note that interest received is includible in Schedule B and interest paid is deductible only for purposes of the complementary tax — never under Schedule B (CC, *Rev.* 1949 No. 628; *Rev.* 1950 No. 688; 1954 No. 168).

tion sheet he attaches to his annual income tax return (Reg. Art. 20[a]).

4. Life insurance premiums. Reg. Art. 20(b) allows a deduction for premiums on life insurance [7] paid during the base year if the insurer is a Brazilian company or a foreign company authorized to operate in Brazil.[8]

The amount of life insurance premiums which is deductible in any taxable year is limited to the lower of Cr$ 100,000 or 1/6th of gross schedular income declared. No deduction whatever is permitted on a single-premium endowment policy (Reg. Art. 20[b]).[9]

5. Extraordinary losses. Reg. Art. 20(c) allows the deduction of extraordinary losses resulting exclusively from fortuitous circumstances or an act of God and not compensated for by insurance or payment of damages. As interpreted in practice, an extraordinary loss presupposes the destruction of, or damage to, the income-producing asset itself and not merely the loss of income.[10]

6. Charitable contributions. Contributions and donations made by the taxpayer to philanthropic institutions which have legal status in Brazil are deductible, provided that the donee's receipt is filed with the taxpayer's return (Reg. Art. 20[d]). The deduction for contributions made in kind is measured by the value of the property at the time it was given.[11]

C. THE RATES OF THE COMPLEMENTARY TAX. The rates of the complementary tax are reproduced in the table below (Reg. Art. 26 as modified by Law No. 2,862 of September 4, 1956, Art. 19). The various tax rates apply to the portions of income within each bracket, so that the effective tax on a given amount of income is less than the rate applicable to the top income bracket would indicate. Fractions of income of less than Cr$ 1,000 are disregarded (Law No. 2,862 Art. 19 §1). As an example, the complementary tax on income of Cr$ 350,950 is the same as that on Cr$ 350,000.

[7] Premiums on other personal insurance, e.g., accident insurance, are not deductible. See CC, *Rev.* 1954 No. 131.

[8] Brazilian law does not allow residents to contract for life insurance abroad unless it is proved that a Brazilian company or a foreign insurance company operating in Brazil will not accept the risk. Sousa, §18.

[9] The abuse at which this provision is directed consisted in the practice of taking out an endowment policy for a large amount immediately before the end of the year, paying the premiums in a lump sum (thereby making them deductible in the following fiscal year), then immediately after January 1 canceling the policy and securing a refund of the premium less a purely nominal discount. The refund of the premium is not taxable income under Reg. Art. 11 §2(c). See Sousa, §18; Rezende, Note 93. As pointed out by Sousa, *loc. cit.*, the present rule is only a very incomplete remedy for the situation; except for single-premium endowment policies, the prohibited objective can still be attained within the present limits for the deduction (1/6th of gross schedular income, or Cr$ 100,000).

[10] Sousa, §19. Regarding the time of deduction, see Rezende, Notes 94 and 95. Losses from theft are not deductible under this heading, CC, *Rev.* 1952 No. 363; 1954 No. 208.

[11] CC, *Rev.* 1949 No. 490 and 1951 No. 906.

Complementary Tax — Statutory Rates

NET INCOME						RATE
Up to	Cr$	60,000				Exempt
Between		61,000	and	Cr$	90,000	3%
"		91,000	"		120,000	5%
"		121,000	"		150,000	8%
"		151,000	"		200,000	11%
"		201,000	"		300,000	14%
"		301,000	"		400,000	18%
"		401,000	"		500,000	22%
"		501,000	"		600,000	26%
"		601,000	"		700,000	30%
"		701,000	"		1,000,000	35%
"		1,001,000	"		2,000,000	40%
"		2,001,000	"		3,000,000	45%
In excess of		3,000,000				50%

Note: This table is reproduced from the text of the law. However, the rates are effective on the entire amount of income between the top of one bracket and the top of the next. Fractions of income under Cr$ 1,000 are disregarded only in determining the total subject to the complementary tax.

12/1.3   Additions to the Tax

The total individual income tax is composed or the sum of the applicable schedular taxes and the complementary tax. This total tax is increased by certain additions.

a. ADDITIONS TO THE TAX UNDER THE LAW FOR THE PROTECTION OF THE FAMILY. Decree-law No. 3200 of April 19, 1941 (called the "Law for the Protection of the Family"), imposes the following percentage increases to the total tax of certain individuals as computed above.

1. 15% for taxpayers over 25 years of age [12] who are either unmarried or widowed without children (Decree-law 3200, Art. 32).
2. 10% for married taxpayers over 25 years of age [13] without children (Decree-law 3200, Art. 32).
3. 5% for taxpayers over 45 years of age [14] with one child only (Decree-law 3200, Art. 33).

The additional tax must be computed on the income tax return of the taxpayer. It is paid together with the income tax if this is paid in one amount, or with the first installment thereof (Decree-law 3200, Art. 34). For the purpose of computing the additions, the age of the taxpayer must be indicated on the income tax return (Decree-law 3200, Art. 35).

[12] The effective date for determining the age is April 30 of the year in which the return is due, not the base year (DIR, *Rev.* 1942 No. 81a; 1951 No. 674). See Rezende, Note 102.
[13] *Ibid.*
[14] *Ibid.*

The administrative provisions in regard to the income tax apply to the additional tax (Decree-law 3200, Art. 36).

b. THE COMPULSORY LOAN. Another addition to the tax, in the nature of a compulsory refundable loan, applies to individuals whose total income tax (including the addition to the tax described under 12/1.3a above) exceeds Cr$ 20,000.[15] The rates of this addition are graduated as follows: [16]

Amount of income tax	Addition
More than Cr$ 20,000 but not more than Cr$ 250,000	15%
More than Cr$ 250,000 but not more than Cr$ 1,000,000	20%
More than Cr$ 1,000,000	25%

The collections made constitute a special fund, which is shown separately in the federal budget; they are to be used for a program of rehabilitation of ports and railroads, increases in the capacity of warehouses, cold storage and slaughterhouse facilities, the generation of electric energy, and the development of basic industries and agriculture.

This additional charge is not a tax,[17] but an enforced subscription to the Brazilian Economic Development Program and in the nature of a compulsory loan. The payments made are refunded to the taxpayer after five years in the form of federal bonds together with a premium of 25% (representing interest at 5% per annum for the time the loan is outstanding) also in federal bonds. The bonds will bear interest at 5% per annum and will mature in 20 equal yearly installments of 5% each, beginning with the year following the one in which they are issued.

12/1.4 Withholding of Income Tax on Wages and Salaries

The withholding table which was in effect for taxable years 1955 and 1956 will be replaced by a new table effective January 1, 1957 (Law No. 2,862 Art. 20 §2).

12/1.5 Individual Tax Computation Illustrated

Example 1

Tax computation in the case of an individual. A is 46 years old, married, has one minor child, and his only income is from salaries, which for the first

---

[15] This charge was introduced by Law No. 1,474 of November 26, 1951, and further regulated by Decree No. 30,812 of May 2, 1952, and Law No. 1,628 of June 20, 1952. Its validity was, under these enactments, limited to the five taxable years from 1952 through 1956 (base years 1951 through 1955). The effective period of the compulsory loan was extended until taxable year 1966 (base year 1965) by Law No. 2,973 of November 26, 1956. The changes in the rates and other modifications effected by Law No. 2,973 are reflected in the text.

[16] Law No. 2,973, Art. 1 and its §1.

[17] Federal Court of Appeals in *Rev.* 1954 No. 144; see Sousa, *Compêndio* (1st ed., 1952) §114.

half of the year 1957 amount to Cr$ 10,000 per month, and for the second half of the year to Cr$ 18,000 per month.

The income tax on the monthly compensation from January to June 1957, inclusive, is withheld by the employer by applying the withholding table effective from January 1, 1957 on.

A is liable to file an income tax return for 1957 because his income from salaries exceeded Cr$ 10,000 during certain months of the year (see 13/1.1 b2). He must include his total annual income in this return (including the part already subjected to taxation at the source); however, the tax so withheld is credited against the total tax computed on the return.

The income tax return of A for the year 1957 may show the following:

Computation of schedular tax:

Gross Schedule C income:		Cr$ 168,000
Less schedular deductions:		
(Traveling expenses, contributions to employees' benefit funds, etc.)		7,500
Net schedular income		160,500
Schedular tax (1%)		Cr$ 1,605

Computation of complementary tax:

Gross income for purpose of the complementary tax		Cr$ 160,500
Less: Allowances and deductions:		
(1) Family allowance (wife and 1 child)	75,000	
(2) Interest on personal debt (Cr$ 50,000 mortgage on home, interest 12%)	6,000	
(3) Life insurance premiums	7,500	
(4) Charitable contributions	1,000	
Total allowances and deductions		89,500
Amount subject to complementary tax		71,000
Complementary tax:		
On first Cr$ 60,000	None	
" Cr$ 11,000 @ 3%	330	
Complementary tax		330
Schedular and complementary tax		1,935
Add: 5% addition under the "Law for the Protection of the Family"	96.75	
Compulsory loan	None	
Total additions to the tax		96.75
Total tax and additions thereto		Cr$ 2,031.75

The amount of income tax withheld at the source is credited against the total tax indicated above, and the balance of tax is paid with the return.

(1)

(Carimbo de data da Repartição recebedora)		DECLARAÇÃO DE RENDIMENTOS

ESTADOS UNIDOS DO BRASIL
MINISTÉRIO DA FAZENDA
DIVISÃO DO IMPÔSTO DE RENDA

Para uso da Repartição

DECLARAÇÃO DE RENDIMENTOS
N.º ....

PESSOA FÍSICA
Exercício de 19.......
Rendimentos no ano de 19.......

NOME ....
(escrever com clareza)

ENDERÊÇO ....
(para a correspondência oficial)

RESIDÊNCIA .... PRÉDIO PRÓPRIO? ....
(se alugado, informar aluguéis pagos: preencher mods 17 e 18)

LOCALIDADE .... MUNICÍPIO .... ESTADO ....

Profissão ....

Nacionalidade .... Idade ....
(dia, mês e ano)

Estado civil .... Regime do casamento ....

Nome do cônjuge ....

Esta declaração abrange os rendimentos do casal? ....

Apresentou declaração para o exercício anterior? ....

Em que Repartição? ....

Sustenta filhos, menores ou inválidos, e filhas solteiras (mesmo maiores), ou filhas viúvas, sem economia própria? ....
Quantos? .... (*)

FILHOS (legítimos, legitimados, naturais reconhecidos e os adotados legalmente: solteiros ou casados, vivos e falecidos) (**)

NOME	NASCIMENTO			ESTADO CIVIL	AUFERIU RENDIMENTOS NO ANO ANTERIOR?
	DATA (Dia, Mês e Ano)	LOCAL DO REGISTRO	SEXO		

(*) Devem ser incluídos nesta declaração quaisquer rendimentos auferidos por êsses filhos.
(**) Inclusão para efeito do Decreto-lei n.º 3.200, de 19 de abril de 1941, que dispõe sôbre a organização e proteção da família.

Declaração de Rendimentos (Pessoa Física), mod. DMF — 5.012

Income Tax Return for Individuals

12/1.6 Translation of Individual Income Tax Return
The following is a translation of the individual income tax return.

(To be stamped with date by receiving office)		

<table>
<tr><td>(To be stamped with date by receiving office)

..

For use of local office</td><td>UNITED STATES OF BRAZIL
MINISTRY OF FINANCE
DIVISION OF INCOME TAX</td><td>DECLARATION OF INCOME
No.........................

INDIVIDUAL
Taxable year 19....
Income for the year 19..</td></tr>
</table>

NAME ....
(write clearly)

ADDRESS ....
(for official correspondence)

RESIDENCE ....OWN PROPERTY?...............
(If rented, indicate rent paid, filling out forms 17 and 18.)

LOCALITY .... CITY OR TOWN .... STATE ....

Occupation ....

Nationality .... Age ....

Married or single .... Separate or community property ....

Name of husband or wife ....

Does this return include income of both husband and wife? ....

Did you file a return for the previous taxable year? ....

In which collector's office? ....

Are you supporting minor or invalid children, unmarried daughters (even if of age), or widowed daughters, who have no income of their own? ....

How many? .... (*)

CHILDREN (legitimate, legitimated, recognized natural children, and legally adopted children: unmarried or married, living or dead)   (**)

NAME	BIRTH			MARITAL STATUS	ANY INCOME LAST YEAR?
	DATE (day, month, year)	PLACE OF REGISTRY	SEX		

(*) Any income received by such children must be included in this return.
(**) Required because of Law No. 3,200 of April 19, 1941 (Law for the Protection of the Family).

Declaration of Income (Individual), form DMF — 5.012

NOTICE: Before filling out this return, preferably by typewriter, please read the appended "Instructions" carefully. In giving information on income which you paid last year, inform the persons concerned that you have given this information to the Division of Income Tax, whether these sums were actually paid or credited to them. In this way you will help such persons avoid being penalized for failing to file a return or for omitting part of their income. In case of doubt, direct your inquiries to your regional office, where the necessary explanations will be given you.

(Second page)
SCHEDULE A

Income from capital invested in nominative securities of federal, state, or local governments, whatever the date of issue, except for those exempted by law from federal taxation.

> GROSS INCOME (specify sources and respective amounts on page 6) Cr$ ....
>   DEDUCTIONS:
> Commissions and brokerage fees (indicate amonts paid: fill in forms
>   17 and 18) .... Cr$ ....
> NET INCOME (*) .... Cr$ ....
> TAX — 3% of net income (*) .... Cr$ ....

SCHEDULE B

Income from capital investments and securities (interest in general, except that derived from government securities)

> GROSS INCOME (specify sources and respective amounts
>   on page 6) .... Cr$ ....
>   DEDUCTIONS:
> Commissions and brokerage fees (indicate amounts paid:
>   fill in forms 17 and 18)..................................... Cr$ ....
> NET INCOME (*) .... Cr$ ....
> TAX — 10% of net income (*) .... Cr$ ....

SCHEDULE C

Compensation for services as an employee, official, or functionary

> GROSS INCOME (**) .... Cr$ ....
>   DEDUCTIONS:
>   1 *Travel and maintenance expenses:*
>   a) Personal expenses for fares, transportation, food,
>   and lodging .... Cr$ ......
>   b) Freight and cartage of goods needed for pur-
>   poses of the trip .... Cr$ ......
>   c) Rent of space for exhibiting goods (indicate
>   amounts paid and fill in forms 17 and 18) ...... Cr$ ......
>   2 Shipping costs and correspondence .... Cr$ ......
>   3 *If indispensable to the carrying on of a skilled or tech-*
>   *nical occupation:*
>   a) Dues to scientific organizations .... Cr$ ......
>   b) Purchase of or subscription to technical books,
>   journals or reviews .... Cr$ ......
>   c) Purchase or rental of materials, instruments
>   and tools .... Cr$ ......
>   4 Contributions to mutual benefit funds, social insurance
>   funds, and organizations .... Cr$ ......
>   5 Per diems and expense reimbursements
>   a) Paid through public funds and private entities .. Cr$ ......
>   6 Syndicate tax .... Cr$ ......
>   7 Tax on industries and professions .... Cr$ ...... Cr$ ....
> NET EARNINGS (*) .... Cr$ ....
> TAX — 1% of net earnings (*) .... Cr$ ....

SCHEDULE D

Income from work not covered in Schedule C, derived from professions and noncommercial occupations and services.

> GROSS INCOME (specify sources and respective amounts on page 6) .. Cr$ ....
>   DEDUCTIONS:
>   1 *Travel and maintenance expenses:*
>   a) Personal expenses for fares, transportation,
>   food and lodging ....Cr$ ......
>   b) Freight and cartage of goods needed for pur-
>   poses of the trip .... Cr$ ......
>   c) Rent of space for exhibitions (indicate amounts
>   paid and fill in forms 17 and 18) .... Cr$ ......
>   2 Shipping costs, correspondence, and advertising .... Cr$ ......
>   3 *When indispensable for the practice of a profession:*
>   a) Dues to scientific organizations .... Cr$ ......
>   b) Purchase of and subscription to technical books,
>   journals, and reviews .... Cr$ ......
>   c) Purchase or rental of materials, instruments, and
>   tools .... Cr$ ......
>   d) Rental or operating costs of vehicles used by
>   physicians or their assistants .... Cr$ ......
>   4 Rental of real property, devoted to the exercise of the
>   income-producing activity. If this professional activity
>   is carried on in your own home, you may deduct only
>   one fifth of the rent (indicate amounts paid: fill in
>   forms 17 and 18)..................................... Cr$ ......

SCHEDULE D continued

SCHEDULE D continued

5 Water, light, power and telephone costs devoted to the exercise of the activity producing income .... Cr$ ......
6 Premiums on insurance for fire and other risks on property devoted to the practice of the activity producing income .... Cr$ ......
7 Salaries, wages, fees, and other payments made for services rendered if necessary to your profession (indicate amounts paid: fill in forms 17 and 18) .... Cr$ ......
8 Syndicate tax .... Cr$ ......
9 Tax on industries and professions .... Cr$ ......
10 Contributions made as employer to social welfare funds .... Cr$ ......
11 Taxes, fees, and legal costs, but only when collected together with fees due you .... Cr$ ......
12 Reasonable rates of depreciation on capital goods, based on purchase price of goods and length of use Cr$ ......
13 Profit participations distributed to third parties (indicate amounts paid: fill in forms 17 and 18) .... Cr$ ...... Cr$ ....

NET INCOME (*) .... Cr$ ....
TAX — 2% of net earnings (*) .... Cr$ ....

(*) To be carried over to page 5.
(**) Specify, on page 6, the sources and respective amounts of earnings indicated under Schedule C, including the amounts received as per diems, expense reimbursements, and representation allowances.

(Third page)
SCHEDULE E

Income from real property, such as that derived from the rental, quitrental, and leasing of real properties, including natural or artificial grazing lands and pastures (if, however, the real property is rented together with movable installations and equipment, the rentals of the real property will be classified under Schedule H, together with that of the movable property).

GROSS INCOME (specify sources and respective amounts on page 6) ...... Cr$ ....
  DEDUCTIONS:
1 *When expenses are paid by owner:*
  a) Federal, state, or municipal taxes, fees and other charges levied on the property or on its use, but not including fines and additional charges for late payment .... Cr$ ....
  b) Maintenance costs, in the case of buildings (up to 10% of declared income) .... Cr$ ....
  c) Commissions for collection of income (up to 5% of declared income). (Indicate amounts paid: fill in forms 17 and 18) .... Cr$ ....
  d) Premiums on fire insurance (indicate number of policy and name of company) .... Cr$ ....
  e) Payment of quitrent in the case of emphyteusis . Cr$ ....
In addition to the deductions listed above, the following will also be permitted:
2 *In the case of joint owners of apartment buildings:*
  a) Share of expenditures for light and electric power .... Cr. ....
  b) Share of wages paid to caretaker and elevator operator .... Cr$ ....
3 *In the case of owners of apartment buildings:*
  a) Expenditures for air conditioning, heat, and cooling of water .... Cr$ ....
  b) Expenditures for light and electric power ...... Cr$ ....
  c) Wages paid to caretaker and elevator operator (indicate amounts paid: fill in forms 17 and 18) .... Cr$ .... Cr$ ....
4 *In the case of buildings constructed in private communities or on private streets:*
  The deductions are those which may apply in the above enumeration.
NET INCOME (*) .... Cr$ ....
TAX — 3% of net income (*) .... Cr$ ....

SCHEDULE F

Income subject to proportional taxation in the hands of legal entities and from any source outside the country.

Specify on page 6 the sources and respective amounts of income here declared.
Actual profit .... Cr$ ....
Presumed or estimated profit .... Cr$ ....
Withdrawals:
  Not charged to general expense or subsidiary accounts .... Cr$ ....
  Not corresponding to services rendered .... Cr$ ....
  Exceeding the limits fixed by law .... Cr$ ....
Bonuses exceeding the limits fixed by law .... Cr$ ....
Dividends on nominative shares and any additional distributions thereon ... Cr$ ....
Value of new shares distributed to holders of nominative shares or distributions other than profits or dividends in the case of:
SCHEDULE F continued

SCHEDULE F continued

Utilization of any funds, including those of amortization, deprecia-
tion, and revaluation of assets .... Cr$ ....
Increase of capital, with funds drawn from any source .... Cr$ ....
Revaluation of assets or sale of a part of assets, without reduction of
capital .... Cr$ ....
Redemption value of founders' shares and other similar participations, as well
as interest and any other earnings on such shares, if nominative .... Cr$ ....
Gains realized by stockholders and members of firms or corporations
through revaluation of assets, in the case of incorporation or the organi-
zation of a new firm .... Cr$ ....
Income produced in other countries, of whatever nature .... Cr$ ....
NET INCOME (*) .... Cr$ ....

(*) To be carried over to page 5.

(Fourth page)
SCHEDULE G

Income from agriculture and stock-raising and from industries processing animal and vegetable products, including the breeding, raising, and fattening of animals of any kind.

FORM A

VALUE OF PROPERTY, consisting of cultivated lands, pasture
lands, constructions, improvements, machinery, agricultural
machinery, perennial crops, work animals and those held
for the production of income (*) .... Cr$ ....
Presumed net profits — 5% of above value (**) .... Cr$ ....

FORM B

ACTUAL NET INCOME; based on books of account, as shown by
appended documents (**) .... Cr$ ....

REQUIRED DATA

I   Designation and location of property ....
....
II Date of purchase (day, month, and year) ....
    Price .... Recording office ....
    Name and address of seller ....
III Date of sale (day, month, and year) ....
    Price .... Recording office ....
    Name and address of purchaser ....

SCHEDULE H

Income from all lucrative occupations not included in other schedules, including that from partnerships on participation account; from leasing or subleasing movable property; from sub-leasing real property; from the leasing of immovable together with movable property; and from the exploitation of industrial or commercial trademarks other than through their direct use. Commercial or industrial profits realized by those who are not regularly engaged in commerce or industry, and net profits from the assignment of any right must also be included in this schedule.

GROSS INCOME (specify sources and respective amounts on p. 6) .... Cr$ ....
DEDUCTIONS:
1 *Travel and maintenance expenses:*
   a) Personal expenses for fares, transportation, food,
      and lodging .... Cr$ ......
   b) Freight and cartage of goods needed for purposes
      of the trip .... Cr$ ......
   c) Rental of space for exhibiting goods (indicate
      amounts paid: fill in forms 17 and 18) .... Cr$ ......
2 Shipping costs, correspondence and advertising ...... Cr$ ......
3 Rental of real property (indicate amounts paid: fill in
   forms 17 and 18) .... Cr$ ......
4 Water, light, power, and telephone .... Cr$ ......
5 Premiums for insurance against fire and other property risks .... Cr$ ......
6 Salaries, wages, bonuses and other remunerations for
   services rendered (indicate amounts paid: fill in
   forms 17 and 18) .... Cr$ ......
7 Reasonable allowance for depreciation of capital
   equipment, based on their purchase price and length
   of use .... Cr$ ......
8 Shares of earnings distributed to third parties (indicate amounts paid: fill in forms 17 and 18) .... Cr$ ......
9 Tax on industry and professions .... Cr$ ......
10 Syndicate tax .... Cr$ ......
11 Employer's contributions to social security institutes .... Cr$ ......
12 *In the case of owners of real property rented together
   with movable property* (only if expenses are paid by
   owner
   a) Federal, state, and municipal taxes, fees, and
      other charges levied on the property or its use,
SCHEDULE H continued

SCHEDULE H continued

but not including fines and additional charges
for late payment .... Cr$ ......
b) Maintenance costs, in the case of buildings (up
to 10% of declared rental) .... Cr$ ......
c) Commissions for collection of rent (up to 5% of
declared rental) indicate amounts: fill in forms
17 and 18 .... Cr$ ......
d) Premiums on fire insurance (indicate number of
policy and name of company) .... Cr$ ......
e) Payment of quitrent, in the case of emphy-
theusis .... Cr$ ......
13 In the case of joint owners of apartment buildings:
a) Share of expenditures for light and electric
power .... Cr$ ......
b) Share of wages paid to caretaker and elevator
operator (indicate amounts paid: fill in forms
17 and 18) .... Cr$ ......
14 In the case of owners of apartment buildings:
a) Expenditures for air conditioning, heat, and
cooling of water .... Cr$ ......
b) Expenditures for light and electric power ...... Cr$ ......
c) Wages paid to caretaker and elevator operator
(indicate amounts paid: fill in forms 17 and
18) .... Cr$ ......   Cr$ ....
15 In the case of buildings constructed in private com-
munities or on private streets:
The deductions are the same as those under
numbers 12, 13 and 14, as far as applicable.
16 In the case of subletting:
The deductions are those specified above, as far
as applicable, if borne by the sublessor.

NET INCOME (**) .... Cr$ ....
TAX — 5% of net income (**) .... Cr$ ....

(*) If the value of the constructions, improvements, machinery, etc., is not known exactly, it is
estimated at 10% of the value of the land, as registered with the state recording offices.
(**) To be carried over to page 5.

(Fifth page)
SUMMARY OF SCHEDULES

SCHEDULE A	— NET INCOME		Cr$	Tax	3%	Cr$ ....
" B —	" "	.... Cr$		"	10%	Cr$ ....
" C —	" "	.... Cr$		"	1%	Cr$ ....
" D —	" "	.... Cr$		"	2%	Cr$ ....
" E —	" "	.... Cr$		"	3%	Cr$ ....
" F —	" "	.... Cr$		"		
" G —	" "	.... Cr$		"		
" H —	" "	.... Cr$		"	5%	Cr$ ....
					Schedular	
GROSS INCOME	.... Cr$			Tax	...... Cr$ ....

CALCULATION OF COMPLEMENTARY TAX

GROSS INCOME (SUM OF NET INCOME UNDER SCHEDULES) .... Cr$ ....

ABATEMENTS:
1 Interest on personal debts, except those on loans made
for the maintenance or development of agricultural
lands. Identify source of indebtedness (indicate
amounts paid: fill in forms 17 and 18) .... Cr$ ......
2 Premiums on life insurance paid to resident companies or to those authorized to operate in this country;
the name of the company and number of the policy
must be indicated for the deduction to be allowed .... Cr$ ......
3 Extraordinary losses, if due exclusively to fortuitous
events or acts of God, such as fire, storms, shipwreck,
or any accident of the same nature, provided that the
losses were not covered by insurance or otherwise in-
demnified (include evidence) .... Cr$ ......
4 Contributions and donations to philanthropic institutions legally established in the country, provided that
documentary proof provided by the institution concerned is included with this return .... Cr$ ......
5 Family allowances:
a) Spouse and children .... Cr$ ......
b) Payments of alimony, in the case of legal separation (include evidence) .... Cr$ ......
6 Support of other persons
a) Contribution to the support of any person as a result of a court order (include evidence) .... Cr$ ......
b) Support given to parents or disabled brothers or
sisters (include evidence) .... Cr$ ......
7 Raising and education of a poor child whom the taxpayer is not legally able to adopt (include evidence) .. Cr$ ......

CALCULATION OF COMPLEMENTARY TAX continued

8 Payments made by taxpayer to physicians and dentists
on behalf of family dependents or for himself, provided
that such payments be specified and documented, indicating the name and address of the recipients (indicate
amounts paid: fill in forms 17 and 18) .... Cr$ ...... Cr$ ....

NET INCOME .... Cr$ ....

COMPLEMENTARY TAX .... Cr$ ....

AMOUNT TO BE PAID

INCOME TAX:
    Schedular (SUM OF SCHEDULAR TAXES) .... Cr$ ......
    Complementary tax .... Cr$ ......
LESS — Discount of   % for prepayment of tax (*) .... Cr$ ....
DIFFERENCE .... Cr$ ....
DECREE-LAW NO. 3,200 of April 19, 1941 (Law for the Protec-
tion of the Family):
    In the case of taxpayer:
    a) Unmarried or widowed over 25, without child:
        Addition of 15% of income tax .... Cr$ ....
    b) Married, over 25, without child:
        Addition of 10% of income tax .... Cr$ ....
    c) Over 45, with only one child:
        Addition of 5% of income tax .... Cr$ ....
TOTAL .... Cr$ ....
FINES FOR DELAYED PAYMENT:
    Income tax — fine of 10% .... Cr$ ......
    Decree-law No. 3,200 — fine of 10% .... Cr$ ...... Cr$ ....
TOTAL TO BE PAID .... Cr$ ....

FOR USE OF COLLECTOR'S OFFICE

Payment of tax shown in above
square must be completed
by ..../....../19......

Table of installments and dates due
1st installment ....Cr$ ....
Decree-law No. 3,200 .... Cr$ ....

Payment in Cash
Receipt No ....
Date ..../.....19.....

2nd installment ....Cr$ ..../...../19....
3rd installment ....Cr$ ..../...../19....
4th installment ....Cr$ ..../...../19....

Signature of Clerk

* See appended "Instructions".

(Sixth page)

DETAILS OF INCOME (*)

SCHEDULES: A, B, C, D, E, F, and H

Schedule	Kind of Income	Name and address of source (*)	Amount	Remarks

SCHEDULES E and H

Schedule	Location of each property and name of tenant (**)	Annual rent	Taxes and fees

Date ....

Signature of taxpayer or his attorney

If signed by attorney:
Power of attorney registered in recording office at .... Date ..../..../19....
Volume .... Page ....
REMARKS:

(*) If this space should not be sufficient, continue on a separate page.
(**) In the case of joint ownership, indicate this fact.

12/2. Entities

12/2.1 Determination of Income

The business income of entities, which is computed as described in Chapter 7, is subject to the uniform tax rates of Reg. Art. 44, regardless of its source and composition.

12/2.2 Entities Exempt from Tax because of Insufficient Income

Entities with *gross annual income* of Cr$ 150,000 or less are entirely exempt from income tax. The exemption does not depend on observing the formalities required for an exemption claimed on the basis of the nature of the taxpayer's operations, as described in (5/6.) (Reg. Art. 28[d]). Exemption from the tax does not imply exemption from other fiscal obligations, such as informing the tax authorities about payments made to others (Reg. Art. 108 *et seq.*, discussed in 13/3.1).

12/2.3 Regular Income Tax Rates

The tax rates on entities with *gross annual income* in excess of Cr$ 150,-000 are 15% on the first Cr$ 500,000 of taxable income, and 20% on the excess over Cr$ 500,000 (Reg. Art. 44).[18]

12/2.4 Additions to the Tax

a. THE COMPULSORY LOAN. The addition to the tax in the nature of a compulsory loan (12/1.3b) applies to legal entities. The rate of the charge is a flat 15% regardless of the amount of the income tax on which it is computed.[19] This additional charge is not a deductible expense and it must be carried on the taxpayer's books as an asset.

b. CHARGE ON RESERVES. For the special charges on reserves, see 7/8.

12/2.5 Tax Computation of Entities Illustrated

Example 2

Income tax computation for a corporation, a partnership, and a branch. The following example presents the tax computation for: 1. a corporation organized in Brazil; 2. a resident partnership; and 3. the Brazilian branch of a foreign corporation (X Corporation in New York).

The tax computation under (1) applies to the Brazilian subsidiary of a foreign corporation except that in this case, all the shares of the Brazilian corporation are owned by a nonresident (the foreign parent company).

The following facts are assumed:

18 As amended by Law No. 2,862 of September 4, 1956, Art. 23.
19 Law No. 2,973, Art. 1 §2.

1. RESIDENT CORPORATION:

The share capital of the corporation is comprised of 40% bearer shares, 30% nominative shares in the hands of residents, and 30% nominative shares in the hands of nonresidents. The corporation has 4 directors.

2. RESIDENT PARTNERSHIP:

The partnership has two partners, one of whom owns 90% and the other 10% of the capital of the partnership.

It is assumed that each of the three organizations shows the following financial statements at the end of the year 1956:

1. Balance Sheet

Assets		Cr$
Current and other assets		4,580,000
Fixed Assets:		
Buildings (cost Cr$ 1,500,000)	2,000,000	
Reserve for depreciation	260,000	
	1,740,000	
Other (cost Cr$ 5,000,000)	5,500,000	
Reserve for depreciation	1,820,000	
	3,680,000	5,420,000
		10,000,000

Liabilities	
Various liabilities	2,142,960
Reserve for indemnities to employees	
(balance at end of previous year: 340,000)	400,000
Reserve for income tax	
(balance at end of previous year: 400,000)	500,000
Reserve for contingencies	
(balance at end of previous year: 300,000)	600,000
Legal reserve (corporation)	350,000
Capital	3,500,000
Surplus	2,507,040
	10,000,000

2. Statement of Profit and Loss and Statement of Surplus

		Cr$
Net profit before other credits and charges		2,435,000
Other credits:		
Dividends received	200,000	
Interest on government bonds (net of withholding tax of 6%)	28,200	228,200
		2,663,200
Other charges:		
Depreciation of buildings	50,000	
Depreciation of revaluation of fixed assets	50,000	
Expense reimbursement to X Corp., New York [a]	80,000	
Directors' fees (corporation) —		
Managers' compensation (branch) or withdrawals (partnership)	600,000	
Bonuses to employees (five employees)	700,000	
Reserve for indemnities to employees	60,000	
Reserve for contingencies	300,000	1,840,000
Net profit before provision for income tax		823,200
Reserve for income tax		500,000
Net profit for the period		323,200
Balance of surplus at the beginning of the period		1,200,000
Revaluation of fixed assets		1,000,000
Net profit for the period	323,200	
Less Allocation to legal reserve [b]	16,160	307,040
Balance of surplus at the end of the period		2,507,040

[a] Withholding tax of 20% (Cr$ 16,000) and compulsory loan (15% of Cr$ 16,000 — Cr$ 2,400) were paid and the net income of Cr$ 61,600 remitted.

[b] Not applicable in case of a branch or partnership. The amount represents 5% of the profit for the period (Cr$ 323,200).

3. Computation of Income Tax under Reg. Art. 44

Description	Corporation		Partnership		Branch of a Foreign Corporation	
	Cr$	Cr$	Cr$	Cr$	Cr$	Cr$
Net profit for the period as per books		323,200		323,200		323,200
Add—Nondeductible expenses						
Depreciation of buildings (7/3.1)	50,000		50,000		50,000	
Depreciation of revaluation of fixed assets (7/3.1)	50,000		50,000		50,000	
Expense reimbursement to X Corp., New York					80,000	
Remuneration of directors, managers or partners:						
Directors' fees (excess over Cr$ 480,000 being equivalent to Cr$ 120,000 for each of 4 directors) (7/5.2)	120,000					
Partners' withdrawals (excess over Cr$ 190,000 computed as follows: partner A, maximum Cr$ 120,000; partner B, maximum 20% of his share of the capital (Cr$ 350,000) or Cr$ 70,000 (7/5.2a)			410,000			
Bonuses to employees (excess over Cr$ 600,000 being equivalent to Cr$ 120,000 for each of 5 employees) (7/5.2 and 8/1.2)	100,000		100,000		100,000	
Reserve for indemnities to employees (7/5.4)	60,000		60,000		60,000	
Reserve for contingencies (7/5.3)	300,000		300,000		300,000	
Reserve for income tax (7/2.7)	500,000		500,000		500,000	
		1,180,000		1,470,000		1,140,000
		1,503,200		1,793,200		1,463,200
Add—Revaluation of fixed assets *credited to surplus* [a]		1,000,000		1,000,000		1,000,000
		2,503,200		2,793,200		2,463,200

Description	(1)	(2)	(3)
Deduct — Income already taxed:			
Dividends earned (7/7.1)	200,000	200,000	200,000
Interest on government bonds (9/1.2a)	28,200	28,200	28,200
	228,200	228,200	228,200
Taxable income	2,275,000	2,565,000	2,235,000
Deduct — Income tax paid during the year, computed on income of the preceding year (7/2.7)	400,000	400,000	400,000
Taxable income	1,875,000	2,165,000	1,835,000
Income Tax:			
15% on first Cr$ 500,000	75,000	75,000	75,000
20% on balance of income	275,000	333,000	267,000
Total income tax	350,000	408,000	342,000
Compulsory loan:			
15% on income tax (12/2.4a)	52,500	61,200	51,300
4% on reserves (7/8.2)	74,681.60 [b]	75,328 [c]	[d]
Total compulsory loan	127,181.60	136,528	51,300

[a] If this item is credited to a revaluation reserve rather than to surplus, taxation thereof may be deferred up to a maximum of four years (see 7/6.2). Revaluations under Law No. 2,862 of September 4, 1956 (14/4.) are not considered in the example.

[b] Computed as follows:

Net profit less legal reserve (Cr$ 323,200 less Cr$ 16,160)		307,040
Revaluation of fixed assets		1,000,000
Increase in reserves:		
Income tax	100,000	
Contingencies	300,000	
Employees' indemnities	60,000	
Depreciation of buildings	50,000	
Depreciation of revaluation	50,000	
		1,867,040
4% thereof	Cr$	74,681.60

[c] 4% of Cr$ 1,883,200 (net profits not reduced by legal reserve).

[d] Not payable because all profits are deemed to be distributed at the end of the year.

4. Taxes in Addition to the Regular Income Tax

1. CORPORATION (30% TAX ON EXCESS RESERVES)

Under the facts of the above example, the corporation is liable to pay (for the account of its shareholders) a tax on excess reserves in the amount of Cr$ 350,112 plus an additional charge of Cr$ 52,516.80 in the nature of a compulsory loan (7/8.3). The tax and additional charge are computed as set forth below.

A comparison of the reserves (including surplus) with the amount of the capital stock at the end of the preceding and of the current year shows the following:

	At end of preceding year	At end of current year
Surplus	Cr$ 1,200,000	Cr$ 2,507,040
Reserves:		
Indemnities to employees	340,000	400,000
Income tax	400,000	500,000
Contingencies	300,000	600,000
Depreciation of buildings	210,000	260,000
Depreciation of revaluation of fixed assets	———	50,000
Legal reserve	333,840	350,000
	2,783,840	4,667,040
Capital	3,500,000	3,500,000
Excess	None	Cr$ 1,167,040

The tax on excess reserves amounts to 30% of Cr$ 1,167,040, or Cr$ 350,112 and the additional charge (compulsory loan) to 15% of Cr$ 350,112, or Cr$ 52,516.80, a total of Cr$ 402,628.80. Both the tax and the additional charge are payable within 30 days of the date of the ordinary general meeting of the shareholders in which the financial statements of the corporation were approved.

Measures to prevent the 30% tax on excess reserves. The tax on excess reserves may be prevented by the distribution of a dividend in an amount at least equal to the excess of surplus and reserves over the capital stock (Cr$ 1,167,040).

It is assumed in the following that the shareholders will decide to distribute a stock dividend of Cr$ 1,000,000 by way of capitalizing the surplus from the revaluation of assets, and furthermore to distribute a cash dividend of Cr$ 200,000.[20]

The distribution of the two dividends and the taxes to be withheld by the corporation in connection therewith are as follows:

[20] The payment of the cash dividend should be resolved in the ordinary general meeting of the shareholders referred to in the text. The increase of capital and distribution of the stock dividend must be resolved in an extraordinary meeting of the shareholders which should be held immediately after the ordinary meeting.

Kind of shares	CAPITAL STOCK Amount	DIVIDEND Stock	Cash	WITHHOLDING TAX
Bearer shares (40%)	Cr$ 1,400,000	Cr$ 400,000	Cr$ 80,000	Cr$ 134,400 [a]
Nominative shares —				
Resident share-holders (30%)	1,050,000	300,000	60,000	none
Nonresident share-holders (30%)	1,050,000	300,000	60,000	72,000 [b]
Totals	Cr$ 3,500,000	Cr$ 1,000,000	Cr$ 200,000	Cr$ 206,400

[a] 28% withholding tax on distributions on bearer shares.
[b] 20% withholding tax on distributions to nonresidents.

Payment of the withholding taxes is due within 30 days of the *publication of the minutes* of the ordinary general meeting of shareholders in reference to the cash dividend, and within 30 days of the *date* of the extraordinary meeting in reference to the stock dividend. There is no withholding of tax as regards dividend payments to resident shareholders; these include the distributions (in stock or in cash) in their personal income tax returns for the succeeding year.

The *cash dividends* due to nonresidents and holders of bearer shares will be paid by the corporation net of the withholding taxes applicable to these distributions. As regards the distribution of the *stock dividend* (especially on bearer shares), it would seem that the corporation can protect itself against ultimate liability for the tax collected from it by retaining the shares and delivering them to the shareholder (or his nominee) against reimbursement of the tax paid on his behalf.

2. PARTNERSHIP (INDIVIDUAL INCOME TAXES OF PARTNERS ON THEIR DISTRIBUTIVE SHARES OF THE PROFITS) [21]

Each partner includes his distributive share of the profits of the partnership in his personal income tax return. The aggregate profit which is distributable is determined as follows:

Net profit for the year	Cr$ 323,200
Revaluation of fixed assets	1,000,000
Increase in reserves (see under 1 above)	560,000
Total profit distributable to partners	Cr$ 1,883,200

Partner A, whose capital share amounts to 90%, has made regular monthly withdrawals of Cr$ 30,000 during the year. He includes the following amounts in his personal return:

Under Schedule C:	
Part of monthly withdrawals (maximum statutory amount)	Cr$ 120,000
Under Schedule F:	
Excess of monthly withdrawals	Cr$ 240,000
90% of total profits as above	1,694,880
	Cr$ 2,054,880

[21] The individual income taxes computed in the following are entirely independent of the income tax imposed on the partnership as such.

Partner B, whose capital share amounts to 10%, has made regular monthly withdrawals of Cr$ 20,000 during the year. The following amounts should be reported in his personal return:

Under Schedule C:
Monthly withdrawals up to the limit of 20% of his
share of the capital (Cr$ 350,000)   Cr$ 70,000

Under Schedule F:
Excess of monthly withdrawals   170,000
10% of total profits as above   188,320
                                                         Cr$ 358,320

3. BRAZILIAN BRANCH OF A FOREIGN CORPORATION (WITHHOLDING TAX)

The profits of the branch are deemed to be distributed to the foreign home office as soon as determined, i.e., as of the balance sheet date.

Within 30 days after publication of its balance sheet, the branch is liable to pay a withholding tax of Cr$ 396,640 plus an additional charge (compulsory loan) amounting to 15% of the tax, computed as follows:

Net profit for the year, as per books   Cr$ 323,200

Add: Revaluation of fixed assets   1,000,000
Increase in reserves:
| | |
Income tax   Cr$ 100,000
Contingencies   300,000
Employees' indemnities   60,000
Depreciation, buildings   50,000
Depreciation, revaluations   50,000   560,000

Excess bonuses to employees   100,000
Income subject to withholding   Cr$ 1,983,200
20% tax   Cr$ 396,640
Compulsory loan (15% of the tax)   59,496
Total   Cr$ 456,136

The withholding tax of Cr$ 396,640 under Reg. Art. 97 is in addition to the income tax of Cr$ 342,000 under Reg. Art. 44.

12/2.6   Preferential Tax Rates for Particular Enterprises

The following entities are subject to income tax at rates different from those listed above (Reg. Art. 44 §2):

1. Public utilities whose annual profits are not in excess of 12% of their invested capital. These taxpayers are subject to a proportional tax of 8% on their profits. The invested capital of these organizations is represented by their paid-in capital and reserves.
2. Civil societies with a capital not in excess of Cr$ 100,000 organized exclusively for the rendering of professional services by physicians, engineers, lawyers, dentists, accountants, painters, sculptors, forwarding agents, and similar services. These societies pay a proportional tax of 5% on their profits (Law No. 2,862 of September 4, 1956, Art. 23 Sole §[b]).
3. The Bank of Brazil pays an income tax equal to the amount of the dividends distributed by it during the preceding year (Reg. Art. 59).

12/2.7   Translation of Income Tax Returns for Juridical Persons (Entities)

The following is a translation of the income tax return for corporations and other entities.

(To be stamped with date by receiving office)		Declaration of Income No ....
	UNITED STATES OF BRAZIL MINISTRY OF FINANCE DIVISION OF INCOME TAX	LEGAL ENTITY Taxable year 19.... Income for the year 19....
For use of local office		

NAME OR FIRM NAME ....
(write clearly)

ADDRESS .... OWN BUSINESS PREMISES? ....
(If rented, indicate rents paid: fill in forms 17 and 18)

LOCALITY .... CITY OR TOWN .... STATE ....

TYPE OF ACTIVITY .... PURPOSE ....
(industrial, commercial, or civil)   (line of activity)

WHERE IS THE FIRM OR COMPANY REGISTERED? ....

NUMBER AND DATE OF REGISTRATION ....

DOES IT HAVE BRANCHES OR AGENCIES? .... WHERE? ....

IS IT A BRANCH OR AGENCY OF A FIRM HAVING ITS SEAT IN A FOREIGN COUNTRY? ....

WHAT IS THE ADDRESS OF THE HOME OFFICE IN THE FOREIGN COUNTRY? ....

DOES THIS DECLARATION INCLUDE THE EARNINGS OF SUBSIDIARIES OR BRANCHES? ....

WHICH ONES? ....

DID YOU FILE A RETURN FOR THE PREVIOUS TAXABLE YEAR? ....

IN WHICH COLLECTOR'S OFFICE? ....

BASE OF TAX (*)

FORM "A"
ACTUAL PROFIT as shown in attached documents (**) .... Cr$ ....

FORM "B"
GROSS RECEIPTS as shown by records of cash sales, installment sales, and other income listed on p. 2 of this form (*) .... Cr$ ....
PRESUMED PROFIT: % OF GROSS RECEIPTS (*) .... Cr$ ....

TAX TO BE PAID

1 Legal entities generally:[a]
   (Up to Cr$ 100,000.00 .... 10% Cr$ ....
      Progressive tax (From Cr$ 100,000.00 to Cr$
      500,000.00) .... 12% Cr$ ....
      (Over Cr$ 500,000.00) .... 15% Cr$ .... Cr$ ....
2 Enterprises licensed to perform public services whose profits do not exceed 12% of invested capital:
   Proportional tax of 8% .... Cr$ ....

[a] The presently valid rates are 15% on the first Cr$ 500,000 of taxable income and 20% on the excess (12/2.3).

(Carimbo da data da Repartição recebidora)

Para uso da Repartição

ESTADOS UNIDOS DO BRASIL
MINISTÉRIO DA FAZENDA
DIVISÃO DO IMPÔSTO DE RENDA

DECLARAÇÃO DE RENDIMENTOS

N.º

PESSOA JURÍDICA
Exercício de 19..........
Rendimentos do ano de 19..........

NOME OU RAZÃO SOCIAL..
(escrever com clareza)
ENDERÊÇO ....PRÉDIO PRÓPRIO ?............
(rua e número)   (se a ugado, informar aluguéis pagos: preencher mods. 17 e18)
LOCALIDADE..MUNICÍPIO....................................ESTADO ....

ESPÉCIE DE ATIVIDADE...FINS...........................
(industrial, comercial ou civil)   (ramo de atividade explorada)
ONDE A FIRMA OU SOCIEDADE ESTÁ REGISTRADA ?...
QUAL O NÚMERO E A DATA DO REGISTRO ?..
TEM FILIAIS, SUCURSAIS OU AGÊNCIAS ?....................................ONDE ?..
É FILIAL, SUCURSAL OU AGÊNCIA DE PESSOA JURÍDICA COM SEDE NO ESTRANGEIRO ?....................................
QUAL O ENDERÊÇO DA SEDE NO ESTRANGEIRO ?...
ESTA DECLARAÇÃO ABRANGE OS RESULTADOS DAS ENTIDADES SUBORDINADAS OU CONGÊNERES ?...................
DE QUAIS ?...
APRESENTOU DECLARAÇÃO PARA O EXERCÍCIO ANTERIOR ?...
EM QUE REPARTIÇÃO ?...

BASE DO IMPÔSTO (*)

FORMA "A"
LUCRO REAL, de acôrdo com os inclusos documentos (**).. Cr$

FORMA "B"
RECEITA BRUTA, de acôrdo com a relação das vendas à vista,
vendas a prazo e outros rendimentos, constante da pág. 2
dêste formulário (*).. Cr$
LUCRO PRESUMIDO: ....% da RECEITA BRUTA (*) .... Cr$

IMPÔSTO A PAGAR

1. Pessoas Jurídicas, em geral:

	Até Cr$ 100.000,00.............. 10% Cr$	
Impôsto progressivo.....	De Cr$ 100.000,00 a Cr$ 500.000,00 12% Cr$	
	Acima de Cr$ 500.000,00......... 15% Cr$	Cr$

2. Emprêsas Concessionárias de Serviços Públicos, cujos lucros não excederem
de 12% do capital invertido:
Impôsto proporcional de 8%.. Cr$

3. Sociedades Civis de capital até Cr$ 100.000,00, quando organizadas exclusivamente
para prestação de serviços profissionais expressamente previstas no regulamento em
vigor:
Impôsto proporcional de 3%... Cr$
MENOS — Desconto de ....% pelo pagamento antecipado do impôsto (***)................ Cr$
DIFERENÇA.. Cr$
MULTA DE MORA DE 10%... Cr$
TOTAL A PAGAR... Cr$

PARA USO DA REPARTIÇÃO

O pagamento do tributo discriminado no quadro acima,
deverá ser realizado integralmente até ..../........../19......

PAGAMENTO NO ATO

Recibo N.º...........................Data.............../19......

Assinatura do servidor

ESCALA DE COTAS E PRAZOS PARA PAGAMENTO

1.ª cota..........	Cr$	......../......./19....
2.ª cota..........	Cr$	......../......./19....
3.ª cota..........	Cr$	......../......./19....
4.ª cota..........	Cr$	......../......./19....

(*) Sòmente as firmas e sociedades com sede no Brasil, cujo capital fôr igual ou inferior a Cr$ 50.000,00 ou cuja receita bruta fôr igual ou inferior a Cr$ 200.000,00 podem optar pelo pagamento do impôsto de renda com base no lucro real (Forma "A") ou no lucro presumido à razão de 8% da receita bruta — art. 40 (Forma "B"). Desde que o capital ou receita bruta seja superior a êsses limites, é obrigatório o pagamento do impôsto com base no lucro real; sendo que, na falta de escrituração legalizada ou quando a escrituração, não satisfizer às exigências legais, a tributação será feita pela Forma "B", mediante o arbitramento do lucro de acôrdo com o estatuído no art 34, § 3.º, do regulamento em vigor.
(**) Demonstrar o lucro real (ou prejuízo) com os documentos referidos no título DOCUMENTOS QUE DEVEM INSTRUIR A DECLARAÇÃO DE RENDIMENTOS das "Instruções" anexas.
(***) Vej "Instruções" anexas.

Income Tax Return for Juridical Persons (Entities)

TAX TO BE PAID continued

3   Civil societies with capital up to Cr$ 100,000.00 organized exclusively for the performance of professional services as stated in the present regulations:

Proportional tax of 3% b .... Cr$ ....

LESS — Discount of   % for prepayment of tax (***) .... Cr$ ....

DIFFERENCE .... Cr$ ....

DELAY PENALTY OF 10% .... Cr$ ....

TOTAL TO BE PAID .... Cr$ ....

FOR USE OF COLLECTOR'S OFFICE

Payment of tax shown in above square must be completed by ..../..../19....

PAYMENT IN CASH	
Receipt No	
Date ..../..../19....	
Signature of clerk	

TABLE OF INSTALLMENTS AND DATES DUE

1st installment .... Cr$ ..../..../19....

2nd installment .... Cr$ ..../..../19....

3rd installment .... Cr$ ..../..../19....

4th installment .... Cr$ ..../..../19....

(*) Only firms and companies with home offices in Brazil whose capital is equal to or less than Cr$ 50,000.00 c and whose gross income is equal to or less than Cr$ 200,000.00 d may choose to pay income tax either on the basis of actual profits or on presumed profits determined at 8% of gross income — art. 40 (Form "B"). If capital or gross income exceed these amounts, payment of the tax on the basis of actual profits is mandatory; but in the absence of certified accounts or of accounts which satisfy the legal requirements, the tax will be computed on Form "B" on the basis of estimated profits, in accordance with art. 34 §3 of the present Regulations.

(**) Indicate actual profit (or loss) with the documents listed under the heading DOCUMENTS WHICH MUST SUPPORT THE INCOME TAX RETURN in the appended "Instructions."

(***) See appended "Instructions."

Declaration of Earnings (Corporate), form DMF. — 5.013

Notice: Before filling out this return, preferably by typewriter, please read the appended "Instructions" carefully. In listing income paid to others last year, inform the persons concerned that you have given this information to the Division of Income Tax, whether the sums were actually paid or credited to them. In this way you will help such persons avoid being penalized for failing to file a return or for omitting part of their income. In case of doubt, direct your inquiries to your regional office, where the necessary explanations will be given to you.

(Second page)

I — STATEMENT OF GROSS INCOME

MONTH	CASH SALES	TERM SALES	OTHER INCOME (*)	GROSS INCOME (total)
January	Cr$	Cr$	Cr$	Cr$ ....
February	Cr$	Cr$	Cr$	Cr$ ....
March	Cr$	Cr$	Cr$	Cr$ ....
April	Cr$	Cr$	Cr$	Cr$ ....
May	Cr$	Cr$	Cr$	Cr$ ....
June	Cr$	Cr$	Cr$	Cr$ ....
July	Cr$	Cr$	Cr$	Cr$ ....
August	Cr$	Cr$	Cr$	Cr$ ....
September	Cr$	Cr$	Cr$	Cr$ ....
October	Cr$	Cr$	Cr$	Cr$ ....
November	Cr$	Cr$	Cr$	Cr$ ....
December	Cr$	Cr$	Cr$	Cr$ ....
TOTALS	Cr$	Cr$	Cr$	Cr$ ....

b The present tax rate is 5% (12/2.6).
c Now Cr$ 100,000 (6/9.1).
d Now Cr$ 500,000 (6/9.1).

II — INFORMATION CONCERNING INDIVIDUAL PROPRIETORSHIPS OR MEMBERS OF COMMERCIAL OR INDUSTRIAL COMPANIES OF ANY KIND
(except corporations and civil societies)

NAME AND ADDRESS	CAPITAL SHARE OR PARTICI-PATION	PROFITS PAID OR CREDITED (Last Balance Sheet)	WITHDRAWALS CHARGED TO "GENERAL EXPENSES" OR SUBSIDIARY ACCOUNTS

III — INFORMATION CONCERNING MEMBERS OF THE FISCAL AND ADMINISTRATIVE COMMITTEE AND DIRECTORS OF CORPORATIONS AND CIVIL SOCIETIES

NAME AND ADDRESS	POSITION	NOMINATIVE SHARES		REMUNERATION FOR SERVICES RENDERED	
		Dividends credited (last balance sheet)	Other Distributions	Fixed monthly salary	Variable

IV — BEARER SECURITIES
(shares, debentures, and participating certificates)

KIND	AMOUNT	NOMINAL VALUE	DEBENTURES			REGULAR GENERAL MEETING	
			DATE OF ISSUE	TOTAL INTEREST PAID	DATE OF PAYMENT	Approving the enclosed balance sheet and authorizing payment of dividends and other distributions	
						DATE OF MEETING	Date of Publication in Official Gazette

Date .... 19....
            Signature ....

(*) Specify on a separate page the nature of "other income." In this column there must also be included all unregistered sales which have been determined for sales tax purposes, and on which sales tax was paid in cash.

CHAPTER 13

TAX ADMINISTRATION

AND PROCEDURE

13/1. Returns and Payment of the Tax

    13/1.1   Individual Taxpayers
        a. Returns — In General
        b. Individuals not Required to File Returns
        c. Joint and Separate Returns of Married
           Taxpayers
        d. Payment of the Tax
    13/1.2   Entities
        a. Returns
        b. Payment of the Tax
    13/1.3   Other Types of Taxpayers
        a. Decedent's Estate

13/2. Review of Returns and Assessment ex officio

    13/2.1   Review
    13/2.2   Assessment ex officio
        a. Scope of Application
        b. Procedure
        c. Basis of the Tax Assessed ex officio

13/3. Information at the Source

    13/3.1   Types of Payments that Must Be Reported
    13/3.2   Persons Who Must Report

13/4. Protests and Review Procedure

    13/4.1   Protests
    13/4.2   Review Procedure

a. Petition for Review by the Taxpayer or
Withholding Agent

b. Petition for Review by the Government

13/4.3 Decision by the Tax Court; Appeals

13/5. Claims for Refund

13/5.1 Procedure

13/6. Time Limits on Assessment and Collection

13/6.1 Assessment

13/6.2 Collection

13/7. Penalties

13/7.1 In General

13/7.2 Late Filing of Return and/or Payment of Tax

13/7.3 Late Payment of Tax Withheld at the Source

13/7.4 Failure to Maintain or Produce Proper Books and Records

a. Books and Records Improperly Maintained

b. Failure to File Required Information

c. Refusal to Produce Books

13/7.5 Failure of the Taxpayer to File the Proper Return

13/7.6 Penalties in the Case of Assessment ex officio

13/7.7 Fraud Penalty

13/1. Returns and Payment of the Tax

13/1.1 Individual Taxpayers

a. RETURNS — IN GENERAL. The income tax return of an individual must include his income from all sources received during the base year. The return covers both the schedular and the complementary tax. The taxpayer must indicate, under the appropriate schedule, the designation and location of the payor of the income and specify the deductions applicable to each type of schedular income (Reg. Art. 65 §1). The return must be prepared on the calendar year basis.

The return must be filed between January 1 and April 30 of the calendar year following the base year [1] with the tax office for the district in

[1] In the case of circumstances beyond the taxpayer's control, one extension of time for filing the return (not exceeding sixty days) may be granted upon the taxpayer's application (Reg. Art. 63 §2). Otherwise, a return filed after April 30 will be accepted only if the taxpayer has not been notified that the administrative process of assessment ex officio (Reg. Art. 77; see 13/2.2) has been initiated.

which the taxpayer maintains his tax residence (Reg. Arts. 63 and 70).[2]
The following information must accompany the return: [3]

1. Statement of payments received. A list of the names and addresses of the parties who during the base year made payments to the taxpayer which the latter included in his gross income.[4]

2. Statement of payments made. A list of the names and addresses of the parties to whom the taxpayer made payments during the base year. This statement is, in general, limited to payments in the nature of interest, profits, dividends, and rent. Other payments which must be reported are those in excess of Cr$ 60,000 made during the year to any one recipient. Annual payments not in excess of Cr$ 60,000 need not be reported, unless the recipient has had income from other sources during that year.[5] (Reg. Art. 108 §3). The obligation to report payments made is not limited to items which constitute deductible expenses to the payor.

3. Proof of deductions claimed. The requirement to file documentary evidence of payments made on items claimed as deductions applies presently only to charitable contributions made by individuals (Reg. Art. 20[d]). In regard to all other deductions, the taxpayer must be prepared to prove the expense if called upon to do so by the government (Reg. Art. 12 §3), but he is not required to submit the evidence with his return.

The deductions and abatements listed in the return may not be increased and new ones may not be claimed after the taxpayer is notified that the tax has been assessed or that an assessment ex officio [6] is being prepared (Reg. Art. 63, §4).

b. INDIVIDUALS NOT REQUIRED TO FILE RETURNS. The following individuals are not required to file returns unless specifically requested to do so by the government:

1. Individuals whose gross annual income is not in excess of Cr$ 60,000,[7] these individuals are not considered taxpayers under Brazilian income tax law (Reg. Arts. 1 and 63 §1[a]).

2. Individuals whose only income is from salaries or wages paid by not more than one employer (Reg. Art. 63 §1[b] and §9) and which is not in excess of Cr$ 10,000 for any one calendar month in the year. Since

[2] The tax residence (or, in Brazilian terminology, "fiscal domicile") of an individual is the place where he has his permanent residence; if the taxpayer exercises a profession or business or a public or other function, it is at the place of his business; if he has several places of residence in Brazil, one will be selected by the authorities as his tax residence (Reg. Art. 171). Changes of residence or business address must be reported within thirty days (Reg. Art. 195).

[3] The tax return as well as the supporting information must be prepared on the official forms provided by the government, Reg. Art. 64.

[4] Reg. Art. 65 Sole §.

[5] The taxpayer cannot presume that the recipient has had no other income during the year; unless he is certain of that fact, he must report annual payments not in excess of Cr$ 50,000 (now Cr$ 60,000) made by him, DIR, *Rev.* 1952 No. 433-I.

[6] 13/2.2.

[7] If gross income is more than Cr$ 60,000, but reduced to an amount below that figure by deductions or abatements, the taxpayer must file a return although there is no tax liability.

in this case, the individual's entire income is subject to withholding of tax at the source, his tax liability is fully satisfied, and he is not required to file a return.

c. JOINT AND SEPARATE RETURNS OF MARRIED TAXPAYERS. Married taxpayers whose marital property rights are governed by the community property system must file a joint return which includes the taxable income of both spouses (Reg. Art. 67). The return is filed by the head of the household, i.e., the husband, and the assessment of the tax is in his name (Reg. Art. 80 Sole §). Besides the income of the spouses, the return must include that of the children (see 12/1.2b). This rule is designed to prevent the splitting of income (for purposes of the complementary tax) between the members of a family.

As regards spouses living under the community property system, a separate return may be filed only by the wife with respect to income from personal work and from property in which exclusive title has been reserved to her or which has been made inalienable or unmortgageable (Reg. Art. 67 §2).[8]

If the settlement between the spouses is one of separation of property, each spouse *may*, if he so chooses, file a separate return and report therein his or her separate income (Reg. Art. 67 §1).

d. PAYMENT OF THE TAX. The collection of the tax begins on June 1 of each year (Reg. Art. 90). After a first review of the return, the taxpayer receives a notice indicating the amount of the tax due (Reg. Art. 76). The tax is payable within 20 days from the date marked in the notice (Reg. Art. 90 §1). If the total tax due is less than Cr$ 500, it must be paid in one amount.[9] Otherwise, payment may be made in four installments.[10] The addition to the tax (compulsory loan [11]) is paid as a fifth installment.

The law provides for the following discounts if payment of the tax is made in full at the time the return is filed (Reg. Art. 85 §2):

1. 5% if payment is made in January;
2. 3% if payment is made in February;
3. 1% if payment is made in March.

13/1.2   Entities

a. RETURNS. Every entity with gross annual income in excess of Cr$ 150,-000 must file an income tax return, whether or not it had net income

---

[8] Separate income of the husband must be reported in the joint return, so that actually only the wife (and not "either spouse," as the wording of Reg. Art. 67 §§1 and 2 would indicate) is entitled to file a separate return reporting separate income; CC, *Rev.* 1952 No. 666; 1953 Nos. 173 and 441; 1954 No. 110; 1955 Nos. 15, 33, and 55.   [9] Reg. Art. 85.

[10] Reg. Art. 85 §1. In this case, the first installment is payable within 20 days after the date indicated on the notice of assessment, and the subsequent installments at intervals of 30 days thereafter (Reg. Art. 90 §1).

[11] Applicable to individuals whose income tax is Cr$ 20,000 or more; see 12/1.3b.

during the base year.[12] The return must be filed between January 1 and
April 30 [13] with the tax office for the district in which the taxpayer maintains its tax residence (Reg. Art. 70). The tax residence of an entity
which has its seat in Brazil and of the Brazilian branch of a foreign
entity is the place where the entity or branch has its business establishment in Brazil (Reg. Art. 172).

The Income Tax Regulations require the filing of a single tax return
for each entity, regardless of the number of its divisions, branches, or
establishments in Brazil. If a Brazilian enterprise has branch offices
located in Brazil, the income of the branches must be included in the
return of the head office (Reg. Art. 69) [14] and the assessment is made
against the latter (Reg. Art. 81). If the home office of the entity is
located abroad, the return is filed by the Brazilian branch and the assessment is made against it (Reg. Arts. 69 and 81 §1); if the foreign
entity has several branches in Brazil, the tax is assessed separately against
each branch, unless the accounting of all Brazilian branches is centralized in one of them (Reg. Art. 81 §1).

Affiliated firms with independent corporate existence, such as subsidiaries, must file separate returns and are assessed separately on their respective taxable income (Reg. Arts. 69 Sole § and 81 §2). There is no provision which would permit the filing of consolidated returns by affiliated
entities.

The return and the information required to be submitted with it must
be prepared on the official forms provided by the government (Reg. Art.
64). The following statements must accompany the return (Reg. Art.
38): [15]

1. Balance sheet.
2. Statement of profit and loss.
3. An analysis of the general expense account by types of expenses included therein.
4. An analysis of the merchandise account, showing the total monthly
   debits and credits to the account and the opening and closing inventories.
5. A list of receivables considered uncollectible and charged to the provision for bad debts or directly to the profit and loss account; the name

[12] Entities with gross annual income not exceeding Cr$ 150,000 are not required
to file a return, DIR, *Rev.* 1955 No. 730.
[13] The provisions regarding an extension of time for filing the return are the same
as in the case of individual taxpayers (see footnote 1 under 13/1.1a). Unless the
taxpayer has been granted an extension, it may file the return after April 30 only
if it has not been notified that the government has initiated the process of assessment
ex officio, Reg. Art. 63 §3 (see 13/2.2).
[14] The branches are merely obliged to report this fact to the tax offices of their
districts, Reg. Art. 69.
[15] Companies which trade in securities must submit additional statistical information, as enumerated in Reg. Art. 38 §1.

and address of each debtor; the amount of his debt; the date it became due; and the reason for its uncollectibility.

6. A statement of payments made similar to the one required from individual taxpayers (13/1.1).
7. An analysis of the surplus account.
8. An analysis of investments in capital items.
9. An analysis of the depreciation reserve.
10. An analysis of the income account (itemizing allowable and unallowable deductions for the purpose of determining taxable income).

The financial statements and other accounting information submitted with the return must be subscribed by qualified accountants who are registered as prescribed by law (Reg. Art. 39).

The accountant certifying to the financial statements of a taxpayer is jointly liable with the latter for any incorrectness of the statements and irregularities of the bookkeeping system which result in an evasion of income tax (Reg. Art. 39 §1). It is important to note that in order to ensure the filing of correct returns by entities, accountants must give the income tax authorities the names and addresses of their clients (Reg. Art. 39 §5).

b. PAYMENT OF THE TAX. The tax may be paid in four equal installments, except a tax of less than Cr$ 5,000, which must be paid in one amount (Reg. Art. 85 and its §1).

The due dates for payment of the tax and the discounts for early payment are the same as for individual taxpayers (Reg. Art. 85 §2; 13/1.1d).

The 4% charge on reserves and the 15% addition to the tax in the nature of a compulsory loan [16] are paid separately as a fifth installment of the total tax due.

13/1.3 Other Types of Taxpayers

a. DECEDENT'S ESTATE. The income tax return of an estate is filed by the administrator (*inventariante*) for each calendar year during which the estate is in process of administration, up to and including the year in which the partition of the estate is confirmed, or the distribution of the estate assets is ordered by judicial decree. The estate is the taxpayer and the tax is assessed against it (Reg. Art. 45 §2).

The income tax return of an estate, like that of an individual taxpayer, is prepared on the basis of the income of the preceding calendar year (Reg. Art. 45). It must be filed on or before April 30 of the year following the base year, except in the last year of the estate's administration. When the judicial decree confirming the partition of the estate or ordering the distribution of the estate assets has been rendered, the administrator must file an income tax return for the estate within ten days from the date of the decree. This return, which is the final income tax return of the estate,

[16] See 12/2.4a.

must include the income from January 1 of the year in which the decree is promulgated to the date of the decree (Reg. Art. 45 §1).

13/2.   Review of Returns and Assessment ex officio

13/2.1   Review

The first review of an income tax return is made in the office of the tax collector (Reg. Art. 74). The income tax authorities may utilize all information which is available to them and may request the taxpayer to give further explanations either orally or in writing, or to submit additional proof.[17] A request for information must be answered by the taxpayer within 20 days after he receives it.[18] If the review discloses no irregularities, the tax is assessed and the taxpayer is notified of the amount of tax due (Reg. Art. 76).

The examination of the books and records of the taxpayer is the duty of the authorities charged with the assessment of the tax (Reg. Art. 124). Formerly, such an examination could proceed only on the basis of written instructions specifically issued by the Director of the Income Tax Division in the Ministry of Finance or his delegate. Now the authorities may make all examinations at the taxpayer's place of business which they deem necessary to establish whether the taxpayer has complied with his fiscal obligations (Reg. Art. 124 §1).[19]

The law imposes a general obligation on all individuals and entities, whether or not they are taxpayers in the particular case under review, to give the information and explanations which revenue agents in the exercise of their functions may require from them. If irregularities are found by the agents, they draw up a statement incorporating the explanations given by the taxpayer, which the latter must sign.[20] Severe penalties are imposed on a taxpayer who refuses to present his books for examination or otherwise obstructs the action of the tax authorities.[21]

13/2.2   Assessment ex officio

a. SCOPE OF APPLICATION. The administrative process of assessment ex officio applies in the case of the following irregularities (Reg. Art. 77):

1. If the taxpayer fails to file a return;
2. If the taxpayer disregards a request for information directed to him by

---

[17] Reg. Art. 74 and its §1.

[18] Reg. Art. 74 §2. If the taxpayer fails to give the required information or explanations, an assessment ex officio will be initiated (Reg. Art. 74 §3).

[19] This procedure is termed "direct, external, and permanent fiscal action."

[20] Reg. Art. 137. However, the signature of the taxpayer to the statement does not signify his consent, and the failure to secure the taxpayer's signature does not invalidate the statement (Reg. Art. 137 §1).

[21] Reg. Art. 149(b); see 13/7.4c. The presentation of the books can be enforced by an order of the court.

the tax authorities, refuses to give the information demanded, or gives it in an unsatisfactory manner;[22]
3. If the taxpayer files an incorrect return, i.e., omits or understates income or claims improper deductions or abatements.

b. PROCEDURE.   An assessment ex officio is initiated by a written request issued by the tax-assessing authority and communicated to the taxpayer, either by registered mail or through publication, to furnish the information desired within 20 days (Reg. Art. 78). If the taxpayer furnishes the information demanded of him, his statements can be questioned by the authorities only if they are in possession of convincing conflicting evidence, or if there are strong indications of the falsehood or inexactness of these statements (Reg. Art. 79 §1).

After the expiration of the 20-day period, the authorities decide whether or not to close the case. If they decide to proceed against the taxpayer, the latter receives a written notice of assessment for the deficiency in income tax and for a fine, which is assessed at the same time.[23]

Entities which qualify for taxation on the basis of presumed profits under Reg. Art. 33 (6/9.1) may exercise this election only if they file a return and submit their financial statements with it. A taxpayer's failure to present the required fiscal information results in the loss of the option to be taxed on the basis of presumed profits.[24] Since this option is exercised and binding for one taxable year only, the failure to file a return or to submit the necessary supporting data for a preceding year does not prevent the taxpayer from making the election for a later taxable year; and an election effectively made in one year is not binding for future taxable years.

c. BASIS OF THE TAX ASSESSED EX OFFICIO.   The income tax law prescribes the following bases for assessing the tax ex officio in the various situations in which this method of assessment applies (Reg. Art. 79):

1. If the taxpayer has failed to file a return, the income will be estimated on the basis of the information available to the government.
2. If the taxpayer has failed or refused to give information demanded by the government, or given unsatisfactory information, taxable income is determined on the basis of the information available to the government, and items which are not sufficiently explained are disregarded.
3. If the return is incorrect, the tax authorities will either compute the

[22] The administrative practice is to consider an explanation given by the taxpayer as satisfactory if he discloses receipts at least equal to those already known to the government, or if he surrenders all his commercial and fiscal books. See CC, *Rev.* 1944 No. 412; Sousa, §49.

[23] Instructions to the Service (*Orden de Serviço*) No. 11 of August 17, 1948, published in *Rev.* 1948 under No. 565.

[24] In this case, an assessment ex officio will be made, Reg. Art. 79 §2. Since the election to be taxed on the basis of presumed profits is made in the return, no such election can effectively be made unless a return is filed by the taxpayer.

amounts omitted in the return, or estimate the entire amount of taxable income, using in either case any information they may have secured.

The tax assessed ex officio must be paid in one lump sum; the option to pay in four equal installments does not apply (Reg. Art. 85 §4).

13/3. Information at the Source

13/3.1 Types of Payments that Must Be Reported

All individuals and entities are obliged to inform the tax authorities [25] before April 30 of each year regarding all payments or credits of income made by them during the preceding calendar year either for their own account or as representatives of third parties. The information to be submitted must indicate the nature and amount of the payments or credits made and the names and addresses of the recipients (Reg. Art. 108).

The following types of income are specifically listed by the statute: salaries, gratuities, bonuses, participations, commissions (8/1.5), fees (8/2.1), interest (9/1.), dividends, profits (9/2.), and rents (9/4.).[26] This enumeration, however, is merely illustrative, and the rule is that the payment or credit of any kind of income must be reported.

Payment of interest, dividends, profits, and rents must be reported irrespective of their amount; other payments must be reported only if the annual amount thereof paid to any one recipient exceeds Cr$ 60,000 (Reg. Art. 108 §3), or if the recipient has no income from other sources. If the payor has no definite information regarding this point, he must report all payments made by him (Reg. Art. 108 §4).

If the income is that of a foreign resident or domiciliary, this fact must be indicated by the informant as well as the name and address of the creditor's representative to whom payment was made (Reg. Art. 108 §5).

13/3.2 Persons Who Must Report

The following persons and organizations, among others, are specifically obliged to furnish fiscal information within the terms outlined above (Reg. Arts. 110 and 111):

1. Banks, brokers, and all other persons and firms whose business it is to collect interest (except interest on the public debt) or to buy and sell foreign exchange or securities traded on an exchange, to the extent that such transactions are carried out in the name and for the account of their clients.

[25] The information required must be filed with the Regional or Sectional Delegates of the Income Tax Division or the federal tax collectors. The informant must use the proper form furnished by the government and attach thereto the information in two copies, one of which will be returned to him with a receipt (Reg. Art. 122).

[26] Reg. Art. 108 §1. Cash payments for traveling and living expenses in the exercise of a business and payments to welfare funds must likewise be reported (Reg. Art. 108 §2). The recipient is required to include these items in his taxable income, taking an equivalent amount as a deduction under Schedule C (7/2.11b and 8/1.3a).

All banks (including the Bank of Brazil) must report every payment or credit of interest made to an individual if the amount thereof exceeds Cr$ 1,000. Information regarding lesser payments or credits of interest as well as information on current commercial accounts must be made available to the government upon its request.[27]

2. Insurance companies (regardless of their form or organization), in reference to pensions paid to the policyholders.

3. Companies dealing in real property, in regard to rents collected by them for their clients.

4. All firms, companies, and associations, with respect to payments of authors' royalties made by them, although such royalties are exempt, at least in the case of resident authors (5/5.3).

5. Brokers' syndicates, in regard to the commissions received by brokers.

The Income Tax Regulations (Arts. 112–121) further provide for the submission of the fiscal information received by various government agencies in the exercise of their functions.

13/4. Protests and Review Procedure

13/4.1 Protests

The taxpayer may, within 20 days after receiving the notice of assessment, file a protest (*reclamação*) with the Regional or Sectional Delegate of the Income Tax Division.[28] This rule applies whether the tax was assessed on the basis of the return filed or whether the assessment was made ex officio. It likewise applies to a withholding agent requested by the government to make payment of tax withheld. The filing of the protest suspends the collection of the tax,[29] and the taxpayer is not required to put up security.[30]

The taxpayer may, by means of his protest, impugn his own tax return by contesting an assessment, even if it corresponds exactly with the return.[31] This is a consequence of the rule that a taxpayer is not legally permitted to resolve doubtful questions regarding the taxability or classification of income or the deductibility of expenses in his own favor by omitting doubtful items of income or claiming doubtful deductions. In order to avoid an assessment ex officio and the imposition of a fine, the taxpayer will include questionable income items in his return and omit vulnerable deductions therefrom and clarify the issues later by filing a protest.

After an adverse decision on the protest has been rendered by the Regional or Sectional Delegate of the Income Tax Division,[32] the taxpayer can petition the Tax Court for review as indicated below.

[27] It should be noted that, under this provision, the government is entitled to full information regarding all bank transactions of an individual or entity.

[28] Reg. Arts. 155, 156. The time limit of 20 days cannot be extended, Reg. Art. 169.

[29] Reg. Art. 155 Sole §.   [30] Sousa, *Compêndio* (2d ed.) §142.

[31] Sousa, *loc. cit.*

[32] Before the revision of Reg. Art. 156 by Law No. 2,354 of November 29, 1954,

13/4.2   Review Procedure

The statute (Reg. Arts. 157, 160) speaks of a "voluntary" petition for review (*recurso voluntário*) if it is brought by the taxpayer or the withholding agent; if brought by the government, the remedy is termed a petition ex officio. While the procedure is similar in both cases, the conditions under which the decision of the Tax Court may be invoked are different.

a. PETITION FOR REVIEW BY THE TAXPAYER OR WITHHOLDING AGENT.

The time limit for filing a petition for review with the Tax Court [33] is 30 days from the date on which the adverse administrative decision was communicated to the taxpayer (Reg. Art. 158). This time limit cannot be extended (Reg. Art. 169). Within the same period of 30 days, the taxpayer must furnish security for the amount in controversy.[34] The payment of the uncontested portion of the deficiency is not deferred by the petition and must be made within the usual time limit (Reg. Art. 158 §1).

The filing of a protest is not a formal requirement of the taxpayer's petition for review. The petition may be brought against an original adverse ruling of the Regional or Sectional Delegate, or against the decision of the Director of the Income Tax Division in the Ministry of Finance which reverses a ruling in favor of the taxpayer by the Regional or Sectional Delegate (see b., below).

b. PETITION FOR REVIEW BY THE GOVERNMENT.

If the Regional or Sectional Delegate of the Income Tax Division reverses (entirely or in part) a ruling of the lower authority which was adverse to the taxpayer, he must at the same time submit the case for further review to the Director of the Income Tax Division in the Ministry of Finance.[35] If the Director of the Income Tax Division issues a ruling

---

only the Regional Delegate was competent to render a decision upon a protest filed by the taxpayer; an adverse ruling by the Sectional Delegate had to be carried first to the Regional Delegate and only the latter's decision could be appealed by the taxpayer to the Tax Court (see CC, *Rev*, 1954 No. 539). Today, only the rulings of the local tax inspectors must first be submitted to the higher administrative authority, see Rezende-Viana, *Consolidação das Leis do Impôsto de Renda*, Note 370.

[33] The substantive requirement of the petition is a decision adverse to the taxpayer or the withholding agent in connection with the interpretation of the law, the collection of the tax, or a violation of the fiscal rules (Reg. Art. 157).

[34] The security may consist of money, of federal government securities, or of fully paid-up shares or debentures of "mixed-economy corporations" (*sociedades mistas*), in which the federal government has a participating share (Reg. Art. 158). Federal bonds are accepted as security at their face value, and shares or bonds of mixed-economy companies at their quoted price on the stock exchange on the day before they are offered as security (Reg. Art. 158 §2). If the amount in controversy exceeds Cr$ 5,000, a suitable surety may be accepted in the discretion of the tax authorities (Reg. Art. 159).

[35] If the decision of the Director of the Income Tax Division is unfavorable to the taxpayer, the latter can petition the Tax Court for review, Reg. Arts. 160 §4 and 157. See under a., above.

favorable to the taxpayer, he must at the same time submit the case to the Tax Court for its decision (Reg. Art. 160 and its §1).

The review procedure outlined above does not apply if either the amount in controversy is less than Cr$ 10,000 or the decision of the lower administrative authority was based on an error of fact (Reg. Art. 160 §3).

13/4.3   Decision by the Tax Court; Appeals

There are two Tax Courts in the nature of administrative tribunals whose respective jurisdiction is determined by the type of tax under review. All matters relating to income tax deficiencies are within the jurisdiction of the *Primeiro Conselho de Contribuintes,*[36] which is referred to throughout this book as the Tax Court. It is composed of six members, of whom three are officials of the Ministry of Finance and three are private citizens (usually lawyers) who are appointed as taxpayers' representatives. Their appointment is for three years and can be extended.

The jurisdiction of the Tax Court does not extend to claims for refunds for overpayments of income tax (13/5.1).

If a decision by the Tax Court is wholly or partly in favor of the taxpayer, the government may petition the court for reconsideration and, if its decision is confirmed, carry the case to the Ministry of Finance whose decision is final (Reg. Arts. 161–163). This administrative appeal does not lie, however, if the decision of the Tax Court was unanimous.[37]

After a decision in favor of the government, the taxpayer has 30 days within which either to pay the amount of the tax due or to bring suit to annul the assessment.[38] The 30-day period, which cannot be extended (Reg. Art. 169), runs from the date on which the decision of the Tax Court is communicated to the taxpayer in one of the ways prescribed by the law.[39] The taxpayer's action to annul the assessment is brought before the competent Federal Court, as regulated in detail in the Code

[36] First Council of Taxpayers. The jurisdiction of this court extends to a number of federal taxes besides the income tax; all other federal taxes (especially the federal excise tax) are within the jurisdiction of the Second Tax Court. There is, furthermore, a third tax court which is in the nature of an administrative Court of Customs Appeals. Regarding the reorganization of the First Tax Court in connection with the reintroduction of the excess profits tax, see 14/8.

[37] Decree-law No. 607 of August 10, 1938, Art. 21; see Min. of Fin., *Rev.* 1951 No. 1012.

[38] The taxpayer may within 20 days from the date on which the decision of the Tax Court is communicated to him as prescribed by law (see Note 39 below), file a petition for reconsideration with the Tax Court (Reg. Art. 161).

[39] The taxpayer may be notified of the decision of the Tax Court personally, by registered mail, or through publication of the decision in the official gazette. The time for filing suit begins to run with the date on which the taxpayer acquires knowledge of the decision if he is notified personally; with the date on which the return receipt is delivered to the Division if notification is made by registered mail; or on the thirtieth day from the date of publication of the decision (Reg. Art. 167).

of Civil Procedure.[40] Within the time limit for the appeal, the taxpayer must deposit the amount in controversy either in money or government securities, unless he has already done so in the course of the administrative proceedings; a surety is not acceptable.[41]

If the taxpayer brings an action for annulment of the assessment, the case is reopened entirely and the administrative decisions rendered therein have no binding effect on the court, which will consider them merely as technical data.[42] An appeal from the decision of the federal court lies with the Federal Appellate Court (*Tribunal Federal de Recursos*). There is, in certain cases,[43] a further appeal to the Supreme Court of Brazil.

13/5. Claims for Refund

13/5.1 Procedure

The refund of an overpayment of income tax, collected from either the taxpayer or the withholding agent, must be claimed within the time limitation for filing a protest (Reg. Art. 170 §2). This time limitation, as set forth above (13/4.1), is twenty days from the date on which the taxpayer received the notice of assessment or the withholding agent the demand for payment (Reg. Art. 155).

The refund of the overpayment of a tax paid on some other basis than assessment or collection at the source may be demanded within one year from the date of payment (Reg. Art. 170 §1). This rule applies, for example, if payment of the tax is made with the return.

The above time limits do not apply, however, if the overpayment of tax was the result of an error of fact. In this case, the right to claim a refund expires at the end of the fifth year following the year for which the tax was paid.[44] The factual error which extends the time limit for claiming a refund is not necessarily that of the taxpayer; it may be an error committed by the government. Giving a liberal interpretation to the provision, the authorities have taken the position that the acceptance of a return containing errors to the detriment of the taxpayer such as the classification of items under the wrong schedule, duplication of income, arithmetical mistakes, etc., constitutes a factual error on the part of the government and results in the application of the five-year statute of limitations for the benefit of the taxpayer.[45]

The Tax Court has no jurisdiction over claims for refund of overpay-

---

[40] Decree-law 1608 of September 18, 1939; see Sousa, *Compêndio* (2d ed.) §43-A.

[41] Decree-law 3336 of June 10, 1941; see Sousa, *loc. cit.*

[42] Supreme Court of Brazil, 151 *Revista dos Tribunais* 771.

[43] As provided in the Constitution of Brazil, Art. 101.

[44] Reg. Art. 170 §3. As an example, the right to claim a refund of income tax paid in and for the year 1955 (i.e., computed on the income of the year 1954) expires on December 31, 1960.

[45] Ministry of Finance, *Rev.* 1933 No. 184; *Rev.* 1941 Nos. 14 and 438; 1943 No. 100. See Rezende, Note 397-A.

ments of income tax.[46] The ultimate administrative decision regarding such claims rests with the Director General of the National Treasury.[47] A refund claim can be carried to the federal courts after it is rejected by the administrative authorities.[48]

The filing of a claim for refund suspends the statute of limitations for assessment and collection of the tax until a final decision is rendered by the administrative agencies of the government.[49]

13/6. Time Limits on Assessment and Collection

13/6.1 Assessment

An original assessment of income tax (on the basis of the taxpayer's return or ex officio) must be made within five years from the end of the taxable year. An additional assessment or supplementary assessment (which presupposes an original assessment made within the five-year period just referred to) must be made within five years from the date on which the taxpayer received notice of the original assessment. The same time limitation applies to revisions of an assessment and to examinations of the taxpayer's books and records for assessment purposes (Reg. Art. 188 and its §1, as amended by Law No. 2,862 of September 4, 1956, Art. 29).[50]

Under the law in its present form (as distinguished from the older law),[51] the five-year periods referred to are substantive periods of limitation which extinguish the right to make an assessment. They cannot be suspended or interrupted by an act of the government.

13/6.2 Collection

The right of the government to collect a tax expires in five years, counted from the last day of the period fixed for the payment of the tax in the notice of assessment.[52] This is a procedural period of limitation which may be interrupted or suspended in certain cases, as shown below.

The five-year period for collection of the tax is interrupted [53] by any

---

[46] Decree-law No. 607 of August 10, 1938; see CC, *Rev.* 1951 Nos. 77 and 1213; *Rev.* 1952 Nos. 372 and 435; 1955 No. 188.

[47] Circular of the Ministry of Finance, *Rev.* 1938 No. 694, cited in Rezende, Note 373.

[48] Supreme Court of Brazil, 74 *Revista Forense* 65; 100 *Revista Forense* 59; 127 *Revista Forense* 290.

[49] Reg. Art. 170 §4.

[50] *Diário Oficial* of October 5, 1956.

[51] The new provision was passed by Congress over the veto of the President.

[52] Reg. Art. 189.

[53] An "interruption" of the statute of limitations, as distinguished from its "suspension," means that the full period of limitation begins to run again with the interrupting event or at the end of the interrupting proceedings, Civil Code of Brazil, Art. 173.

demand for payment of the tax directed to the taxpayer, by the granting of an extension of time for payment of the tax, by a personal citation of the party responsible for payment on the basis of a court order secured by the government, or by presentation of the tax bill before the surrogate or in bankruptcy proceedings for the estate of the taxpayer.[54] It is suspended during proceedings for the collection of the tax.[55]

The five-year period for collection of the tax does not apply in the case of an individual taxpayer claiming the privilege of distributing income earned during several years but collected in one year to the years in which the income was earned; neither does it apply to the collection of income tax required to be withheld at the source.[56]

13/7. Penalties

13/7.1 In General

The Income Tax Regulations impose civil penalties [57] in the form of varying fines upon taxpayers and other parties who violate the tax obligations imposed upon them. Only the more important violations will be discussed below.

13/7.2 Late Filing of Return and/or Payment of Tax

A penalty of 10% for the first month or any fraction thereof of the delay, and of 1% for each following month, computed on the unpaid amount of the tax, applies to a taxpayer (individual or entity) who files his return or pays the tax or any installment thereof after the expiration of the statutory time limit but before action is taken by the tax authorities. The total penalty may in no case exceed 50% of the deficiency. The same penalty applies if the taxpayer, within the period indicated, reports income which he omitted from his return.[58]

13/7.3 Late Payment of Tax Withheld at the Source

If the withholding agent (generally the party paying the income, but in some cases the taxpayer's representative) pays the tax, either voluntarily or upon demand of the tax authorities, after the statutory time limit [59] has expired, the penalty is 10% of the unpaid amount of the tax

[54] Reg. Art. 189 §1.   [55] Reg. Art. 189 §2.

[56] Reg. Art. 191. The Income Tax Regulations do not establish any time limitation regarding the collection of income tax from nonresidents. The matter is regulated by the Civil Code (Art. 177) which provides a general time limitation of 30 years.

[57] Certain violations are subject to criminal penalties, such as the making of false entries or fraudulent alterations in the books of account which are considered public documents, Criminal Code of Brazil, Arts. 240 et seq.

[58] Reg. Arts. 144 and 146, as amended by Law No. 2,862 of September 4, 1956, Art. 27.

[59] As regulated in Reg. Art. 102; see footnote 20 under 11/3.3a.

for the first month or fraction thereof and 1% for each following month of the delay. If, however, it is disclosed in proceedings against the withholding agent that the latter deducted the tax when remitting or crediting the income to the party entitled thereto without turning it over to the government, the penalty is at least 50%.[60] If the withholding agent does not report the income subject to withholding or reports it inaccurately, the penalties listed at 13/7.6 apply in addition to the delay penalty (Law No. 2,862 of September 4, 1956, Art. 28).

In the case of the sale of real property by an individual, the taxpayer's failure to file the required proof regarding the sales price, cost, expenses, and improvements within the time limit set by the law[61] results in a penalty, whether or not a gain was realized on the sale. If the sale did not result in a gain, the penalty is Cr$ 200 to Cr$ 2,000; otherwise, the delay penalty of 10% for the first month and 1% for each month thereafter applies.[62]

13/7.4 Failure to Maintain or Produce Proper Books and Records

a. BOOKS AND RECORDS IMPROPERLY MAINTAINED.   Brazilian companies or the local branches or agencies of foreign entities which fail to keep their books in the language and currency of the country and in the form pre-scribed by the commercial and fiscal law, or which violate any other of the rules of Art. 34 of the Income Tax Regulations are subject to a fine of between Cr$ 500 and Cr$ 5,000 (Reg. Art. 143[a]).

The Income Tax Regulations include detailed provisions,[63] applicable to Brazilian entities and to the Brazilian branches of foreign entities with capital in excess of Cr$ 50,000, governing the individual books to be kept, their registration and authentication by the competent authorities, and the valuation of inventories (6/5.1). A violation of these rules results in fines ranging between Cr$ 5,000 and Cr$ 20,000 (Reg. Art. 149[d]).

b. FAILURE TO FILE REQUIRED INFORMATION.   The failure of an entity to file its balance sheet, statement of profit and loss, or other accounting information with the return, as required by law,[64] results in a fine of between Cr$ 50 to Cr$ 500, if the return is filed by mail.[65]

c. REFUSAL TO PRODUCE BOOKS.   If the taxpayer refuses to produce his books for examination, or otherwise attempts to obstruct the action of the government, the penalty amounts to between Cr$ 2,000 and Cr$ 50,-000 (Reg. Art. 149[b]). A penalty equal to three times the amount of

---

[60] Reg. Art. 147(e). The fine is 50% unless the delay penalty is higher, in which case this latter penalty will be applied.

[61] These rules were discussed in detail in 9/8.2d.

[62] Reg. Art. 147, as amended by Law No. 2,862 of September 4, 1956, Art. 27.

[63] Art. 141; see 6/2.1–6/2.2.

[64] Reg. Art. 38.

[65] Reg. Art. 144(d).

the tax evaded is imposed if the incorrectness of the books or financial statements is established in the course of the tax examination.[66]

13/7.5 Failure of the Taxpayer to File the Proper Return

The following violations result in a penalty of 100% of the deficiency:[67]

1. In the case of an individual taxpayer, the failure to include income from all sources in one return (Reg. Art. 65);
2. The filing of separate returns by a married couple where a joint return is required under Reg. Art. 67;
3. In the case of an entity (or the Brazilian branch of a foreign entity) which centralizes the accounting of its affiliates or which incorporates the business results of these affiliates in its own accounting system, the failure to include all income of the group in one return as required by Reg. Art. 69.

13/7.6 Penalties in the Case of Assessment ex officio

The penalty is from Cr$ 50 to Cr$ 200 in the case of an individual taxpayer able to demonstrate that his net annual income is not in excess of Cr$ 60,000 or of an entity which can explain, within the proper time, that it has not realized profits computed in accordance with the Income Tax Regulations (Reg. Art. 145[a]). Otherwise, the following penalties apply, computed in terms of the unpaid amount of the tax (Reg. Art. 145):

1. 10% if a taxpayer, acting in good faith, has claimed deductions or abatements to which he is not entitled.
2. 30% if a taxpayer called upon to give information,[68] without being informed of the contents of the government record, furnishes satisfactory explanations or declares an income at least equal to the amount already known to the fiscal authorities.
3. 50% if a taxpayer does not respond to a request for information under Reg. Art. 78, or fails to submit satisfactory explanations, or does not declare all his income.

13/7.7 Fraud Penalty

The penalty is 300% of the deficiency in every case where it is evident that the taxpayer acted with fraudulent intent (Reg. Art. 145[e]).

[66] Reg. Art. 149(c). The amount of this fine is equal to that of the fraud penalty under Reg. Art. 145(e), discussed in 13/7.7 below. The wording of Art. 149(c) ("the tax evaded") indicates that this provision, like Art. 145(e), presupposes fraudulent intent.

[67] Reg. Art. 144(c). The deficiency is computed by consolidating the various returns improperly filed into one return.

[68] Reg. Art. 78.

PART III

ANALYSIS OF OTHER TAXES

This part analyzes certain taxes other than the income tax. A summary description of these taxes is included in Part I. In this volume Part III includes the new excess profits tax, sales and excise taxes, stamp taxes, and certain local taxes on business and real property transfers.

CHAPTER 14

THE EXCESS PROFITS TAX

14/1. **In General**

14/2. **The Taxpayer**

14/3. **Income Subject to Excess Profits Tax**

14/4. **The Excess Profits Credit**

    14/4.1   Invested Capital

    14/4.2   Increases of Invested Capital — In General

    14/4.3   Revaluation of Fixed Assets and the Special Tax Thereon

    14/4.4   Capitalization of Reserves and the Special Tax Thereon

    14/4.5   Income Tax Effects of the Revaluation of Assets and the Capitalization of Reserves

14/5. **Computation of the Excess Profits Tax**

    14/5.1   Regular Method of Computation

         a. General Rule

         b. Limitation

    14/5.2   Optional Methods of Computing the Tax

         a. Average Income Method

         b. Percentage of Gross Income Method

    14/5.3   Addition to the Tax

14/6. **Special Types of Taxpayers**

    14/6.1   Commercial Representatives and Enterprises Formed by Brokers, Commission Agents, or Journalists

    14/6.2   Building and Construction Companies

14/7.   Returns and Payment of the Tax
14/8.   Administration of the Tax

14/1.   In General

An excess profits tax was in effect in Brazil from 1944 through 1947.[1] The tax was reintroduced in modified form by Law No. 2,862 of September 4, 1956.[2] Regulations to this law were issued under Decree No. 40,384 of November 19, 1956.[3] The new tax is, like its predecessor, in the nature of an income tax,[4] and it is collected in addition to the regular income tax on business profits under Art. 44 of the Income Tax Regulations (7/1.1). The effective period of the tax is limited to taxable years 1957 through 1960 (base years 1956 through 1959)[5] (Law Art. 1).

In addition to the excess profits tax, the new law also introduced special temporary taxes on increases of capital resulting from the revaluation of certain fixed assets and the capitalization of reserves, provided that these increases were made on or before October 31, 1956. These taxes are discussed in connection with the excess profits credit, i.e., the portion of income which is not subject to excess profits tax (14/4.). It should be understood, however, that a corporation or other entity is free at any time to reappraise its fixed assets or to capitalize its reserves; the resulting increases in capital constitute taxable income both to the entity and to its shareholders, and they are taxed at ordinary income tax rates.[6] The special taxes imposed on the same increases under the new law are in lieu of and considerably lower than the regular income tax, whose rates are 15% on the first Cr$ 500,000 of taxable income and 20% on the excess. The significance of the new law is therefore not to create new possibilities for increasing capital, nor to limit such increases to a reappraisal of assets or a capitalization of reserves under its provisions, but to offer incentive tax rates for making these increases during the limited period from September 4 to October 31, 1956. Apparently, one objective was to obtain immediate revenue from increases in capital

---

[1] Decree-law No. 6,224 of January 24, 1944; regulations issued under Decree No. 15,028 of March 13, 1944, modified by Decree-law No. 9,159 of April 10, 1946. The 1946 law changed the name of the tax from *impôsto de lucros extraordinários* (tax on extraordinary profits) to *impôsto adicional de renda* (additional income tax).

[2] *Diário Oficial* of September 5, 1956. This law is referred to hereinafter as "Law."

[3] *Diário Oficial* of November 20, 1956. This decree is referred to hereinafter as "EPT Reg."

[4] The official name of the new tax is *impôsto adicional sôbre os lucros das pessoas jurídicas em relação ao capital aplicado* (additional tax on profits of juridical persons in relation to invested capital).

[5] For an explanation of the terms "taxable year" and "base year," see 6/3.1.

[6] See discussion at 7/6.2 (tax on entity); 9/2.1d3 (tax on holders of nominative securities); 9/2.2b2 (tax on holders of bearer securities).

thus induced; on the other hand, the yield of the excess profits tax itself is reduced.

14/2. The Taxpayer

The excess profits tax is imposed on "juridical persons" whose taxable income during the base year (14/3.) is Cr$ 300,000 or more. As stated at 2/4.1, the term "juridical persons" (entities) refers to all resident business enterprises regardless of their legal form of organization, and includes sole proprietorships, partnerships, and the Brazilian branch of a foreign corporation or other entity (see also 5/3.4; 11/3.3) (Law Art. 2; EPT Reg. Arts. 1, 5).

The following are exempt from the excess profits tax:

1. Enterprises whose taxable income during the base year (14/3.) is less than Cr$ 300,000 (Law Art. 7; EPT Reg. Art. 5).
2. The civil societies of physicians, lawyers, accountants, etc., described at 12/2.6 (Law Art. 11; EPT; Reg. Art. 5).
3. Enterprises which are exempt from income tax under Arts. 28 and 30 of the Income Tax Regulations (5/6.) (EPT Reg. Art. 6).

14/3. Income Subject to Excess Profits Tax

Taxable income, for purposes of the excess profits tax, is the same as taxable income for purposes of the income tax on business profits discussed in Chapter 7.[7] It is, therefore, identical with the book profits of the base year [8] as adjusted for income tax purposes (7/6.; 7/7.), and without further adjustments for purposes of the excess profits tax. It follows that foreign income is not subject to excess profits tax, and that in the case of activities exercised partly in Brazil and partly abroad, only the portion of the total profit which is allocable to Brazilian sources is included in the tax base (Reg. Art. 35, discussed at 11/2.3; EPT Reg. Art. 6).

The profits on which the tax is computed may be either "actual," "presumed," or "estimated" (Law Art. 3; EPT Reg. Art. 12).[9]

As stated at 7/2.7, the book profits of the base year are reduced by the income tax on business profits paid during that year, and the same would seem to be true for the excess profits tax which, by statutory definition, is in the nature of an additional income tax.

---

[7] Law Art. 3 Sole §. The same rule applied under the prior excess profits tax law; see Rezende, *Impôsto de Lucros Extraordinários* (Rio de Janerio, 1946), pp. 48 *et seq.*

[8] The "base year" or income year may be either the calendar year or a fiscal year (6/3.1) (Law Art. 3).

[9] For an explanation of these terms, see 7/1.1, 6/9.1, 6/9.2. Law Art. 3 speaks only of "actual" and "presumed" profits. EPT Reg. Art. 12 corrected an obvious omission of the law (and at the same time widened its scope) by adding "estimated" profits.

For purposes of the excess profits tax, taxable income as defined above is measured in terms of the taxpayer's invested capital. Only the portion of income which exceeds 30% of the invested capital is subject to excess profits tax. The tax-free portion of income (called "basic profit" in EPT Reg. Art. 13) is hereinafter referred to as the excess profits credit and its computation is discussed at 14/4.

14/4.   The Excess Profits Credit

There are three methods of computing the excess profits credit of the taxpayer, i.e., the amount of its "basic" profits (14/3.) which are not subject to excess profits tax. In the usual case, the credit is computed at 30% of the invested capital as described at 14/4.1. There are, in addition, two optional methods of computing the credit (average income method and percentage of gross income method) which are discussed at 14/5.2. Regarding discretionary increases of the excess profits credit of commercial representatives and certain other taxpayers, see 14/6.1.

14/4.1   Invested Capital

Invested capital consists of the paid-in capital (i.e., the par or nominal value of fully paid-in shares or participations, or the paid-in capital of a partnership or sole proprietorship) and reserves in the technical sense of the term which excludes "provisions" (6/6.1) but includes undistributed profits (Law Art. 4; EPT Reg. Art. 16).[10] The various items of which invested capital is composed are prorated according to the portion of the base year during which they were in existence and entered in the books (Law Art. 4 §2; EPT Reg. Art. 16 §2).[11] This rule applies, in taxable year 1957, to increases in invested capital made during base year 1956 through the revaluation of fixed assets under the temporary provisions of the law (14/4.3).

Borrowed capital does not form part of the invested capital on which the excess profits credit is computed under the present law.[12]

---

[10] Reserves balancing investments in the shares of corporations or parts of other entities were disallowed in computing the invested capital of the taxpayer under the previous excess profits tax law. Although a similar provision was deleted from the draft of Law No. 2,862, it can be assumed that the same interpretation will be applied under the new excess profits tax.

[11] Whether undistributed profits accruing during the base year can be included in invested capital was doubtful under the previous excess profits tax law which also required an allocation. The Excess Profits Tax Council allowed inclusion of the profits on a monthly basis, unless the entire amount thereof was credited or distributed to the partners or shareholders in the closing balance sheet for the year, in which case the required allocation was deemed to have been made as of that date. The Income Tax Division, on the other hand, disallowed the inclusion of undistributed profits of the base year altogether. There is no reference to this question in the present law or its regulations.

[12] This constitutes an important departure from the previous excess profits tax

The method of computing the excess profits credit of the Brazilian branch of a foreign entity cannot be adequately determined at the present time.[13]

14/4.2   Increases of Invested Capital — In General

Law No. 2,862 establishes preferential tax rates of 10% on surplus from the revaluation of certain fixed assets and of 12% on reserves which are capitalized, provided that these increases in capital became effective on or before October 31, 1956.[14] The increases become effective, in the case of a corporation, when approved by the general meeting of shareholders; in the case of a sole proprietorship, with the entry of the transaction in the books of account.[15] The required filing and registration of the changes with the Commercial Registry may be performed after October 31, 1956 (Law. Art. 5 §4; Decree Art. 9).[16]

14/4.3   Revaluation of Fixed Assets and the Special Tax Thereon

Only fixed assets acquired on or before December 31, 1950, could be revalued. The revaluation was performed by multiplying the original cost of the asset (before depreciation) by the following "coefficients" or index numbers (Law Art 5[a]; Decree Art. 1):

under Decree-laws No. 6,224 and 9,159 (footnote 1) which permitted the inclusion of 30% of the amount of loans received and owed by the taxpayer during the base year. Thus, a loan of Cr$ 1,000,000 taken up on January 1 and repaid on June 30 increased the excess profits credit by one half of Cr$ 300,000, or Cr$ 150,000. Dividends declared but unpaid and profit shares credited to partners but not withdrawn were considered as loans. There is no comparable provision in the present excess profits tax law or regulations.

[13] As stated at 6/6.1, the unincorporated branch of a foreign entity is not considered capable of having reserves of its own for purposes of the income tax under Reg. Art. 97. Following the same theory, it was held by the Income Tax Division and the Excess Profits Tax Council under the prior excess profits tax law that the invested capital of the branch consisted exclusively of its paid-in capital, i.e., the portion of the entire capital of the foreign firm which was allocated to its Brazilian branch as required by Art. 65 Sole § of the Corporation Law; this was, in the usual case, only a nominal amount. An express provision to the same effect was included in the original draft of Law No. 2,862, but later deleted from the bill. The question referred to, therefore, appears entirely open at present, as is the further one whether undistributed profits of the branch are counted in computing its excess profits credit.

[14] The temporary provisions of Law No. 2,862 relating to the revaluation of assets and the capitalization of reserves have been the object of regulations issued under Decree No. 39,995 of September 13, 1956 (published in the *Diário Oficial* of the same date). They are referred to hereinafter as "Decree."

[15] Since a sole proprietorship cannot have reserves or surplus in the technical sense of the term (6/6.1), these entities can increase their capital through a revaluation of fixed assets but not through the capitalization of reserves. The same applies to branches of foreign corporations or other entities; their revaluation of assets must be approved by the foreign head office.

[16] The same is probably true of the required government approval of an increase in the capital of the Brazilian branch of a foreign entity (Corp. Law Arts. 61 §5, 64).

For assets acquired	in or	before	1929 [17]				10
"	"	"	from	1930	through	1934	9
"	"	"	"	1935	"	1937	8
"	"	"	"	1938	"	1939	7
"	"	"	"	1940	"	1942	6
"	"	"	"	1943	"	1944	5
"	"	"	"	1945	"	1946	4
"	"	"	"	1947	"	1948	3
"	"	"	"	1949	"	1950	2

The surplus arising from the revaluation is added to the invested capital and increases the excess profits credit. If the fixed assets, or any part thereof, were previously reappraised under the rule of an older income tax law (7/6.2), only the excess of the present revaluation over the previous revaluation may be added to invested capital, in order to prevent a duplication of the credit (Law Art. 5[c]; Decree Art. 1 §3). The taxpayer is not permitted to compute depreciation or amortization on the increase in the book value of the reappraised assets for income and excess profits tax purposes, and he must always show the amount of the increase separately in his books of account (Law Art. 5[e]; Decree Art. 1 §4).

The revaluation surplus [18] is subject to a special tax of 10%, increased by an addition of 15% of the tax in the nature of a compulsory refundable loan (12/2.4a) (Law Art. 15; Decree Art. 13). The tax is imposed on the business enterprise whose assets are revalued and it is in lieu of all income taxes ordinarily imposed both on the enterprise and on its owners, partners, or shareholders in connection with a revaluation of assets [19] (Law Arts. 2, 5 §9; Decree Art. 1). If the assets were reappraised under an older income tax law, only the difference between such prior revaluation and a revaluation conducted under the new law is covered by its provisions (Law Art. 5[c] and Decree Art. 1 §3). The assets are reappraised by applying the coefficients listed above to their original cost and the result of the prior revaluation is deducted from the present reappraised value. The effect of this method is shown by the following examples.

[17] Law Art. 5(a) lists assets acquired *prior to* 1929, and Decree Art. 1, assets acquired *until* 1929. However, it was obviously not intended to leave out assets acquired in 1929.
[18] Revaluation surplus is equal to the reappraised value of the asset (cost multiplied by the appropriate coefficient), less original cost (Decree Art. 1 §1).
[19] These taxes are: the business income tax under Reg. Art. 44 on the entity whose fixed assets are reappraised (7/6.2); the complementary tax under Reg. Art. 8(d) on the owners, partners, or shareholders if the shares or participations are nominative, whether or not the increase in value is distributed in the form of a stock dividend (9/2.1d3); and the withholding tax on the shareholders under Reg. Art. 96(3)(c) in the case of bearer shares (9/2.2b2).

Example 1

Revaluation under Law No. 2,862 (original cost of the asset x coefficient, less original cost)	Cr$ 2,000
Prior revaluation	1,500
Permissible present revaluation, both for purposes of increasing the excess profits credit and of the special 10% tax	Cr$ 500

Example 2

Revaluation under Law No. 2,862 (as above)	Cr$ 2,000
Prior revaluation	2,000
Permissible present revaluation (as above)	None

Example 3

Revaluation under Law No. 2,862 (as above)	Cr$ 2,000
Prior revaluation	2,500
Permissible present revaluation (as above)	None

The special tax of 10% also applies to increases in capital through the capitalization of reserves which originated from the revaluation of assets made under Decree-law No. 9,407 of June 27, 1946, or under Art. 43 §1(h)(I) of the present Income Tax Regulations (Law Art. 5[d]; Decree Art. 1 §2). As explained at 7/6.2, revaluations under Decree-law No. 9,407 were tax-free, while those made under Reg. Art. 43 §1(h)(I) are subject to income tax at ordinary rates, with an option to defer payment of the tax for four years. Under the new provisions, the capitalization of these reserves is taxed under the rules applying to revaluations of assets, i.e., at the rate of 10%, and not under the rules which apply generally to the capitalization of reserves (14/4.4), i.e., at the rate of 12%, for the reason that these reserves have their origin in a revaluation of assets. The cited provisions are intended to offer an incentive, in the form of the lower 10% tax rate as against the ordinary income tax rates, to capitalize before November 1, 1956, certain reserves which were either formed tax-free or on which payment of the income tax was deferred.[20]

The 10% tax is payable over three years. The first installment amounts to 30% of the tax and is due within one month from the date on which the

20 The reserves in question are the following:

1. Reserves which were formed tax-free through a revaluation of assets under Decree-law No. 9,407. These reserves were immediately taxable to the shareholders (as a constructive dividend) but they became taxable income of the corporation or other entity (at ordinary income tax rates) only upon their capitalization or actual distribution, for which no time limit was set under Decree-law No. 9,407.
2. Reserves which were formed through a revaluation of assets under the present Income Tax Regulations, in exercise of the option offered by Reg. Art. 43 §1(h)(I) to defer payment of the income tax by both the corporation and the shareholders for up to four years. The new provisions are aimed at persuading corporations to waive the privilege of deferring payment of the balance of the tax in return for a special tax rate of 10%.

revaluation became effective (14/4.2). The balance is payable in equal installments during the following 35 months, i.e., at the monthly rate of 2% of the tax, or 0.2% of the taxable revaluation surplus (Law Art. 5 §§2[a], 4; Decree Art. 8[a]).

It appears that the 10% tax is deductible in computing business profits for purposes of the income tax and the excess profits tax.[21]

The benefit of the special tax of 10% is forfeited, and the regular income taxes both on the entity and on its owners, partners, or shareholders are imposed in the following situations.

1. If the entity, within three years from the date of revaluation, reduces its capital or is merged or consolidated with another firm or dissolved, except in the cases of death (of an individual owner) or bankruptcy (Law Art. 5 §§1, 6; Decree Art. 2).

2. If the first installment of the tax is not paid within the prescribed time (Law Art. 5 §6; Decree Art. 10).

3. If payment of any subsequent installment of the tax is delayed for more than four months, except if the taxpayer is absolutely unable to pay the tax (Law Art. 5 §5; Decree Art. 10 Sole §).[22] If the delay in payment does not exceed four months, the usual penalties for late payment (13/7.2) apply.

4. If the ownership of the reappraised assets is transferred within five years from the date of revaluation, except in the cases of death or bankruptcy (see [1] above) (Law Art. 5 §7; Decree Art. 3).

The special tax does not apply to the extent that the shares of the company whose assets are reappraised are owned by a government (federal, state, or municipal) or by an *autarquia*[23] (Law Art. 5 §10; Decree Art. 5).

14/4.4 Capitalization of Reserves and the Special Tax Thereon

Invested capital may be increased by the capitalization of reserves (appropriations of surplus) which were formed on or before December 31, 1955 (Law Art. 5; Decree Art. 4). The resulting increase in capital is subject to a special tax of 12% imposed on the entity in lieu of all income taxes for which the partners or shareholders would otherwise be liable as a result of a capitalization of reserves[24] (Law Art. 5[b] and §9;

[21] Law Art. 5 §3 merely states that the 12% tax on the capitalization of reserves (14/4.4) is *not* deductible. The various installments of the 10% tax are apparently deductible in the base years during which they are paid (7/2.7).

[22] This inability must be recognized by the Ministry of Finance whose decision is final. The Ministry may, in cases of this kind, authorize a limitation of the increase in capital in proportion to the tax already paid.

[23] I.e., government agencies with independent administration and finances, such as the Brazilian Coffee Institute, the various social security institutions, etc.

[24] These taxes are listed in footnote 19 above. Since reserves in the technical sense are tax-paid amounts, the question of an imposition of the business income tax on the entity does not arise.

Decrees Arts. 6, 7). The 12% tax discussed here is not deductible in computing taxable income for income and excess profits tax purposes (Law Art. 5 §3; Decree Art. 4 §2). The 15% addition in the nature of a compulsory refundable loan applies to this 12% tax (Law Art. 15).

The tax is paid in 30 monthly installments. The first installment, amounting to one third of the tax (or 4% of the capitalized reserves) is due within one month from the date on which the capitalization of reserves became effective (14/4.2). The balance is payable in 29 equal monthly installments (Law Art. 5 §2[b]; Decree Art. 8[b]). Nonpayment of the first installment within the prescribed time or a delay of more than four months in the payment of any subsequent installment results in the imposition of the regular income tax on the shareholders or partners in lieu of the 12% tax on the entity; a delay of less than four months entails the usual penalties for late payment (Law Art. 5 §§4, 5; Decree Art. 10).

The special tax does not apply if and to the extent that the shares (if nominative) or participations of the entity are held by an organization which is exempt from income tax under Reg. Art. 28 (5/6.), by a government (federal, state, or municipal), or by an *autarquia* [25] (Law Art. 5 §§8, 10; Decree Art. 4 §1, Art. 5).

14/4.5   Income Tax Effects of the Revaluation of Assets and the Capitalization of Reserves

If an entity (corporation, limited liability company, partnership, etc.) holds shares or participations of another entity which reappraises its assets or capitalizes reserves under the provisions discussed at 14/4.3 and 14/4.4, the capital of both entities is equally increased. An increase in the assets and capital of the investing company usually results from the distribution of new shares or participations by the entity which revalues its assets or capitalizes its reserves.

According to Law Art. 5 §9 and Decree Art. 6, no income tax [26] is imposed in connection with the transactions referred to either on the investing company or on its shareholders or partners. The effect of this important provision which enlarges the field of tax-free transactions under existing income tax law may be illustrated by the following example.

Example 4

Company A is a shareholder (or partner) of Company B, which increases its capital through a revaluation of fixed assets or the capitalization of reserves under the provisions of Law No. 2,862. Company B distributes new

[25] See footnote 23.
[26] I.e., any of the various forms of income tax imposed under the Income Tax Regulations, including the schedular and complementary income tax on individuals, the income tax on the business profits of entities, and the withholding tax on both individuals and entities.

shares (or participations) to Company A equivalent to the amount by which its capital has been increased. Company A now increases its own capital by an amount equal to the par value of the new shares (or participations) received from Company B, and in turn issues new shares of its own stock to its shareholders.

The par value of the new shares received from Company B is not taxable income to Company A. This follows from the rule of Art. 43 §2(c) or (d) of the Income Tax Regulations (depending on whether the shares received from Company B are nominative or bearer shares), as explained in detail at 7/7.1 and 7/7.2. In this respect, Law No. 2,862 adds nothing to the older provisions.

In addition, the increase in Company A's capital and the distribution of its shares do not result in taxable income either to Company A or to its shareholders. To this extent the new provisions modify the rules of the Income Tax Regulations discussed at 7/6.1, 9/2.1c, and 9/2.2e.

14/5.   Computation of the Excess Profits Tax

14/5.1   Regular Method of Computation

a. GENERAL RULE. The tax is graduated according to the proportion existing between the "excess" profits (i.e., the portion of profits which exceeds the excess profits credit) and the "basic" profits (i.e., the amount equivalent to the excess profits credit).[27]

The tax rates are listed in the following table (Law Art. 8; EPT Reg. Art. 17).

Percentage which excess profits are of basic profits	Tax Rate
Not more than 50%	20%
More than 50%, but not more than 100%	30%
More than 100%, but not more than 200%	40%
More than 200%	50%

Example 5

The "actual profits" of a taxpayer for base year 1956 (as adjusted for purposes of the income tax on business profits under Reg. Art. 44) are Cr$ 500,000 and its excess profits credit (including increases on account of a revaluation of fixed assets and the capitalization of reserves), Cr$ 70,000. The excess profits tax amounts to Cr$ 190,500, computed as follows:

Taxable income for income tax purposes	Cr$ 500,000
Less: Excess profits credit	70,000
Income subject to excess profits tax	Cr$ 430,000

[27] Assume that the invested capital of the taxpayer is Cr$ 1,000,000 and its business profits (as adjusted for income tax purposes) are Cr$ 325,000. The excess profits credit is Cr$ 300,000 (30% of Cr$ 1,000,000). Of the total profits, Cr$ 300,000 are "basic" and Cr$ 25,000 are subject to excess profits tax.

Tax on Cr\$ 35,000 (first 50% of basic profits)   at 20% Cr\$ 7,000
"   "   35,000 (50%–100% of basic profits)   at 30%   10,500
"   "   70,000 (100%–200% of basic profits) at 40%   28,000
"   "   290,000 (excess over 200% of basic
                              profits) at 50%   145,000
                  Excess profits tax   Cr\$ 190,500

b. LIMITATION. Law Art. 7 Sole § and EPT Reg. Art. 18 state, in effect, that if the net income of the base year exceeds Cr\$ 300,000, but is reduced to an amount below that figure after deducting the excess profits tax computed thereon, the tax shall not be greater than the difference between the amount of net income (computed without deducting the excess profits tax applicable thereto) and Cr\$ 300,000. The effect of this rule is illustrated by the following example.

Example 6
The same facts as in Example 5, except that the excess profits credit is Cr\$ 30,000. The excess profits tax on Cr\$ 470,000 (before application of the limitation) amounts to Cr\$ 224,500, computed as follows:
Tax on Cr\$ 15,000 (first 50% of basic profits)   at 20% Cr\$ 3,000
"   "   15,000 (50%–100% of basic profits)   at 30%   4,500
"   "   30,000 (100%–200% of basic profits) at 40%   12,000
"   "   410,000 (excess over 200% of basic
                              profits) at 50%   205,000
        Excess profits tax, before limitation   Cr\$ 224,500

The tax as thus computed reduces net income to Cr\$ 275,500 (Cr\$ 500,-000 less Cr\$ 224,500), i.e., an amount of less than Cr\$ 300,000.
In this case, the tax is reduced by Cr\$ 24,500 (Cr\$ 300,000 less Cr\$ 275,-500), so that the excess profits tax payable amounts to Cr\$ 200,000.

14/5.2 Optional Methods of Computing the Tax

In the discretion of the taxpayer, the income subject to excess profits tax may be computed under one of the following two alternative methods.[28]

a. AVERAGE INCOME METHOD. Under the average income method, the income subject to excess profits tax is equal to the excess of actual business profits during the base year over twice the amount of the average profits of the three-year period from base year 1947 to base year 1949 [29] (Law Art. 6, EPT Reg. Art. 13 §2).

b. PERCENTAGE OF GROSS INCOME METHOD. Under the percentage of gross income method, the income subject to excess profits tax is equal to the

[28] The election made by the taxpayer is effective and irrevocable only for the taxable year for which it is made (EPT Reg. Art. 13 §4).
[29] I.e., taxable years 1948 through 1950; see footnote 8.

excess of actual business profits during the base year over the following percentages of gross income [30] during that base year (Law Art. 6; EPT Reg. Art. 13 §3).

6% of gross income up to Cr$ 3,500,000.

5% on the portion of gross income exceeding Cr$ 3,500,000 but not exceeding Cr$ 5,000,000.

4% on the portion of gross income exceeding Cr$ 5,000,000.

14/5.3   Addition to the Tax

The excess profits tax is increased by an addition in the nature of a compulsory refundable loan amounting to 15% of the tax (12/1.3b).

14/6.   Special Types of Taxpayers

14/6.1   Commercial Representatives and Enterprises Formed by Brokers, Commission Agents, or Journalists

Commercial representatives and companies formed by brokers, commission agents, or by journalists may separate their profits as between those which are attributable to capital and those which result from personal labor. If these taxpayers do not separate their profits, their excess profits credit may be increased up to 40% of the invested capital and the tax rates (14/5.) may be lowered to one half. Taxpayers' requests for an application of these provisions are decided upon by the Director of the Income Tax Division in the Ministry of Finance (Law Arts. 9, 13; EPT Reg. Arts. 19, 23).[31]

14/6.2   Building and Construction Companies

Under the rule of the Income Tax Regulations (Reg. Art. 56; see 6/4.2), the total profits of a firm engaged in construction work extending over more than one year (especially the building of railroads and highways) must be accrued in the year during which a particular job is completed. For excess profits tax purposes, however, the profits may be allocated to the years during which the work was done. The allocation is made on the basis of the expenses incurred in each of those years (Law Art. 10; EPT Reg. Art. 12 §1).[32]

[30] Gross income is the same as for purposes of the income tax (EPT Reg. Art. 13 §3; Income Tax Reg. Art. 40 §1), i.e., it includes the total income from transactions carried out for the taxpayer's own account and the amounts received for services rendered. Discounts and allowances are excluded from gross income.

[31] While Law No. 2,862 gives no indication regarding the criteria to be applied by the Ministry of Finance in the exercise of its discretion, this question may be clarified by future administrative rulings.

[32] The five-year periods of limitation on assessment and collection (13/6.) are not counted from the end of the year to which income is allocated nor from the due date of the income tax for that year (Law Art. 10, Sole §; EPT Reg. Art. 12 §2),

14/7.   Returns and Payment of the Tax

Excess profits tax returns must be prepared on the official forms issued by the Income Tax Division. The returns must be filed together with the taxpayer's income tax return on or before April 30 of each of the taxable years 1957 through 1960, except as noted below (EPT Reg. Art. 7):

1. An entity which is formed and liquidated in the course of the same taxable year (between 1957 and 1960) must file a return for the period during which it was in existence, if its taxable income during that period amounted to Cr$ 300,000 or more. Regarding the due date of the return, see 6/3.6 (EPT Reg. Art. 7 §1).
2. An entity which is dissolved during one of the taxable years 1957 through 1960 must file a return for the period from the beginning of the year until the date of dissolution, if its taxable income during that period amounted to Cr$ 300,000 or more.[33] The return is due within 30 days from the date on which the liquidation was terminated (EPT Reg. Art. 7 §2).
3. The rules set forth under (2) apply in the case of a change in the taxpayer's accounting period (6/3.) with respect to the period (of more or less than 12 months) between the date of the balance sheet accompanying the last income tax return filed and the most recent balance sheet prepared, if the taxable income for that period amounted to Cr$ 300,000 or more (EPT Reg. Art. 4).

One single extension of time of not more than 60 days for filing the return may be granted by the Income Tax Division upon application if the taxpayer was prevented by circumstances beyond its control from filing the return within the prescribed time (EPT Reg. Art. 7 §3). Otherwise, a return will be accepted after April 30 only if the taxpayer has not been notified that an assessment ex officio (14/8.; 13/2.2) has been initiated (EPT Reg. Art. 7 §4).

If the tax for the year amounts to Cr$ 5,000 or less, it must be paid in one amount at the time the return is filed.[34] Otherwise, payment may be made in four equal installments under the rules set forth at 13/1.2b; the discounts for early payment of the tax do not apply (EPT Reg. Art. 20).

14/8.   Administration of the Tax

The substantive and procedural rules of the Income Tax Regulations, including those on penalties, apply to the excess profits tax (Law Art.

but apparently from the end of the year which is the taxable year for income tax purposes.

[33] This return must be filed in addition to the excess profits tax return covering the preceding (base) year.

[34] Payment of the excess profits tax in one amount is also required if the tax is assessed ex officio and in respect of the final tax of a dissolved entity (EPT Reg. Art. 20).

14, EPT Reg. Art. 31). The first administrative decision on taxpayers' requests for rulings is rendered by the Director of the Income Tax Division in the Ministry of Finance. The rules on protests and appeals set forth at 13/4. apply (Law Arts. 13, 14). The provisions on assessments "ex officio" (EPT Reg. Arts. 9–11) are substantially the same as those set forth at 13/2.2.

As a result of the reintroduction of the excess profits tax, certain changes in the organization of the administrative tribunals became necessary. The First Council of Taxpayers (Tax Court) now consists of two divisions.[35] The jurisdiction of the first division includes all controversies relating to the income tax, the excess profits tax,[36] and all other additional income taxes. Other matters formerly within the jurisdiction of the First Council of Taxpayers are referred to its second division (Law Art. 16).

[35] Each division is composed of six members who are appointed as explained at 13/4.3.

[36] I.e., the new excess profits tax introduced by Law No. 2,862 and the older tax referred to at 14/1. Pending controversies under the older excess profits tax laws are decided by the Tax Court, and the former Excess Profits Tax Council (*Junta de Ajuste de Lucros*) is abolished. In respect of the older excess profits tax, the decisions of the Tax Court (like those of its predecessor) are not open to administrative appeal (Law Art. 16). The right of the taxpayer to appeal to the regular courts is, of course, preserved.

CHAPTER 15

SALES AND EXPORT TAXES

15/1. Background of the Sales Tax
    15/1.1   Scope of Chapter
    15/1.2   History of the Sales Tax
    15/1.3   Interstate Sales
          a. Constitutional Provisions
          b. Statutory Regulation

15/2. Taxpayer and Taxable Event
    15/2.1   Merchants and Producers
    15/2.2   Taxable Sale
    15/2.3   Extension of the Scope of the Sales Tax
    15/2.4   Sale and Delivery
    15/2.5   Exchanges
    15/2.6   Contributions to Capital
    15/2.7   Consignments
    15/2.8   Exemptions
          a. Minor Producers
          b. Cooperatives
          c. Exempt Transactions

15/3. Tax Base
    15/3.1   Gross Invoice Price
    15/3.2   Inclusion of Other Items in Tax Base
          a. Excise Tax
          b. Export Bonuses and Overprices

15/4. Tax Rates and Computation of the Tax
    15/4.1   In General
    15/4.2   Comparison of Rates
    15/4.3   Fees and Other Additions to Sales Taxes

15/5. Administration of the Tax
  15/5.1   Assessment
  15/5.2   Payment of Tax and Required Records
          a. Cash Sales
          b. Term Sales
          c. Common Requirements
  15/5.3   Refunds
  15/5.4   Fines

15/6. The Export Tax
  15/6.1   Description of the Export Tax
  15/6.2   Taxable Event
  15/6.3   Substitutes for the Export Tax

15/7. Concurrent Sales Taxes
  15/7.1   Constitutional Background
  15/7.2   The Transactions Tax

15/1. Background of the Sales Tax

15/1.1   Scope of Chapter

This chapter covers the general principles of the sales taxes, which are now state taxes imposed on commercial sales and certain other transactions, and the related state export taxes and transaction taxes.

15/1.2   History of the Sales Tax

The history of the sales tax is closely related to that of negotiable instruments. Prior to the enactment in 1908 of a federal statute on bills and notes, commercial invoices were generally treated as negotiable instruments. The new law, however, cast doubt on the qualification of invoices to serve as negotiable instruments. To remove this doubt, the Congress of Brazilian Chambers of Commerce proposed to the federal government legislation creating a peculiar type of negotiable instrument called the *duplicata,* to be issued by registered merchants in connection with any bill of sale payable 30, or more than 30, days from date. It also suggested that the government might use the *duplicata* as the vehicle for collecting a sales tax; by requiring each *duplicata* to carry stamps and by making correct stamping a prerequisite of negotiability, the government would, in effect, make each bearer of the instrument a controller of the tax. Both suggestions were eventually adopted, and the federal government was authorized in 1922 [1] to recognize commercial

[1] Law No. 4,625 of December 31, 1922.

invoices as negotiable instruments and to impose a tax on sales evidenced by these documents.

The sales tax remained a federal tax until 1934 when the Constitution of that year allocated it to the states as an "exclusive" tax (1/3.2), partly as compensation for reserving the income tax to the federal union.[2] The federal law [3] included, side by side, provisions of business law regulating the *duplicata* as a negotiable instrument and provisions of tax law regulating the sales tax. The former were retained in force by another federal statute [4] while the latter were abrogated as being no longer within the legislative domain of the federal union.[5]

15/1.3   Interstate Sales

As the history of sales tax indicates, it is now reserved to the states as an "exclusive" tax. The disadvantages of allocating the sales tax to the states are that the difference in tax rates from one state to another may act as a barrier to interstate commerce [6] and that the Brazilian states are sharply divided into producer states and consumer states.

a. CONSTITUTIONAL PROVISIONS.   Some remedy for these disadvantages is provided by a constitutional provision against rate discrimination as between sales of locally produced goods and those originally produced in other states, as well as between sales for local consumption and those made for shipment to other states.[7]

b. STATUTORY REGULATION.   The basic problem in interstate sales is, however, the conflict of laws between a producer state and a consumer state which both exert taxing power on the same transaction. A federal law [8] directed toward this problem states that when goods produced in one state are shipped to a branch or agent of the producer in another state to be sold there, the sales tax is due to the producer state at the time of shipment; any balance of tax due that arises from a markup of price when the goods are actually sold is also due to the producer state and not to the state where the sale took place. In spite of this law,

---

[2] Up to the Constitution of 1934, the income tax had been a "nonexclusive" tax which could be levied by the states. Actually there is no instance of a state income tax, at least in systematic form.

[3] Decree No. 22,061 of November 9, 1932.

[4] Law No. 187 of January 15, 1936.

[5] The tax provisions of Decree No. 22,061 remain in force, however, in the federal territories, where the tax is levied by the federal union.

[6] A national conference of State Secretaries of the Treasury achieved in 1940 a uniform rate agreement, observance of which was, however, short-lived and counteracted indirectly by local measures such as the institution of "additional rates" or of "fees" actually amounting to rate increases.

[7] Const., Art. 19, §5.

[8] Decree-law No. 915 of December 1, 1938.

consumer states have tried to impose the sales tax on every public sale made in their territory, regardless of the origin of the goods sold.

Certain states require payment of the sales tax on all merchandise, regardless of its origin, when it leaves the state's territory. This practice has been declared unconstitutional as extending the scope of the federal legislation which, as previously indicated, applies only to sales of state-produced goods.[9]

15/2. Taxpayer and Taxable Event

15/2.1 Merchants and Producers

Where sales tax is due, the seller is liable for the tax. To determine whether a sale is subject to the tax, one has to look at the characteristics of the seller, the nature of the sale, and, in some cases, the characteristics of the buyer.

The characteristics of the taxpayer are of importance in determining the imposition of the sales tax because earlier federal statutes specifically defined it as a tax on "mercantile" sales; and, according to Art. 191 of the Commercial Code of Brazil, a sale is mercantile when at least one of the parties to it is a registered merchant, the object of the sale is movable property,[10] and the purpose of the transaction from the point of view of the buyer is to resell the goods or to rent their use. The Constitution of 1934, when assigning the tax to the states, omitted any reference to the mercantile character of the sale, but spoke of a tax on "sales made by merchants or producers, including manufacturers." It appears from this language that the previous limitations on the scope of the tax still apply, at least in part.[11]

The sales tax is, therefore, applied whenever the seller is a merchant. The term "merchant" obviously includes manufacturers; the specific reference to manufacturers in the Constitution is therefore redundant. The reference to "producers," on the other hand, is intended to apply to activities other than mercantile activities, i.e., to agriculture and livestock raising.[12] Most states, however, also impose the sales tax on transactions

[9] Supreme Court, 105 *Revista Forense* 294 (1946); 100 *Arquivo Judiciário* 249 (1951).

[10] Brazilian business law does not govern transactions involving real (immovable) property which are, therefore, regulated by the Civil Code alone and are not regarded as mercantile. From the standpoint of taxation, moreover, sales of real property fall under a different specific tax, the transfer tax inter vivos. See Chapter 19.

[11] Similar language appears in Art. 19(IV) of the Constitution of 1946, which is presently in force.

[12] Agriculture and livestock raising are not regarded as mercantile activities for the purpose of other taxes such as the income tax (see 10/2.2a), provided the raw material is not purchased from third parties. As an example, a rancher selling his own native cattle is not a merchant, whereas an *invernista*, i.e., a rancher who does not breed cattle but merely buys, fattens and resells, is a merchant. São Paulo State

in which only the *buyer* is a merchant. The allegation that this application is unconstitutional because it converts a tax on sales into one on
purchases was rejected by the courts on the ground that purchase and
sale are parts of one and the same transaction.[13]

15/2.2 Taxable Sale

As indicated above, the definition of a sale for tax purposes is based
exclusively upon the characteristics of the parties to the transaction rather
than the purpose of the sale. Consequently, the purchase by a merchant
of articles not intended for resale (such as store fixtures, office furniture,
and the like) is subject to the tax, notwithstanding the fact that the transaction is not a mercantile one under business law. Conversely, all sales
made by a merchant, even if not in the regular course of his business, such
as sales of furniture, fixtures, delivery trucks, etc., are subject to the tax.
It should be noted that since a corporation (*sociedade anônima*) is defined by statute as a merchant whatever its object,[14] all sales of any
kind made by a corporation constitute mercantile transactions and are
therefore subject to the tax.[15]

In every case, however, the object of the sale must be movable property. Sales of real property are subject to a different tax (see Chapter
19) if either or both parties to the transaction are merchants.

15/2.3 Extension of the Scope of the Sales Tax

The more developed states often extend the scope of the sales tax to
transactions in which neither party is a merchant, manufacturer, or producer. Thus, the states of São Paulo and Rio Grande do Sul levy the
tax on sales of automobiles by private parties. The argument that such
sales are obviously not mercantile has been circumvented by describing
the tax on them either as a state stamp tax (17/3.3) or as a registration
fee.

The tax is also extended to cover contracts entered into by architects,
building contractors, and other taxpayers which provide for the render-

Board of Tax Appeals, 241 *Revista dos Tribunais* 681 (1955). The reference to
"producers," in the case of the sales tax, is intended to make both types of rancher
subject to the tax.

[13] The practice referred to in the text is obviously inspired by fiscal expediency,
since there can be no effective control unless the tax is collected from the party
who is a merchant, and therefore required to keep books. In these cases, the tax is
in effect borne by the seller, because the buyer will offer a proportionately reduced
price.

[14] Corp. Law Art. 2.

[15] São Paulo State Board of Tax Appeals, 236 *Revista dos Tribunais* 565 (1955);
São Paulo State Court of Appeals, 107 *Revista Forense* 302 (1946); different if the
corporation is a public utility company (interstate carrier), 212 *Revista dos Tribunais*
370 (1953).

ing of services combined with the supplying of materials. The Supreme Court has ruled that a building contract under which the builder supplies materials is a combination of a sale and a contract for services.[16] This decision has been variously interpreted by the states to imply that the sales tax can be collected either on the price of the materials alone or on the combined price of materials and services. The state of São Paulo has adopted a different approach to the question by instituting a specific tax called the transaction tax. This tax, whose rates are identical with those of the sales tax, falls on the price of services when these alone are supplied, as in the case of establishments which dye cloth for textile mills; if, however, materials are supplied along with the services, the tax is imposed on the combined price of both (15/7.2).

15/2.4 Sale and Delivery

Under the civil and commercial law of Brazil, a sale is an agreement for the transfer of property in consideration of a price expressed in money.[17] The essential point in this definition is that a sale is an executory contract in which the parties exchange mutual promises to transfer title to the property sold and to pay the price. Neither delivery nor payment is an element of the sales contract itself but merely its subsequent consummation.

For purposes of the sales tax, however, execution of the agreement through delivery of the goods sold is essential.[18]

Delivery of the goods includes constructive as well as actual delivery. Actual delivery exists if the goods are physically placed into the possession of the buyer. Constructive delivery, recognized by the Commercial Code, refers to acts which enable the buyer to acquire physical possession, such as the endorsement of a bill of lading or the handing over of the keys of the warehouse where the goods are deposited. The usual form of constructive delivery is the transmission by the vendor of a bill of sale; if the latter is not contested by the buyer within 10 days, delivery is presumed by law.[19]

[16] Supreme Court, 90 *Revista Forense* 387 (1942), 92 *Revista Forense* 94 (1942).

[17] Civil Code Art. 1,122; Commercial Code Art. 191.

[18] São Paulo State Board of Tax Appeals, 1951 *Revista Fiscal de São Paulo* No. 113; São Paulo State Court of Appeals, 221 *Revista dos Tribunais* 233 (1951). These decisions refer to sales agreements cancelled before delivery. Cancellation of a sale after delivery, according to the principle adopted by the courts, amounts to a resale and therefore, in theory at least, a second tax could be collected. Existing rulings, however, confine themselves to refusing refund of the tax paid on the cancelled sale, even though cancellation was freely decided by the parties instead of being an outcome of a court decision declaring the sales contract null and void; São Paulo State Board of Tax Appeals, 241 *Revista dos Tribunais* 678 (1955).

[19] Commercial Code, Art. 200. The provision states that the buyer must contest the bill of sale "immediately." The 10-day period referred to in the text is pro-

15/2.5 Exchanges

An exchange of goods between two merchants is defined [20] as a combination of two reciprocal sales in which each article exchanged constitutes the price for the other. On the basis of this provision, exchanges have been declared subject to the sales tax.[21]

15/2.6 Contributions to Capital

Whether a contribution of movable property to a corporation in exchange for its shares is subject to the sales tax is doubtful. The title to property contributed passes to the corporation;[22] the Constitution states expressly that the transfer tax falls on contributions of real property.[23] Acting on these premises, some states impose the sales tax on contributions of movable property in connection with the incorporation of an individual business or the transfer of stock in trade during a merger. The imposition of a sales tax in this situation has been held unconstitutional because the contribution of property in exchange for shares, although resulting in a change of ownership, is not a sale.[24] No similar objection arises, however, if the appraised value or market value of the property contributed exceeds the par value of the shares issued and the corporation pays an equalization price in cash to the contributor.[25]

15/2.7 Consignments

According to Art. 19(IV) of the Constitution the sales tax may be imposed on consignments. Brazilian commercial law and practice [26] recognize two types of consignment: "agency consignment" and "sales consignment." In the first, the agent sells to the customer in the name

vided by Art. 211 as an exception, applying only to cases in which the merchandise is delivered packed, crated, or otherwise under cover. Therefore, the 10-day period should be understood to run from actual delivery of the goods and not from constructive delivery through the issuance of the bill of sale. Common usage, however, extends this 10-day period to all cases. In tax practice, a sale is regarded as final if the merchandise is not returned, or if no objection to the bill of sale is raised by the buyer within 10 days from delivery of either the merchandise or the bill of sale.

[20] Commercial Code, Art. 221.

[21] Federal Tax Court, *Revista Fiscal* 1949, No. 30 (applying to the sales tax in the federal territories); São Paulo State Board of Tax Appeals, *Revista Fiscal de São Paulo* 1950, No. 131 (overruling an earlier decision of the Board, *id. No. 6*).

[22] Corp. Law, Art. 7.

[23] Const. Art. 19(III). See Chapter 19.

[24] São Paulo State Court of Appeals, 230 *Revista dos Tribunais* 207 (1954), 236 *Revista dos Tribunais* 214 (1955).

[25] São Paulo State Board of Tax Appeals, 228 *Revista dos Tribunais* 530 (1954).

[26] Commercial Code, Arts. 165 *et seq.*; Jorge Alberto Romeiro, opinion in 144 *Revista Forense* 84 (1952). Both types of consignment are regulated by the federal statute on *duplicatas*: Law No. 187 of January 15, 1936, Arts 8 and 9.

and for the account of the principal, and title to the goods passes directly from the principal to the customer. In the second, the consignee sells to the customer in his own name and for his own account, and title to the goods passes first from the consignor to the consignee and from him to the customer.

While the sales tax was a federal tax under the Constitution of 1891, which contained no express reference to consignments, it was accepted without dispute that only one sales tax was imposed on an agency consignment because there was only one sale. Two sales taxes were payable in the case of a sales consignment, however, because there were two sales: the "actual" sale by the consignee to the customer, and the "constructive" sale by the consignor to the consignee. This distinction has become doubtful since the Constitution of 1934 first introduced an express reference to consignments. Interpreting this reference to mean that consignments as such had become taxable transactions, it has been argued that a double sales tax may now be imposed also on agency consignments. The treatment of this matter is not uniform in state legislation and the administrative and judicial decisions are still in conflict.[27]

15/2.8 Exemptions

a. MINOR PRODUCERS. The Constitution provides for a general exemption from the sales tax for all sales or consignments effected by "minor producers" as defined by state legislation.[28] This relief applies only to producers as distinguished from merchants (15/2.1). State legislation usually defines "minor producers" in terms of annual gross turnover. Furthermore, sales of articles produced by private institutions for destitute or disabled persons, reform schools, and the like benefit from the general immunity granted by Art. 31 of the Constitution to charitable and educational institutions (1/3.5).

b. COOPERATIVES. State legislation is as a rule not liberal in granting exemptions in consideration of the circumstances of the taxpayer, an attitude which is prompted by the nature of the sales tax as a tax on the transaction and not on the person executing it. A disputed case is that of cooperative societies, to which a blanket exemption is granted by federal statute.[29] Most states have refused to apply the exemption, sometimes on the ground that a personal exemption is not applicable

---

[27] São Paulo State Board of Tax Appeals, 211 *Revista dos Tribunais* 598 (1953); Supreme Court, 88 *Arquivo Judiciário* 89 (1948) (not specific, but leading to the conclusion that two taxes are due only in the case of a "sales consignment").

[28] Const., Art. 19(IV).

[29] Decree No. 22,239 of December 19, 1932, as amended by Decree-laws No. 5,893 of October 19, 1943, and No. 8,401 of December 19, 1945.

to a tax on transactions, but more often by questioning the power of the federal government to grant exemptions from a state tax.[30] Another argument against the exemption[31] is that the cooperative society is actually not a taxpayer in its own right but merely a collecting agent for taxes which are owed by the producers or manufacturers of the goods sold by the cooperative.

c. EXEMPT TRANSACTIONS. The only exemption from sales tax based on the nature of the goods sold that is directly provided in Art. 31 of the Constitution is a general immunity from federal, state, and local taxation granted for paper used exclusively for printing newspapers, periodicals, and books. Under this provision, sales of printing paper are exempt from the sales tax.[32]

Other exemptions of the same nature granted by state legislation differ largely from one state to another. They cover sales of such essential commodities as food, medicines, and clothing, and they are usually restricted to the first sale by the producer or manufacturer, or to retail sales below a certain price.

Sales of bonds, shares of stock, and securities in general are specifically exempt from the sales tax under most state statutes, except for securities which represent title to merchandise, such as warehouse receipts and similar certificates of ownership. It could be argued that the sales tax would not be due on such transactions even in the absence of a specific statutory exemption, because contracts by which the ownership of securities is transferred are regarded under Brazilian law as assignments rather than sales[33] and as such subject to the federal stamp tax (17/2.6).

[30] São Paulo State Court of Appeals, 236 *Revista dos Tribunais* 273 (1955), 237 *Revista dos Tribunais* 346 (1955).

[31] Antão de Morães, opinion in 31 *Revista de Direito Administrativo* 474 (1953); argument adopted by São Paulo State Court of Appeals, 238 *Revista dos Tribunais* 289 (1955).

[32] In the State of São Paulo, the sale or consignment of printed books is also exempt from the sales tax. Whether an independent printer working for a publisher is subject to the transaction tax (which is essentially a substitute for the sales tax applying to nonmercantile sales or to the performance of services with or without the supply of material) is doubtful. The argument against taxation is that the tax would indirectly amount to a tax on the paper, whereas, if the transaction tax were to be assessed on the price of the services alone, the exemption granted by state law for the sale of books would be circumvented. It should be pointed out in this connection that the state exemption does not distinguish between sales made by booksellers or publishers and those made by the manufacturer of the books.

[33] In the State of São Paulo, the provision exempting sales of securities also refers to "sales of money." As the national currency obviously cannot be regarded as merchandise, this provision applies only to exchange transactions, described as sales of foreign currency. Since this description seems hardly fitting from a strictly legal point of view, the provision in question was of limited application; but it recently acquired a peculiar importance in connection with the bonus paid to exporters by the Bank of Brazil; see footnote 38.

15/3. Tax Base

15/3.1 Gross Invoice Price

The sales tax is based on the price stated in the bill of sale, the *duplicata*, or other similar document exchanged between the parties.

The price for sales tax purposes is the gross invoice price unless the seller grants rebates or discounts which are not dependent upon payment by the buyer within certain time limits. For example, if an invoice reads "Price Cr$ 100 with 5% discount," the tax is computed on Cr$ 95. But if an invoice maturing in 90 days reads "Price Cr$ 100, 5% discount if paid within 30 days," the tax is computed on Cr$ 100 regardless of whether the buyer avails himself of the discount. Discounts must be entered in full on the invoice and the corresponding *duplicata* (15/5.2b) in order to be considered in the computation of the tax.

The tax authorities insist that freight, cartage, insurance, and packing and handling expenses must be included in the price to prevent tax evasion achieved by increasing the cost of such items at the expense of the price of the merchandise. There can be no dispute with this viewpoint in the matter of c.i.f. and c. & f. sales, but the situation is more doubtful as regards f.o.b., f.a.s., or local sales. Although in these latter cases administrative practice invariably requires the inclusion of additional expenses in the invoice for sales tax purposes,[34] there are conflicting judicial decisions on this point.[35]

15/3.2 Inclusion of Other Items in Tax Base

a. EXCISE TAX. A question has arisen regarding the mandatory inclusion in the sales price of the federal excise tax, which is imposed upon the producer, manufacturer, or importer, but charged by him to the first purchaser of the goods. Because excise tax must be shown as a separate item on the bill of sale (16/2.10a), it was recently held that this tax is not part of the price for sales tax purposes as regards the first sale made by the producer.[36] On subsequent sales, the excise tax becomes merged in the price, and is thus included in the base of the tax. There is no similar rule concerning the sales tax itself, because this tax is cumulative (except in the State of Amazonas); its base is successively increased by the sales taxes collected on prior sales, as well as by profits and incidental expenses.[37]

[34] Rulings of São Paulo State Treasury Revenue Department in 1952 *Revista Fiscal de São Paulo* Nos. 100 and 135.
[35] Supreme Court, 128 *Revista Forense* 457 (1950); Minas Gerais State Court of Appeals, 107 *Revista Forense* 101 (1946); São Paulo State Court of Appeals, 218 *Revista dos Tribunais* 584 (1953).
[36] São Paulo State Court of Appeals, 232 *Revista dos Tribunais* 283 (1955).
[37] In order to minimize the consequent progressive enlarging of the tax base it has been suggested that the sales tax should be revised along the lines of the French

The theory underlying the judicial decisions which exclude the federal excise tax from the base of the sales tax is that a payment made by the buyer to a party other than the seller cannot be regarded as part of the price.

b. EXPORT BONUSES AND OVERPRICES. An analogous argument has been used to support the contention that an incentive bonus paid by the Bank of Brazil to exporters (1/2.7) is not part of the sales price of the exported goods and should not, therefore, be taken into account in computing the sales tax on export sales.[38] A comparable question arises in the matter of sales by importers. The question here is whether the various premiums which the importer must pay to the Bank of Brazil, in addition to the uniform price of the foreign exchange depending upon the nature of the imported merchandise, and which are charged by him to the first buyer, must be included in determining the base of the sales tax.[39]

15/4. Tax Rates and Computation of the Tax

15/4.1 In General

Art. 19, §5 of the Constitution states that the rate of the sales tax must be uniform in each state, regardless of the origin or destination of the goods sold. This provision prohibits rate discrimination between sales of goods produced within the state and sales of imported goods, as well as between sales for local consumption and those for export.[40] The Constitution of 1934 and the Charter of 1937, in addition, prohibited rate differentials based on the nature of the goods sold. This restriction prevented the states from gaining additional revenue by using the sales tax as a luxury tax. Although the Constitution of 1946 eliminated the restriction, it is generally considered that a luxury tax, discriminating according to the nature of goods sold, would be unconstitutional as conflicting with the federal excise tax.[41]

"value-added" tax; in other words, that it should be computed on the full price (and incidental expenses) of the first sale, but only on the accretions resulting from subsequent sales. It is doubtful whether this system could be adopted in Brazil without constitutional amendment, as the tax (except on the first sale) would no longer be, strictly speaking, a sales tax. Gomes de Sousa, "A Tributação das Vendas" in O Impôsto sôbre Vendas e Consignações no Sistema Tributário Brasileiro, Rio de Janeiro, 1956, p. 9.

[38] Gomes de Sousa, opinion in 229 Revista dos Tribunais 37 (1954). The São Paulo State Court of Appeals upheld this contention and ruled that the sales tax should not be computed on the amount of the bonus: 237 Revista dos Tribunais 342 (1955).

[39] This problem is more acute with regard to the federal excise tax, where the question is one of determining the cost of the merchandise to the importer; see 16/2.6.

[40] On this last point, see 15/6.

[41] In a recent and still unreported case, the Rio Grande do Sul State Court

15/4.2   Comparison of Rates

Uniformity of rates in all states has not in fact been imposed by the Constitution, and attempts to achieve uniformity by covenant have not been successful (15/1.3). The free play of interstate commerce has, however, brought about a relative uniformity. The following chart [42] gives the rates in force as of January 1, 1956.

	% Rate
State of Amazonas	8
States of Ceará and Pará	3.5
States of Bahia, Espírito Santo, Maranhão, Paraná, Rio Grande do Norte, Rio Grande do Sul, Rio de Janeiro,[43] Santa Catarina and São Paulo	3
State of Alagôas	2.85
State of Sergipe	2.7
States of Pernambuco and Piauí	2.6
States of Goiás and Paraíba	2.5
State of Mato Grosso	2.4
State of Minas Gerais	1.4
Federal District	4
Federal Territories	1.25

The reason for the conspicuously higher rate in the State of Amazonas is that there the tax is collected only once on the first sale, whereas in all other states the tax is collected on each transaction.

15/4.3   Fees and Other Additions to Sales Taxes

In most states the rate of the sales tax is indirectly increased through "additions" or so-called "fees" of various descriptions. These increases sometimes apply only to the sales tax, but in other cases they are superimposed on all state taxes. The revenue from these additions and fees is invariably allocated to specific expenditures or public services. Consequently, the only difference between an addition and a fee is that the "addition" is always a percentage of the amount or rate of the tax, whereas a "fee" is computed on the same base as the tax, i.e., on the sales price.[44]

of Appeals declared that a state law imposing a higher rate of tax on state-produced beverages using imported raw materials violated the constitutional provision against rate discrimination based on the origin of goods sold. The court, however, declined to rule on other provisions of the same statute that provided for rate differentials based on the nature of the goods.

On this question, see opinion of Gomes de Sousa in 32 *Revista de Direito Administrativo* 453 (1953).

[42] Adapted from 15 *Revista de Finanças Públicas* No. 172 (1955) p. 18.

[43] Not to be confused with the City of Rio de Janeiro (Federal District).

[44] Thus, in the State of São Paulo a general addition to all state taxes was instituted in 1954 at the rate of 10% of the tax due in each case. The proceeds of

The increases of the sales tax by means of fees vary too much from one state to another to be reduced to a general pattern. In some states the fees also differ according to the type of sale (wholesale, retail, or sales by manufacturers as opposed to sales by merchants) or with the amount of the transaction.

In many cases the constitutionality of such fees may be questioned because they discriminate on the basis of the origin, destination, or nature of the goods sold, or, more generally, because they violate the constitutional requirement of equality of treatment. They may be considered general taxes because their burden falls upon persons who do not benefit from the service for which the fee is imposed. A typical example are the fees, common in the northern and northeastern states, which are levied on sales but used to finance the social institutions of the state. Another example is a fee on sales imposed by the State of Pernambuco throughout its territory, but collected to finance the fire department in the state's capital city of Recife.

15/5. Administration of the Tax

15/5.1 Assessment

The sales tax is regarded in Brazil as a self-assessed tax in the sense that the taxpayer (i.e., the seller) is required by law to pay the tax on his own initiative, usually in stamps which are purchased from the Treasury and affixed to the sales document. The burden of collection thus falls upon the taxpayer, not only in the matter of bookkeeping, but especially in determining whether the tax is due and the proper amount thereof. Deficiencies detected after the sale cannot be recovered from the buyer.

15/5.2 Payment of Tax and Required Records

The usual method of payment of the sales tax differs slightly between cash sales (those payable in less than 30 days) and term sales.

a. CASH SALES. In cash sales, most of which are over-the-counter retail sales, the vendor is required by tax regulations to issue to the buyer a sales slip describing the merchandise and listing the price and date of the sale. The amount of the sales tax need not be shown on the sales

this addition are used to consolidate the state's floating debt. As of January 1, 1956, the addition was increased to 13.75%, the increase being destined to finance a plan for the development of the state's electric power production and distribution. The effective rate of the sales tax, therefore, is 3.4125% on each sale. The authorities require the two additions (10% and 3.75%) to be computed separately by the taxpayer. Fractions of Cr$ 1.00 are always rounded off in tax computations.

slip.[45] At the close of each business day, the number and amount of each slip are entered in a special register previously authenticated by the tax authorities, and the amount of the tax on each entry is then computed and recorded. Periodically, usually every two weeks, the daily entries are added up and the tax is paid on the total amount by affixing stamps to the register. The register must be open throughout business hours for inspection by the tax authorities and preserved for a stipulated length of time, usually 5 years.

By special application to the tax authorities, retail stores may be permitted to dispense with the sales slip. Control of sales is then made through the cash register.

b. TERM SALES. In term sales, the seller is required by commercial law to issue an invoice and a *duplicata* to the buyer. The invoice is subject to the same requirements as the cash sales slip except that it must further contain the name and address of the buyer. The seller then draws on the buyer a *duplicata*, which is similar in form to a promissory note and contains, besides a serial number of its own, the number and amount of the corresponding invoice,[46] the names and addresses of both seller and buyer, the discounts granted, if any, and the dates of issuance and maturity. The *duplicata* is signed by the seller and presented to the buyer (usually through a bank) for acceptance. Failure to return the *duplicata* within the prescribed time or to pay on maturity entitles the seller (or the lawful bearer) to protest it against the buyer and to sue for payment under the procedure applicable to a promissory note.[47]

Since the *duplicata* is a negotiable instrument, the tax regulations require that the tax be paid by the seller by affixing stamps to the *duplicata* itself at the time of its issuance. Consequently the tax is, in this instance, advanced by the seller until the maturity date. All bearers (especially banks accepting *duplicatas* for discount) are re-

---

[45] Sales slips must be numbered consecutively in print and detached from a book in which a carbon copy is made and preserved for tax inspection for a variable period of time, usually 5 years. In the State of São Paulo where control is most elaborate, printing shops are required to print an identifying mark on all sales slip blanks supplied by them and to preserve a record of all such supplies for 5 years.

[46] Invoices issued during the month to the same customer may be combined in one *duplicata* drawn at the end of the month.

[47] Failure to accept a *duplicata* does not lead to the same consequences. An unaccepted *duplicata* is not a promise to pay and therefore does not entitle the bearer to protest. São Paulo State Court of Appeals, 233 *Revista dos Tribunais* 453 (1955); Federal Court of Appeals for the Federal District, 233 *Revista dos Tribunais* 473 (1955). Consequently, the bearer in this case can only sue in the ordinary manner for breach of contract. But if the buyer fails to return the *duplicata* or returns it without stating his reasons for not accepting it, the vendor (but not the bearer if the *duplicata* has been negotiated) is entitled to issue a *triplicata* and protest it immediately.

quired to verify that the tax has been correctly paid. In addition, all *duplicatas* issued must be recorded in a special register which is subject to the same requirements as the register of cash sales.

c. COMMON REQUIREMENTS. Besides the registers of cash sales slips, of cash sales, and of *duplicatas*, all taxpayers are required to keep separate books for recording purchases, consignments made or received, and shipments of merchandise made to or received from their branches, agents, or representatives in other states. The object of all these records is to facilitate control of the sales made through a comparison of the sales records with purchases and inventories at the time of the inspector's visit. The register of shipments made to the taxpayer's establishments in other states is used to determine the tax due on the excess of the sales price over the value of the shipments.

15/5.3   Refunds

When a tax is payable in stamps, the purchase of the stamps by the taxpayer does not constitute a payment of the tax, which occurs only when the stamps are affixed to a book or document. The tax authorities have taken the position that tax stamps are sold by the Treasury like ordinary merchandise which the buyer utilizes at his own risk and they have therefore denied refunds for unused stamps.[48] The courts have rejected this contention as a denial of due process of law, as it would foreclose a consideration of refund claims on their merits purely on the formal ground of the method of payment; besides, tax stamps are not ordinary merchandise but a type of currency which is legal tender for tax debts only.

15/5.4   Fines

Fines are usually made up of two elements: one is a fixed amount which is determined, in the discretion of the tax authorities, between a minimum and a maximum established by law; the second, which is imposed in addition to the first, is a percentage of the defaulted tax. If the taxpayer voluntarily corrects a deficiency, he is subject only to the percentage fine at the minimum rate. Conversely, the percentage is increased if the deficiency is fraudulent. In some states, incorrect bookkeeping with intent to defraud or failure to keep books entitles the authorities to estimate the tax on the basis either of the average inventory of the firm or the average turnover of similar establishments. A wide margin of discretion is usually allowed the authorities in such cases by legislation and court decisions.

[48] The same contention is also advanced by the federal authorities in connection with the federal stamp tax; see 17/1. below.

15/6. The Export Tax

15/6.1 Description of the Export Tax

The export tax is reserved to the states by Art. 19(V) of the Constitution. It is in effect an extension of the sales tax. It is defined as a tax on the export of goods limited in rate to 5% ad valorem but it may be increased to as much as 10% if a special temporary permit is granted to the state by the federal Congress. It can only be levied by the state in which the goods (referred to as "state-produced" goods) were produced.[49]

The courts have decided that the sales tax and the export tax can be imposed simultaneously on an export sale on the ground that the sale of merchandise and its shipment abroad are two different taxable events and not elements of one and the same transaction.[50]

15/6.2 Taxable Event

The fact that the export tax is imposed by the states rather than by the federal government raises numerous problems. The major problem of this kind concerns the definition of "state-produced goods," especially in cases where a manufacturer ships merchandise produced in one state to a branch or agent in another state prior to its exportation. Preliminary shipment to another state is sometimes unavoidable, as in the case of inland states, but it is occasionally arranged in an attempt to evade the tax, e.g., when merchandise produced in a state imposing the tax is first transferred to another state not imposing it and then exported from the latter. Multiple problems of constitutional law are raised by this practice.

Other problems arise when merchandise produced in one state is processed or improved in any way in a second state before it is exported. In such cases, both states usually demand payment of the export tax on the ground that the merchandise was manufactured in their territory. In these cases the "original package doctrine" is usually invoked.[51] This doctrine, however, is often difficult and sometimes impossible to apply, especially to natural products which require refining before export, such as coffee, cotton, plant oils, and fats, or which are shipped in bulk, such as grain. Most states seek to protect themselves against tax evasion by demanding payment of the export tax on all locally-produced goods at the time they leave the territory of the state, regard-

[49] Const., Art. 19(V); see also Art. 27 of the Constitution, which prohibits interstate or intermunicipal taxes except for road fees or tolls.
[50] São Paulo State Court of Appeals, 220 Revista dos Tribunais 229 (1954); 221 Revista dos Tribunais 240 (1954). For the contrary opinion, Francisco Campos, opinion in 37 Revista de Direito Administrativo 480 (1954).
[51] Carlos Maximiliano, opinion in 4 Revista de Direito Administrativo 375 (1946). Gomes de Sousa, opinion in 25 Revista de Direito Administrativo 404 (1951).

less of their destination. The tax is later refunded on evidence that the goods were not exported.

15/6.3   Substitutes for the Export Tax

The constitutional limitation of the rate of the export tax to 5% is avoided in some states by assessing the tax at fixed rather than percentage rates; obviously, an export tax of Cr$ 50 per ton is more than 5% if the price of a ton is less than Cr$ 1,000. Yet this device sometimes succeeds by describing what is clearly an export tax as a "fee" on the clearance of goods shipped or as a "port charge" or a "toll." Exactions of this type sometimes appear in the state's budget not as taxes but as industrial revenue, such as charges for the use of state-operated port facilities.

In the State of São Paulo, no export tax is imposed as such, but state-produced goods which are exported must be accompanied by a special invoice or export document on which a state stamp tax is collected, computed as a percentage of the invoice value. This so-called "stamp tax" is obviously a substitute for an export tax but it is kept within the constitutional limitations by not exceeding 5% ad valorem. In effect, its rate is always kept equal to that of the sales tax. Thus the aggregate amount of the sales tax and the export tax in São Paulo is less than it is in other states.

15/7.   Concurrent Sales Taxes

15/7.1   Constitutional Background

As previously noted (15/2.2), the sales tax can, as an "exclusive" tax, be levied by the states only within certain constitutional limitations, especially with respect to the characteristics of the parties to the transaction. In order to tax transactions which cannot properly be made the object of an "exclusive" sales tax — such as those regulated by the civil law, or the rendering of services without the furnishing of materials — the states have frequently imposed taxes which are complementary to the sales tax. These taxes, however, can be imposed by the states only as "concurrent" taxes (1/3.3), the revenues from which they must share with the federal government and the municipalities.

15/7.2   The Transactions Tax

One example of such a concurrent tax is the transactions tax imposed by the State of São Paulo on persons supplying materials and performing services, where the price includes the value of both. This tax is levied on hotels, business agents, architects and smaller establishments such as laundries, garages and repair shops in general. The rate of the transactions tax is always kept equal to the rate of the sales tax, which indicates that it is intended to be complementary to that tax.

CHAPTER 16

EXCISE TAXES

16/1. Introductory
    16/1.1 Scope of Chapter

16/2. Description of the Federal Excise Tax
    16/2.1 General
    16/2.2 Federal Legislation
    16/2.3 Taxable Event
    16/2.4 Taxpayers
          a. Manufacturers and Importers
          b. Exemptions
    16/2.5 Base and Rates of the Tax
    16/2.6 Table A — "Ad Valorem" Tax
    16/2.7 Table B — Tax on "Ceiling" Price
    16/2.8 Table C — Tax Computed According to Quantities or Technical Characteristics
    16/2.9 Table D — Miscellaneous
    16/2.10 Administration
          a. Payment and Collection
          b. Refunds
          c. Penalties

16/3. The "Impôsto Unico"
    16/3.1 Constitutional Background
    16/3.2 Fuels and Lubricants
    16/3.3 Electric Power
    16/3.4 Minerals
    16/3.5 Tax on Waterfalls

16/4. State and Municipal Excise Taxes
    16/4.1 Agricultural and Industrial Exploitation Tax

16/1. Introductory

16/1.1 Scope of Chapter

The taxes treated in this chapter are the federal excise tax (the official name of which is *impôsto de consumo,* or consumption tax) which is the basic tax of this type, the *impôsto unico,* and certain minor taxes.

Excise taxes have always played an important part in the Brazilian revenue system. Invariably intended as taxes on the use or consumption of goods, collected from the producer but recovered by him from the consumer as an element of the price, they have presented the revenue authorities with the double advantage of arousing little protest from the public and of requiring a relatively simple mechanism for their assessment and collection.

16/2. Description of the Federal Excise Tax

16/2.1 General

The federal excise tax (or consumption tax) is imposed under the provision of the Constitution which reserves to the federal government the exclusive right to impose consumption taxes.[1] The tax is imposed at specific rates on enumerated articles, and it affects substantially all goods manufactured in or imported into Brazil except those subject to the *impôsto unico* (16/3). Though the tax is intended to be borne by the consumer, it is imposed on the manufacturer or importer, and the law does not prohibit absorption of the tax by the latter (16/2.4). The tax imposes a considerable burden on the manufacturer because its rules of interpretation and administration are extremely complex, frequently changed, and often confusing. Control by the authorities is very strict, and comparatively minor breaches of regulations may result in heavy fines (16/2.10c).

16/2.2 Federal Legislation

The legislation on the federal excise tax is now consolidated in one comprehensive enactment which is divided into two parts.[2] The first part, entitled "General Rules," contains the provisions which are applicable to all taxable products. The second part is composed of 29 "schedules" or lists of articles subject to the tax, which are sometimes specifically described. The schedules also indicate the various tax rates and sometimes contain specific rules which, in regard to the articles to which the schedule refers, constitute exceptions to the provisions of the "General Rules."

[1] Const., Art. 15 (II).
[2] Decree No. 26,149 of January 5, 1949, as amended by Law No. 2,974 of November 26, 1956.

16/2.3 Taxable Event

Under the federal excise tax the taxable event occurs at the moment when merchandise is put into circulation. This is, in the case of a domestic product, the time when it leaves the factory, and in the case of a foreign product, the time when it enters through customs. While the tax is designated as "consumption tax," the term "consumption," in this context, refers to the use of merchandise in a manner consistent with its nature, and it thus acquires a wider meaning than that which implies the destruction of the merchandise in the use for which it was produced. Hence, the fact that the merchandise is put into circulation is sufficient to give rise to the tax. Further, the legal nature of the event through which this occurs, i.e., sale, loan, gift, etc., is immaterial. Since the impact of the tax does not depend on a sale, the shipment of merchandise from the factory to a warehouse, a sales department, or an agent of the manufacturer constitutes a taxable event, and the same is true if merchandise is given away gratuitously (e.g., to charity, or as a prize, etc.), or exchanged for goods previously sold but returned by the buyer as defective or for other reasons.

Applying the same principle, semi-finished articles which leave one factory for completion in another (even if both factories are owned and operated by the same manufacturer) are subject to the tax if they can be used in their present state of completion. The tax is imposed again when the finished product leaves the second factory. The basis of this second assessment differs depending on whether the final stage of manufacture constitutes an "improvement" or a "transformation." "Improvement" is an industrial operation which merely increases the value of the product; in this case, the additional excise tax is calculated only on the added value. "Transformation" is an industrial operation which renders a product capable of use different from that in its prior condition; [3] here, the additional excise tax is imposed on the full value of the final product.

16/2.4 Taxpayers

a. MANUFACTURERS AND IMPORTERS. Although the tax is intended to be borne by the consumer, the manufacturer or the importer of articles affected by the tax is the taxpayer, and most legal provisions and control measures are directed at him (for joint liability of the buyer in certain cases, see 16/2.10a). The manufacturer is personally liable to pay the tax and he is responsible for any deficiencies which may be found after

[3] This is expressed rather differently in the act which speaks of an industrial operation rendering the product liable to a different fiscal classification (i.e., to classification under a different schedule). General Rules, Sec. 7. The practical result of this definition, however, is as stated in the text.

the goods have left the factory even though he may no longer be in a position to recover the tax from his buyer. These facts sufficiently demonstrate that the excise tax is primarily of interest to the manufacturer and to the importer rather than to the ultimate consumer.[4]

b. EXEMPTIONS. Exemptions based upon the nature of the taxpayer, i.e., the manufacturer or importer, are very few in number. They apply to charitable institutions and government departments in regard to articles imported or manufactured for their own consumption; [5] and to industrial establishments in regard to articles manufactured and exported directly by them to foreign countries. It should be noted that the federal, state, and municipal governments are not exempt from the excise tax either on articles sold to the public or on articles imported or purchased locally. The administrative rulings hold that the general immunity from taxation provided by the Constitution [6] does not apply because the tax falls not on government property, services, or revenue, but on a transaction.

Exemptions from the tax based on the nature of the product are usually listed under the applicable schedule. The General Rules of the statute provide for such exemptions only in two cases; namely, (1) samples and (2) articles constituting the minimum commodities required for the housing, feeding, clothing, and medical treatment of "persons of limited economic capacity." While this last-named exemption is already granted by Art. 15, §1 of the Constitution, it had to be implemented by a special statute,[7] which defines the exempted goods in terms of their prices.[8] However, the statute referred to prescribed such strict rules and heavy penalties that most manufacturers preferred to set their prices just above the legal limit in order to exclude their product from the exemption and thereby escape the specific regulations.[9]

16/2.5 Base and Rates of the Tax

The base and rates of the federal excise tax are defined in 29 schedules or lists of manufactured articles which are grouped together according to their characteristics or the nature of their basic material. The schedules are designated by Roman numerals and by generic titles; they contain the applicable rates and specific rules and exemptions

---

[4] It is important to note in this connection that the federal excise tax, if improperly collected, is not refunded to the manufacturer or importer. See 16/2.10b.

[5] But the raw materials are not included in this exemption, except in the cases of perfume, paper, paints and textiles; see 16/2.6, 16/2.9.

[6] Const. Art. 31, discussed at 1/3.5.

[7] Law No. 494 of November 26, 1948.

[8] The price limits set by Law No. 494 have been doubled by Law No. 2,653 of November 24, 1955.

[9] The excessive strictness of the regulations has been somewhat eased by Decree No. 38,492 of December 31, 1955.

which, as far as they apply, supersede the General Rules of the statute.

Problems of classification are resolved by the specific, as opposed to the generic, nature of the article in question. Thus, a revolver would, according to its generic nature, be classified in Schedule I (metal products); actually, it is classified in Schedule II (weapons), which describes its specific nature more closely. Where a product is composed of more than one material, the component material which is predominant in volume determines the classification. Borderline cases are decided by a ruling of the Director of Internal Revenue.

The 29 schedules are grouped into 4 Tables (designated by letters) according to common characteristics of the computation and payment of the tax.

The following is a summary of the definitions, rates,[10] and significant specific rules under each of the 29 schedules. Under the new law, the rates for domestic and for imported articles are the same, except in some individual cases as indicated below.

16/2.6   Table A — "Ad Valorem" Tax

Table A includes the products on which the tax is paid "ad valorem," i.e., on the basis of the manufacturer's invoice price. This table includes the greatest number of products and is therefore the most important. The treatment of discounts follows the same rules as those which apply under the sales tax (15/3.1).

There are four cases, however, when the price on which the tax is computed is that charged by the *first buyer* to his subsequent buyer rather than that charged by the manufacturer. In all of these cases, there is at least the possibility that the price charged by the manufacturer to the first buyer is not the result of arm's length bargaining. They are: (1) When the manufacturer and first buyer are departments of the same firm, (2) When the first buyer is a legal entity of which the manufacturer (or its controlling shareholder or partner) is in turn a controlling shareholder or partner,[11] (3) When the first buyer acquires more than 50% of the entire output of the manufacturer, (4) When the first buyer acquires the entire output of the manufacturer in any one of the latter's lines of production.

The excise tax on imported products is, under the new law, first tentatively computed on the exporter's invoice price plus freight, insurance,

[10] The tax rates are those introduced by Law No. 2,974 of November 26, 1956, which are effective beginning January 1, 1957. These rates supersede those of Decree No. 26,149 of January 5, 1949, as well as the temporary additions to those rates established by Law No. 2,653 of November 24, 1955, which were in effect during 1956.

[11] A controlling partner or shareholder is defined for this purpose as one holding more than 50% of the capital, but this definition is obviously useless in the case of bearer shares.

customs duties, and other incidental expenses; this tentative tax is paid
at the time when the merchandise enters through customs. In computing
this tax, prices in foreign currency are converted at the average rate of
exchange prevailing in the calendar month prior to the date of entry.
Exchange premiums paid by the importer under Law No. 2,145 are includible in the tax base as an item of additional cost.

The final tax is computed on the basis of the local sales price of the
merchandise. The mechanics of the adjustment of the tentative tax to
the final tax still require clarification through administrative regulations.

Schedule I: Metal machines and manufactures not specifically covered in
other schedules: 5%. Exemptions: industrial machinery in general, agricul-
tural instruments, electric or fuel engines, and works of art. Automobiles:
15%. Exemptions: buses, trucks, and ambulances.
Schedule II: Cutlery, weapons, ammunition, and fireworks: 15%.
Schedule III: Manufactured articles of animal or vegetable materials: leather
goods, ivory, bone, wood (except furniture) and plastic articles: 6%. Furs
and tanned skins: 10%.
Schedule IV: Toys, sports articles, and games: 6%.
Schedule V: Ceramics and glass manufactures: 5%.
Schedule VI: Hats: 6%.
Schedule VII: Cement, domestic: 10%; imported: 15%. Alabaster, marble, or
granite slabs, domestic: exempt; imported: 2%; manufactured articles of those
materials (domestic or imported): 5%.
Schedule VIII: Electric power: see *impôsto unico* (16/3).
Schedule IX: Brushes, paint-brushes, and brooms: 5%.
Schedule X: Precious or semi-precious stones and any articles of wear wholly
or partly made of or ornamented with such stones or with pearls, gold, silver,
platinum, or their alloys: 16%. Clocks and watches: 7%. New articles covered by both this schedule and another are taxed under *both* schedules.
Articles sold second-hand by dealers are taxed only under Schedule X.
Schedule XI: Paper and cardboard in sheets, blotting paper, carbon paper,
stencil, and manufactured paper or cardboard articles: 4%. Exemptions:
printing paper and paper or cardboard used as raw material in manufactured
articles.
Schedule XII: Processed foods. Cereal, domestic: exempt; imported: 4%.
Flour, biscuits, meat or fish preserves, edible animal or vegetable fats,
domestic: 3%; imported: 4%. Edible oils, butter, margarine, cheese, and con-
densed milk, domestic: exempt; imported: 6%. Sugar, domestic: 4%; imported: 6%. Fruit or vegetable preserves, spices, sauces, chocolate, roast or
ground coffee, and tea, domestic: 5%; imported: 7%.
Schedule XIII: Pharmaceutical, medical, dental, and veterinary products in
general, produced industrially, domestic: 4%; imported: 6%. Exemptions:
prescriptions and free samples to doctors, hospitals, or dispensaries, if
plainly labeled as such.
Schedule XIV: Paints, enamels, and varnishes: 5%. This schedule includes
finished articles as well as raw materials, such as pigments, dyes, and sol-
vents. However, raw materials used by manufacturers of articles included in
this or any other schedule are not taxed provided the manufacturer puts up
a bond of up to Cr$ 100,000 to guaranty payment of the tax if he should
sell the materials in their original condition.
Schedule XV: Candles: 6%.

16/2.7   Table B — Tax on "Ceiling" Price

Different from the method applied under Table A, the tax under Table B is not based on actual prices but on the maximum prices of certain commodities within certain price brackets. These "ceiling" prices are fixed in the law for purposes of the federal excise tax; they must not be confused with ceiling prices under price control regulations. Table B includes only two kinds of merchandise (shoes and furniture).

Schedule XVI: Shoes. The tax is computed on the *retail* price which must be marked on the sole by the *manufacturer.* The manufacturer therefore marks a higher price than he receives (up to the limit of the next higher tax bracket) and the difference represents the retailer's markup. This marked price is the "ceiling" price for tax purposes, but domestic shoes with a retail price not exceeding Cr$ 200 are exempt under the rules discussed at 16/2.4b. On higher-priced articles, the tax rates are: over Cr$ 200 to Cr$ 300: Cr$ 20.00; over Cr$ 300 to Cr$ 500: Cr$ 2.50 on each Cr$ 25.00; over Cr$ 500: Cr$ 5.00 on each Cr$ 50.00.

Schedule XVII: Furniture. The "ceiling" price for tax purposes is the *manufacturer's* price which must be marked on each piece, including those sold in sets. The retailer's markup is therefore free of tax. The rate is 6% computed on the "ceiling" price.

16/2.8   Table C — Tax Computed According to Quantities or Technical Characteristics

Under Table C, the tax is based on quantities or certain technical characteristics which are apparent from the detail of the schedules listed below.

Schdule XVIII: Alcohol: the tax is a fixed amount per bottle [12] (Cr$ 0.08) or half-bottle (Cr$ 0.04), or by liter (Cr$ 0.12) or half-liter (Cr$ 0.06); if sold in containers of greater capacity, the fraction of these measures is taxed as a full measure. The tax on imported alcohol is the same amount, increased by 50%.

Schedule XIX: Beverages. Soft drinks: 10%; beer: 30%. The tax on all other beverages is at fixed amounts per bottle or liter, according to the rules of Schedule XVIII, but the rates vary widely according to alcoholic content and to the nature of the manufacturing process (fermented or distilled). The average tax rate, on a price basis, is about 25%. Imported beverages pay the same rates, increased according to the same rules by up to 400% (champagne).

Schedule XX: Playing cards, per pack: 30%.

Schedule XXI: Electric bulbs: 5%.

Schedule XXII: Vinegar: domestic, fixed amounts per bottle or liter according to the rules of Schedule XVIII, but such amounts vary according to the nature of the basic material (wine, sugar, cane, etc.). Imported, same amounts increased by 30%.

[12] A bottle is 0.66 of a liter.

16/2.9   Table D — Miscellaneous

The schedules classified under Table D likewise include products
which are taxed under a special method.

Schedule XXIII: Matches, at fixed amounts according to number of units
in box or folder: Cr$ 0.12 up to 30 units, or Cr$ 0.16 up to 60 units, plus
an additional Cr$ 0.08 for each 30 units in excess of the first 60. Lighters:
20%.

Schedule XXIV: Tobacco. Cigarettes: domestic, per box or pack of up to
20 units: price up to Cr$ 4.00: 45%; over Cr$ 4.00 to Cr$ 10.00: 50%; over
Cr$ 10.00: 55%. Imported cigarettes, Cr$ 6.50 per box or pack of up to 20
units regardless of price. Cigarette or pipe tobacco: domestic, in fixed
amounts between Cr$ 0.40 and Cr$ 2.00, equivalent to about 40% of price
in every case; imported, Cr$ 2.00 per unit weight of 25 grams gross regard-
less of price. Imported tobacco leaves, crude or treated, Cr$ 1.00 per kilo.
The retail price applied under this schedule is the price marked by the
manufacturer, the same as under Schedule XVI.

Schedule XXV: Fuels and lubricants. See below under *impôsto unico*
(16/3.).

Schedule XXVI: Umbrellas (domestic or imported), in fixed amounts according to price (about 15% of price in every case).

Schedule XXVII: Toiletries, domestic or imported. Soap: 20%; lotions, hair
tonic, bath salts, lipstick, nail polish, and similar articles: 30%; natural or
artificial oils and aromatic chemicals used as raw materials: 50%. Exemption: raw materials, subject to same rules as under Schedule XIV. Retail
price under this schedule is the price marked by the manufacturer according to the rules of Schedule XVI.

Schedule XXVIII: Salt in bulk: domestic, Cr$ 0.03 per kilo, imported
Cr$ 0.12 per kilo. Kitchen salt in containers: domestic Cr$ 0.03, imported
Cr$ 0.06, in both cases per unit weight of 25 grams net.

Schedule XXIX: Textiles of any material: 10%; sewing thread, twine, and
rope, of any material: 6%. Exemption: domestic cotton textiles, the manufacturer's price of which is not more than Cr$ 10.00 per meter.

16/2.10   Administration

a. PAYMENT AND COLLECTION. The federal excise tax is paid in two different ways; either by a direct payment in cash to the Treasury, or by
affixing tax stamps to the articles. The first method of payment applies to
all articles in Table A, the so-called ad valorem tax. The manufacturer or
importer pays the tax in cash, credits the corresponding amount to a
current account maintained in a special register, and debits this account
for the amount of tax due on each article which leaves the factory or
warehouse.

Payment of the tax in stamps applies to all articles in Tables B, C, and
D (Schedules XVI through XXIX), except that the excess of tax due on
imported articles over that payable on similar domestic articles is paid
ad valorem, i.e., in cash. Payment by affixing stamps (sometimes called
"the tax by direct stamping") is a much more complicated process than

direct payment in cash. The manufacturer or importer must purchase special excise tax stamps and either affix them to the articles leaving the factory or warehouse or deliver them to the customer along with the merchandise. Stamps are affixed to articles which are sold either directly to the customer or to a dealer in packages ready for resale at retail. If the articles are sold to a dealer in larger containers which must be broken down into smaller units for retail sale, the manufacturer or importer must deliver the tax stamps in sheets so that the retailer can affix the individual stamps to the articles before exhibiting them for sale.

The manufacturer or importer is obliged to cancel the stamps issued by him (regardless of whether they are affixed to the merchandise or delivered in sheets) so that his initials and the number of the applicable schedule appear on the face of each individual stamp. In addition, stamps delivered in sheets must be cancelled by the manufacturer or importer on the reverse side with a notation indicating his name and address as well as that of the purchaser, the number and date of the bill of sale, and the number of units in the shipment. Some part of this inscription must appear on the reverse side of each stamp.

Producers (manufacturers and importers) are required to keep a register showing the excise tax stamps purchased by them and those used or delivered. Each shipment of merchandise from the factory or warehouse must be accompanied by a bill (*nota fiscal*) describing the merchandise and its price, the amount of tax paid, and the names and addresses of the producer and purchaser. These bills are numbered consecutively and issued in duplicate. The original of the bill is preserved by the purchaser (if a registered merchant), and the duplicate by the producer, for not less than five years. Merchants are required to satisfy themselves that the producer has complied with all these requirements, and they become liable for any deficiency in tax if they disregard this obligation.

b. REFUNDS. Perhaps the most striking feature of the administration of the excise tax is the refusal of the tax authorities to refund the tax to the manufacturer or importer, even if there is no doubt that the tax has been improperly collected. The attitude of the government and the courts is that the tax is indirect in nature and that the producer is obligated by express provision of the law to recover it from the consumer. Therefore, the decisions hold that the manufacturer or importer has no right to a refund, because he is already reimbursed by the consumer, and a further refund by the Treasury would be without cause.[13]

---

[13] DIR, *Rev.* 1946 No. 621, CC, *Rev.* 1947 No. 169; Federal Court of Appeals, 24 *Revista de Direito Administrativo* 60 (1951). The denial of refund occurs even when the manufacturer or importer can prove that he did not recover the tax, but this situation can legally arise only in two cases; namely, (1) when the producer imports or manufactures for his own consumption, or (2) when the tax is collected

While it may be doubtful whether the seller or the buyer should be entitled to the refund, the present system results in the Treasury's retaining all taxes collected.

c. PENALTIES. The penalties for nonpayment of the tax [14] are as follows:

If the deficiency is discovered upon inspection of the merchandise while in transit, the penalty is 100% of the unpaid tax, but not less than Cr$ 500.

If the deficiency is discovered upon inspection of the books or records, the penalty is 100% of the unpaid tax, but not less than Cr$ 2,500.

If in either of the above cases the deficiency is due to wilful intent to defraud, the penalty is 200% of the unpaid tax, but not less than Cr$ 5,000.

The penalties are greatly reduced if the taxpayer makes a voluntary disclosure and tenders payment of the unpaid tax before the merchandise is seized, or an inspection of his books or records is initiated. In this case, the penalty is 10% of the unpaid tax if payment is tendered not later than 15 days after the merchandise has left the factory or warehouse; 20% if tendered later than 15 but not later than 30 days; and 50% after 30 days.

The statute of limitations for imposing the above penalties is five years. This limitation does not apply to the collection of the deficiency.

16/3.   The "Impôsto Unico"

16/3.1   Constitutional Background

Art. 15 (III) of the Constitution provides that the federal government shall have the "exclusive" power to levy taxes on the "production, commerce, distribution, and consumption, as well as on the import and export of lubricants and of liquid or gaseous fuels of whatever origin or nature, this regulation to be extended, insofar as applicable, to domestic minerals and to electric power." In paragraph 2 of the same Article, the Constitution provides further that "the tax under Section III of this Article shall be in the form of a single tax to be levied on each type of product."

The principle of imposing only one tax on fuels and lubricants originated in two amendments to the Constitutional Charter of 1937, which were introduced in 1940. The first deprived the states and municipalities of the power to tax such products, while the second granted that power to the federal government. Both amendments were the outcome of a report submitted to the President by the National Petroleum Com-

from the producer after the goods have been sold. The second instance is by far the more important.

[14] There are, furthermore, a large number of fines for various breaches of regulations. These fines are expressed in fixed amounts.

mittee, which pointed out the inconveniences arising from the multiple taxation then prevailing. That report also clearly recommended that the proposed single tax (*impôsto unico*) should not be a federal tax in the sense of an "exclusive" tax as previously defined (1/3.2) but a "national" tax assessed and collected by the federal government, the revenue from which should be apportioned among the states and municipalities in lieu of their own former taxes on the commodities and activities included in the scope of the new tax.[15]

The Constitution of 1946 preserved the same system and extended it to include, "insofar as applicable," electric power and domestic minerals. The Constitution further outlines, in Art. 15, §2, the method of apportioning the proceeds of the tax by stating that at least 60% shall be distributed among the states and municipalities according to their respective areas, population, consumption, and production, as implemented by law.

In spite of the national character which the Constitution intends to confer on the *impôsto unico,* some states and municipalities have tried to assess certain of their own taxes or fees on oil companies. Such attempts have not, as a rule, met with the approval of the courts, except in the case of the municipal business tax (18/2.4g). The Supreme Court has recently held that that tax is a tax on the importer, manufacturer, or merchant, and not a tax on the goods themselves or on industrial or commercial activities, and that it can, therefore, be assessed in addition to the *impôsto unico.*[16]

Similarly, the federal stamp tax on the exploitation of waterfalls for electric power is in addition to the taxation of one of the products covered by the *impôsto unico.*

16/3.2 Fuels and Lubricants

The *impôsto unico* on fuels and lubricants is assessed and collected in the form of an excise tax on domestic products and in the form of customs duties on imported products, superseding respectively Schedule XXV of Table D of the Excise Tax Act (16/2.9) and part of Chapter 17 of Section III of the Tariff Act (1/2.6). The tax is computed on the average c.i.f. price as determined from time to time by the National Petroleum Committee,[17] at the following rates:

[15] On the background and scope of the single tax, see Gilberto de Ulhôa Canto, opinion in 25 *Revista de Direito Administrativo* 410 (1951) and Gomes de Sousa, opinion in 41 *Revista de Direito Administrativo* 486 (1955).

[16] Supreme Court, 42 *Revista de Direito Administrativo* 61 (1955). For a criticism of this interpretation, see works cited in footnote at 15/2.3a and also Gilberto de Ulhôa Canto, opinion in 29 *Revista de Direito Administrativo* 279 (1952), commenting on earlier decisions by state courts.

[17] Law No. 2,975 of November 27, 1956, effective January 1, 1957. Under the prior law (Law No. 1,749 of November 28, 1952), the tax was assessed on weight.

Table of Rates

A. Imported Products

Liquefied gases	80%
Aviation gasoline:	
In 1957	65%
In 1958	75%
In 1959 and thereafter	85%
Ordinary gasoline	150%
Premium gasoline	200%
Kerosene:	
In 1957	80%
In 1958	90%
In 1959 and thereafter	100%
Gas oil, signal oil, Diesel oil:	
In 1957	55%
In 1958	65%
In 1959 and thereafter	80%
Fuel oil:	
In 1957	50%
In 1958	60%
In 1959 and thereafter	70%
Simple, compound, or emulsive lubricants:	
In bulk	150%
Packed	200%
Crude oil	Exempt

B. Domestic Products

Liquefied gases, aviation gasoline, ordinary gasoline, and premium gasoline	75% of the amount computed under Table A
Kerosene, gas oil, signal oil, Diesel oil, and fuel oil	50% of the amount computed under Table A
Simple, compound, or emulsive lubricants	Exempt during 1957–1961, then taxed at 25% of the amount computed under Table A
Crude oil	Exempt

Apportionment of the proceeds of the *impôsto unico* on fuels and lubricants is regulated by other acts [18] which establish that 40% of such proceeds shall go to the Federal Highway Department and 60% shall be apportioned among the states, the municipalities and the Federal District according to the following schedule: 36% on the basis of consumption, 12% on the basis of population, and 12% on the basis of area. Production is not taken into account, since domestic production of petro-

---

[18] Decree-law No. 8,463 of December 27, 1945, as amended by Law No. 22 of February 15, 1947, and by Law No. 302 of July 13, 1948.

leum products is still relatively small and not evenly distributed in the national territory.

16/3.3 Electric Power

The *impôsto unico* on electric power is assessed and collected in the form of an excise tax, superseding Schedule VIII of Table A of the Excise Tax Act (16/2.6). The tax is collected from public utility companies and must be charged by them to the consumer, at fixed rates of Cr$ 0.20 per kilowatt-hour of light, or of Cr$ 0.10 per kilowatt-hour of power. Forty per cent of the proceeds of the tax are apportioned to the Federal Electric Power Commission,[19] and 60% to the states, the municipalities and the Federal District, according to the following schedule: 50% on the basis of population, 45% on the basis of consumption, 4% on the basis of area, and 1% on the basis of production.[20]

16/3.4 Minerals

The *impôsto unico* on domestic minerals is not yet regulated by specific legislation. There are, therefore, still federal, state and local taxes on mining; but under Art. 68 of the Code of Mines,[21] the total of such taxes, except for the income tax, may not exceed 8% of the market value of the product f.o.b. at the mine.

16/3.5 Tax on Waterfalls

Under Art. 152 of the Constitution, the exploitation of a waterfall is distinct from the ownership of the land where the waterfall is located. The Federal Code of Waterways [22] makes the exploitation of a waterfall for producing electric power dependent upon a concession of the federal government, and Decree-law No. 2,281 of June 5, 1940, instituted a tax payable semiannually on the charter of such a concession. The tax is computed on the kilowatt power of the falls, but its rate is fixed annually by a special law based on the recommendation of the National Council for Waterways and Electric Power. Thus the tax is actually on the concession to exploit the waterfall for electric power and is not levied if the waterfall is not so exploited. It is payable by a stamp affixed to the charter granting the concession. It is not part of the *impôsto unico* levied on the production of electric power, but must be paid in addition to it. It is levied under Art. 15 (VI) of the Constitution, which provides for the Federal Stamp Tax (17/2.).

---

[19] The Federal Electric Power Commission also participates in the proceeds of the tax on exchange remittances (4/10).
[20] Law No. 2,308 of August 31, 1954.
[21] Decree-law No. 1,985 of January 29, 1940.
[22] Decree No. 24,643 of July 10, 1934.

16/4.   State and Municipal Excise Taxes

16/4.1   Agricultural and Industrial Exploitation Tax

In most states other than São Paulo (especially in the north and northeast of Brazil), a tax of basically the same nature as the federal excise tax is imposed under the name of an agricultural and industrial exploitation tax. This tax is assessed at the producer level, at varying percentage rates, and according to the nature of the goods. When assessed by a state, this tax may be justifiable under the concurrent power of taxation (1/3.3), except that on certain commodities its legality may be doubtful as impinging on the exclusive jurisdiction of the federal excise tax. For this reason, certain state courts have distinguished between "consumer" and "producer" excises. By classifying these taxes under the latter heading, they differentiate them from the federal excise tax, which is intended to be borne by the consumer (16/2.1).

CHAPTER 17

············

STAMP TAXES

17/1. Description of Stamp Taxes
    17/1.1   Scope of Chapter
    17/1.2   Constitutional and Legislative Background

17/2. The Federal Stamp Tax
    17/2.1   Scope of the Tax in General
    17/2.2   Official Documents
    17/2.3   Private Written Agreements
    17/2.4   Loans
    17/2.5   Capital Issues and Liquidations
    17/2.6   Transfer of Securities
    17/2.7   Installment Sales and Promises to Sell
    17/2.8   Exchange Transactions
    17/2.9   Unspecified Documents
    17/2.10 Additions to Federal Stamp Tax

17/3. State and Municipal Stamp Taxes
    17/3.1   In General
    17/3.2   State Stamp Taxes on Interstate Sales
    17/3.3   State Stamp Taxes on Automobile Registrations

17/1. Description of Stamp Taxes

17/1.1 Scope of Chapter

The expression "stamp tax" obviously describes no particular tax, but rather a method of collection. Although taxes other than those referred to in this chapter are collected by means of affixing stamps (e.g., under certain schedules of the federal excise tax as described at 16/2.10a), this chapter is limited to those taxes which are defined by the Constitution as falling on papers issued by a government at the request of taxpayers, such as licenses, permits, etc., on forms issued by a government; and on transactions evidenced by documents that are regulated by a law of the government imposing the tax, or that have an economic consequence within such government's territory. It covers both the federal stamp tax and certain state and municipal taxes of the same nature.

17/1.2   Constitutional and Legislative Background

Under the Constitution, each of the three governments may levy a tax of this description as an exclusive tax.[1] That the federal, state, and municipal stamp taxes are not intended to be superimposed is evidenced by the fact that the power of taxation granted to each government extends only to matters within that particular government's jurisdiction.

The basic rule of assessment of all stamp taxes is that liability for them depends upon the existence of a formal deed or instrument, irrespective of its legal or economic effectiveness. Thus, whenever an agreement is executed in legal form, the tax is due, even if the agreement is never given actual performance by the parties or is subsequently voided by the courts. Conversely, the tax is not due merely because a legal or economic result is obtained so long as there is no formal instrument, e.g., if a house is rented and occupied, and rent is paid, purely on the basis of a verbal agreement.

However, to prevent some of the more usual forms of stamp tax avoidance, the law sometimes provides that the existence of any document or instrument showing that a taxable agreement exists is sufficient to give rise to the tax. Thus, in the cited example of a house rented without written contract, the tax is payable on the rent receipt issued by the owner to the tenant.[2]

17/2.   The Federal Stamp Tax

17/2.1   Scope of the Tax in General

The federal stamp tax is far more important than state or municipal stamp taxes. Since it is a tax on "legal documents and instruments regulated by federal law," and civil and commercial law are federal matters, the tax affects, in theory at least, practically all legal documents

---

[1] Const., Art. 15(VI), Art. 19(VI), Art. 29(V).

[2] On the theory of the stamp tax, see Gomes de Sousa, "O Princípio Documental no Impôsto do Sêlo," in *Estudos de Direito Tributário*, São Paulo, 1950, p. 292.

including those embodying transactions that are also subject to state and municipal taxes. In order to avoid double taxation, the Constitution [3] provides that legal documents embodying transactions which are the object of a state or municipal *exclusive* tax shall be exempt from the federal stamp tax. Thus, a mercantile deed of sale, being regulated by federal law (Commercial Code, Art. 191 *et seq.*), could be subject to the federal stamp tax; but, as the transaction is subject to an exclusive state tax (the sales tax), it is exempted from the former.

The federal stamp tax is at present regulated by a consolidated act [4] which comprises, apart from a set of general rules applicable to all cases, a table divided into 123 paragraphs which lists in alphabetical order all legal documents or papers subject to the tax. Since the nature of such documents is highly diverse, the scope of the tax is different in each case, being in some a tax proper, while in others it is more in the nature of a fee.

17/2.2 Official Documents

In the case of most legal documents, such as affidavits, petitions presented to the authorities, or briefs submitted to courts, the stamp tax is a fixed charge per page, and is, essentially, a fee for the formalization of a private statement. Similarly, the stamp tax on documents issued by public authorities at the request of private parties, such as certificates, licenses, passports, and the like, or on the mandatory registration of private deeds with public officials (e.g., deeds for the conveyance of land, or minutes of corporations) is in the nature of a fee to defray the cost of a service performed, irrespective of its value to the private party.

17/2.3 Private Written Agreements

Of much greater importance is the stamp tax levied on private instruments, which is in the nature of a tax on a contract. In these cases the tax is proportional to the value of the undertaking or obligation, and the tax rate is 0.6% or Cr$ 6 for each Cr$ 1,000 of such value. The value of an agreement, for tax purposes, includes principal, interest, and all other obligations incidental to it. If a surety is given, the tax will fall on it also, but the tax on the surety may not exceed the tax on the obligation. If the value of an agreement is impossible to determine at the outset, e.g., if the duration of the contract is indeterminate, or if only a rate of commission is stipulated, then the tax is paid on the basis of an estimate submitted by the taxpayer, the agreement

[3] Const., Art. 15, §5.
[4] Decree No. 32,392 of March 9, 1953.

is registered with the collecting agency, and the original payment is readjusted every year while the contract is in force.

All parties to an agreement are jointly responsible for the tax. Where the tax is payable in the form of a fixed rate, it is paid by affixing stamps to the document and cancelling them with the date and the taxpayer's signature. When the tax due is more than Cr$ 2,000 (as is usually the case with the proportional tax on a contract), it is paid in cash to the collecting agency, which affixes an identifying stamp to all copies of the document.

The stamp tax itself is not a heavy burden on most contracts but if not paid, or paid incorrectly, it may easily become a serious factor, because the fine is five times the tax or, if fraudulent intent is proved, twenty times the tax. Even when reasonable care is exercised, a stamp tax deficiency may be incurred, for certain paragraphs of the table are very broad in scope and their language is vague.

17/2.4 Loans

Loans are subject to the tax, whether in the form of bank overdrafts (§1), debentures (§50), or promissory notes (§69). Apart from these specific cases, §49 also taxes as a loan any book entry to the credit of a third party, the origin of which is not shown to be other than a loan. However, in certain cases, the transaction is held to be taxable as a loan even if the origin of the credit entry is shown to be different, e.g., in the case of dividends declared which are credited individually to shareholders, or of bonuses or other remuneration credited to a corporation's officials or employees (see also 17/2.7).

17/2.5 Capital Issues and Liquidations

Partnership or corporation agreements are subject to the tax in various ways (§110). Thus, when a partnership or corporation is formed, the tax is due on its authorized capital, even if not fully paid up; the same applies to subsequent increases in capital through new cash or assets or the capitalization of existing reserves or surplus, but not through a revaluation of assets. In reorganizations, the tax is due on any increase or reduction of capital, unless the reduction is effected to cover losses. On liquidation the tax is due on the full amount (capital and profits) distributed to partners or shareholders.

17/2.6 Transfer of Securities

The transfer of nominative shares of stock by a shareholder is subject to the tax, which is computed on the par value of the stock transferred

(§26).[5] The transfer of bearer shares cannot be similarly taxed, but the tax is imposed on the conversion of nominative shares into bearer shares (§43).

17/2.7 Installment Sales and Promises to Sell

As previously indicated, the stamp tax does not apply to agreements for the sale of movable property, as these are subject to the state sales tax, which is an exclusive tax; nor can the stamp tax be imposed on agreements for the sale of real property, as these are subject to a state transfer tax. But when property, real or personal, is sold on installments, it is usual for the parties to execute an agreement or promise to sell under which, even if the buyer is immediately put in possession, title will pass to him only when the price is paid in full. The stamp tax is imposed on such agreements (§94). Instead of the basic 0.6% rate, the tax rates on installment sales are graduated according to price, starting at 0.4% for the portion of the price up to and including Cr$ 150,000, and rising to 3% on the portion of the price in excess of Cr$ 3,000,000. Loans secured by real property, such as mortgages, are also subject to this tax in lieu of the regular tax under §49 (17/2.4).

17/2.8 Exchange Transactions

All remittances in national and foreign currency to or from Brazil are subject to the stamp tax (§120) in addition to the special tax on exchange remittances discussed at 4/10. Another very important provision in this connection (§82) imposes the tax on all book entries to the debit or credit of a nonresident person (individual or company). According to the prevailing administrative interpretation, this broad provision is intended to complement §120 by imposing the tax on "constructive" exchange transactions effected through book entries, where there is no actual remittance of funds. Consequently, when the tax is payable under §120 it is not due under §82 and vice versa.

17/2.9 Unspecified Documents

Unspecified documents containing an undertaking or promise to pay, deliver, or perform, are subject to the stamp tax under the blanket provision of §83. It is important to note, however, that the provision applies to *unspecified* documents only, meaning that §83 does not by itself impose an independent tax, but is a provision merely complementary to the entire act and designed to apply to cases where a similar result is obtained through legal means different from those specifically

---

[5] In this case there is no infringement of the state sales tax because a transfer of ownership of securities is not a sale but an assignment. See 15/2.8c.

referred to in other sections of the act. The courts have refused to expand the scope of §83 beyond those limits.

17/2.10   Additions to Federal Stamp Tax

The education and health stamp, described by statute as a "fee," actually is an addition to the federal stamp tax. It is due at the fixed rate of Cr$ 1.50 on every document which is subject to that tax. The education and health stamp was instituted and regulated by Decree No. 21,335 of April 29, 1932, which allocated its proceeds in equal parts to federal sanitation of rural areas and to federal research in higher education and grants-in-aid to universities. Under Decree-law No. 9,486 of July 17, 1946, however, one half of the total proceeds was allocated to the pension fund for federal civil servants.

17/3.   State and Municipal Stamp Taxes

17/3.1   In General

State and municipal stamp taxes are of minor importance, chiefly because of the prevalence of the federal stamp tax (17/2.1). They are mostly in the nature of fees for government services, such as dispatching petitions, issuing certificates or licenses, etc.

Occasionally, certain states or municipalities take advantage of the imprecise definition of a stamp tax in order to impose a tax of a substantially different nature under that name.

17/3.2   State Stamp Taxes on Interstate Sales

The state stamp tax on export invoices is a case in point. As previously indicated (15/6.2), the states are permitted to levy an export tax only on the export of state-produced goods to foreign countries, but by imposing a stamp tax on invoices some states manage, in effect, to impose an export tax on interstate sales. This device is used by most of the consumer states to counteract the effects of federal Decree-law No. 915 of December 1, 1938, which regulates, to the advantage of the producer states, the taxation of interstate sales. By imposing a stamp tax, the consumer state in which such sales actually take place succeeds in taxing sales of goods shipped from another state.

17/3.3   State Stamp Taxes on Automobile Registrations

A stamp tax is imposed by some states (such as São Paulo and Rio Grande do Sul) on the registration of automobiles with the state police. This registration is required of every new owner of a car, and the stamp tax is imposed on every registration at the same rate as the sales tax, except where a sales tax has been paid on the purchase.

CHAPTER 18

. . . .

BUSINESS TAXES

18/1.   Background of the Business Tax

    18/1.1   Scope of Chapter
    18/1.2   History of the Business Tax

18/2.   Classes of Taxpayers

    18/2.1   Persons Subject to the Tax
    18/2.2   Taxable Activities
    18/2.3   Actual Exercise of an Activity
    18/2.4   Exempt Activities
          a. Newspapers, Radio, and Television
          b. Charitable and Educational Establishments
          c. Cooperative Societies
          d. New Industries
          e. Exemptions Based on Size of Establishment
          f. Corporate Executives
          g. Oil Companies

18/3.   Base and Rates

    18/3.1   Base of Business Tax
    18/3.2   Administration of the Tax

**18/4.   Other Taxes on Business and on Miscellaneous
Activities**

    18/4.1   Amusements Tax
    18/4.2   The Lottery Tax
    18/4.3   The Tax on Games of Chance
    18/4.4   Miscellaneous Taxes

18/1. Background of the Business Tax

18/1.1 Scope of Chapter

This chapter covers the general municipal business taxes here called "the business tax," as well as some other taxes of similar character.

18/1.2 History of the Business Tax

In 1812, while Brazil was a kingdom united with Portugal, the Bank of Brazil was created as a mixed corporation in which the government subscribed the major part of the capital. Since Portugal was in no position to supply the funds needed to cover the subscription, a temporary tax was enacted on all shops engaged in public business in the city of Rio de Janeiro to finance the government's participation. The tax was soon extended to other parts of the country, and it remained in force after the government's share in the Bank's capital was paid up.

When the Republic was established, the tax was allocated exclusively to the states. Later, the states were required to return 50% of the revenue from the tax to the municipalities in which it was collected. Finally, under the Constitution of 1946,[1] the business tax was allocated to the municipalities as an exclusive tax.

Many difficulties, both practical and theoretical, have arisen in the imposition and administration of the business tax. The chief one concerns the multiple taxation of businesses carried on in more than one municipality. Another is that the assessment and control of this tax are particularly difficult for smaller townships, which therefore, are unable to enforce the tax properly, or are forced to use simpler methods of assessment.[2]

To meet the problem of multiple taxation of businesses operating in more than one municipality, a federal bill providing an elaborate method of apportionment among the different municipalities in which a business is carried on has been incorporated in the draft of a national fiscal code (1/4.3). This method, in simplified form, has been voluntarily adopted by the city of São Paulo for businesses carried on there and in other municipalities of the State of São Paulo. Only in one state (Bahia) has a general solution been adopted. It is in the form of a covenant under which the municipalities have agreed to a uniform tax act administered by the state, which collects the tax and returns the proceeds to the municipalities of origin after deducting 5% as a service charge.

[1] Const., Art. 29(III).
[2] The usual method is to assess the business tax as a percentage of the state sales tax paid annually by each business.

18/2. Classes of Taxpayers

18/2.1 Persons Subject to the Tax

The tax, originally instituted as a tax on "shops," an expression which included chiefly commercial establishments but also the rudimentary industry of the time, has now evolved into a tax on the exercise of commercial, industrial, or professional activities. The tax is part of the taxpayer's overhead and is reflected in the price of commodities and services.[3]

18/2.2 Taxable Activities

Court decisions have interpreted the constitutional definition of the business tax as a tax on "industries and professions" to include manufacturing, commerce, nonindustrial production such as agriculture, livestock raising, etc., and the exercise of a profession. The latter term comprises all commercial services, such as transportation, and the exercise of a profession by a doctor, lawyer, accountant, engineer, etc.

Some state courts have limited the application of the tax to commercial activities, as defined for the purpose of the sales tax (15/2.1).[4] Other state courts have held that the tax may be imposed with respect to all activities exercised as a means of livelihood (in the case of an individual) or to further a contractual purpose (in the case of a partnership or corporation).[5] The Supreme Court has resolved the conflict in favor of the second, and wider, definition.[6]

18/2.3 Actual Exercise of an Activity

Earlier rulings held that the mere fact of being organized for business constituted sufficient basis for an assessment of the tax. This applied, for instance, in the case of a firm which had filed its partnership agreement with the Commercial Registry, had rented business premises, acquired stock-in-trade, and secured a license to operate from the appropriate authorities, although no actual business had been transacted during the taxable year.[7] Subsequently, however, the same court reversed this decision and held that the tax was due only when the activity was *actually* exercised. This is now the prevailing interpretation as shown by cases in which the taxpayer was relieved of the tax for that part of the taxable year during which the business was closed for

[3] Theotonio Monteiro de Barros, in 200 *Revista dos Tribunais* 64 (1952).
[4] Minas Gerais State Court of Appeals, 120 *Revista Forense* 195 (1948).
[5] São Paulo State Court of Appeals, 143 *Revista dos Tribunais* 240 (1943), 166 *Revista dos Tribunais* 582 (1947).
[6] Supreme Court, 122 *Revista Forense* 134 (1949).
[7] São Paulo State Court of Appeals, 144 *Revista dos Tribunais* 116 (1943).

repairs ordered by the health authorities or following a seizure foɪ nonpayment of other taxes.[8]

Actual exercise of an activity refers to the transaction of business even if no profit is shown at the close of the taxable year.[9] The failure to realize a profit does not preclude the application of the tax, as the business tax is not an income tax. Some courts have qualified this statement to exclude certain activities undertaken without intent to make a profit,[10] i.e., where certain activities are carried on as a sideline to the main business of the taxpayer, as the operation of a nonprofit canteen for the benefit of employees.

18/2.4 Exempt Activities

Exemptions vary widely from one municipality to another, but the following derive from, or may be linked to, constitutional limitations and are fairly general.

a. NEWSPAPERS, RADIO, AND TELEVISION. The Constitution grants immunity from direct taxation only to the salaries of journalists (Art. 203), but exemption from the business tax is also usually granted to newspapers, news agencies, and radio and television networks by local statutes.

b. CHARITABLE AND EDUCATIONAL ESTABLISHMENTS. Art. 31(V)(b) of the Constitution grants a general immunity from taxation to charitable and educational institutions, provided only that all their income is used in Brazil for charitable or educational purposes. The same educational purpose also motivated the general immunity from taxation granted by Art. 31(V)(c) of the Constitution to "paper to be used exclusively in the printing of periodicals and books." For purposes of the business tax, this immunity applies to importers or local manufacturers of such paper, but it is frequently extended by local statute to the printing, manufacturing and distribution of periodicals and books.

c. COOPERATIVE SOCIETIES. Cooperative societies are granted a general exemption by federal statute, but most states and municipalities have refused to comply on the ground that it is ultra vires. The Ministry of Agriculture, however, has actively promoted cooperatives, with the result that a large number of municipalities grant them full or partial exemption for the first years of their operation.[11]

---

[8] São Paulo State Court of Appeals, 184 *Revista dos Tribunais* 96 (1950).

[9] Minas Gerais State Court of Appeals, 95 *Revista Forense* 139 (1943), 100 *Revista Forense* 508 (1944); São Paulo State Court of Appeals, 144 *Revista dos Tribunais* 299 (1943).

[10] São Paulo State Court of Appeals, 181 *Revista dos Tribunais* 865 (1949); 1 *Revista Fiscal de São Paulo* 9 (1950).

[11] In most cases the exemption is 100% of the assessed tax in the first year of operation, 75% in the second, 50% in the third and 25% in the fourth. From the fifth year on, the tax is collected in full.

d. NEW INDUSTRIES. New industries are frequently exempted by municipalities. The prerequisites of the exemptions, and their scope, differ considerably from one municipality to another. In some cases exemptions are specified by local statute, while in others the law gives the municipal executive power to grant exemptions in its discretion. Sometimes the exemption is reduced in later years, as in the case of cooperatives,[12] but it is always temporary; the maximum length of time is usually five years for full exemption, or ten years for partial exemption. The hotel industry enjoys a temporary exemption from federal, state, and municipal taxes under the terms of Decree-law No. 6,761 of July 31, 1944 (but see 3/2.8).

e. EXEMPTIONS BASED ON SIZE OF ESTABLISHMENT. Exemptions are usually granted by local statute to small taxpayers, such as tradesmen with a turnover not in excess of a stipulated amount, and to home industries.

f. CORPORATE EXECUTIVES. There is some dispute concerning directors of corporations and certain professionals (such as lawyers, doctors, and accountants) employed full-time by corporations; many municipalities impose the tax in such cases, provided the professional activity in question would be taxable if exercised independently.[13]

g. OIL COMPANIES. There has been much litigation over whether both the business tax and the *impôsto unico* (16/3.2) may be levied on oil companies. It would seem rather obvious that the latter tax is intended by the Constitution to fall on the "production, commerce, distribution and consumption, as well as on the import and export of lubricants and of liquid or gaseous fuels" to the exclusion of all other taxes. The Supreme Court, however, recently ruled that the business tax, being a tax on the person of the importer, manufacturer, or merchant, can be imposed on oil companies simultaneously with the *impôsto unico,* which is a tax on certain goods or on the industrial or commercial activities exercised with regard to such goods.[14]

Similar attempts, made by municipalities, or even by states, in regard to the tax on mining companies have been defeated by the courts.[15] No similar problem arises in respect of electric power companies because they are public utilities and, as such, enjoy specific exemption from local taxation either by law or by contract.

[12] *Supra,* note 11.

[13] Decisions of the São Paulo State Court of Appeals upholding taxation have been confirmed by the Federal Supreme Court in 121 *Revista Forense* 100 (1949) and in 16 *Revista de Direito Administrativo* 117 (1949). The case for nontaxation is expressed by Haroldo Valladão, opinion in 28 *Revista de Direito Administrativo* 414 (1952).

[14] See decision quoted in footnote 16 in 16/3.1, and criticism cited therein.

[15] *Impôsto unico* on mining companies held exclusive of municipalities' business tax by São Paulo State Court of Appeals, 36 *Revista de Direito Administrativo* 196 (1954) and of state sales tax, 201 *Revista dos Tribunais* 442 (1952).

18/3. Base and Rates

18/3.1 Base of Business Tax

The imprecise definition of the tax as one "on the actual exercise of an industry or profession" is reflected by the many different factors on which the tax is based in the various municipalities. Usually the tax is assessed simultaneously on two bases: (1) As a fixed percentage (usually 10%) of the rental value of the premises in which the activity is carried out [16] and (2) either as a fixed amount or (less frequently) as a percentage of gross annual turnover, in either case combined with other factors related to the nature of the activity and to the manner of its exercise.

The second base is the more complicated of the two. Although methods of assessment vary, the law in force in the City of São Paulo is illustrative, since it is the most comprehensive and because other local laws are patterned after it.[17]

The law itself contains only general rules. The actual tax which is applicable in the individual case is determined from 38 schedules which are attached to the law. Of these, the first two are designated by Arabic numerals 1 and 2, the following thirteen by Roman numerals I to XIII, and the remaining twenty-three by letters A to X. The taxpayer first looks for the description of his activity in Schedule 1 to determine whether he is taxable at all and if so, under which of Schedules I to XIII or A to X. He then compares the facts of his case with those listed in the applicable schedule and thus finds the category number of Schedule 2 that applies to him. By referring to that category, he finds the amount of tax due in his case.

Schedule 1 is an alphabetical list of 597 types of taxable activity which are numbered consecutively. The description of each activity is followed by either a Roman numeral or a letter which refers to one of the following schedules (e.g., No. 597 — Zinc plates for roofing etc., manufacturer or merchant of — C).

Schedule 2 is a list of categories designated by numbers from 1 to 140, which indicate the amount of annual tax due (e.g., Category 1 — Annual tax Cr$ 10; Category 140 — Annual tax Cr$ 2,000,000).

Schedules I to XIII apply to activities for which gross turnover is not an element, or not the only element, of assessment. These schedules list various combinations of factors such as invested capital, annual rental value, number of employees, gross annual turnover, location of the establishment in one or another district of the city, and occasionally others

---

[16] As determined for the purposes of the tax on improved real property (3/2.7c).

[17] The business tax in the City of São Paulo is imposed under Municipal Law No. 3,683 of December 31, 1947, regulated by Decree No. 1,044 of January 8, 1948, both consolidated (together with all other local tax legislation) in Decree No. 1,436 of September 27, 1951 (Arts. 132 to 180).

which are peculiar to a particular activity. As an example, the combination of factors under Schedule VI (barbershops and beauty parlors) is invested capital, plus annual rental value, plus the number of chairs. For each combination of factors, the schedules indicate a category number corresponding to one of the 140 categories in Schedule 2.

Schedules A to X apply to activities for which gross turnover is the sole element of assessment. The concept of "gross turnover" (*movimento econômico*), although far from settled, is roughly equivalent to gross receipts. It includes sales receipts, commissions, and fees for services rendered. These letter schedules are, therefore, merely compilations of annual turnover figures which are keyed to the category numbers in Schedule 2. There are twenty-three schedules in this group (the letter W is omitted) because the tax is intended to differ according to the nature of the activity, although the turnover may be the same; consequently, very different amounts of tax apply to the same amount of turnover under the various schedules.

18/3.2   Administration of the Tax

The business tax is not "self-assessed." The taxpayer, after determining the pertinent factors as explained above, reports them, together with the rental value of the premises he occupies, on an appropriate form. On the basis of this report, the authorities issue a tentative assessment for the entire year, but usually payable in quarterly installments. At any time before the close of the taxable year the tentative assessment may be revised on the basis of an actual inspection of the taxpayer's books, records, and other pertinent data. If the tentative assessment is found to be deficient, the difference is collected (without fine, except in case of fraud) through a write-up of the unpaid installments; or, if the revision took place after the fourth installment fell due, as a fifth installment. The revision must be made, however, before the close of the taxable year. Conversely, if the tentative assessment is found to be in excess of the tax due, no refund is granted unless the revision is made after payment of the year's last installment; otherwise, the correction is effected through a reduction of the outstanding installments.

18/4.   Other Taxes on Business and on Miscellaneous Activities

18/4.1   Amusements Tax

The amusements tax is granted exclusively to the municipalities by Art. 29 (IV) of the Constitution. An amusements tax would seem to be simply a form of taxing business, but since the business tax is also granted exclusively to the municipalities, a distinction was made by defining the business tax as a tax on the establishment and the amusements tax as a tax on the public. The two taxes are therefore not held to be mutually exclusive.

The amusements tax is usually assessed simultaneously as (1) a fixed amount based on the capacity of the house and collected at stipulated intervals irrespective of actual attendance, and (2) a percentage of all charges on spectators or patrons, usually collected by means of stamps affixed to admission tickets, reservation cards, waiters' checks, etc. In most cases, a substantial portion of the proceeds of the amusements tax is allocated to welfare work and to local charities.

18/4.2   The Lottery Tax

Lotteries are regulated by Decree-law No. 854 of November 12, 1938, which makes them dependent on a federal or state concession. Art. 13 of the same act institutes a federal tax of 5% on the total price of the tickets, which is paid by the concessionaire and charged to the ticket-buyer. In addition, there is a 10% tax payable by the concessionaire on the cash value of all prizes distributed in lotteries.[18]

18/4.3   The Tax on Games of Chance

Gambling is illegal in Brazil,[19] but games of chance in amusement parks, etc., are allowed. They are subject to a federal license tax of Cr$ 500 per year and to a tax of Cr$ 0.03 per ticket sold, both payable in the form of stamps.[20] As with lotteries, there is a tax of 10% payable by the concessionaire on the cash value of all prizes distributed in games of chance operated for commercial purposes.[21]

18/4.4   Miscellaneous Taxes

Decree-law No. 1,726 of November 1, 1939, imposes a federal license tax of 0.5% to 5% on (1) the price of admission to races, fights, and similar professional sporting events, (2) the capital of establishments manufacturing or selling alcoholic beverages, tobacco, playing cards, and firearms. The same act also imposes a 10% tax payable by the defendant on the amount of bail set by the courts in criminal cases. All the taxes imposed by this act are paid in the form of stamps. About one half of the proceeds from them is used for federal assistance to state prison reform programs and to the improvement of conditions in federal penitentiaries.

[18] Decree-law No. 7,930 of September 3, 1945. This tax should not be confused with the income tax on such prizes, which is discussed at 10/4.1b2.

[19] Decree-law No. 9,215 of April 30, 1946.

[20] Law No. 4,440 of December 31, 1921, amended by Law No. 4,625 of December 31, 1922.

[21] See note 18 *supra*.

THE REAL PROPERTY

TRANSFER TAX

19/1.   In General
    19/1.1   Scope of Chapter

19/2.   Classes of Taxpayers
    19/2.1   Persons Subject to the Tax
    19/2.2   Constitutional Exemptions
    19/2.3   Legislative Exemptions
        a. Churches
        b. Certain Acquisitions by Veterans, etc.
        c. Real Property Acquired by Foreign
           Governments
        d. Acquisition of a Dwelling Place

19/3.   Taxable Event
    19/3.1   Taxable Transfers
    19/3.2   Special 30-year Tax in Rio de Janeiro

19/4.   Base of the Tax
    19/4.1   In General
    19/4.2   Real Property by Nature
    19/4.3   Real Property by Destination
    19/4.4   Real Property by Operation of Law

19/5.   Rates and Computation of the Tax
    19/5.1   Tax Rate
    19/5.2   Additions to the Tax

19/6.   Administration of the Tax
    19/6.1   Execution and Registration of Deeds

19/6.2   Collection of Tax "by Anticipation"
19/6.3   Appraisal
         a. Preliminary Appraisal
19/6.4   Taxpayers' Remedies
19/6.5   Fines and Penalties

19/1. In General

19/1.1   Scope of Chapter

Article 19 (III) of the federal Constitution authorizes the states to impose a tax on the transfer of immovable property inter vivos. The taxable transfer may be either gratuitous or for a consideration. For the reasons stated at 3/3.1, the gift tax on gratuitous transfers of real property is described under taxes on capital in Chapter 3 and the tax on transfers of real property for a consideration in this chapter.

19/2. Classes of Taxpayers

19/2.1   Persons Subject to the Tax

The taxpayer is always the individual or entity *acquiring* the property. In the case of a deficiency the property itself may be seized in the hands of the taxpayer.

19/2.2   Constitutional Exemptions

Since the taxpayer is the party acquiring the property, persons who are exempt from taxation under the Constitution,[1] such as federal, state and local governments, charitable or educational associations, and political parties, may acquire real property free of this tax.

19/2.3   Legislative Exemptions

Apart from the constitutional exemptions, all states specifically exempt acquisitions of real property effected by certain persons under specified circumstances.

a. CHURCHES. Although churches of every denomination are granted tax immunity by the federal Constitution, the application of this provision is frequently disputed by the states in respect of the transfer tax on the ground that the immunity is restricted to taxes on property held but does not extend to taxes on its acquisition. In practice, however, the exemption is always granted by a special statute.

[1] Const., Art. 31(V)(a) and (b).

b. CERTAIN ACQUISITIONS BY VETERANS, ETC. The purchase of a residence by Brazilian military veterans, by persons suffering from certain disabilities, or by public servants or other individuals eligible to acquire property in government housing developments is exempt. The exemption is usually restricted as to price and is always contingent on the fact that the beneficiary does not own other real property.

c. REAL PROPERTY ACQUIRED BY FOREIGN GOVERNMENTS. Buildings or plots purchased by foreign governments for the use of their embassies or consulates are exempted on the basis of reciprocity.

d. ACQUISITION OF A DWELLING PLACE. The purchase of a "dwelling place" [2] is always exempt. However, the exemption is usually restricted to acquisitions below a stipulated price, which, in view of current property values is of little practical significance.

19/3. Taxable Event

19/3.1 Taxable Transfers

The taxable event for purposes of this tax is the acquisition of any of the properties defined in Art. 43 of the Civil Code (see 3/2.1) or of certain of the rights treated as real property under Art. 44 of the Civil Code.[3] Whenever real property is purchased or otherwise acquired (except by gift or inheritance), and whenever transferable rights in real property, such as uses, usufructs, and easements, are assigned for a consideration, the real property transfer tax falls due. The transfer of rights which merely secure a debt, such as mortgages and other liens, is not subject to this tax.

Art. 19(III) of the Constitution, in allocating this tax exclusively to the states, also refers specifically to the contribution of such property, or rights in property, to the capital of a legal entity. This specific provision is intended to eliminate a doubt whether these assets become the property of the entity. Under the Constitution and the Corporation Law [4] it is now clear that the transfer tax is due both on the contribu-

[2] A dwelling place, as defined by Art. 70 of the Civil Code, is exempt from seizure for debt (except for unpaid taxes on the building itself) while occupied by the owner, his wife, or his minor children.

[3] Civil Code, Art. 44: The following rights constitute real property under the law:
   I. Rights in real property, including agricultural pledges, and legal remedies provided for the protection or enforcement of those rights.
   II. Inalienable government bonds.
   III. The right to a distributive share of a decedent's estate.

The rights in real property referred to in Art. 44(I) are enumerated in Art. 674 of the Civil Code. The remedial rights also listed in that section and the inalienable rights referred to in Art. 44(II) (government bonds transferred by gift or inheritance with a clause that they cannot be alienated by the donee, heir, or legatee or attached by his creditors) are of no interest for purposes of the real property transfer tax.

[4] Decree-law No. 2,627 of September 26, 1940, Art. 7.

tion of assets to the capital of a legal entity and on their distribution to partners or shareholders upon its liquidation.[5]

The transfer tax may be avoided by creating a corporation which holds title to real property and by transferring the shares of that corporation rather than the property. In trying to curb this practice, most states have, at one time or another, made unsuccessful attempts to impose the transfer tax on sales or assignments of shares or participations in corporations or partnerships organized primarily for the purpose of holding real property. The courts, however, have firmly adhered to the principle that a corporation or partnership is a legal entity distinct from its shareholders or partners and that a share or participation is movable property which does not represent title to an undivided portion of the real property held by the corporation or partnership.[6] It should be noted, however, that the states' contention has gained a certain measure of recognition from the requirement of the Corporation Law (Art. 177) that shares of real property corporations must be nominative. This provision is obviously designed to make it possible for the states to tax transfers of such shares, which they would not be able to do if the shares were made out to bearer. On the other hand, the states' claim to the transfer tax is recognized by the courts in reorganizations, such as a merger, in which all or a part of the real property of corporations or partnerships is transferred.

19/3.2   Special 30-year Tax in Rio de Janeiro

The Federal District (City of Rio de Janeiro) imposes a tax, at the same rate as the transfer tax, every 30 years on the fair market value of real property owned by legal entities, provided such real property is located in the Federal District, even if the seat of the entity is elsewhere. The 30-year period in which the tax recurs is selected as the average length of time between transfers of property not owned by a legal entity. This tax is within the concurrent tax jurisdiction of the Federal District.

19/4.   Base of the Tax

19/4.1   In General

In every state, the base of the tax is the fair market value of the

---

[5] Some states grant an exemption in this case, provided that the real property is returned on liquidation to the partner or shareholder who had contributed it originally. This exemption can obviously be justified only as a tax benefit intended to promote partnership or corporate investment. Clearly with the same object, some states also apply reduced rates to transfers of real property to a partnership or corporation in payment for capital subscribed, as compared with the rates applicable to transfers for other purposes.

[6] São Paulo State Court of Appeals, 181 *Revista dos Tribunais* 362 (1949); 195 *Revista dos Tribunais* 327 (1952); Supreme Court, 28 *Revista de Direito Administrativo* 185 (1952).

property at the time of its transfer (19/6.2). Consequently, the gain or loss realized by the transferor is not a factor in determining the base of assessment.[7]

Fair market value for tax purposes is determined by an appraisal conducted by the tax authorities, usually according to Harper's formula (3/2.5b), and subject to protest by the taxpayer as to the method of appraisal applied.

Regarding the effect, on the tax base, of the price for which the property is transferred, see 19/6.2.

19/4.2 Real Property by Nature

Difficulties have arisen regarding the classification of certain items as "real property by nature," as defined in the Civil Code.[8] Thus, although trees and growing crops qualify under the definition (as natural accretions to the soil), it has been decided by state courts (in nontax cases) that sales of standing trees or of unpicked crops, to be felled or picked by the buyer, are sales of movable property.[9] The Supreme Court, in a later case, confirmed this view by ruling that the application of the real property transfer tax to such sales is unconstitutional.[10]

Since forests are granted a general exemption from taxation by federal law,[11] it would seem that their value should be deducted for the purposes of the transfer tax when they are sold together with the land. While general exemptions by federal statute are often questioned by the states, most states grant similar exemptions, through their own legislation, to natural forests and reforestation projects.

The case of mineral deposits involves the unsettled question of whether the *impôsto unico* embraces taxation of the property value of mines or only that of their industrial exploitation (16/3.4). State courts have ruled that the value of mineral deposits, whether in the course of exploitation or not, is not deductible in determining the value of the property for transfer tax purposes.[12]

[7] The contention that the Constitution does not justify the fair market value as the base of the tax has been rejected by the São Paulo State Cour+ of Appeals on the ground that the Constitution did not intend the tax to be an income or capital gains tax; 193 *Revista dos Tribunais* 938 (1951). Similarly, it has frequently been contended that the income tax on gains from the sale of real property (9/8.) is unconstitutional as impinging on the real property transfer tax, but the Supreme Court rejected this contention in an early case; 77 *Arquivo Judiciário* 353 (1946). Thus the two taxes are entirely separate and do not conflict with each other.

[8] For definition of real property in Civil Code, Art. 43, see 3/2.1.

[9] São Paulo State Court of Appeals, 131 *Revista dos Tribunais* 632 (1941); Minas Gerais State Court of Appeals, 155 *Revista dos Tribunais* 771 (1945).

[10] Supreme Court, 118 *Revista Forense* 401 (1948).

[11] Federal Code of Forestry, Decree No. 23;793 of January 23, 1934, Art. 17.

[12] São Paulo State Court of Appeals, 187 *Revista dos Tribunais* 360 (1950); 190 *Revista dos Tribunais* 939 (1951).

Concerning the assignment of the federal concession which is required to exploit a mine, it has been held that the concession is a right in real property and that, therefore, the transfer tax is due on the assignment.[13] Similarly, it has been decided that if real property containing a mineral deposit is rented with the right to the tenant to extract ore, the contract is not a lease but a sale, since the extracted ore becomes the property of the tenant. This ruling was given in a nontax case, but its tax implications are obvious.[14]

19/4.3 Real Property by Destination

"Real property by destination" (3/2.1) is real property only as long as it is permanently affixed to, or kept on, the land or the building. Consequently, the tax is due in regard to this property only when it is sold, or otherwise alienated, together with the land or building to which it adheres.

Conversely, a sale of machinery which is separated from the factory is a sale of movable property and not subject to the transfer tax.[15] The taxpayer must show that the separation was bona fide. Thus, the simultaneous sale to the same buyer of machinery by one deed, and of the factory building by another deed, has been considered an ineffective device to escape the transfer tax.[16]

19/4.4 Real Property by Operation of Law

When rights treated as real property [17] are assigned separately from the real property to which they are attached, the tax is computed on the full fair market value of the rights assigned. This value is defined by law in each state as being from one third to two thirds of the full fair market value of the real property to which the rights are attached.

Conversely, when real property is transferred separately from the rights attached to it, the fair market value of the real property is reduced by the fair market value that the rights would have for tax purposes if assigned separately.

[13] The decision is by the Santa Catarina State Court of Appeals; by refusing to review the case, the Supreme Court implicitly admitted that there had been no violation either of the Constitution (as to the scope of the *impôsto unico*) or of a federal statute (such as the Civil Code as to the definition of rights in real property, or the Code of Mines as to the definition of a mining concession); 130 *Revista Forense* 79 (1950).

[14] Minas Gerais State Court of Appeals, confirmed by the Supreme Court in 118 *Revista Forense* 107 (1948).

[15] São Paulo State Court of Appeals, 116 *Revista Forense* 183 (1948). But note that such a sale, as a mercantile sale of movable property, is subject to the sales tax (15/2.2).

[16] São Paulo State Court of Appeals, 173 *Revista dos Tribunais* 340 (1948).

[17] *Supra*, note 3 in 19/3.1 for translation of Civil Code, Art. 44, where such rights are defined.

19/5. Rates and Computation of the Tax

19/5.1 Tax Rate

The rate of the transfer tax varies from state to state; the average rate is 10%.[18] Except for the addition discussed in 19/5.2 below, the rate of the real property transfer tax is proportional and does not vary with the value of the property transferred.

19/5.2 Additions to the Tax

Many states impose an addition of 1% to the real property transfer tax rate on transfers whose value exceeds Cr$ 100,000. The revenue from this addition is usually earmarked for state housing agencies.

19/6. Administration of the Tax

19/6.1 Execution and Registration of Deeds

Under the civil law of Brazil, a transfer of real property can only be effected through a deed executed before a notary (*tabelião*) and title passes when the deed is filed with a special office called the Registry of Real Property (*Registro de Imóveis*). The same is true of any right in real property. A deed for the alienation of real property, or for the creation or the assignment of a right in real property, is binding *between the parties* as soon as it is executed before a notary, but it is effective against third parties only after it is filed with the Registry. By using the Registry's records, which are public, to facilitate the administration, collection, and control of the tax, the state authorities have made tax evasion nearly impossible.

19/6.2 Collection of Tax "by Anticipation"

Since a transfer of real property is binding between the parties when the deed is executed, although registration is needed to make it effective as against third parties, the tax is in most states collected "by anticipation," i.e., when the deed is executed. If the filing of the deed is subsequently denied by a final decision of the courts, the tax is refunded. On the other hand, proof of payment of the tax is a prerequisite of registration.

As a general rule, the tax is tentatively computed on the price as stipulated by the parties, with the express provision that the authorities reserve the right to appraise the property for tax purposes and to collect the difference, if any, within a prescribed time limit (usually

[18] As stated at 19/3.1, reduced rates apply to contributions of real property to the capital of corporations and other entities. These rates vary between 5% and 8%.

one year), after which the payment made by anticipation becomes final.

One notable exception is the Federal District (the city of Rio de Janeiro) where the tax is not collected by anticipation but only after appraisal of the property by the authorities. This system eliminates subsequent collections of deficiencies, but it frequently delays the registration of a deed for several months, during which the buyer may have difficulties in negotiating the property.

19/6.3 Appraisal

Appraisals of property are made by the tax authorities according to technical methods which are designed to determine individual fair market values.

Once the fair market value of the land is ascertained (see 3/2.5b on Harper's formula), the improvements are appraised by methods appropriate to their nature. Thus, buildings are usually appraised on the basis of current construction costs, with corrective factors for age and depreciation. Obviously, the authorities exercise a much wider margin of discretion in appraising improvements than they do in appraising land, and this margin is greatest in their appraisals of industrial machinery, where valuation is most difficult technically.

a. PRELIMINARY APPRAISAL. The hazards of property appraisal can be minimized through a petition for the appraisal to be conducted preliminary to the transaction. In most states the authorities will comply with such requests for a nominal fee. If the tax is paid on the appraised value, the parties to the transaction are secure even if the stipulated price is higher than the appraised value.

19/6.4 Taxpayers' Remedies

The conclusions of the appraising authority can be contested by the taxpayer under the normal administrative or judicial procedure for the review of tax assessments (1/5.). It is clear, however, that the taxpayer may only contest the application of the technical method adopted by the authority making the appraisal. In such cases, the courts usually rely on the opinion of valuation experts appointed by them.

19/6.5 Fines and Penalties

In the usual instance, when a deficiency in tax is asserted solely because the appraised value of the property is higher than the price, the difference is collected without fine or interest. On the other hand, penalties up to 20% of the defaulted tax are imposed if it is shown that the deficiency is due to fraud, the usual form of which is that the parties stipulate a lower price in the deed than the one which was actually paid. The property law helps the tax authorities because, if the contract between the parties is rescinded, the seller's liability is limited to the stipulated price, which tends to discourage understatements thereof in the agreement.

REFERENCES

Table of Statutes

Federal Constitution of 1946

Art.	
15	1/3.2; 1/6.2
15 (II)	1/6.2b; 16/2.1
15 (III)	10/1.1; 16/3.1
15 (III) § 2	10/1.1
15 (V)	4/10.
15 (VI)	16/3.5; 17/1.2
15 § 1	16/2.4b
15 § 2	16/3.1
15 § 3	9/1.2
15 § 5	17/2.1
19	1/3.2; 1/6.3
19 (I)	3/2.1
19 (II)	3/3.1; 3/3.7
19 (III)	3/3.1; 15/2.6; 19/1.1; 19/3.1
19 (IV)	15/2.1; 15/2.7; 15/2.8
19 (V)	15/6.1
19 (VI)	17/1.2
19 § 2	3/3.2
19 § 3	3/3.2
19 § 5	15/1.3; 15/4.1
21	1/3.3; 1/6.3g
27	15/6.1
29	1/3.2; 1/6.4
29 (I)	3/2.1
29 (III)	18/1.2
29 (IV)	18/4.1
29 (V)	17/1.2
30 Sole §	1/3.4
31	1/3.5; 3/2.3; 3/3.3; 5/6.1; 15/2.8a; 15/2.8c; 16/2.4b
31 (V) (a)	19/2.2
31 (V) (b)	18/2.4b; 19/2.2
31 (V) (c)	18/2.4b
65	1/4.5c
66	1/4.5c
66 (I)	1/4.5d
86 § 2	1/4.5c
87	1/4.5c
101	13/4.3
141	6/1.3a
141 § 2	1/4.5a
141 § 24	1/5.5
141 § 34	1/3.1; 1/4.5a
152	16/3.5

Art.	Constitution (continued)
203	3/3.5; 5/5.3; 6/1.2e; 6/1.3a; 9/5.1a; 18/2.4a

Civil Code of Brazil

Art.	
16	5/2.3
43	3/2.1; 3/2.7b; 9/8.2; 19/3.1; 19/4.2
43 (3)	3/2.7b
44	3/3.4; 9/8.2; 9/8.2b; 19/3.1; 19/4.4
44 (I)	19/3.1
44 (II)	19/3.1
48	3/3.4
70	19/2.3d
173	13/6.2
177	1/5.10; 13/6.2
178 (7) (II)	1/5.10
368	12/1.2b
369	12/1.2b
396–405	12/1.2b
674	19/3.1
677	1/5.7
678	9/4.1b
1,122	15/2.4
1,572	3/3.6

Commercial Code of Brazil

Art.	
11	6/2.2
12	6/2.2
13	6/2.2
14	6/2.2
17	1/5.3b
165, *et seq.*	15/2.7
191, *et seq.*	15/2.1; 15/2.4; 17/2.1
200	15/2.4
211	15/2.4
221	15/2.5
311–314	1/4.2e
315–316	1/4.2b
317–324	1/4.2c
325–328	1/4.2d

Corporation Law (Decree-law No. 2,627 of September 26, 1940)

General	1/4.2e; 1/4.2f; 1/4.2g
Art.	
2	15/2.2
5	7/3.6
6	7/3.6
7	15/2.6; 19/3.1
15	9/9.5a
16	9/9.5a
16 Sole §	9/9.5a
17	9/9.5a
18	9/9.5a
19	9/9.5a
31	9/2.1e
60	11/3.2
61 § 5	14/4.2
64	5/2.1; 11/3.2; 14/4.2
65 Sole §	14/4.1
68	6/2.1
98	6/4.1a
98 Sole §	6/4.1a
105 (a)	9/9.5a
105 (d)	9/9.5a
105 (e)	9/9.5a
105 (g)	9/9.5a
107	9/9.5a
116	7/5.2b
129 Sole § (a)	6/5.1; 6/5.4
129 Sole § (b)	6/5.1; 6/5.3
129 Sole § (c)	6/5.2
130	6/6.2; 7/5.3; 7/8.2
130 § 1	6/6.2
130 § 2	6/5.4; 6/6.2; 7/8.3
152	9/2.1f; 9/9.4
153	9/2.1f; 9/9.4
163–166	1/4.2e
177	19/3.1

Federal Mining Code (Decree-law No. 1,985 of January 29, 1940, as amended by Decree-law No. 5,247 of February 12, 1943)

Art.	
11	10/1.2
68	10/1.1; 16/3.4
68 § 2	10/1.1

Federal Code of Forestry (Decree No. 23,793, of January 23, 1934)

Art. 17	3/2.3e; 19/4.2

Federal Code of Civil Procedure

General	1/5.5

Criminal Code of Brazil

Art.	
240, *et seq.*	13/7.1
325	1/5.8
334	1/5.8

Other Laws

No. and Date	
3,708, 10 I 1919	
Art. 18	1/4.2f
4,440, 31 XII 1921	18/4.3
4,625, 31 XII 1922	15/1.2; 18/4.3
Art. 31	2/1
187, 15 I 1936	15/1.2
Art. 8	15/2.7
9	15/2.7
22, 15 II 1947	16/3.2
154, 25 XI 1947	2/1.; 7/3.4; 7/4.4
156, 27 XI 1947	4/10.
302, 13 VII 1948	16/3.2
313, 30 VII 1948	1/2.6
494, 26 XI 1948	16/2.4b
842, 4 X 1949	1/2.6
854, 10 X 1949	1/3.4
1,433, 15 IX 1951	4/10.
1474, 26 XI 1951	2/1; 7/6.2; 12/1.3b
Art. 1 §§ 2–4	7/8.1
2	7/8.3
2 § 2	7/8.3
2 § 3	7/8.3
3	7/8.1
3 (b)	7/8.2
3 § 2 (III)	7/8.2
3 § 3	7/8.2
1,533, 31 XII 1951	1/5.5
1,628, 20 VI 1952	7/8.2; 12/1.3b
1,749, 28 XI 1952	16/3.2
1,772, 18 XII 1952	7/6.2; 7/8.1
2,145, 29 XII 1953	16/2.6
2,308, 31 VIII 1954	4/10; 16/3.3
2,354, 29 XI 1954	2/1.; 5/6.6; 6/3.2; 6/9.1; 8/1.5a; 11/2.3; 11/2.4; 13/4.1
Art. 6, § II	7/5.4
17	7/3.4; 7/5.1
30	11/3.5c
2,653, 24 XI 1955	16/2.4b; 16/2.5
2,862, 4 IX 1956	1/5.1; 2/1; 2/3.3; 2/6; 7/6.2; 12/2.5
	Chapter 14
Art. 1	14/1.
2	14/2; 14/4.3
3	14/3.
3 Sole §	14/3.
4	14/4.1
4 § 2	14/4.1
5	14/4.4
5 (a)	14/4.3
5 (b)	14/4.4
5 (c)	14/4.3
5 (d)	14/4.3

Other Laws (continued)

2,862, 4 IX 1956 (continued)
Art.

5 (e)	14/4.3
5 § 1	14/4.3
5 § 2 (a)	14/4.3
5 § 2 (b)	14/4.4
5 § 3	14/4.3; 14/4.4
5 § 4	14/4.2; 14/4.3; 14/4.4
5 § 5	14/4.3; 14/4.4
5 § 6	14/4.3
5 § 7	14/4.3
5 § 8	14/4.4
5 § 9	14/4.3; 14/4.4; 14/4.5
5 § 10	14/4.3; 14/4.4
6	14/5.2a; 14/5.2b
7	14/2.
7 Sole §	14/5.1b
8	14/5.1a
9	14/6.1
10	14/6.2
10 Sole §	14/6.2
11	14/2.
13	14/6.1; 14/8.
14	14/8.
15	14/4.3; 14/4.4
16	14/8.
19	5/1.1; 8/1.5a; 12/1.2a; 12/1.2c
19 § 1	12/1.2c
19 § 2	8/1.5a
20	8/1.5a
20 § 1	8/1.5a
20 § 2	8/1.5a; 12/1.4
20 § 3	8/1.5a
20 § 5	8/1.5a
21	8/1.5a
21 Sole §	8/1.5a
22	12/1.2b
23	12/2.3
23 Sole § (b)	12/2.6
25	7/8.3; 9/1.6; 9/2.2a; 9/2.2d; 9/2.4; 9/9.5b
26	9/9.5a
26 Sole §	9/9.5a
27	13/7.2; 13/7.3
28	13/7.3
29	13/6.1
2,973, 26 XI 1956	1/2.3b; 2/4.4b; 7/8.1; 7/8.2; 12/1.3b
Art. 1 § 1	12/1.3b
1 § 2	12/2.4a
1 § 3	7/8.2
2,974, 26 XI 1956	16/2.2; 16/2.5
2,975, 27 XI 1956	16/3.2
2996, 10 XII 1956	1/6.2g

Decree-laws

No. and Date

5, 13 XI 1937	1/5.9
42, 6 XII 1937	1/5.9

Decree-laws (continued)

No. and Date

300, 24 II 1938	1/2.6
607, 10 VIII 1938	13/5.1
Art. 21	13/4.3
854, 12 XI 1938	18/4.2
Art. 13	18/4.2
915, 1 XII 1938	1/6.3h; 15/1.3b; 17/3.2
960, 17 XII 1938	1/5.7
Art. 60	1/5.7
1,608, 18 IX 1939	1/5.5; 13/4.3
1,726, 1 XI 1939	18/4.4
1,985, 29 I 1940	See Federal Mining Code
2,063, 7 III 1940	
Arts. 57–66	10/3.2a
2,281, 5 VI 1940	16/3.5
2,416, 17 VII 1940	1/3.4
2,627, 26 IX 1940	See Corporation Law
2,878, 18 XII 1940	1/2.6
3,200, 19 IV 1941	12/1.3a
Art. 32	12/1.3a
33	12/1.3a
34	12/1.3a
35	12/1.3a
36	12/1.3a
3,336, 10 VI 1941	1/5.9; 13/4.3
4,014, 13 I 1942	1/5.6
4,178, 13 III 1942	2/1.
5,247, 12 II 1943	See Federal Mining Code
5,452, 1 V 1943	1/5.7
5,844, 23 IX 1943	2/1.
5,893, 19 X 1943	15/2.8b
6,016, 22 XI 1943	1/3.5; 3/2.3
6,224, 24 I 1944	14/1.; 14/4.1
6,761, 31 VII 1944	3/2.8; 18/2.4d
7,903, 27 VII 1945	
Art. 39	7/3.6
138	7/3.6
7,930, 3 IX 1945	18/4.2
8,401, 19 XII 1945	15/2.8b
8,463, 27 XII 1945	16/3.2
9,159, 10 IV 1946	14/1.; 14/4.1
9,215, 30 IV 1946	18/4.3
9,407, 27 VI 1946	7/6.2; 14/4.3
9,486, 17 VII 1946	17/2.10
9,832, 11 IX 1946	1/5.6

Decrees

No. and Date

14,946, 15 VIII 1921	9/1.2a
19,412, 19 XI 1930	9/1.2a
20,910, 6 I 1932	1/5.10
21,335, 29 IV 1932	17/2.10
21,554, 20 VI 1932	2/1.
21,717, 10 VIII 1932	9/1.2a
22,061, 9 XI 1932	15/1.2

Decrees (continued)

No. and Date	
22,239, 19 XII 1932	15/2.8
22,456, 10 II 1933	10/3.2a
22,866, 28 VI 1933	1/5.7
23,535, 1 XII 1933	9/1.2a
23,793, 23 I 1934	See Federal Code of Forestry
24,233, 5 V 1934	9/1.2a
24,268, 19 V 1934	4/10.
24,643, 10 VII 1934	16/3.5
15,028, 13 III 1944	14/1.
24,239, 22 XII 1947	2/1.
25,474, 10 IX 1948	1/2.6
26,149, 5 I 1949	16/2.2; 16/2.5
27,541, 3 XII 1949	1/2.6
30,812, 2 V 1952	12/1.3b
Art. 4 § 1 (b)	7/8.2
4 § 5	7/8.2; 8/8.2
4 § 11	7/8.2; 8/8.2
32,392, 9 III 1953	17/2.1
34,893, 5 I 1954	1/2.7b
36,773, 13 I 1955	See Income Tax Regulations
38,492, 31 XII 1955	16/2.4b
39,995, 13 IX 1956	2/1.; Chapter 14
Art. 1	14/4.3; 14/4.4
1 § 1	14/4.3
1 § 2	14/4.3
1 § 3	14/4.3
1 § 4	14/4.3
2	14/4.3
3	14/4.3
4	14/4.4
4 § 1	14/4.4
4 § 2	14/4.4
5	14/4.3; 14/4.4
6	14/4.4; 14/4.5
7	14/4.4
8 (a)	14/4.3
8 (b)	14/4.4
9	14/4.2
Art. 10	14/4.3; 14/4.4
10 Sole §	14/4.3
13	14/4.3
40,384, 19 XI 1956	Chapter 14
Art. 1	14/2.
4	14/7.
5	14/2.
6	14/2.; 14/3.
7	14/7.
7 § 1	14/7.
7 § 2	14/7.
7 § 3	14/7.
7 § 4	14/7.
9	14/8.
10	14/8.
11	14/8.
12	14/3.
12 § 1	14/6.2
12 § 2	14/6.2

Decrees (continued)

40,384, 19 XI 1956 (continued) Art.	
13	14/3.
13 § 2	14/5.2a
13 § 3	14/5.2b
13 § 4	14/5.2
16	14/4.1
16 § 2	14/4.1
17	14/5.1a
18	14/5.1b
19	14/6.1
20	14/7.
23	14/6.1
31	14/8.

Income Tax Regulations
(promulgated under Decree No. 36,773 of January 13, 1955)

Reg. Art.	
1	5/1.1; 5/5.1; 5/6.6; 6/1.3a; 8/1.5a; 13/1.1b
1 Sole §	6/8.1
3	9/1.2a
4	9/1.3; 9/1.4
4 § 1	9/1.4b
4 § 3	8/2.2; 9/1.5
4 § 4	9/1.5
4 § 5 (a)	9/1.4b
4 § 5 (b)	9/9.5a
4 § 5 (c)	9/1.4c
4 § 5 (d)	10/4.1b
4 § 6	9/1.3a
5 § 1 (a)	8/1.2a
5 § 1 (I) (c)	7/5.2a; 8/1.2b
5 § 1 (II)	8/1.2a; 9/3.1
5 § 2	7/5.2a; 8/1.2b
5 § 3	7/5.2a; 8/1.2b
5 § 4	7/5.2a; 8/1.2b
5 § 5	7/5.2a; 8/1.2b
5 § 6	7/5.2a; 8/1.2b
6	8/2.2
6 (g)	9/5.1.a
7	9/4.1a
7 Sole § (a)	9/4.1a
7 Sole § (b)	9/4.1a
8	7/4.3
8 Sole §	11/2.2; 11/3.4c
8 (a)	9/2.1a
8 (b)	7/5.2a
8 (c)	7/7.2; 9/2.1b
8 (d)	9/2.1c; 9/2.1d; 9/2.1f; 9/9.5a; 14/4.3
8 (d) (I)	9/2.2b
8 (d) (II)	9/2.2b
8 (e)	9/2.1e; 9/9.5a
8 (f)	9/2.1f; 9/9.4
9	10/2.2a
10	10/4.1a
10 Sole §	9/4.1a
10 (b)	9/4.3a

Income Tax Regulations (continued)

Reg. Art.		Reg. Art.	
10(c)	9/4.3a	27 § 2	5/2.4; 11/3.2
10(d)	9/5.2a	28	5/6.1; 5/6.2; 14/2; 14/4.4
10(e)	7/1.3	28 Sole §	5/6.4
10(f)	10/4.1a	28(d)	5/6.6; 12/1.1; 12/2.2
11 § 1(a)	7/1.1; 8/1.2b; 8/2.2	30	5/6.5; 11/4.1; 14/2
11 § 1(c)	8/1.2a; 8/1.3a	31	5/6.6; 10/1.1; 11/2.2
11 § 2	6/1.2e	32	6/1.1; 6/2.1; 7/1.1
11 § 2(a)	9/1.4b; 9/3.1	33	6/9.1; 13/2.2b
11 § 2(c)	12/1.2b	33 § 1	6/9.1; 11/3.3b
11 § 3	6/1.2e	33 § 2	6/9.1
12	6/1.2	33 § 3	6/9.1
12 § 1	6/4.1b	34	6/2.1; 6/4.2; 11/2.3; 13/7.4a
12 § 3	7/2.1; 13/1.1a	34 § 1	6/2.1; 11/2.3
13	9/1.2b; 9/1.3b	34 § 2	6/7.1
14	8/1.3; 11/3.4c	34 § 3	11/3.3a
14(a)	8/1.2a	34 § 4	6/3.7; 6/9.2
15	8/2.3; 9/5.1a	35	10/4.2; 11/2.3; 14/3
15 § 1(a)	8/2.3	35 § 1	11/2.3
15 § 1(b)	8/2.3	35 § 2	11/2.3
15 § 2	8/2.3	37	7/1.1; 7/4.2
16	9/4.1b; 11/3.4	37(a)	6/4.2; 7/2.1; 7/2.2; 7/2.3;
16 § 1(a)	9/4.1b		7/2.5; 7/2.8
16 § 1(b)	9/4.1b	37(b)	7/2.4
16 § 2	9/4.1b	37(c)	6/6.1; 7/2.9; 7/4.1
17	9/4.3a; 9/5.2a; 10/4.1a	37(d)	6/6.1; 7/3.1
18	6/1.1	37(e)	7/3.4; 7/5.1
20	6/4.1b; 7/2.1	37(f)	6/6.1; 10/1.2
20(a)	7/2.1; 12/1.2b	37(g)	7/2.10
20(b)	7/2.1; 9/3.1; 12/1.2b	37 § 1(a)	6/6.1; 10/3.2a
20(c)	7/4.1; 12/1.2b	37 § 1(b)	10/3.2b
20(d)	7/2.1; 7/2.10; 12/1.2b	37 § 2	11/3.3c
	13/1.1a	37 § 3	11/3.3c
20(e)	12/1.2b	38	6/3.1; 6/7.1; 13/1.2a; 13/7.4b
20(e) (I)	12/1.2b	38(e)	7/4.1
20(e) (II)	12/1.2b	38 § 1	13/1.2a
20(f)	12/1.2b	38 § 2	6/3.2
20(g)	12/1.2b	39	13/1.2a
20(h)	12/1.2b	39 § 1	13/1.2a
20(i)	12/1.2b	39 § 5	13/1.2a
20 § 1	12/1.2b	40	6/3.6; 6/9.1; 11/3.3b
20 § 2	12/1.2b	40 § 1	6/9.2; 11/2.3; 14/5.2b
20 § 3	12/1.2b	40 § 2	6/9.2; 11/2.3
20 § 4	12/1.2b	41	6/9.1
21	6/1.1	42	6/9.1
22	5/4.4; 6/3.1	43	7/1.1; 7/4.2
22 § 1	6/4.1a	43 § 1(a)	7/5.1
22 § 3	6/2.2	43 § 1(b)	7/5.2; 7/5.2a
23(a)	8/3.3	43 § 1(c)	7/5.2; 7/5.2a
23(d)	8/3.2	43 § 1(d)	7/5.2b
24 § 3	5/5.3; 6/1.2e; 9/5.1a	43 § 1(e)	7/5.2c
24 § 6	8/1.5a	43 § 1(f)	6/6.1; 7/1.1; 7/5.3;
24 § 7	7/8.3		9/2.2b
25	5/3.2; 7/1.3; 8/1.4; 8/2.5;	43 § 1(g)	6/6.1; 7/6.1
	9/1.2c; 9/4.1c; 9/4.3a;	43 § 1(h)	6/6.1; 7/4.2; 7/6.2;
	9/5.1a; 9/5.2a; 9/9.5a;		7/6.3; 9/9.4
	10/4.1a; 12/1.1	43 § 1(h) (I)	7/6.2; 14/4.3
26	12/1.2a; 12/1.2c	43 § 1(i)	6/6.1; 7/6.1
27	5/2.3; 5/3.4; 6/1.1	43 § 1(j)	6/6.1; 7/6.1
27 § 1	5/3.4; 10/1.1; 10/4.1a	43 § 1(k)	6/6.1; 7/5.3

Income Tax Regulations (continued)

Reg. Art.		Reg. Art.	
43 § 1(l)	6/6.1; 7/5.3	64	13/1.1a; 13/1.2a
43 § 1(m)	6/6.1; 7/5.3; 7/5.4	65	13/7.5
43 § 2(a)	7/2.12	65 Sole §	13/1.1a
43 § 2(b)	7/2.13	65 § 1	13/1.1a
43 § 2(c)	7/7.1; 9/2.3; 9/9.5b; 11/3.3b; 14/4.5	67	12/1.2b; 13/1.1c; 13/7.5
43 § 2(d)	7/7.2; 9/2.3; 9/9.5b; 11/3.3b; 14/4.5	67 § 1	12/1.2b; 13/1.1c
		67 § 2	12/1.2b; 13/1.1c
43 § 2(e)	7/2.8; 7/7.3; 9/3.2	69	13/1.2a; 13/7.5
43 § 3	7/4.2; 7/4.4	69 Sole §	13/1.2a
43 § 4	7/4.2	70	13/1.1a; 13/1.2a
43 § 5	7/6.2	73	5/1.1; 5/4.1; 6/1.3b
44	5/3.1; 5/4.8; 6/9.1; 6/9.2; 7/1.1; 7/4.4; 7/6.1; 7/6.3; 7/7.1; 9/1.7; 9/2.2b; 9/2.3; 9/4.1a; 9/4.3b; 9/5.1b; 9/5.2b; 9/8.1; 9/9.5b; 10/1.1; 10/2.3; 10/4.2; 11/3.1; 11/3.3a; 11/3.3b; 11/3.3c; 11/3.3e; 11/3.4a; 11/3.5a; 12/2.1; 12/2.3; 12/2.5; 14/1.; 14/4.3; 14/5.1a	74	13/2.1
		74 § 1	13/2.1
		74 § 2	13/2.1
		74 § 3	13/2.1
		76	13/1.1d; 13/2.1
		77	13/1.1a; 13/2.2a
		78	13/2.2b; 13/7.6
		79	13/2.2c
		79 § 1	13/2.2b
		79 § 2	13/2.2b
44 § 2	12/2.6	80 Sole §	13/1.1c
45	13/1.3a	81	13/1.2a
45 § 1	13/1.3a	81 § 1	13/1.2a
45 § 2	13/1.3a	81 § 2	13/1.2a
45 § 3	5/3.5	85	13/1.1d; 13/1.2b
48	5/3.5	85 § 1	13/1.1d; 13/1.2b
48 Sole §	5/3.5	85 § 2	13/1.1d; 13/1.2b; 13/2.1d
51	9/9.2	85 § 4	13/2.2c
52	6/3.6; 6/3.7; 9/9.2	90	13/1.1d
52 Sole §	9/9.2	91	5/3.6
53	9/9.2	90 § 1	13/1.1d
54	9/9.3; 9/9.3c	92	5/4.3; 7/1.2; 9/8.2; 9/8.2c
54 (a)	99/9.3; 9/9.3a	92 § 1	9/8.2; 9/8.2a; 9/8.2b
54 (b)	9/9.3; 9/9.3b	92 § 1(a)	9/8.2b
54(c)	9/9.3	92 § 1(b)	9/8.2b
56	6/4.2; 14/6.2	92 § 1(c)	9/8.2b
57 § 1	10/2.2a	92 § 2	9/8.2b
57 § 2	10/2.2a	92 § 3	9/8.2b
57 § 3	10/2.2a	92 § 4	9/8.2b
57 § 4	10/2.2b	92 § 5	9/8.2a
58	10/2.2a	92 § 6	9/8.2b
58 § 1	10/2.2b	92 § 7	9/8.2b
58 § 2	10/2.2a	93	9/8.2
59	12/2.6	94	9/8.2d
60	5/4.4	94 § 3	9/8.2d
60 § 1	5/4.4	95	9/8.2d
61	5/4.4	96	5/4.3; 7/6.2; 9/2.1; 9/2.1f
61 § 1	5/4.4	96(1)	5/4.3; 9/1.6; 9/1.8
62	6/3.6	96(2)	5/4.3
62 § 1	6/3.6	96(2)(a)	9/9.5a
62 § 2	6/3.6	96(2)(b)	9/1.6
63	13/1.1a	96(2)(c)	9/2.2c
63 § 1(a)	6/1.2c; 8/1.5a; 13/1.1b	96 (3)	7/8.3; 9/9.4; 9/9.5b
63 § 1(b)	8/1.5a; 13/1.1b	96(3)(a)	7/7.2; 9/2.2a; 9/2.3; 9/9.5b
63 § 2	13/1.1a		
63 § 3	13/1.2a	96(3)(b)	9/2.2d
63 § 4	7/2.1; 13/1.1a	96(3)(c)	9/2.1f; 9/2.2b; 9/9.5a; 14/4.3
63 § 9	8/1.5a; 13/1.1b		

Income Tax Regulations (continued)

Reg. Art.		Reg. Art.	
96(3)(c)(I)	9/2.2b	144	13/7.2
96(3)(c)(II)	9/2.2b	144(c)	13/7.5
96(4)	10/4.1b	144(d)	13/7.4b
96(5)	9/9.5a; 10/4.1b	145	13/7.6
96 § 1	14/1.3	145(a)	13/7.6
96 § 2	9/1.6; 9/2.2a; 9/2.2c; 9/2.2d;	145(e)	13/7.4c; 13/7.7
	9/9.5a	146	13/7.2
96 § 3	7/6.2	147	13/7.3
97	5/4.3; 5/4.4; 5/4.8; 6/1.3a; 7/4.4;	147(e)	13/7.3
	7/6.1; 11/3.1; 11/3.3b; 11/3.3c;	149(b)	13/2.1; 13/7.4c
	11/3.3d; 11/3.3e; 11/3.4; 11/3.4a;	149(c)	13/7.4c
	11/3.5b; 12/2.5; 14/4.1	149(d)	13/7.4a
97(1)	5/1.1; 5/4.1; 5/4.2; 9/1.8;	155 Sole §	13/4.1
	9/2.4; 9/4.2; 9/9.5c; 10/4.3;	155	13/4.1; 13/5.1
	11/3.3a; 11/3.3c; 11/3.4; 11/3.4a;	156	13/4.1
	11/3.4c	157	13/4.2; 13/4.2a; 13/4.2b
97(2)	5/4.2; 9/5.1c; 9/5.2c;	158	13/4.2a
	11/3.4; 11/3.5c	158 § 1	13/4.2a
97(2)(c)	5/4.8	158 § 2	13/4.2a
97(2)(d)	5/1.1; 5/4.1	159	13/4.2a
97 § 1	9/4.3d	160	13/4.2; 13/4.2b
97 § 2	6/1.3b	160 § 1	13/4.2b
97 § 2(a)	6/1.3a	160 § 3	13/4.2b
97 § 2(b)	6/1.3a	160 § 4	13/4.2b
97 § 2(c)	11/3.3d	161–163	13/4.3
97 § 3	9/4.3d	167	13/4.3
97 § 4	5/4.3; 9/1.8; 11/3.4	169	13/4.1; 13/4.2a; 13/4.3
97 § 5	1/4.5b; 5/4.2; 9/1.8; 9/2.4;	170 § 1	13/5.1
	9/4.2; 9/4.3c; 9/5.1c; 9/5.2c;	170 § 2	13/5.1
	9/9.5c; 10/4.3; 11/3.4; 11/3.4a	170 § 3	13/5.1
98 Sole §	8/1.5a	170 § 4	13/5.1
98(2)	8/1.5a	171	13/1.1a
99	7/8.3	172	13/1.2a
99 Sole §	7/8.3	188	13/6.1
102	11/3.3a; 13/7.3	188 § 1	13/6.1
102 § 2	9/2.2a	189	13/6.2
102 § 4	8/1.5a	189 § 1	13/6.2
108	12/2.2; 13/3.1	189 § 2	13/6.2
108 § 1	13/3.1	191	9/8.2d; 13/6.2
108 § 2	13/3.1	195	13/1.1a
108 §3	13/1.1a; 13/3.1	195 Sole §	5/4.4b
108 § 4	13/3.1	198	9/9.5a
108 § 5	13/3.1	199	11/2.4
110	13/3.2	206	6/2.1; 11/2.4
111	13/3.2	206 Sole §	6/2.1
112–121	13/3.2	210 § 1	7/8.3; 11/3.4a
122	13/3.1	211	6/4.1a
124	13/2.1		
124 § 1	13/2.1		
126	5/3.6		
134	5/4.4b	**State of São Paulo Code of Taxation**	
137	13/2.1	(Decree No. 22,022, 31 I 1953)	
137 § 1	13/2.1		
141	6/2.2; 6/5.1; 13/7.4a	Book V, Appendix I 3/3.7	
141 § 3	6/5.1; 7/5.3	City of São Paulo Business Tax Legislation	
141 § 4	6/5.1; 7/5.3		
141 § 5	6/5.1	Law No. 3,683, 31 XII 1947	18/3.1
141 § 9	6/2.1	Decree No. 1,044, 8 I 1948	18/3.1
143(a)	13/7.4a	Decree No. 1,436 27 IX 1951	
		Arts. 132–180	18/3.1

INDEX

Detailed contents appear at beginning of each chapter
All references to Chapters 5/ through 13/ are to the income tax

A

Abajemientos (Abatements)
- allowance for dependents. *See* Allowances
- charitable contributions. *See* Charities
- defined, 6/1.2d
- extraordinary losses. *See* Losses
- insurance premiums. *See* Insurance
- interest on personal debts. *See* Deductions
- penalty for improper claim of, 13/7.6

Absence from country
- citizens, residence as affected by, 5/1.1
- government service, on, 6/1.3b
- nonresidence as determined by, 5/4.1
- students, 6/1.3b

Accounting
- accountants. *See* Independent services
- balance sheet in return, 13/1.2a
- books and records. *See* Books and records
- change of accounting period
- · calendar to fiscal year, 6/3.2
- · fiscal year to another fiscal year, 6/3.4
- · fiscal year to calendar year, 6/3.3
- entities
- · cash or accrual method, 6/4.2
- · centralized and decentralized, 6/7.1
- · period, 6/3.1
- · reorganizations, 6/3.5
- · systems, 6/2.1
- individuals
- · cash or accrual method, 6/4.1
- · period, 6/3.1
- inventories, valuation of, 6/5.1

Additional assessments. *See* Assessment of tax

Additions to tax
- excess profits tax, 14/5.3
- federal stamp tax, 17/2.10
- *impôsto unico*, 16/3.5
- income tax

- · compulsory loan to government. *See* Compulsory loan to government
- · entities, payment by, 13/1.2b
- · individuals, payment by, 13/1.1d
- · law for the protection of the family, 12/1.3a
- · reserves, charge on, 7/8.2
- real property transfer tax, 19/5.2
- sales tax, 15/4.3

Administration, 1/5.
- administrative organization
- · federal, 1/5.1
- · state and municipal, 1/5.2
- collection of tax. *See* Collection and payment of tax
- enforcement measures, 1/5.7–1/5.9
- · assessment ex officio, 13/2.2
- · estimated profits as tax base, 6/9.2
- · penalties. *See* Penalties
- · presumed interest, 9/1.4b
- income tax, 13/
- information required by government. *See* Information required by government
- inheritance and gift taxes, 3/3.8
- payment of tax. *See* Collection and payment of tax
- penalties. *See* Penalties
- remedies. *See* Taxpayers' remedies
- returns. *See* Returns
- time limits. *See* Time limits
- violations, investigations to determine, 1/5.3

Advertising expenses
- entities, 7/2.11a
- independent services, incurred in, 8/2.3; 8/2.4

Agências. See Branches

Agents
- business. *See* Independent services
- independent, acting for foreign corporations, 11/3.2

Agriculture, 10/2.

Detailed contents appear at beginning of each chapter
All references to Chapters 5/ through 13/ are to the income tax

Agriculture (*Continued*)
• agricultural and industrial exploitation tax, 16/4.1
• agricultural machinery
• • federal excise tax, 16/2.6–Sch. J
• • import duties, 1/2.6a
• • rates of depreciation, 7/3.3
• agricultural production, 1/2.2
• entities engaged in, 10/2.3
• general, 10/2.1
• individuals engaged in, 10/2.2

Airlines, foreign, 5/6.5

Alcoholic beverages. *See* Beverages

Allocation of tax revenue, 1/6.1
• business tax, 18/1.2
• education and health stamp, 17/2.10
• *impôsto unico,* 16/3.1–16/3.3
• mining, tax on, 10/1.1
• public construction, fees for, 3/2.10
• sales tax, 15/1.2
• • additions to, 15/4.3

Allowances
• dependents, for
• • abatement for complementary tax, 12/1.2b1
• • withholding at source, 8/1.5a
• medical and dental expenses, 12/1.2b2
• minimum income
• • abatement for complementary tax, 12/1.2b1
• • decedents' estates, 5/3.5
• • entities, 12/2.2
• • individuals, 13/1.1b
• • schedular tax, for, 6/1.2; 12/1.1
• • withholding at source, 5/1.2

Amortization
• intangibles, of, 7/3.6
• investment, of
• • natural resource extraction, 10/1.2
• • public utilities, 10/3.2b
• reappraised assets, increase in value of, 14/4.3
• shares, of, 9/9.5a1

Amusement and gaming devices. *See* Gambling

Amusement taxes, 18/4.1

Appeals. *See* Taxpayers' remedies

Appraisal
• inheritance and gift taxes, for, 3/3.6
• protest of, 13/4.1
• real property transfer tax, for, 19/6.3
• surplus, taxability of, 9/9.4

Architects. *See* Independent services *and* Partnerships, professional

Artistic organizations, 5/6.1

Assessment, taxation by
• acquisition of residence, effect of, 5/4.1; 5/4.4a
• branches of foreign entities, 5/4.8
• • loss deduction for, 7/4.4
• corporations subject to, 5/2.2a
• individuals subject to, 5/1.1
• nonresidents, 5/4.2
• taxable year, 5/4.4a

Assessment ex officio, 13/2.2
• penalties for avoiding, 13/7.6
• protests of, 13/4.1

Assessment of tax
• business tax, 18/2.3; 18/3.2
• export tax, 15/6.2
• federal excise tax, 16/2.3
• *impôsto unico,* 16/3.2; 16/3.3
• income tax
• • entities, 13/1.2d
• • individuals, 13/1.1d
• • time limits for suspended by claim for refund, 13/5.1
• inheritance and gift taxes, 3/3.8
• protest of. *See* Taxpayers' remedies
• sales tax, 15/5.1
• stamp taxes, 17/1.2

Assessments, special, 1/3.4

Assets
• book value of as basis of estimated profits, 6/9.2
• deductibility of cost of, 7/5.1
• depreciation of. *See* Depreciation
• fixed (*ativo imobilizado*)
• • increase in, results of, 14/4.5
• • revaluation of, tax on, 14/4.3
• • valuation of, 6/5.4
• inventories as. *See* Inventories
• profits on sale of, 7/6.3
• receivables as, 6/5.2
• revaluation of. *See* Valuation
• securities. *See* Securities

Assignments of income. *See* Attribution of income

Assignments of rights
• profits from, 10/4.1a

Athletic associations, 5/6.1

Ativo imobilizado. *See* Assets, fixed

Attribution of income, 6/8.1
• head of household, to, 13/1.1

Automobiles
• depreciation rates on, 7/3.3
• federal excise tax on, 16/2.6–Sch. I

Automobiles (*Continued*)
- sales tax on, 15/2.3
- stamp tax on, 17/3.3

B

Bachelorhood, tax on. *See* Law for the protection of the family

Bad debts. *See* Debts

Balance sheet. *See* Accounting

Bank Loans Fund (*Caixa de Mobilização Bancária*), 1/2.4

Bank of Brazil
- described, 1/2.4
- foreign exchange control, 1/2.7b; 4/10.
- foreign trade department (*Carteira do Comercio Exterior* or *CACEX*), 1/2.7b
- income tax rates on, 12/2.6
- payments to includable in sales tax base, 15/3.2b

Bankrupts' estates, 5/3.6

Banks and banking, 1/2.4

Base of tax. *See* Tax base

Base year, 6/3.1
- excess profits tax, for, 14/3.
- first year of residence, 5/4.4a

Bearer shares. *See* Securities

Beverages
- federal excise tax on, 16/2.8–Sch. XIX
- tax on manufacture and sale of alcoholic beverages, 18/4.4

Bonds. *See* Securities

Bonuses
- compensation, as. *See* Compensation for services
- export
- • general, 1/2.7
- • sales tax base, in, 15/3.2b
- premiums, import, 1/2.7

Books and records. *See also* Accounting
- depreciation shown in, 7/3.1
- expenses proved by, 7/2.1
- income determined by, 7/1.1
- inspection of, 1/5.3b; 13/2.1
- loss or destruction of
- • estimated profits in case of, 6/9.2
- • presumed profits in case of, 6/9.1
- losses determined by, 7/4.1
- penalties for irregularities in
- • estimated profits in case of, 6/9.2

- • failure to show, 13/7.4c
- • false entries, 13/7.1, n. 57
- • improper maintenance, 13/7.4a
- • sales tax, 15/5.4
- presumed profits based on, 6/9.1
- requirements, 6/2.
- • agriculture, for, 10/2.2a
- • allocation of income between foreign and domestic sources, 11/2.3
- • branches, for, 6/7.1
- • branches of foreign entities, for, 6/2.1; 11/3.3a
- • compensation for services to be recorded in, 7/5.2a
- • currency to be kept in, 6/2.1
- • language to be kept in, 6/2.1
- • legalization, 6/2.2

Branches (*Filiais, sucursais* or *agências*)
- accounting, centralized and decentralized, 6/7.1
- books and records, 6/7.1
- foreign entities, of. *See* Branches of foreign entities
- returns, consolidation of with head office, 13/1.2a

Branches of foreign entities, 5/4.8; 11/3.3. *See also* Branches
- books and records, 6/2.1
- compulsory loans to government, charge on reserves, 7/8.2
- deductions allowed, 11/3.3c
- entities, as, 5/4.8; 11/3.3a
- excess profits credit, 14/4.1
- home office expenses, 11/3.3c
- income of
- • actual profits, 11/3.3b
- • estimated profits, 6/9.2; 11/3.3b
- • presumed profits, 6/9.1; 11/3.3b
- • when deemed received by parent, 11/3.3a
- incorporation of, 9/9.3b3
- increase of capital, 7/6.1
- interest paid to home office, 7/2.4
- losses, 7/4.4
- profits reinvested in equipment, 11/3.3d
- reserves, 6/6.1
- returns, 13/1.2a
- • penalties for not consolidating, 13/7.5
- subsidiaries compared, 11/3.3e
- withholding tax as deduction. *See* Deductions

Broadcasting. *See* Radio and television

Brokers. *See* Independent services

Building. *See* Construction

Detailed contents appear at beginning of each chapter
All references to Chapters 5/ through 13/ are to the income tax

Buildings
- depreciation on, 7/3.1; 10/1.2

Business income, 7/
- actual profits, 2/4.3; 6/2.1; 11/3.3b
- allocation of between foreign and domestic source, 11/2.3
- defined, 2/4.1; 6/1.1; 7/1.1
- excess profits tax on. See Excess profits tax
- exclusions from, 7/7.
- gross profits, 7/1.1
- gross receipts distinguished, 6/1.1
- items of
  - agricultural, 10/2.3
  - agricultural industry, from, 10/2.2a
  - assignment of rights, 10/4.1a
  - bearer shares, from, 7/7.2
  - cancellation of debts, 7/1.1
  - capital gains, 7/1.2; 9/8.1
  - compensation for nonexercise of contractual rights, 10/4.1a
  - compensation for services. See Compensation for services
  - damages for breach of contract, 10/4.1a
  - dissolution of provision accounts, 7/6.1
  - dividends and other distributions, 7/7.1; 9/2.3
  - excess provisions for bad debts, 7/2.9
  - excess provisions for depreciation, 7/3.3
  - futures and report operations, from, 10/4.1b*l*
  - improvements made by lessee, 7/3.5
  - increase in capital, 7/6.1; 9/2.1d
  - insurance benefits, 7/7.3; 9/3.2
  - interest, 9/1.7
  - mining, from, 10/1.1
  - miscellaneous receipts, 10/4.2
  - premiums on securities issued, 7/1.1
  - real property, from sale of, 7/1.2
  - recovery of charged-off debts, 7/2.9
  - redemption of securities, 9/9.5b
  - rent from movable property, 9/4.3b
  - rent from real property, 9/4.1a
  - revaluation of assets, 7/6.2
  - royalties, 9/5.1b; 9/5.2b
  - sale of assets, 7/6.3
  - sales price of obsolete assets, 7/3.4
  - stock dividends, to issuing entity, 7/6.1
- nonresidents, of. See Foreign entities *and* Nonresidents
- presumed profits, 6/9.1
- return of capital distinguished, 6/1.1
- returns must include analysis of, 13/1.2a
- tax rates on, 2/4.2; 12/2.3
- when deemed received, 6/4.2
  - branch profits by parent, 11/3.3a
  - constructive dividends, 9/2.1b
  - improvements to rented property, 7/3.5, n. 59

Business organizations. See also Corporations; Partnerships, commercial; *and* Limited liability companies
- corporations (*sociedades anônimas*), 1/4.2g
- individual proprietorship, 1/4.2a
- limited liability company (*sociedade por quotas de responsibilidade limitada*), 1/4.2f
- partnerships, types of, 1/4.2b–1/4.2e

Business tax, 18/
- exemptions, 18/2.4
- history of, 18/1.2
- persons subject to, 18/2.1
- substitutes for, 18/4.
- summarized, 4/8
- tax base, 18/3.1
- tax rates, 18/3.1
- taxable activities, 18/2.2; 18/2.3
- violations, 18/3.2

C

Caixa de Mobilização Bancária (Bank Loans Fund), 1/2.4

Cancellation of indebtedness. See Debts

Capital
- contributions to (*suprimentos*)
  - income to recipient entity, as, 7/6.1
  - patents and trademarks as, 7/3.6
  - premiums on securities as, 7/1.1
  - real property transfer tax on, 19/3.1
  - sales tax on, 15/2.6
- estimated profits as measured by, 6/9.2
- foreign, accruals on, 4/10.
- impairment of, 6/6.2
- increase of
  - effect for income tax purposes, 14/4.5
  - excess profits credit, 14/4.2
  - income to entity as, 7/6.1
  - tax on revaluation of fixed assets, 14/4.3
- invested
  - excess profits credit, 14/4.1
- issues, 17/2.5

Detailed contents appear at beginning of each chapter
All references to Chapters 5/ through 13/ are to the income tax

Capital (*Continued*)
• return of through reorganization, 9/9.5a
• taxes on, 3/

Capital expenditures. *See* Nondeductible expenditures

Capital gains
• entities, to, 7/1.2; 9/8.1
• individuals, to, 9/8.1
• • commercial or industrial profits as, 7/1.3
• • real property transactions, as, 9/8.2
• nonresidents, to, 11/3.5b
• • real property transactions as, 5/4.3

Capitalization bonds. *See* Securities

Capitalization companies (*Sociedades de capitalização*)
• technical reserves of
• • deductions, as, 10/3.2a
• • exemption of from compulsory loan, 7/8.2

Carteira do Comercio Exterior (*CACEX*). *See* Bank of Brazil

Cash
• accounting method, 6/4.1; 6/4.2
• assets, as, for measuring estimated profits, 6/9.2, n. 98
• sales, 15/5.2a

Casualty losses. *See* Losses

Charge on reserves, 7/8.2

Charities
• contributions to
• • abatements for complementary tax, as, 12/1.2b6
• • deductibility of by entities, 7/2.10
• exemptions
• • business tax, from, 18/2.4b
• • constitutional provisions, 1/3.5
• • federal excise tax, from, 16/2.4b
• • income tax, from, 5/6.1
• • inheritance and gift taxes, from, 3/3.3b1
• • real property taxes, from, 3/2.3d
• • real property transfer tax, from, 19/2.2
• • sales tax, from, 15/2.8a

Churches. *See* Religious organizations

Cigarette tax. *See* Tobacco

Civil companies
• entities, constituting, 5/2.3

Civil service employees. *See* Government service

Civil societies. *See* Partnerships, professional

Claims for refunds. *See* Taxpayers' remedies

Clerics, 5/5.4. *See also* Religious organizations

Clothing, federal excise tax on. *See* Federal excise tax

Coffee
• export of, 1/2.2
• • export tax on, 15/6.2
• • licensing by Brazilian Coffee Institute, 1/2.7b

Collection and payment of tax
• business tax, 18/3.2
• capitalization of reserves, tax on, 14/4.4
• excess profits tax, 14/7.
• export tax, 15/6.2
• federal excise tax, 16/2.10a
• *impôsto unico*, 16/3.1
• income tax
• • assessment ex officio, 13/2.2c
• • entities, 13/1.2b
• • gains from sale of real property, 9/8.2d
• • individuals, 13/1.1d
• • surplus from revaluation of assets, 7/6.2
• • time limits for payment. *See* Time limits
• inheritance and gift taxes, 3/3.8
• penalties. *See* Penalties
• real property transfer tax, 19/6.2
• revaluation of assets, tax on, 14/4.3
• sales tax, 15/5.2
• stamp taxes, 17/1.1
• tax on waterfalls, 16/3.5

Commencement and termination of operations
• commencement of operations, 6/3.6
• • capital, stamp tax on issues of, 17/2.5
• • new industries, 18/2.4d
• • organizational requirements, 1/4.2g
• reorganization, resulting from. *See* Reorganizations
• same year, in
• • excess profits tax, 14/7.
• • income tax, 6/3.6
• termination of operations
• • continuation of business after dissolution, 9/9.3c
• • excess profits tax, 14/7.
• • liquidation, 9/9.2
• • returns, 6/3.7
• • stamp tax on, 17/2.5

Detailed contents appear at beginning of each chapter
All references to Chapters 5/ through 13/ are to the income tax

Commercial partners. *See* Partnerships, commercial

Commercial Registry (*Junta Comercial* or *Registro do Comercio*), 5/2.4
• books and records, legalization of, 6/2.2
• increases in capital to be filed with, 14/4.2

Commercial services. *See* Individuals engaged in business

Commissions
• employees. *See* Compensation for services
• independent services. *See* Independent services

Community property
• joint returns in case of
• • computation, 12/1.2b*1*
• • who must file, 13/1.1c

Compensation for services
• amounts includible in Schedule C, 8/1.2
• attributable to several taxable years
• • employees, 8/3.2
• • independent services, 8/3.3
• • when deemed received, 8/3.1
• deductibility of, 7/2.3
• • bonuses, 7/5.2a
• • commissions paid for collecting rent, 9/4.1b
• • commissions paid to officers, partners, etc., 8/1.2b
• • independent services, against income from, 8/2.3
• • limitations, 7/5.2a
• • nonresident directors, 7/5.2b
• • owners and directors, 7/5.2a
• • salaries paid by branches of foreign entities, 11/3.3e
• deductions allowed against, 8/1.3
• income from foreign sources, as, 11/2.2
• materials and services combined, 15/7.1; 15/7.2
• occasional services as employee, 10/4.1a
• officers, directors, etc., 8/1.2b
• retainers as, 8/1.2a
• withholding at source on, 2/3.3b; 8/1.5
• • compensation paid by foreign employer, 8/1.5a
• • nonresidents, 11/3.4c

Complementary tax, 6/1.2; 12/1.2
• abatements, 6/1.2d; 12/1.2b
• decedents' estates, 5/3.5

• exclusions from gross income for, 6/1.2e
• general, 2/3.2
• income from foreign sources, 11/2.2
• income subject to, 6/1.2c; 12/1.2a
• income-spreading provisions for, 8/3.
• tax rates, 12/1.2c

Compra (Repurchase of shares of stock), 9/9.5a*1*

Compulsory loan to government, 1/2.3b
• entities, 12/2.4a; 13/1.2b
• • charge on reserves, 7/8.2
• • deductibility of, 7/2.7
• individuals, 12/1.3b; 13/1.1d

Computation of taxes. *See* Tax base *and* Tax rates

Consignments, sales tax on, 15/2.7

Consolidation (*Incorporação*). *See* Reorganizations

Constitutional tax provisions
• exemptions, 1/3.5. *See also* Exemptions
• history, 1/1.3
• jurisdiction to tax
• • concurrent, 1/3.3
• • exclusive, 1/3.2; 1/6.2
• • summarized, 1/3.1
• types of levies, 1/3.4

Construction
• accounting periods, 6/4.2; 14/6.2
• contracts
• • defined, 15/2.3
• • sales tax on, 15/2.3
• • stamp tax on, 17/2.3
• deductibility of expenses of, 7/2.5
• excess profits tax on, 14/6.2
• exemptions to encourage, 3/2.8
• materials, federal excise tax on. *See specific items*

Contracts
• construction, 15/2.3
• corporate, 17/2.5
• independent services, for. *See* Independent services
• materials and services, for. *See* Independent services
• private written, 17/2.3

Contributions
• capital, to (*suprimentos*). *See* Capital
• deductibility of
• • charitable, 7/2.10; 12/1.2b6
• • political, 7/2.10
• employees' benefit funds, to

Contributions, employees' benefit funds, to
(*Continued*)
 · · employers, by, 8/2.3
 · · independent services, deductibility
  from, 8/2.3

Conventions and treaties, 1/4.5d; 11/4.1

Cooperatives, exemptions
 · business tax, from, 18/2.4c
 · income tax, from, 5/6.2
 · sales tax, from, 15/2.8b

Copyrights. *See* Intellectual property

Corporations (*Sociedades anónimas*). *See
also* Entities *and* Foreign corporations
 · classification of as entities for tax purposes, 5/2.3
 · defined, 1/4.2g
 · domicile, 5/4.6
 · excess reserves, tax on, 7/8.3
 · executives, exemption from business
  tax, 18/2.4f
 · income of as business income. *See*
  Business income
 · nationality of stockholders as affecting
  residence, 5/2.1
 · organizational requirements, 1/4.2g
 · reorganization. *See* Reorganization
 · reserves required, 6/6.2
 · residence, determination of, 5/2.1
 · shareholders in. *See* Shareholders
 · shares, repurchase of (*compra*), 9/9.5a1
 · taxation of profits to shareholders, 5/2.5
 · taxes on
 · · federal stamp tax, 17/2.5
 · · real property transfer tax, 19/3.1
 · · sales tax, 15/2.2; 15/2.6
 · valuation and revaluation of assets. *See*
  Valuation

Cost
 · depreciation based on, 7/3.1
 · fixed assets, of, 6/5.4
 · goods sold, of
 · · computation for tax purposes, 7/1.1
 · · items included in, 6/5.1
 · inventories, of. *See* Inventories
 · real property
 · · basis, as, 9/8.2a
 · · gains on sale of, 9/8.2b
 · replacement of obsolete assets, 7/3.4
 · securities, of, 6/5.3

Credits
 · dividends received, 9/2.3
 · excess profits, 14/4.
 · foreign tax, 11/4.1

Cultural organizations, 5/6.1

Currency. *See also* Foreign exchange
 · books and records to be kept in, 6/2.1
 · issue of, 1/2.4
 · losses on exchange of, 7/4.5

Customs duties, 1/2.6; 4/4. *See also*
Imports

D

Debts
 · amortization of foreign, 4/10.
 · bad
 · · deductibility of, 7/2.9
 · · dissolution of provision for, 7/6.1
 · · entities' returns to include list of,
  13/1.2a
 · · provisions for, 7/2.9; 7/8.2
 · cancellation of as income to debtor
 · · entities, 7/1.1
 · · independent services, for, 8/2.2
 · interest on, *See* Interest
 · recovery of debts previously charged
  off, 7/2.9

Decedents' estates
 · inheritance tax. *See* Inheritance tax
 · returns, 13/1.3a
 · taxable entities, as, 5/3.5

Declaratory judgment. *See* Taxpayers'
remedies

Decrees. *See* Tax law

Deduction at source. *See* Withholding
at source

Deductions
 · accounting methods — cash or accrual
 · · entities, 6/4.2
 · · individuals, 6/4.1b
 · advertising, 7/2.11a
 · agricultural income, from, 10/2.2b
 · amortization. *See* Amortization
 · bad debts. *See* Debts
 · bonuses, 7/2.5a
 · brokers' fees. *See* Independent services
 · business, 7/2.1
 · capitalization companies, technical reserves of, 6/6.1
 · charitable contributions. *See* Charities
 · claims for, 7/2.1
 · · doubtful, 13/4.1
 · · improper, 13/7.6
 · commissions. *See* Compensation for
  services *and* Independent services
 · compensation for services, from, 8/1.3
 · compensation for services as. *See* Compensation for services

Detailed contents appear at beginning of each chapter
All references to Chapters 5/ through 13/ are to the income tax

Deductions (*Continued*)
- compulsory loan to government, 12/2.4a
- cost of capital assets, 7/5.1
- depletion of natural resources, 10/1.2
- depreciation. *See* Depreciation
- entertainment expenses, 7/2.11a
- extraordinary losses, 12/1.2b5
- foreign exchange losses, 7/4.5
- home office expenses, 11/3.3c
- • paid by subsidiary to foreign parent, 11/3.3e
- indemnifications prescribed by labor law, 7/5.4
- installation expenses, 7/2.5
- insurance companies, technical reserves of, 6/6.1
- insurance premiums. *See* Insurance
- interest as. *See* Interest
- interest income, from, 9/1.3b
- investment in natural resource extraction, 10/1.2
- losses. *See* Losses
- maintenance expenses, 7/2.5
- medical and dental expenses, 12/1.2b2
- obsolescence, 7/3.4
- payments to officers, directors, etc., 7/5.2a
- period claimed for, 7/2.1
- presumed profits, for purposes of, 6/9.1
- profit participations
- • employees, 7/2.12
- • government, 7/2.13
- • holders of participating certificates, 7/2.14
- proof of, 7/2.1; 13/1.1a
- provisions as, 6/6.1
- rent, 7/2.2
- rental income, from, 9/4.1b
- rented property
- • improvements made by lessee, 7/3.5
- repairs, 7/2.5
- reserves, 6/6.1
- • insurance companies, 10/3.2a
- • required by law, 6/6.2
- schedular, 6/1.2b
- Schedule A through Schedule H, under. *See* Schedule A *through* Schedule H
- travel expenses, 7/2.11b; 8/1.3a
- wages. *See* Compensation for services
- worthless securities, 7/2.6

Deeds. *See* Real property

Deficiencies. *See also* Penalties
- business tax, 18/3.2
- deficiency assessments, 13/6.1
- federal excise tax, 16/2.10c

- real property transfer tax, 19/6.2
- sales tax, 15/5.4

Dependents
- allowances for, 12/1.2b1
- statements required concerning, 8/1.5a

Depletion. *See* Natural resource extraction

Depreciation
- amortization. *See* Amortization
- buildings, 7/3.1; 10/1.2
- cost basis, 7/3.1
- income from independent services, from, 8/2.3
- methods allowed, 7/3.2
- movable property, 7/3.1
- natural resource extraction, 10/1.2
- obsolescence as affected by, 7/3.4
- provisions for
- • charge on excess, 7/3.3
- • returns must include analysis of, 13/1.2a
- rates of, 7/3.3
- reappraised assets, increase in value of, 14/4.3
- transfer of funds for as income, 7/3.1; 7/6.1
- who may claim, 7/3.1

Designs. *See* Intellectual property

Despachantes, 1/5.6

Development expenses for natural resource extraction, 10/1.2

Diplomatic representatives, foreign. *See* Foreign governments

Directors (*Diretores*)
- deductibility of compensation of to entity, 7/5.2a
- life insurance on, with entity as beneficiary, 7/7.3
- nonresident, 7/5.2b

Discount operations, 9/1.4c

Discounts
- early payment of tax, for, 13/1.1d
- sales tax base, as affecting, 15/3.1

Dissolution. *See* Commencement and termination of operations

Dividends and other distributions
- attribution rules, 6/8.1
- bearer shares, on, 2/3.3a; 9/2.2a; 9/2.2b
- capitalization bonds, on, 9/2.2c
- constructive dividends, 9/2.1b
- declared but unpaid, 14/4.1, n. 12

Detailed contents appear at beginning of each chapter
All references to Chapters 5/ through 13/ are to the income tax

Dividends and other distributions
(*Continued*)
- discounts on securities of other entities sold to shareholders, 7/6.3
- dissolved entity, of, 9/9.3a2
- entities as recipients, 7/7.1; 9/2.3
- exchange remittance tax, 4/10.
- foreign sources, from, 11/2.2
- increase in value of securities from revaluation as, 7/6.2; 14/4.3
- individuals as recipients, 9/2.1
- information required by government, 13/3.1
- interest. *See* Interest
- nominative securities, on, 9/2.1b
- nonresidents as recipients, 5/4.3; 9/2.4
- participating certificates, on. *See* Profit participations
- profits of commercial partners, 9/2.1a
- provisions for depreciation, paid from, 7/3.1
- revaluation of assets in reorganization, from, 9/2.1f
- Schedule F income, as, 9/2.1
- shares bought below par as, 7/6.3
- stock dividends
- - bearer shares, 9/2.2b
- - income to issuing entity, as, 7/6.1
- - nominative securities, 9/2.1c
- - valuation of, 9/2.1d
- tax paid by distributing entity, 7/2.7
- when deemed received, 6/4.1a

Documents
- stamp tax on, 17/2.1
- - official, 17/2.2
- - unspecified, 17/2.9

"Doing business in Brazil," 11/3.2
- authorization required for foreign corporations, 5/2.1, n. 3
- services which constitute, 11/3.4b

Domicile. *See* Residence

Dues
- deductibility of by employees, 8/1.2b

Duplicata
- defined, 15/1.2
- issuance of, 15/5.2b
- tax base, effect on, 15/3.1

E

Economic background, 1/2.
Education and health stamp, 17/2.10
Educational institutions, exemptions
- business tax, from, 18/2.4b
- constitutional provisions, 1/3.5
- income tax, from, 5/6.1

- inheritance and gift taxes, from, 3/3.-3b1
- real property taxes, from, 3/2.3d
- real property transfer tax, from, 19/2.2
- sales tax, from, 15/2.8a

Election available to taxpayer
- accounting periods, 6/3.1–6/3.5
- bad debts, charge-off of provisions for, 7/2.9
- depreciation methods, 7/3.2
- determination of tax base
- - agricultural income, 10/2.2a
- - blanket deduction, 8/2.4
- - presumed profits, 6/9.1
- excess profits
- - credit, computation of, 14/4.
- - tax, methods of computing, 14/5.1; 14/5.2
- income-spreading provisions, 8/3.1
- payment of tax in installments
- - entities, 13/1.2b
- - individuals, 13/1.1d
- revaluation of assets, 7/6.2

Electricity. *See also* Public utilities
- electric light bulbs, 16/2.8–Sch. XXI
- electric power, 16/3.3
- electric power companies, 18/2.4g
- electrical installations, 7/3.3

Emphyteusis
- deductibility of ground rent, 9/4.1b

Employees, 8/1.
- compensation for services. *See* Compensation for services
- deductions allowed against compensation, 8/1.3
- employment contracts, 8/1.2a
- expenses reimbursed, as income, 8/1.2a
- indemnification of
- - deductibility of to employer, 7/5.4
- - income, as, 6/1.2e
- life insurance on, entities as beneficiaries, 7/7.3
- officers as, 8/1.2b
- participations in profits, 7/2.12
- pensions and retirement pay of, 9/3.1
- withholding at source, 8/1.5a
- - compensation paid by foreign employer, 8/1.5a
- - rates, 12/1.4

Engineers. *See* Independent services

Entertainment expenses. *See* Deductions

Entities
- accounting methods and periods. *See* Accounting

Detailed contents appear at beginning of each chapter
All references to Chapters 5/ through 13/ are to the income tax

Entities (*continued*)
- agriculture, engaged in, 10/2.3
- allowances, minimum income, 12/2.2
- base of tax on, 6/1.4
- • actual profits, 2/4.3
- • estimated profits, 6/9.2
- • presumed profits, 6/9.1
- beneficiaries of life insurance, as, 7/7.3
- books and records of. *See* Books and records
- branches of foreign corporations as, 5/4.8
- civil companies as, 5/2.3
- deductions. *See* Deductions
- defined, 5/2.3
- depreciation allowed. *See* Depreciation
- dividends received, 7/7.1; 9/2.3
- excess profits tax on, 14/2.
- foundations as, 5/2.3
- income of. *See* Business income
- mercantile companies as, 5/2.3
- nonresident, defined, 5/4.6
- ownership of property by, 19/3.2
- partnerships
- • commercial, 5/3.1
- • professional, 12/2.6
- payment of tax, 13/1.2b
- profits determined from books and records, 6/2.1
- registration required, 5/2.4
- returns of. *See* Returns
- *sociedade em conta de participação*, 5/3.2
- tax computation, 12/2.5
- tax rates, 12/2.3
- tax status, 5/2.5

Estates
- bankrupts', 5/3.6
- decedents'. *See* Decedents' estates
- inheritance tax on. *See* Inheritance tax

Estimated profits as tax base
- excess profits tax, 14/3.
- income tax, 6/9.2
- • assessment ex officio, 13/2.2c1
- • branches of foreign entities, 11/3.3b, n. 24
- • termination of operations, 6/3.7

Excess profits credit
- fixed assets, revaluation of
- • income tax effects, 14/4.5
- • tax on, 14/4.3
- invested capital, 14/4.1
- • increases in, 14/4.2
- reserves, capitalization of
- • income tax effects, 14/4.5

- • tax on, 14/4.4

Excess profits tax
- additions to, 14/5.3
- administration of, 14/8.
- computation of
- • average income method, 14/5.2a
- • percentage of gross income method, 14/5.2b
- • regular method, 14/5.1
- credit. *See* Excess profits credit
- general, 14/1.
- income subject to, 14/3.
- payment of, 14/7.
- returns, 14/7.
- taxpayers, 14/2.
- • building and construction companies, 14/6.2
- • commercial representatives and enterprises, 14/6.1

Exchange. *See* Foreign exchange

Exchange remittance tax, 4/10.

Exchanges
- sales tax on
- • property for property, 15/2.5
- • property for shares, 15/2.6

Excise taxes, 16/
- agricultural and industrial exploitation, 16/4.1
- federal. *See* Federal excise tax
- *impôsto de consumo*. *See* Federal excise tax
- *impôsto unico*. *See* Impôsto unico
- municipal, 16/4.
- state, 16/4.
- summarized, 4/5.
- waterfall exploitation, 16/3.5

Executive powers, 1/1.5a

Exemptions
- agents of Brazilian shipping lines, 6/1.3b
- agricultural machinery
- • federal excise tax, from, 16/2.6– Sch. I
- • import duties, from, 1/2.6a
- athletic organizations, 5/6.1
- authors' royalties. *See* Intellectual property
- books, 4/10.
- branch profits reinvested in Brazil, 11/3.3d
- charities. *See* Charities
- clerics, 5/5.4
- constitutional, summary of, 1/3.5
- cooperatives. *See* Cooperatives

Detailed contents appear at beginning of each chapter
All references to Chapters 5/ through 13/ are to the income tax

Exemptions (*Continued*)
• cost of living. *See* Allowances
• decedents' estates, 3/3.5
• determination of, 5/6.3
• disabled persons, 19/2.3b
• dwelling place (homestead), 19/2.3d
• educational institutions. *See* Educational institutions
• electric power companies, 16/3.1
• entities
• • dividends from bearer securities, 7/7.2
• • dividends received, 7/7.1; 9/2.3
• • income from foreign sources, 11/2.3
• • insurance payments, 7/7.3
• essential commodities
• • exchange remittance tax, from, 4/10.
• • federal excise tax, from, 16/2.4b
• • import duties, from, 1/2.6a
• • sales tax, from, 15/2.8c
• exchange obligations between banks, 4/10.
• executives, corporate, 18/2.4f
• executors and administrators, 3/3.1b3
• exporters of Brazilian products, 6/1.3b
• exports, 16/2.4b
• foreign airlines, 5/6.5
• foreign capital, repayment of, 4/10.
• foreign debt, amortization of, 4/10.
• foreign diplomatic representatives, 5/5.2
• foreign exchange, 15/2.8c, n. 33
• foreign governments. *See* Foreign governments
• foreign steamship lines, 5/6.5
• forests and forestation projects. *See* Forests and forestation
• fuels and lubricants. *See* Fuels and lubricants
• gains from sale of real property, 9/8.2
• government. *See* Government
• government securities, income from, 9/1.2a
• government service, persons engaged in. *See* Government service, persons engaged in
• individuals, general, 5/5.1
• industrial machinery. *See* Industries
• industries. *See* Industries
• intellectual property. *See* Intellectual property
• journalists, 5/5.3
• loss of, 5/6.4
• minimum income. *See* Allowances
• mining and refining equipment, 1/2.6a
• municipalities, 1/3.5
• new industries, 18/2.4d
• newspapers and news agencies, 18/2.4a

• nonresidents, 6/1.3b
• • authors' royalties, 6/1.3a
• oil companies, 16/3.1
• paper. *See* Paper
• pigments used by manufacturers as raw materials, 16/2.6–Sch. XIV
• political parties. *See* Political parties
• printing, 18/2.4b
• professional associations
• • excess profits tax, from, 14/2.
• • income tax, from, 5/6.1
• professional partnerships, 14/2.
• professional personnel, corporate, 18/2.4f
• radio and television networks, 18/2.4a
• recreational organizations, 5/6.1
• religious organizations. *See* Religious organizations
• reserves required by law, 6/6.2
• samples, 16/2.4b
• savings bank deposits, 3/3.5
• securities, sale of, 15/2.8c
• states, 1/3.5
• students studying abroad, 6/1.3b
• surviving spouse, 3/3.3b2
• teachers, 5/5.3
• textiles, 16/2.9–Sch. XXIX
• veterans, 19/2.3b
• works of art, 16/2.6–Schs. I *and* VII

Expenditures, public, 1/2.3c. *See also* Allocation of tax revenue

Expenses
• • books and records as proving, 7/2.1
• deductibility of. *See* Deductions
• nondeductible. *See* Nondeductible expenditures
• returns must include analysis of, 13/1.2a

Export tax, 15/6.
• defined, 15/6.1
• general, 4/3.
• sales tax on same transaction, 15/6.1
• substitutes for, 15/6.3
• tax rates, 15/6.1
• taxable event, 15/6.2

Exports
• agents for, 6/1.3b
• export tax on. *See* Export tax
• federal excise tax on, 16/2.4b
• foreign exchange. *See* Foreign exchange
• sales tax on. *See also* Sales tax
• • prohibition against discrimination, 15/4.1
• • tax base, 15/3.2b

Extraordinary losses, 12/1.2b5

Detailed contents appear at beginning of each chapter
All references to Chapters 5/ through 13/ are to the income tax

F

Family, law for the protection of, 12/1.3a

Federal Appellate Court (*Tribunal Fed-erál de Recursos*), 13/4.3

Federal excise tax (*Impôsto de consumo*). See also Excise taxes
* collection and payment of tax, 16/2.10a
* defined, 16/2.1
* exemptions, 16/2.4b
* federal legislation, 16/2.2
* penalties, 16/2.10c
* refunds, 16/2.10b
* summarized, 4/5.
* tax base, 16/2.5
* • ad valorem, 16/2.6
* • ceiling price, 16/2.7
* • technical characteristics, computed by, 16/2.8
* • units, computed by, 16/2.9
* tax rates, 16/2.5
* • alcohol, 16/2.8–Sch. XVIII
* • animal products, 16/2.6–Sch. III
* • automobiles, 16/2.6–Sch. I
* • beverages, 16/2.8–Sch. XIX
* • brushes and brooms, 16/2.6–Sch. IX
* • candles, 16/2.6–Sch. XV
* • cement, 16/2.6–Sch. VII
* • ceramics and glass, 16/2.6–Sch. V
* • classification, method of, 16/2.5
* • clocks and watches, 16/2.6–Sch. X
* • cutlery, 16/2.6–Sch. II
* • electric light bulbs, 16/2.8–Sch. XXI
* • electric power. See *Impôsto unico*
* • foods, processed, 16/2.6–Sch. XII
* • fuels and lubricants. See *Impôsto unico*
* • furniture, 16/2.7–Sch. XVII
* • furs, 16/2.6–Sch. III
* • games, sporting goods, toys, 16/2.6–Sch. IV
* • hats, 16/2.6–Sch. VI
* • leather goods, 16/2.6–Sch. III
* • lighters, 16/2.9–Sch. XXIII
* • matches, 16/2.9–Sch. XXIII
* • metal products, 16/2.6–Sch. I
* • metals, precious, 16/2.6–Sch. X
* • paints and varnishes, 16/2.6–Sch. XIV
* • paper products, 16/2.6–Sch. XI
* • pharmaceutical products, 16/2.6–Sch. XIII
* • plastic goods, 16/2.6–Sch. III
* • playing cards, 16/2.8–Sch. XX
* • salt, 16/2.9–Sch. XXVIII
* • shoes, 16/2.7–Sch. XVI
* • stone, 16/2.6–Sch. VII
* • stones, precious and semi-precious, 16/2.6–Sch. X
* • textiles, 16/2.9–Sch. XXIX
* • tobacco, 16/2.9–Sch. XXIV
* • toiletries, 16/2.9–Sch. XXVII
* • umbrellas, 16/2.9–Sch. XXVI
* • vegetable products, 16/2.6–Sch. III
* • vinegar, 16/2.8–Sch. XXII
* • weapons, 16/2.6–Sch. II
* taxable event, 16/2.3
* taxpayer, 16/2.4a

Federal stamp tax, 17/2.
* additions to, 17/2.10
* background of, 17/2.1
* summarized, 4/7.
* tax base. See *specific taxable docu-ment, infra., this heading*
* tax rates. See *specific taxable docu-ment, infra., this heading*
* taxable documents
* • capital issues, on, 17/2.5
* • contracts, private written, on, 17/2.3
* • exchange transactions, on, 17/2.8
* • installment sales, on, 17/2.7
* • liquidations, on, 17/2.5
* • loans, on, 17/2.4
* • official documents, 17/2.2
* • unspecified documents, 17/2.9

Fees, 1/3.4

Filiais. See Branches *and* Branches of foreign entities

Financial institutions, 1/2.4; 10/3.1. See *also* Bank of Brazil

Fines. See Penalties

Firma individual. See Individuals en-gaged in business

Fiscal year. See Accounting

Fixtures
* real property transfer tax on, 19/4.3
* sales tax on, 15/2.2

Food
* coffee. See Coffee
* essential commodity, exemption as
* • federal excise tax on, 16/2.4b
* • import duties, 1/2.6a
* • sales tax on, 15/2.8c
* processed, 16/2.6–Sch. XII
* salt, 16/2.9–Sch. XXVIII
* vinegar, 16/2.8–Sch. XXII

Foreign airlines, 5/6.5

Detailed contents appear at beginning of each chapter
All references to Chapters 5/ through 13/ are to the income tax

Foreign entities
- branches of and subsidiaries of compared, 11/3.3e
- branches of in Brazil. *See* Branches of foreign entities
- "doing business in Brazil," 11/3.2
- • authorization required, 5/2.1, n. 3
- • investment, 1/2.7c
- permanent establishments of, 5/2.1
- tax residence in Brazil
- • affected by subsidiaries of, 11/3.2
- • determination of, 5/4.6
- • effect of, 5/4.7

Foreign exchange
- control of, 1/2.7
- exchange remittance tax on, 4/10.
- export bonuses, 15/3.2b
- federal stamp tax on, 17/2.8
- losses, 7/4.5
- rates, computation of, 1/2.7a
- • books and records, for, 6/2.1; 7/2.5
- • federal excise tax, for, 16/2.6
- • income from foreign sources, for, 11/2.4
- reserves required for banks, 1/2.4

Foreign governments, exemptions
- exchange remittance tax, from, 4/10.
- income tax, from, 5/2.3
- • diplomatic representatives, 5/5.2
- real property transfer tax, from, 19/2.3c

Foreign investment, 1/2.8c

Foreign shipping lines, 5/6.5

Forests and forestation
- deduction for, 10/1.2
- exemption of
- • real property taxes, from, 3/2.3e
- real property transfer tax on, 19/4.2

Foundations
- entities, as, 5/2.3
- exemptions, 5/6.1

Fraud
- books and records, in
- • income tax, penalties for, 13/7.7
- • sales tax, penalties for, 15/5.4
- estimation of profits in cases of, 6/9.2

Fuels and lubricants. *See also* Petroleum industry
- exchange remittance tax, exemption from, 4/10
- *impôsto unico* on, 16/3.2

Fusão. See Reorganizations

Futures, sales of, 10/4.1b1

G

Gambling
- games of chance, 18/4.3
- income from, 10/4.1b2
- lotteries, 18/4.2

Gift tax, 3/3.
- appraisal, 3/3.6
- assessment and collection of, 3/3.8
- background of, 3/3.1
- exemptions, 3/3.3b; 3/3.5
- jurisdiction to tax, 3/3.2
- tax base, 3/3.4
- tax rates, 3/3.7
- taxpayer, 3/3.3a

Gifts
- *causa mortis* as distinguished from *inter vivos,* 3/3.1
- federal excise tax on, 16/2.3
- gift tax on. *See* Gift tax
- income, as, 6/1.2e

Government
- branches of, 1/1.5
- exemptions, 1/3.5
- • federal excise tax, from, 16/2.4b
- • inheritance and gift taxes, from, 3/3.3b1
- • real property taxes, from, 3/2.3a
- • real property transfer tax, from, 19/2.2
- expenditures, 1/2.3c. *See also* Allocation of tax revenues
- history of, 1/1.1–1/1.3
- national economy. *See* National economy
- petition for review, 13/4.2b
- revenue sources other than taxes
- • compulsory loans, 1/2.3b
- • foreign exchange overprices, 1/2.7b
- • social security contributions, 1/2.3a
- securities. *See* Securities
- subdivisions of, 1/1.4

Government service, persons engaged in
- exemptions
- • real property transfer tax, from, 19/2.3b
- • withholding tax, from, 6/1.3b

Gross income. *See also* Income *and* Profits
- entities, 7/1.1
- estimated profits as measured by, 6/9.2
- excess profits tax computed on, 14/5.2b
- gross receipts distinguished from, 6/1.1
- individuals, 6/1.1

Detailed contents appear at beginning of each chapter
All references to Chapters 5/ through 13/ are to the income tax

Gross income, individuals (*Continued*)
  • • complementary tax, for, 6/1.2c
  • • exclusion from for schedular tax, 6/1.2e
  • nonresidents
  • • tax on basis of, 11/3.4
  • • withholding of tax at source, 5/4.7
  • presumed profits as measured by, 6/9.1
  • return of capital distinguished from, 6/1.1
  • when deemed received. *See* Business income *and* Income of individuals

Gross profits. *See* Gross income *and* Profits

H

Harper's formula, 3/2.5b

Head of household
  • income of dependents reported by, 13/1.1c

History of taxation in Brazil, 1/1.1–1/1.3

Home office expenses, 11/3.3c

Hotels
  • business tax on, 18/2.4d
  • depreciation available to, 7/3.3, n. 48
  • real property taxes on, 3/2.8
  • transaction tax on, 15/7.2

I

Immovable property. *See* Real property

Implied interest, 9/1.4b

Imports
  • exchange remittance tax on, 4/10.
  • federal excise tax on, 16/2.4a; 16/2.6
  • foreign exchange controls, 1/2.7b
  • import duties on, 1/2.6; 4/4.
  • sales tax on, 15/3.2b

Impôsto de consumo. *See* Federal excise tax

Impôsto unico, 16/3.
  • background, 16/3.1
  • electric power, on, 16/3.3
  • fuels and lubricants, on, 16/3.2
  • general, 4/6.
  • minerals, on, 16/3.4
  • tax rates. *See specific taxable items, supra., this heading*

Income. *For items of, see* Business income *and* Income of individuals. *See also* Gross income *and* Profits
  • additions to, 7/6.
  • attribution of, for tax purposes. *See* Attribution of income
  • business. *See* Business income
  • complementary tax, subject to, 6/1.2c
  • estimated, 6/9.2
  • excess profits tax, subject to, 14/3.
  • exclusions from, 6/1.2e
  • income-spreading provisions. *See* Compensation for services, attributable to several taxable years
  • individuals, of. *See* Income of individuals
  • presumed, 6/9.1
  • presumptive, 9/6.1
  • recipients of
  • • bankrupts' estates, 5/3.6
  • • corporations. *See* Business income
  • • entities. *See* Business income
  • • individuals. *See* Income of individuals
  • • nonresident entities. *See* Business income
  • • nonresident individuals. *See* Income of individuals
  • • nonresidents generally, 5/4.2
  • • partnerships, members of, 6/4.1a
  • • professional persons. *See* Independent services
  • subject to excess profits tax, 14/2.
  • when deemed received. *See this title under* Business income *and* Income of individuals

Income from foreign sources
  • entities as recipients, 11/2.3
  • excess profits tax on, 14/3.
  • individuals as recipients, 11/2.2

Income of individuals
  • allocation of between foreign and domestic sources, 11/2.2
  • defined, 6/1.1
  • exclusions from, 6/1.2e
  • gross receipts distinguished, 6/1.1
  • individuals engaged in business, 5/3.4. *See also* Individuals engaged in business
  • items of
  • • agricultural, 10/2.2
  • • assignment of rights acquired under contract of sale, 10/4.1a
  • • capital gains, 9/8.1
  • • compensation for nonexercise of contractual rights, 10/4.1a

Detailed contents appear at beginning of each chapter
All references to Chapters 5/ through 13/ are to the income tax

Income of individuals, items of
(*Continued*)
· · compensation for services. *See* Compensation for services
· · damages for breach of contract, 10/4.1a
· · dividends and other distributions. *See* Dividends and other distributions
· · estimated profits, 6/9.2
· · futures and report operations, profits from, 10/4.1b*1*
· · gambling, from, 10/4.1b*2*
· · improvements made by lessee, 7/3.5
· · insurance benefits. *See* Insurance
· · insurance premiums refunded, 6/1.2e
· · interest. *See* Interest
· · lotteries, from, 10/4.1b*2*
· · mining, profits from, 10/1.1
· · miscellaneous, 10/4.1
· · occasional commercial or industrial transactions, 7/1.3
· · partnership profits, 6/4.1a
· · pensions, 9/3.1
· · presumptive income, 9/6.1
· · professional services, from. *See* Independent services
· · real property transactions, 9/8.2
· · recovery of charged-off debts, 7/2.9
· · redemption of securities, 9/9.5a
· · rent. *See* Rent
· · rental value of real property occupied by owner, 6/1.2e
· · royalties. *See* Intellectual property
· nonresident individuals, 6/1.3a
· presumed profits, 6/9.1
· when deemed received, 6/4.1a
· · improvements to rented property, 7/3.5
· · services rendered during more than one year. *See* Compensation for services, attributable to several taxable years

Income tax
· administration of, 13/
· business income, on, 7/
· capital, on income from, 9/
· computation of, 12/
· income determination, principles of, 6/
· international aspects of, 11/
· personal services, on income from, 8/
· special activities and miscellaneous sources, on income from, 10/
· summary of, 2/
· taxpayers, classes of, 5/

Incorporação. *See* Reorganizations
Independent services

· blanket deduction, 8/2.4
· brokers' fees and commissions, 8/2.2
· · brokers' syndicates, paid by, 13/3.2
· · excess profits tax, 14/6.1
· · government securities, from transactions in, 9/1.2b
· business tax, subject to, 18/2.2
· compensation for, 8/2.2
· · occasional services, 10/4.1a
· · tax rates, 8/2.5
· deductions, 8/2.3. *See also* Deductions
· excess profits tax on, 14/2.
· rendered over more than one year, 8/3.3
· tax practice, persons engaged in, 1/5.6
· transaction tax, subject to, 15/7.2

Individuals. *See also* Income of individuals
· accounting methods. *See* Accounting
· allowances. *See* Allowances
· assessment of tax, 5/1.1; 13/1.1d
· base year, 6/3.1
· exemptions, 5/5.1. *See also* Exemptions
· payment of tax, 13/1.1d
· returns. *See* Returns

Individuals engaged in business (*Firma individual*)
· capital
· · gains on sale of, 7/6.3
· · increases in subject to excess profits tax, 14/4.2
· compensation for services of owner
· · deductibility of, 7/5.2a
· · withholding at source on, 8/1.5b
· depreciation. *See* Depreciation
· individual proprietorship described, 1/4.2a
· losses, 7/4.3
· profits of owner, 6/4.1a; 9/2.1a
· registration of, 5/3.4
· reorganization
· · succession of ownership, 9/9.3a*1*
· · transformation, 9/9.3b*1*
· reserves, 6/6.1; 7/8.2
· returns, 5/3.4; 13/1.2a
· revaluation of assets, 7/6.2
· taxable income, 6/1.1

Industries
· agricultural and industrial exploitation tax, 16/4.
· exemptions
· · industrial machinery, 16/2.6–Sch. I
· · new industries, 18/2.4d
· · pigments used by as raw materials, 16/2.6–Sch. XIV
· · small industries, 18/2.4e

Detailed contents appear at beginning of each chapter
All references to Chapters 5/ through 13/ are to the income tax

Industries (*Continued*)
· industrial production, 1/2.2
· manufacturers
· · federal excise tax on, 16/2.4a
· · sales tax on, 15/2.1

Information required by government
· assessment ex officio, in, 13/7.6
· financial statements of entities, 13/2.2b
· payments made, 13/3.1
· · identity of payees, 13/3.1
· · payors who must report, 13/3.2
· penalties
· · failure to file, 13/7.4
· · failure to supply, 13/2.2a
· · nondisclosure of sale of real property, 13/7.3
· returns, to be filed with
· · entities, 13/1.2a
· · individuals, 13/1.1a
· review of returns, in, 13/2.1

Inheritance tax
· appeals, 3/3.8
· appraisal for, 3/3.6
· collection and payment of, 3/3.8
· exempt persons, 3/3.3b
· exempt transfers, 3/3.5
· general, 3/3.1
· jurisdiction to tax, 3/3.2
· tax base, 3/3.4
· tax rates, 3/3.7
· taxpayer, 3/3.3a

Inheritances
· income, as, 6/1.2e
· tax on. *See* Inheritance tax

Insufficient income exemption. *See* Allowances, minimum income

Insurance
· deductibility of premiums
· · abatements for complementary tax, as, 12/1.2b4
· · entities, 7/2.8
· · income from independent services, from, 8/2.3
· · rental income, from, 9/4.1b
· · single-premium endowment policies, 9/3.1; 12/1.2b4
· endowment policy benefits, 9/3.1
· expenses of as computed in sales tax base, 15/3.1
· life
· · entities as beneficiaries, 7/2.8; 7/7.3
· · partners as beneficiaries, 7/2.8
· · proceeds as gross income, 6/1.2e
· premiums refunded, 6/1.2e

Insurance companies
· depreciation, 7/3.3, n. 48
· payments made by, reports of required by government, 13/3.2
· technical reserves of
· · deductibility of, 6/6.1; 10/3.2a
· · exemption of from compulsory loan, 7/8.2

Intangibles
· amortization of, 7/3.6

Intellectual property
· amortization of, 7/3.6
· authors' royalties, requirement to report payment of, 13/3.2
· contributions to capital, as, 7/3.6
· exemption of income from
· · authors' royalties, 5/5.3; 9/5.1
· · nonresident authors' royalties, 6/1.3a
· inheritance and gift taxes, exemption from, 3/3.5
· licensing of, 11/3.4a
· recipients of royalties
· · entities as, 9/5.1b; 9/5.2b
· · individuals as, 9/5.1a; 9/5.2a
· · nonresidents as, 9/5.2c; 11/3.4a
· sale of, 11/3.5c

Interest
· bank accounts, on, 9/1.3a
· bearer shares, from, 9/1.6
· compensation for independent services, on, 8/2.2
· deductibility of
· · debts of entities, on, 7/2.4
· · debts of individuals, on, 12/1.2b3
· · debts of nonresidents, on, 7/2.4
· · loans to acquire or develop agricultural property, on, 10/2.2b
· · mortgages, on, from rental income, 9/4.1b, n. 40
· · paid by branches to foreign home office, 7/2.4
· · paid to owners and partners, 7/5.2c
· deposits and current accounts, on, 9/1.4a
· entities as recipients, 9/1.7
· foreign capital, on, 4/10.
· government securities, on, 9/1.2a; 9/1.6
· implied, 9/1.4b
· individuals as recipients, 9/1.1
· loans, on, 9/1.3a
· miscellaneous, 9/1.5
· nominative securities, on, 9/1.3
· nonresidents as recipients, 9/1.8
· payments of, reported to government, 13/3.1; 13/3.2

Detailed contents appear at beginning of each chapter
All references to Chapters 5/ through 13/ are to the income tax

Interest (*Continued*)
• presumed, 9/1.4b
• tax exempt items, on, 6/1.2e
• withholding at source on, 9/1.6

Internal Revenue Department, 1/5.1C

International trade, 1/2.6. *See also* Exports *and* Imports

Inventories
• reserves for decline in value of, 6/5.1; 7/5.3
• valuation of, 6/5.1

J

Joint venture (*Sociedade em conta de participação*), 5/3.2

Journalists
• excess profits tax on, 14/6.1
• income tax, exempt from, 5/5.3

Judicial decisions. *See* Tax law

Judicial remedies. *See* Taxpayers' remedies

Judicial system, 1/1.5c

Junta Comercial. *See* Commercial Registry

Juridical persons. *See* Entities

Jurisdiction to tax, 1/3.1
• business tax, 18/1.2
• concurrent, 1/3.3
• exclusive, 1/3.2
• federal stamp tax, 17/2.1
• *impôsto unico,* 16/3.1
• inheritance and gift taxes, 3/3.2
• real property transfer tax, 19/3.1
• sales tax, 15/1.2
• stamp taxes, 17/1.2

Jurisprudência. *See* Tax law

L

Law for the protection of the family, 12/1.3a

Laws. *See* Tax law

Lawyers. *See* Independent services *and* Partnerships, professional

Leaseholds. *See also* Rented property
• emphyteusis, 9/4.1b

Legal expenses, deductibility of, 8/2.3

Legislative branch, 1/1.5b

Licenses. *See* Intellectual property

Liens
• refund claim as, 1/5.5
• tax claim as, 1/5.7

Life insurance. *See* Insurance

Limitations. *See* Time limits

Limited liability company (*Sociedade por quotas de responsibilidade limitada*), 1/4.2f; 5/3.3
• incorporation of, 9/9.3b2
• increase in value of quotas, 7/6.1

Liquidations. *See* Commencement and termination of operations

Literary organizations, 5/6.1

Livestock raising. *See* Agriculture

Loans
• Bank Loans Fund (*Caixa de Mobilização Bancária*), 1/2.4
• capital, of, 14/4.1
• compulsory. *See* Compulsory loan to government
• federal stamp tax on, 17/2.4
• interest on as income, 9/1.3a

Lotteries
• income from, 10/4.1b2
• tax on, 18/4.2

Losses, 7/4.
• branches of foreign entities, 7/4.4
• carry-over of, 7/4.2
• deductible, 7/4.1
• depreciation as affecting, 7/3.1
• extraordinary, 12/1.2b5
• foreign exchange, 7/4.5
• individuals engaged in business, 7/4.3
• partnerships, commercial, 7/4.3
• securities transactions, 7/2.6

Luxury tax, 15/4.1

M

Machinery
• depreciation rates on, 7/3.3
• federal excise tax on, 16/2.6–Sch. I
• import duties on, 1/2.7b
• real property transfer tax on, 19/4.3

Maintenance expenses. *See* Deductions

Mandamus, writ of (*Mandado de segurança*). *See* Taxpayers' remedies

Manufacturers and manufacturing. *See* Industries

Detailed contents appear at beginning of each chapter
All references to Chapters 5/ through 13/ are to the income tax

Married persons
· allowance for spouse, 8/1.5a; 12/1.2b*1*
· returns
· · joint and separate, 13/1.1c
· · penalties for improper filing, 13/7.5

Medical and dental expenses, 12/1.2b2

Medicines and drugs. *See* Pharmaceutical products

Mercantile companies, 5/2.3

Mercantile sales. *See* Sales

Merchandise account
· entities, of, 13/1.2a

Merger (*Fusão*). *See* Reorganizations

Metals
· *impôsto unico* on, 16/3.4
· mining of. *See* Natural resource extraction
· precious, 16/2.6–Sch. X
· products, 16/2.6–Sch. I

Mining. *See* Natural resource extraction

Mortgages
· stamp tax on, 17/2.4

Motion pictures, compensation for use of, 9/4.3

Movables
· depreciation of, 7/3.1
· inheritance and gift taxes on, 3/3.1; 3/3.4
· rental income from, 9/4.3

Municipalities
· autonomy of, 1/1.4
· exemption from taxation, 1/3.5
· Municipal Organization Acts (*Leis Organicas dos Municipios*), 3/2.1
· planning through real property taxes, 3/2.8
· real property taxes
· · improved urban real property, on, 3/2.7
· · unimproved urban real property, on, 3/2.6
· sources of revenue summarized, 1/6.4
· tax authorities, 1/5.2

N

National economy, 1/2.
· agricultural and industrial production, 1/2.2
· character of, 1/2.1
· income, 1/2.2

· international trade, 1/2.5
· public finance, 1/2.3

Natural resource extraction, 10/1.
· allocation of income from between foreign and domestic sources, 11/2.3
· amortization of investment in, 10/1.2
· concession for, 19/4.2
· depletion, 10/1.2
· · charge on excess provisions for, 14/1.2
· · dissolution of provision for, 7/6.1
· generally, 1/2.1
· *impôsto unico* on, 16/3.4
· jurisdiction to tax, 10/1.1
· machinery for, 1/2.6b

Net income. *See* Income

Nondeductible expenditures
· capital expenditures, 7/5.1
· · deductible expenses distinguished, 7/2.5
· payments to owners, officers, partners, etc., 7/5.2
· political contributions, 7/2.10
· reserves, 7/5.3
· · indemnifications prescribed by labor law, for, 7/5.4
· retirement pay to partners, 7/2.3

Nonresidents. *See also* Foreign entities *and* Branches of foreign entities
· assessment, taxation by, 5/4.2
· branches of foreign corporations as. *See* Branches of foreign entities
· capital gains of, 11/3.5b
· collection of tax on, 13/6.2, n. 56
· directors of entities, 7/5.2
· entities. *See* Foreign entities
· exemptions, 6/1.3
· gains from sale of real property, 11/3.5b
· gross income as base of tax on, 11/3.4
· income of, 6/1.3a; 11/3.1
· · capital, from, 9/7.2
· · dividends and other distributions as, 9/2.4
· · interest, 9/1.8
· · motion picture lessors, 9/4.3d
· · real property, from, 5/4.2; 9/4.2
· · real property subleases, from, 9/4.3c
· · redemption of securities, 9/9.5c
· · royalties, authors', 6/1.3a
· · royalties, other, 9/5.1c; 9/5.2c; 11/3.4a
· · taxed at source to residents, 5/4.3
· · withholding at source on, 10/4.3; 11/3.4
· individuals
· · determination of nonresidence, 5/4.1

Detailed contents appear at beginning of each chapter
All references to Chapters 5/ through 13/ are to the income tax

Nonresidents, individuals (*Continued*)
- • income subject to tax, 5/4.2
- • inheritance and gift taxes on, 3/3.7
- • interest payments to, 7/2.4
- • profits from sales to Brazil, 11/3.5
- • taxation of, generally, 2/5.
- • withholding at source on, 5/4.9
- • • penalties for late payment of tax withheld, 13/7.3
- • • rates, 5/4.2

O

Obsolescence, 7/3.4

Office expenses
- • deductibility of by employees, 8/1.3b

Office furniture
- • depreciation of, 7/3.3
- • federal excise tax on, 16/2.7–Sch. XVII
- • sales tax on, 15/2.2

Officers of entities
- • business tax on, 18/2.4f
- • compensation for services, 8/1.2b
- • • deductibility of, 7/5.2
- • life insurance on, 7/7.3

Oil companies. *See* Petroleum industry

Ordens de serviço. See Tax law

Original package doctrine, 15/6.2

Overpayment of tax. *See* Taxpayers' remedies

Owners of entities. *See also* Individuals engaged in business *and* Partnerships, commercial
- • compensation for services, 8/1.2b
- • • deductibility of, 7/5.2a
- • distributions to
- • • interest, 7/5.2c
- • • when entity taxed on estimated profits, 6/9.2
- • life insurance on, 7/7.3
- • withdrawals, 7/5.2a

P

Paper, exemptions. *See also* Publications
- • business tax, from, 18/2.4b
- • exchange remittance tax, from, 4/10.
- • federal excise tax, from, 16/2.6–Sch. XI
- • sales tax, from, 15/2.8c

Participating certificates. *See* Profit participations

Partnerships, commercial
- • books and records of, 6/2.2
- • capital
- • • invested, 14/4.1
- • • tax on increases of, 14/4.2
- • compensation for services of partners, 7/5.2a
- • deductions. *See* Deductions
- • entities, as, 5/3.1
- • excess profits tax on, 14/2.
- • federal stamp tax on, 17/2.5
- • income from, assignment of by partners, 6/8.1
- • incorporation of, 9/9.3b2
- • losses, 7/4.3
- • profits of partners, 5/3.1; 9/2.1a
- • • when deemed income to, 6/4.1a
- • reserves, 6/6.1
- • • capitalization of, tax on, 14/4.4
- • • charge on, 7/8.2
- • retirement pay to partner, 7/2.3
- • revaluation of assets
- • • partners taxed on surplus, 7/6.2
- • • tax on, 14/4.3
- • tax computation for, 12/2.5
- • types of, 1/4.2b–1/4.2e

Partnerships, professional
- • assignments of income, 6/8.1
- • books and records of, 6/2.2, n. 32
- • excess profits tax, exemption from, 14/2.
- • income tax rates on, 12/2.6

Patents. *See* Intellectual property

Payment of tax. *See* Collection and payment of tax

Payments
- • constructive, deductibility of,
- • • entities, to, 6/4.2
- • • individuals, to, 6/4.1b
- • deductibility of. *See* Deductions *and* Nondeductible expenditures
- • reports of required by government, 13/3.1. *See also* Information required by government
- • • entities, 13/1.2a
- • • individuals, 13/1.1
- • • payors who must report, 13/3.1; 13/3.2

Penalties
- • business tax, under, 18/3.2
- • collection of delinquent taxes, 1/5.9
- • criminal, 1/5.8
- • enforcement measures, 1/5.7
- • excess profits tax, under, 14/8.

Detailed contents appear at beginning of each chapter
All references to Chapters 5/ through 13/ are to the income tax

Penalties (*Continued*)
- federal excise tax, under, 16/2.10c
- fines, 1/5.8
- income tax, under
- • assessment ex officio, 13/7.6
- • books and records, failure to maintain or show, 13/7.4
- • deductions claimed but not allowed, 7/2.1; 13/7.6
- • estimated profits as, 6/9.2
- • failure to file return properly, 13/7.5
- • fraud, 13/7.7
- • late filing of return, 13/7.2
- • late payment of tax, 13/7.2
- • late payment of tax by withholding agent, 13/7.3
- • sale of real property, failure to report, 13/7.3
- real property transfer tax, under, 19/6.5
- sales tax, under, 15/5.4
- tax officials, on, for improper practices, 1/5.8

Pensions
- based on illness, 6/1.2e
- income, as, 9/3.1
- payment of by insurance companies, 13/3.2

Personal exemptions. *See* Allowances

Petitions. *See* Taxpayers' remedies

Petroleum industry
- exemptions
- • business tax, from, 18/2.4g
- • exchange remittance tax, from, 4/10.
- *impôsto unico* on, 16/3.2

Pharmaceutical products
- federal excise tax on, 16/2.6–Sch. XIII
- sales tax on, 15/2.8c

Philanthropic institutions. *See* Charities

Physicians. *See* Independent services *and* Partnerships, professional

Political parties
- contributions to, 7/2.10
- exemptions
- • constitutional provisions, 1/3.5
- • inheritance and gift taxes, from, 3/3.3b1
- • real property taxes, from, 3/2.3c
- • real property transfer tax, from, 19/2.2

Portarias. See Tax law

Power companies. *See also* Public utilities
- *impôsto unico* on, 16/3.3

- waterfall tax on, 16/3.5

Power of attorney
- attribution of income to holder of, 6/8.1

Premiums
- import, 1/2.7b
- insurance. *See* Insurance
- securities, on, 7/1.1

President of Brazil, 1/1.5a

Presumed interest, 9/1.4

Presumed profits as tax base
- excess profits tax, 14/3.
- income tax, 6/9.1
- • branches of foreign entities, 6/9.1; 11/3.3b
- • commencement and termination in same year, 6/3.6
- • returns and information required for, 13/2.2b

Presumptive income, 9/6.1

Primeiro Conselho de Contribuintes. See Tax Court

Processes. *See* Intellectual property

Producers. *See also* Industries
- defined, 15/2.1
- excise tax on, 16/4.1
- exemptions
- • minor producers, 15/2.8a; 18/2.4e
- • new producers, 18/2.4d
- sales tax on, 15/2.1

Professional associations, exemptions. *See* Exemptions

Professional services. *See* Independent services

Professors, 5/5.3

Profit and loss statements. *See also* Accounting
- failure to file with return, 13/7.4b

Profit participations
- certificate holders, effect of distribution to, 7/2.14
- deductibility of, 8/2.3
- distributions
- • Schedule F income, as, 9/2.1e
- • taxable at source, 9/2.2d
- employees as participants, 7/2.12
- government as participant, 7/2.13
- sale of interest in, 9/9.3a3

Profits. *See also* Business income; Gross income; Income; *and* Income of individuals

Detailed contents appear at beginning of each chapter
All references to Chapters 5/ through 13/ are to the income tax

Profits (*Continued*)
· accumulated. *See* Surplus
· actual
· · excess profits tax, based on, 14/3.
· · income tax, based on, 2/4.3
· appropriations of to reserves, 6/6.2
· books and records as determining, 7/1.1
· defined, 7/1.1
· discount operations, from, 9/1.4c
· entity, of, taxed to shareholders, 5/2.5
· estimated. *See* Estimated profits as tax base
· excess profits tax. *See* Excess profits tax
· foreign capital, on, 4/10.
· participation in. *See* Profit participations
· partnerships, commercial
· · taxation of, 5/3.1
· · when deemed income to partners, 6/4.1a
· presumed. *See* Presumed profits as tax base
· undistributed
· · compulsory loan to government, based on, 7/8.2
· · excess profits credit, 14/4.1

Proof of deductions, 7/2.1; 13/1.1a

Protest (*Reclamação*), 1/5.4; 13/4.1. *See also* Taxpayers' remedies

Provisions (*Provisões*)
· bad debts, for, 7/2.9
· defined, 6/6.1
· depreciation, for. *See* Depreciation
· dissolution of as income, 7/6.1
· excess. *See* Reserves
· excess profits credit, 14/4.1
· exemption of from compulsory loan, 7/8.2

Public corporations, 5/2.3

Public sector, 1/2.3

Public utilities. *See also* Power companies
· amortization of capital investments, 10/3.2b
· determination of income, 10/3.1
· tax rates, 12/2.6

Publications
· business tax, exemptions from
· · newspapers and news agencies, 18/2.4a
· · paper, 18/2.4b
· · printing, 18/2.4b
· copyrights and royalties on. *See* Intellectual property

· excess profits tax on associations of journalists, 14/6.1
· exchange remittance tax, exemptions from
· · books, 4/10.
· · paper, 4/10.
· federal excise tax, exemption of paper from, 16/2.6–Sch. XI
· income tax, exemptions from
· · journalists, 5/5.3
· · literary organizations, 5/6.1
· sales tax, exemption of paper from, 15/2.8c

R

Radio and television networks
· business tax on, 18/2.4a

Rates
· amortization
· · improvements made by lessee, 7/3.5
· · intangibles, 7/3.6
· · investment in natural resource extraction, 10/1.2
· depletion, 10/1.2
· depreciation, 7/3.3
· tax. *See* Tax rates

Rates of exchange. *See* Foreign exchange

Real property
· contributions to capital, as, 15/2.6
· decedents' estates, receipt by heir or legatee of more than share, 3/3.8
· deeds
· · execution and registration of, 3/2.2; 19/6.1
· · federal stamp tax on, 17/2.2
· defined, 3/2.1; 19/3.1, n. 4
· depreciation of. *See* Depreciation
· fair market value of, 3/2.5b; 19/4.1
· fees on, 3/2.10
· fixtures as, 19/4.3
· gains from sale of, 9/8.2
· · individuals engaged in business, 7/6.3
· · nonresidents, 11/3.5b
· · withholding at source on, 2/3.3c
· income from, 9/4.1. *See also* Rent
· information required concerning sale of, 13/7.3
· mineral leases and concessions, 19/4.2
· mortgages on, 17/2.4
· nonresidents as owners, 9/4.2
· occupant, tax on, 3/2.2
· rental of
· · value of, 3/2.7c

Detailed contents appear at beginning of each chapter
All references to Chapters 5/ through 13/ are to the income tax

Real property, rental of (*Continued*)
- • value of as income when occupied by owner, 6/1.2e
- rights constituting, 19/3.1, n. 4
- rural land tax, 1/6.3a
- summary of taxes on, 3/1.1
- transfers of
- • conduct of business, as, 5/3.4
- • inter vivos other than by gift, 19/1.1
- • means of effecting, 19/6.1
- • taxes on. *See* gains from sale of, *supra,* this heading *and* Real property transfer tax
- urban real property tax, 1/6.4a
- waterfalls, tax on, 16/3.5

Real property transfer tax
- additions to, 19/5.2
- appraisal of value, 19/6.3
- background, 19/1.1
- collection of, 19/6.2
- deeds, execution and registry of, 19/6.1
- distribution of inherited property in excess of share subject to, 3/3.8
- exemptions
- • constitutional, 19/2.2
- • statutory, 19/2.3
- penalties, 19/6.5
- persons subject to, 19/2.1
- property subject to
- • destination, property by, 19/4.3
- • nature, property by, 19/4.2
- • operation of law, property by, 19/4.4
- refunds, 19/6.2
- summarized, 4/9.
- tax base, 19/4.1
- tax rates, 19/5.1
- taxable event, 19/3.1
- taxpayers' remedies, 19/6.4
- thirty-year tax, 19/3.2
- underpayment of tax, 19/6.2

Receipts returned by taxpayer, 6/4.1a

Receivables
- uncollectible. *See* Debts, bad
- valuation of, 6/5.2

Reciprocity, exemption by
- foreign air and shipping lines, 5/6.5
- foreign governments, 5/2.3

Reclamação (Protest), 1/5.4; 13/4.1

Recreational organizations, 5/6.1

Recurso voluntário (Petition for review), 13/4.2

Reembolso (Payment to dissenting stockholder), 9/9.5a1

Refunds. *See* Taxpayers' remedies

Regional delegate, protest to, 13/4.1

Registration
- entities, 5/2.4
- foreign corporations, 11/3.2
- individuals engaged in business, 5/3.4

Registration fee, 15/2.3

Registro de Comercio (Commercial Registry), 3/2.2; 5/2.4

Registry of Deeds (*Registro de Imóveis*), 19/6.1

Religious organizations, exemptions
- constitutional provisions, 1/3.5
- income tax, from, 5/6.1
- inheritance and gift taxes, from, 3/3.3b1
- real property taxes, from, 3/2.3b
- real property transfer tax, from, 19/2.3a

Remedies. *See* Taxpayers' remedies

Rent, 9/4.
- assignment of, 6/8.1
- commissions paid for collection of, 13/3.2
- deductibility of
- • entities, to, 7/2.2
- • income from independent services, from, 8/2.3
- deductions from, 9/1.4b
- income, as
- • prepaid, when deemed received, 6/4.1a
- • report of to government, 13/3.1
- nonresidents as recipients
- • motion pictures, from, 9/4.3d
- • movable property, from, 9/4.3c
- • real property, from, 9/4.2
- residents as recipients
- • movable property, from, 9/4.3a; 9/4.3b
- • real property, from, 9/4.1

Rented property
- agricultural income from, 10/2.2a
- depreciation on, 7/3.1
- improvements made by lessee, 7/3.5
- value of, 3/2.7c
- • owner-occupier, as income to, 6/1.2e

Reorganizations, 9/9.
- accounting periods, 6/3.5
- consolidation (*incorporação*), 9/9.3a
- excess profits credit, forfeiture of, 14/4.3
- federal stamp tax on, 17/2.5
- general, 9/9.1
- increase in stock value from, 9/2.1f
- legal form of business, change of, 9/9.4
- merger (*fusão*), 9/9.3a

Detailed contents appear at beginning of each chapter
All references to Chapters 5/ through 13/ are to the income tax

Reorganizations (*Continued*)
- revaluation of assets in
- - dividends paid from, 9/**2.1f**
- - surplus from, 7/6.2
- succession, 9/9.3a
- transformation, 9/9.3b

Reserves (*Reservas*), 6/6.; 7/8. *See also* Provisions
- capitalization of, 14/4.3; 14/4.4
- cash, required for banks, 1/2.4
- charge on, 7/8.2
- compulsory loan to government on. *See* Compulsory loan to government
- deductibility of, 7/5.3
- - bad debts, for, 7/2.9
- - declines in value of inventory, for, 6/5.1
- - declines in value of securities, for, 6/5.3
- - depletion, for, 10/1.2
- - depreciation, for, 7/3.3
- - indemnifications prescribed by labor law, for, 7/5.4
- - losses on foreign exchange, for, 7/4.5
- - taxes, for, 7/2.7
- - technical reserves of insurance and capitalization companies, 10/3.2a
- defined, 6/6.1
- excess, 7/8.3
- general, 2/4.4
- loss carry-over as affected by, 7/4.2
- nondeductible, 2/4.4a
- regulation of, 6/6.2
- revaluation of assets, for, 7/6.2
- taxes on, general, 2/4.4b; 7/8.1

Residence
- acquisition of, 5/4.4a
- entities, 5/2.1; 5/4.6; 11/3.1
- individuals, 5/1.1; 11/3.1
- permanent establishment affecting, 5/4.1
- services rendered in Brazil affecting, 11/3.4b
- termination of, 5/4.4b

Resources. *See* Natural resource extraction

Retainers, 8/1.2a. *See also* Compensation for services

Retirement pay. *See* Pensions

Return of capital, 6/1.1

Returns
- accounting periods. *See* Accounting
- acquisition of residence, 5/4.4a
- base period for, 6/3.1
- branches, 6/7.1
- branches of foreign entities, 13/1.2a
- challenge of by taxpayer, 13/4.1

- commencement of operations, 6/3.6
- decedents' estates, 13/1.3a
- dependents, 13/1.1c
- doubtful deductions, 7/2.1
- entities, 13/1.2a
- - penalties for not consolidating, 13/7.5
- - receipts for charitable contributions to be filed with, 7/2.10
- errors in, 13/2.2a
- excess profits tax, 14/7.
- failure to file, 13/2.2a
- falsifications of, 6/9.2
- filed improperly, 13/2.2a
- filed late, 13/7.2. *See also* Penalties
- forms, 12/2.7
- gains from sale of real property reported in, 9/8.2d
- government officials absent from country, 6/1.3b
- individuals, 13/1.1
- individuals engaged in business, 5/3.4
- - loss carry-over included in owner's personal return, 7/4.3
- married persons
- - joint and separate, 12/1.2b1; 13/1.1c
- - penalties for improper filing, 13/7.5
- omissions from, 6/9.2
- partners, commercial
- - individual returns as affected by partnership losses, 7/4.3
- - partnership income reported in, 5/3.1
- partners, professional
- - partnership income reported in, 12/2.5
- presumed profits as tax base, election of made in, 6/9.1
- refunds claimed on basis of error in, 13/5.1
- review of by government, 13/2.1
- tax for protection of the family computed on, 12/1.3a
- taxable year for, 6/3.1
- termination of operations, 6/3.7
- termination of residence, 5/4.4b

Revaluation of assets. *See* Valuation

Review, petition for (*Recurso voluntário*), 13/4.2b. *See also* Taxpayers' remedies

Royalties. *See* Intellectual property

Rural real property tax, 3/2.5

S

Salaries. *See* Compensation for services
Sales
- business tax on, 18/3.1

Detailed contents appear at beginning of each chapter
All references to Chapters 5/ through 13/ are to the income tax

Sales (*Continued*)
- cash, 15/5.2a
- consignment, 15/2.7
- contractual rights, of, 10/4.1a
- course of business, in
- • entities. *See* Business income
- • individuals. *See* Individuals engaged in business
- defined, 15/2.4
- export tax on, 15/6.1; 15/6.2
- installment
- • federal stamp tax on, 17/2.7
- • sales tax on, 15/5.2b
- interstate
- • sales tax on, 15/1.3
- • stamp tax on, 17/3.2
- mercantile, 15/2.1
- occasional, income from
- • entities, by, 7/1.1
- • individuals, by, 7/1.3; 10/4.1
- patents, trademarks, copyrights, processes, licenses, of. *See* Intellectual property
- promises to sell, 17/2.7
- real property, of, income from
- • entities as vendors, 7/1.2
- • individuals as vendors, 9/8.2
- • real property transfer tax on, 19/3.1
- remittances in foreign currency, 17/2.8
- sales tax on. *See* Sales tax
- securities. *See* Securities
- stamp tax on, 17/2.7; 17/2.8; 17/3.1
- term, 15/5.2b

Sales tax
- additions to, 15/4.3
- assessment of, 15/5.1
- capital, contributions to, 15/2.6
- concurrent taxes
- • background, 15/7.1
- • transactions tax, 15/7.2
- consignments, 15/2.7
- delivery, 15/2.4
- *duplicata,* 15/1.2; 15/3.1; 15/5.2
- exchanges, on
- • property for property, 15/2.5
- • property for shares, 15/2.6
- exemptions from, 15/2.8
- extension of scope of, 15/2.3
- fees, 15/4.3
- general, 4/2.
- interstate sales, on
- • constitutional provisions, 15/1.3a
- • statutory provisions, 15/1.3b
- materials and services, on, 15/7.1; 15/7.2
- merchants, on, 15/2.1

- penalties, 15/5.4
- producers, on, 15/2.1
- refunds, 15/5.3
- states, allocation to, 15/1.2
- tax base
- • export bonus included in, 15/3.2b
- • federal excise tax included in, 15/3.2a
- • gross invoice price included in, 15/3.1
- • overprices included in, 15/3.2b
- tax rates, 15/4.1
- • comparison of, 15/4.2
- taxable sale, 15/2.2
- transaction tax, 15/2.3; 15/7.2

Schedular taxes
- deductions applying to more than one schedule, 8/2.3
- exclusions from gross income for, 6/1.2e; 12/1.1
- general, 2/3.1
- income subject to, 12/1.1
- tax rates, 6/1.2; 12/1.1

Schedule A (income from government securities)
- deductions, 9/1.2b
- income included in, 9/1.2a
- tax rates, 9/1.2c

Schedule B (miscellaneous interest)
- deductions, 9/1.3b
- income included in
- • bank accounts, from, 9/1.3a
- • deposits and current accounts, from, 9/1.4a
- • discount operations, from, 9/1.4c
- • excess over face value paid on insurance policies, 9/1.4
- • gain on conversion of insurance policies, 9/3.1
- • loans, from, 9/1.3a
- • nominative securities, from, 9/1.3
- • report operations, from, 10/4.1b*1*
- • sales of futures, from, 10/4.1b*1*
- tax rate, 9/1.3c

Schedule C (income from wages and salaries)
- deductions
- • contributions to employees' benefit funds, 8/1.3d
- • dues, 8/1.3c
- • office expenses, 8/1.3b
- • travel expenses, 8/1.3a
- income included in, 8/1.2
- • pensions and retirement pay, 9/3.1
- • withholding at source on, 8/1.5b
- tax rates, 8/1.4

Detailed contents appear at beginning of each chapter
All references to Chapters 5/ through 13/ are to the income tax

Schedule D (income from independent services)
· deductions, 8/2.3
· · blanket deduction, 8/2.4
· income included in, 8/2.2
· · royalties, from, 9/5.1a
· tax rates, 8/2.5

Schedule E (income from rent)
· deductions, 9/4.1b
· income included in, 9/4.1a
· tax rates, 9/4.1c

Schedule F (income from dividends and other distributions)
· income included in
· · commercial partnerships, profits of, 5/3.1; 9/2.1a
· · foreign sources, from, 11/2.2
· · increase in stock value in reorganizations, 9/2.1f
· · individuals engaged in business, profits of, 9/2.1a
· · nominative shares, from, 9/2.1b
· · profit participations, from, 9/2.1e
· · stock dividends, from, 9/2.1c
· · surplus, from, 9/2.1d
· losses, effect of, 7/4.3

Schedule G (agricultural and related income)
· deductions, 10/2.2b
· income included in, 10/2.2a
· tax rates, 10/2.2a

Schedule H (miscellaneous income)
· deductions, 10/4.1a
· income included in, 10/4.1a
· · joint ventures, profits of participants in, 5/3.2
· · mining, profits from, 10/1.1
· · rental of movable and immovable property combined, from, 9/4.1a
· · sublease of real property, from, 9/4.3
· tax rates, 10/4.1a

Schools. *See* Educational institutions

Scientific organizations, 5/6.1

Securities
· capital gains on sales of
· · entities, 7/1.2
· · individuals, 9/8.1
· capitalization bonds, anticipated retirement of, 9/9.5a3
· dividends and other distributions on. *See* Dividends and other distributions
· government, income from, 9/2.1
· information required in returns of entities dealing in, 13/1.2a

· losses on, 7/2.6
· participating certificates. *See* Profit participations
· redemption of, 9/9.5
· · bearer shares, 9/9.5a4
· · nominative shares, 9/9.5a2
· sales tax on
· · exchange of property for, 15/2.6
· · exemption from, 15/2.8c
· stock dividends
· · income to issuing entity, as, 7/6.1
· · valuation of, 9/2.1c
· value of, increase in from revaluation of assets
· · complementary tax on, 7/6.2
· · special tax on, 14/4.3

Security for payment of tax. *See* Taxpayers' remedies

Shareholders. *See also* Dividends and other distributions *and* Securities
· corporate profits as income to, 5/2.5
· dissenting, 9/9.5a1
· dividends, when deemed received by, 6/4.1a
· life insurance on, 7/7.3
· securities sold below par to, 7/6.3
· withholding at source of tax on excess reserves, 7/8.3

Shares. *See* Securities

Shipping lines, foreign, 5/6.5

Ships
· depreciation rates on, 7/3.3

Social security, 1/2.3a

Sociedades anônimas, 1/4.2g. *See also* Corporations

Sociedades com firma, 1/4.2b. *See also* Partnerships, commercial

Sociedades de capital e indústria, 1/4.2c. *See also* Partnerships, commercial

Sociedades de capitalização. See Capitalization companies

Sociedades em comandita, 1/4.2e. *See also* Partnerships, commercial

Sociedades em comandita por ações, 1/4.2e. *See also* Partnerships, commercial

Sociedades em conta de participação (Joint venture), 1/4.2d; 5/3.2

Sociedades em nome coletivo, 1/4.2b. *See also* Partnerships, commercial

Detailed contents appear at beginning of each chapter
All references to Chapters 5/ through 13/ are to the income tax

Sociedades por quotas de responsibili-dade limitada, 1/4.2f. *See also* Limited liability companies

Sole proprietorship. *See* Individuals engaged in business

Source of income
- determination of
- • entities as recipients, 11/2.3
- • individuals as recipients, 11/2.2
- sales by nonresidents to Brazil, 11/3.5a

Stamp taxes, 17/
- background of, 17/1.2
- export tax, substitute for, 15/6.3
- federal. *See* Federal stamp tax
- general, 4/7.
- municipal, 17/3.1
- sales tax, substitute for, 15/2.3
- state, 17/3.1
- • automobiles, registration of, 17/**3.3**
- • interstate sales, on, 17/3.2

States
- autonomy of, 1/1.4
- exemptions from taxation, 1/3.**5**
- interstate sales, 1/6.3h
- real property, tax base for, 3/**2.1**
- sources of revenue, 1/6.3
- tax authorities, 1/5.2

Statutes. *See* Tax law

Students, 6/1.3b

Subsidiaries, 11/3.3e
- parent company's residence as affected by, 11/3.2
- returns of, 13/1.2a

Sucursais. See Branches *and* Branches of foreign entities

Supplementary assessments, 13/6.1

Supreme Court of Brazil
- appeals to, 13/4.3
- described, 1/1.5c

Suprimentos (Contributions to capital). *See* Capital

Surplus
- compulsory loan to government on, 7/8.2
- entities, of, analyzed in returns, 13/1.2a
- loss carry-over as affected by, 7/4.2
- revaluation of assets, from, 14/4.3

T

Tax administration. *See* Administration

Tax base
- assessment ex officio, for, 13/2.2c
- business tax, for, 18/3.1
- entities
- • actual profits as, 6/1.1
- • estimated profits as, 6/9.2
- • presumed profits as, 6/9.1
- federal excise tax, for
- • ad valorem, 16/2.6
- • ceiling price, 16/2.7
- • technical characteristics, computed by, 16/2.8
- • units, computed by, 16/2.9
- federal stamp tax, for
- • corporate agreements, 17/2.5
- • foreign exchange transactions, 17/2.8
- • installment sales, 17/2.7
- • private written agreements, 17/2.3
- • securities, on transfer of, 17/2.6
- individuals, 6/1.1
- inheritance and gift taxes, for, 3/3.4
- real property taxes, 3/2.4
- • improved urban real property, 3/2.7a; 3/2.7b
- • rural real property, 3/2.5a
- • unimproved urban real property, 3/2.6
- real property transfer tax, for, 19/4.1
- • deductibility of *impôsto unico* from, 19/4.2
- • rights treated as real property, 19/4.4
- sales tax, for,
- • Bank of Brazil, payments to included in, 15/3.2
- • export bonus included in, 15/3.2b
- • federal excise tax included in, 15/3.2a
- • gross invoice price included in, 15/3.1
- • overprices included in, 15/3.2b
- • prior sales tax included in, 15/3.2a
- tax on revaluation of fixed assets in, 14/4.3
- taxes on capital, 3/2.1

Tax Court (*Primeiro Conselho de Contribuintes*)
- jurisdiction, 13/4.3
- petition for review by
- • government, filed by, 13/4.2b
- • taxpayer or withholding agent, filed by, 13/4.2a

Tax evasion
- export tax, 15/6.2
- penalties for. *See* Penalties
- real property transfer tax, 19/3.1

Tax law
- National Fiscal Code, 1/4.3
- persons permitted to practice, 1/5.6

Detailed contents appear at beginning of each chapter
All references to Chapters 5/ through 13/ are to the income tax

Tax law (*Continued*)
- sources of
- - constitutional, 1/3.
- - miscellaneous, 1/4.6
- - statutory, 1/4.5

Tax rates
- Bank of Brazil, on, 12/2.6
- business tax, 18/3.1
- capitalization of reserves, tax on, 14/4.4
- decedents' estates, income of, 5/3.5
- distributions on bearer securities, 9/2.2a
- - issued by government, 9/1.6
- education and health stamp, 17/2.10
- entities, on, 12/2.3
- estimated profits, on, 6/9.2
- excess profits tax, 14/5.
- exchange remittance tax, 4/10.
- export tax, 15/6.1
- federal excise tax
- - list of, 16/2.6–16/2.9
- - method of classification, 16/2.5
- federal stamp tax, 17/2.3; 17/2.7
- gains from sale of real property, on, 9/8.2c
- *impôsto unico*, 16/3.2–16/3.4
- individuals
- - complementary tax, 12/1.2c
- - compulsory loan to government, 12/1.3b
- - law for the protection of the family, 12/1.3a
- inheritance and gift taxes, 3/3.7
- nonresidents, 11/3.4
- - royalties, on, 9/5.1c; 9/5.2c
- partnerships, professional, 12/2.6
- presumed profits, on, 6/9.1
- public utilities, 12/2.6
- real property transfer tax, 19/5.1
- revaluation of assets, tax on, 14/4.3
- rural real property tax, 3/2.9a
- sales tax
- - comparison of, 15/4.2
- - prohibitions against discrimination in, 15/1.3; 15/4.1
- schedular taxes, 6/1.2
- Schedule A, 9/1.2c
- Schedule B, 9/1.3c
- Schedule C, 8/1.4
- Schedule D, 8/2.5
- Schedule E, 9/4.1c
- Schedule G, 10/2.2a
- Schedule H, 9/4.3a
- transaction tax, 15/7.2
- urban real property tax, 3/2.9b

Taxable income. *See* Business income; Income; *and* Income of individuals

Taxable year
- assessment, taxation by, 5/4.4a
- definition, 6/3.1

Taxation by assessment. *See* Assessment, taxation by

Taxes
- additions to. *See* Additions to tax
- agricultural and industrial exploitation, 16/4.1
- allocation of revenue from. *See* Allocation of tax revenue
- amusements, 18/4.1
- assessment of. *See* Assessment of tax
- business, 18/
- capital, on, 3/
- capitalization of reserves, on, 14/4.4
- collection of. *See* Collection and payment of tax
- constitutional provisions. *See* Constitutional provisions
- consumption, 16/2.
- deductibility of
- - entities, by, 7/2.7
- - excess profits tax, 14/3.
- - foreign taxes, 11/2.2
- - income from independent services, from, 8/2.3
- - individuals, by, 12/1.2b
- - liability for tax contested, 7/2.7
- - rental income, from, 9/4.1b
- - tax on revaluation of assets, 14/4.3
- - withholding agents, 7/2.7
- excess profits, 14/
- excess reserves of corporations, on, 7/8.3
- excise, 16/
- export, 15/6.
- federal excise, 16/2.
- federal stamp, 17/2.
- fees
- - clearance of goods, on, 15/6.3
- - defined, 1/3.4
- games of chance, on, 18/4.3
- historical and political background of, 1/1.1–1/1.4
- *impôsto de consumo*, 16/2.
- *impôsto unico*, 16/3.
- *impôstos*, defined, 1/3.4
- income, 2/; 5/–13/
- lottery, 18/4.2
- luxury, 15/4.1
- municipal excise, 16/4.
- municipal stamp, 17/3.1
- payment of. *See* Collection and payment of tax

Detailed contents appear at beginning of each chapter
All references to Chapters 5/ through 13/ are to the income tax

Taxes (*Continued*)
- playing cards, on manufacture and sale of, 18/4.4
- port charges, 15/6.3
- protection of the family, for, 12/1.3a
- real property, summarized, 3/2.1
- real property transfer, 19/
- refunds of. *See* Taxpayers' remedies
- registration fee, 15/2.3
- revaluation of fixed assets, on, 14/4.3
- sales, 15/1.–15/5.
- sources of revenue, as
- • federal, 1/6.2
- • municipal, 1/6.4
- • state, 1/6.3
- special assessments, defined, 1/3.4
- sporting events, on admission to, 18/4.4
- stamp, 17/
- state excise, 16/4.
- state stamp, 17/3.
- tax receipts, 1/2.3
- thirty-year, 19/3.2
- toll, 15/6.3
- transaction, 15/7.2
- transactions, on, 4/
- *tributo,* defined, 1/3.4
- waterfalls, on, 16/3.5

Taxpayers
- business tax, 18/2.1
- excess profits tax, 14/2.; 14/6.1; 14/6.2
- federal excise tax, 16/2.4a
- inheritance and gift taxes, 3/3.3a
- penalties on, 1/5.7–1/5.9. *See also* Penalties
- private written agreements, 17/2.3
- real property transfer tax, 19/2.1
- remedies of. *See* Taxpayers' remedies
- sales tax, 15/2.1

Taxpayers' remedies
- advisors, 1/5.6
- appeal (*recurso*)
- • administrative, 1/5.4
- • judicial, 1/5.5
- appraisal of real property, contest of, 19/6.4
- claim for refund
- • business tax, 18/3.2
- • export tax, 15/6.2
- • federal excise tax, 16/2.10b
- • income tax, 13/5.1
- • sales tax, 15/5.3
- • suit for refund, 1/5.5
- income tax laws, under, 13/4.1–13/4.3
- protest (*reclamação*), 1/5.4; 13/4.1

- review, petition for (*recurso voluntário*), 13/4.2
- review of assessment, 13/4.3
- review of return, 13/2.1
- security for payment of tax
- • protests, during, 13/4.1
- • review, during, 13/4.2a
- • suit to annul assessment, during, 13/4.3
- Tax Court. *See* Tax Court

Termination of operations. *See* Commencement and termination of operations

Termination of residence, 5/4.4b

Textiles
- export of, 1/2.6
- federal excise tax on, 16/2.9–Sch. XXIX
- transaction tax on, 15/2.3

Time limits
- assessment of tax, 13/6.1
- • gains from sale of real property, 9/8.2d
- claims for refund, 13/5.1
- collection of tax, 13/6.2
- filing protests, 13/4.1
- filing suit to annul assessment, 13/4.3
- general, 1/5.10
- information requested by government
- • assessment ex officio, in, 13/2.2b
- • review of returns, in, 13/2.1

Tobacco
- federal excise tax on, 16/2.9–Sch. XXIV
- manufacture and sale of, tax on, 18/4.4

Tools, depreciation rates on, 7/3.3

Trademarks. *See* Intellectual property

Transportation
- automobiles. *See* Automobiles
- expenses of as deduction, 7/2.11b; 8/1.3a
- foreign air and steamship lines, 5/6.5
- fuels and lubricants, 16/3.2. *See also* Petroleum industry
- ships, 7/3.3

Travel expenses
- employees, deductibility by, 8/1.3a
- entities, deductibility by, 7/2.11b

Treaties, 1/4.7d

Tributo, 1/3.4. *See also* Taxes

Trustees
- attribution of income to, 6/8.1

Detailed contents appear at beginning of each chapter
All references to Chapters 5/ through 13/ are to the income tax

U

Underpayment of tax. *See* Deficiencies *and* Penalties

Undistributed profits, 7/8.2

Universities. *See* Educational institutions

Urban real property tax
- improved property
- • base, 3/2.7a
- • exclusions from tax base, 3/2.7b
- • rates, 3/2.9b
- • valuation of, 3/2.7c
- unimproved property, 3/2.6

Usufructs
- attribution of income from, 6/8.1
- real property transfer tax on assignment of, 19/3.1

Utilities
- deductibility of from income from independent services, 8/2.3
- public. *See* Public utilities

V

Valuation
- agricultural property, 10/2.2a
- constructive dividends, 9/2.1b
- depreciable property, 7/3.1
- fixed assets, 6/5.4
- inventories, 6/5.1
- patents, 7/3.6
- real property
- • fair market value of, 3/2.5b; 19/4.1
- • gains from sale of, 9/8.2b
- receivables, 6/5.2
- replacement of obsolete assets, 7/3.4
- revaluation of assets, 7/6.2
- • depreciation as affected by, 7/3.1
- • reorganizations, in, 9/2.1f; 9/9.4
- • tax on, 14/4.3
- securities, 6/5.3
- stock dividends, 9/2.1c
- trademarks, 7/3.6

Vehicles. *See* Automobiles

Violations. *See* Penalties

Visitors, 5/4.5

W

Wages. *See* Compensation for services

Withholding at source
- acquisition of residence as terminating, 5/4.4a
- allowances, 5/1.2
- bearer shares, 2/3.3a
- • entities as recipients, 7/7.2
- • revaluation of assets as affecting, 7/6.2
- • stock dividends, on, 9/2.2b
- branches of foreign entities, 5/4.8
- • loss deduction for, 7/4.4
- deductibility of taxes withheld, 7/2.7
- exemptions
- • persons abroad on government service, 6/1.3b
- • persons studying abroad, 6/1.3b
- • reinvested branch profits, 5/4.8
- general, 2/3.3; 5/1.2
- income subject to
- • compensation of employees, 8/1.5; 2/3.3b
- • compensation of officers, directors, owners and partners, 8/1.5b
- • excess reserves of corporations, 7/8.3
- • gains from sale of real property, 2/3.3c; 9/8.2
- • income from capital, nonresidents as recipients, 9/7.2
- • income from capital, residents as recipients, 9/7.1
- • nonresident individuals as recipients, 5/4.2
- • profits of branches of foreign entities, 11/3.3
- • profits of nonresident corporations, 5/4.7
- • profits of other nonresident entities, 5/4.9
- late payment of tax withheld, 13/7.3
- nonresidents
- • compensation for services, 11/3.4c
- • dividends and other distributions, 9/2.4
- • gains from sale of real property, 5/4.3
- • gross income as base of, 11/3.4
- protest by withholding agent, 13/4.1
- residents, 5/4.3
- termination of residence as resulting in, 5/4.4b
- time limit on collection of tax withheld, 13/6.2
- visitors, 5/4.5

CONTRIBUTORS

Abbott Laboratories
Aluminum Company of America
American Cable & Radio Corporation
American Chicle Company
American Cyanamid Company
American Express Company
American Smelting and Refining
Company
American Zinc, Lead and Smelting
Company
Anaconda Company
Anderson, Clayton & Co.
Armour and Company
Automatic Electric Company
The Borden Company
Borg-Warner Corporation
Burroughs Corporation
Godfrey L. Cabot, Inc.
Cargill, Incorporated
The Chase Manhattan Bank
Chrysler Corporation
The Coca-Cola Company
Columbia Broadcasting System, Inc.
Corn Products Refining Company
Crown Zellerbach Corporation
E. I. du Pont de Nemours & Company
The First National Bank of Boston
Ford Motor Company
General Foods Corporation
General Motors Corporation
The General Tire & Rubber Company
The Gillette Company
The B. F. Goodrich Company
The Goodyear Tire & Rubber Company
W. R. Grace & Co.
Gulf Oil Corporation
Haytian Purchasing Corporation

Hercules Powder Company
International General Electric
Company
International Harvester Company
International Telephone and
Telegraph Corporation
Johnson & Johnson
Lambert & Co.
Eli Lilly International Corporation
Lockheed Aircraft Corporation
Olin Mathieson Chemical Corporation
Mine Safety Appliances Company
National Dairy Products Corporation
Owens-Illinois
Pan American World Airways,
Inc.
Parke, Davis & Company
Philco Corporation
The Procter & Gamble Company
Radio Corporation of America
Raymond Concrete Pile Company
Robertshaw-Fulton Controls Company
Socony-Vacuum Oil Company
E. R. Squibb & Sons Overseas
Division
Standard Oil Company of California
Standard Oil Company (New Jersey)
Standard-Vacuum Oil Company
Trans World Airlines, Inc.
Union Carbide and Carbon
Corporation
United States Rubber Company
United States Steel Corporation
Vick Chemical Company
Westinghouse Air Brake Company
Westinghouse Electric International
Company

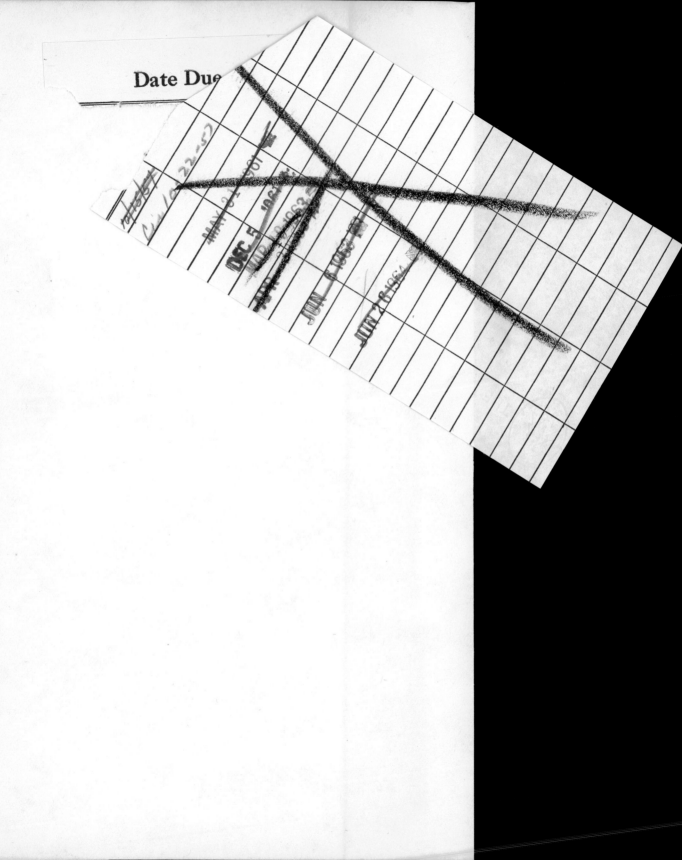